# THE NEW LIVES OF IMAGES

• • •

**Sensing Media**

Aesthetics, Philosophy, and Cultures of Media

EDITED BY WENDY HUI KYONG CHUN AND SHANE DENSON

# THE NEW LIVES OF IMAGES

## Digital Ecologies and Anthropocene Imaginaries in More-Than-Human Worlds

ADRIAN J. IVAKHIV

**STANFORD UNIVERSITY PRESS**
Stanford, California

Stanford University Press
Stanford, California



Library of Congress Cataloging-in-Publication Data
Names: Ivakhiv, Adrian J., author.
Title: The new lives of images : digital ecologies and anthropocene imaginaries in more-than-human worlds / Adrian J. Ivakhiv.
Description: Stanford, California : Stanford University Press, [2025] | Series: Sensing media : aesthetics, philosophy, and cultures of media | Includes bibliographical references and index.
Identifiers: LCCN 2025001417 (print) | LCCN 2025001418 (ebook) | ISBN 9781503643505 (cloth) | ISBN 9781503643987 (paperback) | ISBN 9781503643994 (ebook)
Subjects: LCSH: Image (Philosophy) | Imagination (Philosophy)
Classification: LCC B105.I47 I93 2025 (print) | LCC B105.I47 (ebook) | DDC 128/.3—dc23/eng/20250303
LC record available at https://lccn.loc.gov/2025001417
LC ebook record available at https://lccn.loc.gov/2025001418

Cover design: Martyn Schmoll
Cover art: Annie Spratt from Unsplash

The authorized representative in the EU for product safety and compliance is: Mare Nostrum Group B.V. | Mauritskade 21D | 1091 GC Amsterdam | The Netherlands | Email address: gpsr@mare-nostrum.co.uk | KVK chamber of commerce number: 96249943

# CONTENTS

# ACKNOWLEDGMENTS

Where does one book end and another begin? This book has been many years in the making, and its writing has benefited from the insights and support of multiple people and institutions. Some of them have already been mentioned in the acknowledgments of previous books that led to this one, especially *Shadowing the Anthropocene* (2018) and to a lesser degree *Ecologies of the Moving Image* (2013). To keep things manageable, I will refer here mainly to the six years of work that followed the publication of the later of those two volumes.

First and foremost, I wish to thank the Cinepoetics Centre for Advanced Film Studies at Freie Universität Berlin, which generously sponsored a senior research fellowship and hosted me through a Fulbright scholarship that together became a wonderful year spent in Berlin in 2022–23. In particular, I am grateful to Mattias Grotkopp, Michael Wedel, Hermann Kappelhoff, Michael Ufer, Jan-Hendrik Bakels, and the other staff and students of the Center for their support during that year, and to the Cinepoetics fellows-colleagues who helped to create a most stimulating intellectual environment as I worked on this volume. The latter include Francesco Casetti, Inga Pollmann, Mark B. N. Hansen, Robert Sinnerbrink, Antonio Somaini, Holger Schulze, T. J. Demos, Birgit Schneider, Alex Galloway, Erika Balsom, Angelos Koutsourakis, Enis Dinç, Elisa Linseisen, Jennifer Barker, and Steffen Hven.

The University of Vermont supported me through sabbatical funding; a REACH grant offered by its Office for the Vice-President for Research, which funded the work of research assistant Michael McGuire, who helped me with finding and analyzing several of the videos examined in chapter 6; three years of funding as Steven Rubenstein Professor, with support from the Steven and Beverly Rubenstein Charitable Foundation; and funds from the Gund Institute for Environment and the UVM Humanities Center. Simon Fraser University also provided generous research time to complete the book as part of my activity (since 2024) as J. S. Woodsworth Chair in the Humanities, and through a previous speaking invitation from the university's Institute for the Humanities.

Various pieces of this book have been presented in talks and written materials prepared at the invitation of multiple people and institutions. These have included the University of California Santa Barbara Film and Media Studies department and the Carsey-Wolf Center, which hosted me as a visiting scholar in the spring of 2022; Paola Spinozzi at the University of Ferrara's PhD Programme in Environmental Sustainability and Wellbeing; Bernd Herzogenrath at Goethe-Universität Frankfurt's American Studies program; Angela Krewani and Alessandra Boller at Philipps-Universität's Marburg Centre for Canadian Studies, which sponsored a keynote lecture at their 2019 "Echoing Ecologies" conference; Nicolai Skiveren at Aarhus University ("The Garden and the Dump" conference, 2021); Zoriana Rybchynska and the 2021 Congress of Culture in Lviv, Ukraine; Zhou Haitian at Shanghai University; Vermont Humanities, which sponsored two talks of mine in 2021 and 2024; Nadia Foty-Oneschuk at the University of Saskatchewan, who kindly invited me to give the 24th Annual Mohyla Lecture in 2022; Patrick Van Ginkel and the Free Cultural Spaces network, who invited me to speak at the "Towards the Symbiocene?" symposium in Amsterdam, 2023; and ACCRA's Écologies visuelles conference for a keynote presented at the Université de Strasbourg in January 2025. Portions of chapters 4 and 7 have appeared in "Image Ecologies, Spiritual Polytropy, and the Anthropocene," *Journal for the Study of Religion, Nature, and Culture* 13.4 (2019), and "Reimagining Religious Imagination, in Theory and in Practice," *Journal for the Study of Religion, Nature, and Culture* 15.3 (2021); both are fully revised here.

Colleagues, collaborators, and students in the environmental humanities and film/media studies fields who have been helpful along the way include (in alphabetical order) Maria Boguszewicz, David Brahinsky, Joshua Brahinsky, Kristian Brevik, Alenda Chang, Stephen Collis, Sean Cubitt, Ludo de Roo, Lucy Drummond, Samir Gandesha, Bishnupriya Ghosh, Antonio López, Sabina Magliocco, Laura Marks, Svitlana Matviyenko, Sarah Pike, Patricia Pisters, Bhaskar Sarkar, Lisa Sideris, Bron Taylor, Janet Walker, Kunyu Wang, John Whalen-Bridge, and others too numerous to list. Erica Wetter has been wonderful to work with at Stanford University Press, as has Natalie Gabriela Rovero, Tiffany Mok, David Zielonka, Melissa Jauregui Chavez, and the Sensing Media series coeditors, Shane Denson and Wendy Hui Kyong Chun.

Finally, the love and support of my partner Auriel and our son Zoryan are always deeply appreciated. We have moved around a lot in the last few years; I dedicate this book to our continued journey together, and to the memory of Auriel's late mother, Ethne Bertram Gray, whose deep love for the image will always remain infectious.

# PREFACE

*Our civilization doesn't have adequate images, and I think our civilization is doomed, is gonna die out like dinosaurs if it does not develop an adequate language or adequate images.*

—WERNER HERZOG, Werner Herzog Eats His Shoe, *1980*[1]

*Without an image of tomorrow, one is trapped by blind history, economics and politics beyond our control. . . . Only by having clear and vital images of the many alternatives, good and bad, of where one can go, will we have any control over the way we may actually get there in a reality tomorrow will bring all too quickly.*

—SAMUEL DELANY, Starboard Wine: More Notes on the Language of Science Fiction[2]

*The imaginal is not a world, but it is what makes a world possible in the first place. . . . [T]he imaginal is a field of possibilities.*

—CHIARA BOTTICI, Imaginal Politics: Images Beyond Imagination and the Imaginary[3]

This book is rooted in a conviction that I have pursued in my writing for the last few decades: that most modern accounts of the human imagination misunderstand and underestimate its role in shaping the world that humans inhabit. Imagination is not something that is "just in our heads"; it is not merely an error-prone way of making sense of the data brought to us from the world by our senses. On the contrary, imagination is something like the medium in which we and others live. There *is* a universe outside of the one we can grasp with our imagination(s), but it is not a universe that is free of the kinds of meanings we impart to it. This is because meaning is inherent in the universe for meaning-bearing beings. We humans are one such being, though far from the only one, and the idea that our (human) ability to bear or create meaning is not only special but somehow separate from the physical universe is a flawed premise.

In this sense, I begin with a rejection of what Alfred North Whitehead called the "bifurcation of nature." This is the idea that our experience of reality is divided between "the nature apprehended in awareness"—"the greenness of the trees, the song of the birds, the warmth of the sun, the hardness of the chairs, and the feel of the velvet"—and "the nature which is the *cause* of awareness," that is, the "molecules and electrons" known to science, and that the former is ontologically secondary and therefore less real than the "primary qualities" that make up the latter.[4] Each of the first category presumes a perception, an interpretation, or a meaning. Rejecting this bifurcation means rejecting the idea that meaning is an adjunct to reality, and that it somehow separates us, enclosing us in a subjective mental bubble, from the universe. On the contrary, Whitehead's radical proposal is that meaning situates and emplaces us within reality. If this is the case, then I believe it is also true to say that the main way in which meaning-bearing beings grasp or bear meaning is through what can be called "images." As I will explain in the first chapter, images are central to understanding what it means to live in a world, or to "live a world." Images are neither subjective nor objective, or, rather, they are both; they are what links subject and object, and what connects our concrete experience with the abstraction that makes sense of that experience. They are small and they are large. As Gilbert Simondon has put it, "Images impregnate civilizations and energize them with their power."[5]

Understanding our capacity to make and use, or at least to bear, images—which is how I will define the imagination—is central to understanding both ourselves and our universe. What is most important, and what I will attempt to shed light on, is what we do with those images and how they shape, enable, and constrain us as we navigate our relationship with the more-than-human world around us. Our capacity to bear images is inherent to our perception of the world, but also to our creative transformation of that world. This dual aspect of images—as perceptual and as creative, as reproductive and productive—will be our key. As philosopher Jennifer Gosetti-Ferencei writes in *The Life of Imagination: Revealing and Making the World,* imagination both *reveals* and *makes* the world for us. It is "the presentational and transformational activity of human consciousness," where "presentational" refers to "something that is brought to the fore or made present for consciousness," and "transformational" refers to the possibility of "change" in the "object or expression of imagining."[6]

Two modern philosophers whose work provides rich insight into this, if in quite different ways, will be my touchstones here. Whitehead is one of them; the other is Charles Sanders Peirce. The work of both has been applied to the interpretation of images and to understanding media, including today's digital media, but not necessarily in the way that I will do this. Their work is not entirely unique, and it is related to and echoed by a diverse cast of others today and in the past—westerners and non-westerners, women and men, philosophers and poets, scientists and shamans.[7] Even as Whitehead and Peirce frame my own thinking about images and imagination, neither of them detailed the full implications of the "bifurcation of nature" they each, in their own way, identified. That has required generations of philosophers, historians of science, and others who have probed the ways in which this bifurcation has shaped and been shaped by histories of colonialism, extractive capitalism, and cultural and ecological practices marked by gender relations and other variables unfolding over centuries.[8] All of this work remains to be successfully synthesized into a popularly resonant form.[9]

What I tease out of the work of these thinkers is this idea that the *perceptual* and the *creative*—what and how we perceive, and what we do with those perceptions—constitutes a kind of unified field within which images, or imag*ing*, plays a central role. Today that field is shaped increasingly by the world of digital media, and it is my overarching goal to understand how that world affects and changes the possibilities for imagining the world into existence. The reason such an understanding is needed, to quote political artists Mihnea Mircan and Jonas Staal, is in order to address the "crisis of the imagination," which they define as "a lack of imagination to understand our disastrous present as much as to project our desired future."[10]

This book is the fourth in a series devoted directly to some dimension of this image-centered understanding of the contemporary world. The first, *Claiming Sacred Ground*, focused on how imagination features in conflicts over land and in perceptions and interpretations of its meanings. Those interpretations included claims for land's alleged significance or "sacredness" in places where environmental conflicts appeared outsizedly acute. While its analysis of images was more implicit than explicit, the book's attempt to theorize "place-images" in the context of human activities—"practices of place" that shape those places into what they become—is something that is directly relevant to the present volume. Most especially, the way in which that volume moved between activities thought to be religious or spiritual and those considered secular or modern—between ceremonial rituals on one hand and tourist promotion, recreation, and real estate speculation on the other—is something I will pick up again in this book. All such activities are still with us, but now they are found within a context shaped increasingly by digital media.

In light of that first volume, the second in the series, *Ecologies of the Moving Image*, may have appeared a detour into an altogether different line of study, though it is the book that most directly leads into this one. Understanding images today necessitates a rigorous analysis of the kinds of images that came, most dramatically, to populate and to shape the world over the course of the twentieth century: moving images. *Ecologies of the Moving Image* attempted not only a thorough refashioning of our understanding of moving images, but a kind of excavation of them from within a world reshaped by them. It presented a multileveled analysis of cinema in terms of the worlds it produces, which are material, social, and perceptual (or animate); the ways we viewers engage with those worlds—their moment-by-moment spectacularity, their sequential narrativity (or one-thing-after-anotherness), and their referentiality to all kinds of other worldly and imagined things; and the ways our engagements with film-worlds changes the worlds that precede and outlast those film-viewing experiences (which, again, it does materially, socially, and perceptually). *Ecologies of the Moving Image* was in this sense both phenomenological, to do with how we experience films, and ontological, to do with what films and their worlds (film-worlds) are and how they relate to other dimensions of reality.

The next volume, *Shadowing the Anthropocene*, deepened the philosophical basis of my previous work, relating it especially to the "speculative realisms," "new materialisms," and "ontological turns" that have marked certain segments of the philosophically inclined academy (though not so much analytic philosophy departments as cultural studies, media studies, and the arts and social sciences). Then I applied this philosophy to the *practice* of living and to the theorization of cultural and religious "image wars" or "iconoclashes," all within the context of the "Anthropocene predicament," which an increasing number of intellectuals take to mark the present time. With its forays into the practical and the "iconoclashic," *Shadowing* returned me more directly to the concerns of the first volume in this tetralogy.

The present volume effectively brings all of these concerns together. It proposes, in the most complete form to date, a theory of the imagination that is also a theory of images—what they are and what they do—and that accounts for a broad spectrum of people's use of images, from the religious and political to the scientific and aesthetic, and from the premodern to the world of digital media. If anything, it takes such categorical distinctions—between religion, science, magic, aesthetics, politics, as well as modernity, secularism, and others—as categories to be set aside so that their common substance can be recognized. That common substance is imagination and the forms it takes: images or imaginings (image-events), image ecologies (or imaginaries), image regimes, and the icono-couplings and iconoclashes that occur in the mixtures of images we find in the world; all these terms will be defined soon enough. And it continues the work of analyzing moving images—images that *move* us—in a world where those images have gone if not viral, then at least digital.

This book is, in a sense, both a genealogy and the beginnings of an analysis of the heavily mediated present. That makes it an ambitious book. Fortunately, its division into two parts absolves me of some of that ambition. Where the first half presents the theory in its most holistic form, the second selectively focuses on a series of locations or sites of interest to understanding the Anthropocene condition. Like the three books preceding it, this one aims to help us navigate the set of circumstances humans collectively find ourselves inhabiting today. I (and others) have argued that the term "Anthropocene" is a misnomer, both because the "Anthropos" is hardly a responsible and unified agent—

the causes of the Anthropocene are far more complex than the term suggests—and because humans are far from equally implicated in this condition. At any rate, the case I make is that the Anthropocene *condition* or *predicament*—a shared situation rather than a geological epoch (as geologists themselves have recently asserted)—is not just one in which human activities today risk the physical and biological foundations on which we depend, so that those activities need to be reassessed and remade. It is also a predicament that requires epistemological and ontological regrounding. This book hopes to contribute to that task by helping us understand the image-world in which we live.

I use this term "image-world" in a double sense. It is, on the one hand, the world of images that surround us increasingly, and that do this by virtue of imaging technologies that are primarily electronic and digital. This is the *digital* image-world, and while the digital is not reducible to images, digital technology makes possible the networked, participatory, and hypermediated world that so many of us live with and, to a large degree, live within. It is where we find the bulk of the images, as well as the stories and texts, that shape and make sense of our lives. On the other hand, I also intend to recognize that *every* human world is an image-world; it is a world brought forth in and through our imaginative capacities and acts. The book aims to contribute to both of these: an ontology of *the* image-world (which is every world) and an ontology of the *particular* image-world—that of digital images and networks—that grows around us and enfolds us increasingly today.

I will do this, first, by identifying a series of patterns or configurations, which I call "image regimes," according to which humans have negotiated their relationships with the larger world through the use of images. These present multiple variations on the humans–images–reality triad. Since human ideas about each of these—about images, about reality, and about humans ourselves—have changed over time, this will be a way to establish some reference points amidst an ensemble of moving pieces. In the second part of the book, I will apply this understanding of image regimes to three sites of image production. The first pertains to the Anthropocene itself, in the shape of a set of multimedia artworks dealing with ecological, climatic, and geological changes affecting humanity today. The second examines an array of online audiovisual materials documenting and commenting on transspecies animal encounters, that is, encounters that cross commonly assumed boundaries between humans and nonhuman animals. The third looks at art, music, and poetry that refer to and engage, or at least claim to engage, with agential forces that exceed or transcend humanity as it is currently understood in its dominant formulation.

I have chosen these three sites in order to give us a sense of what is at stake in our imagination both of ourselves—the human, the *Anthropos*—and of three significant kinds of others-to-the-human. The first of these others is the Earth as a whole, the geological or biogeochemical other in its unity. The second includes the ranks of animal species to which we humans belong, as animals ourselves, but from which we have disavowed our belonging insofar as we have considered ourselves humans and *not* animals. The third of these others is less easy to pinpoint: it is not one that is obviously scientifically knowable, and depending on one's convictions, it may or may not exist except as a product of imagination. And yet it represents the kind of other that has been looked to as the most significant by many societies over millennia: the other referred to in discourses commonly labeled religious, spiritual, mythological, supernatural, or at the very least poetic. Together with the animal other, this third other raises a question that has haunted humanity across the period marked by the rise of what is loosely called humanism: *Are we alone?* If most forms of humanist thought, including the very humanist idea of the Anthropocene, suggest that humans constitute a central character on the stage of the world, then this question "Are we alone?" becomes a complex and open site: a site of denial, of haunting, of speculation, and of utopian imagining. And if we are to move to a "posthumanist" embrace of the more-than-human world, a more-than-humanism, this question will need to be taken seriously.

To that end, the three chapters that make up part 2 of this volume will treat these three image formations, in effect, as construction sites. It is these kinds of sites that are, to use Chiara Bottici's words (cited above), "what makes a world possible in the first place." They are part of the "imaginal" that can prepare us, or fail to prepare us, for the world Werner Herzog and Samuel Delany foresee in the accompanying epigraphs. I will name them "scenes"—the "Anthroposcene," the "Therioscene," and the "Theoscene"—to highlight the ways in which they serve as settings for image-formation unfolding at three kinds of boundaries, thresholds, crossroads, or encounter zones: those between humans and the Earth, between humans and other animals, and between humans and the more mysterious relations that anchor us in our sense of passage between the past that grounds us and the future that beckons.[11] It is this sense of movement within temporality, and in fact within multiple temporalities, that makes this project a "chronopolitical" one, a way of navigating time that encompasses aesthetic, ethical, and political dimensions.

For all this talk of the "anthro" and its "(s)cene(s)," I wish to make clear, and hope that my analysis bears out, that the human world is neither singular—one shared human world—nor is it exclusively human. Humans are one kind of being that bears worlds; many worlds do we bear, and their convergence and divergence is a real issue for us to contend with today. The argument developed in this book builds up to a focus on how certain decolonial, Indigenous, and Afrofuturist artists are contributing to the elicitation of imaginaries that may help us with this world-crafting. This is a world-crafting that involves redefining ourselves as well as our animal kin and our *other* others—those ancestral, invisible, and mysteriously present to us in ways that may be accessible via the imaginal practices of artists and other "diviners." My premise here is that grappling with a world of growing ecological precarity, political and economic instability, late-imperial resource rivalry, and general feverishness—the twenty-first century world of late-capitalist crisis—requires cultural and imaginative resources from beyond its dominant, institutionalized strains, and significant creativity in their uptake.

Many other worlds exist alongside our human worlds, and some of them elude even the least of our human contributions. Each of them points to a larger, all-encompassing reality within which these worlds arise and by which they get subsumed. We can call that reality "the more-than-human world," as my subtitle does, or we can call it, much more broadly, the universe, even if physicists (and anthropologists) aren't sure if it is one universe or many, a multiverse or a pluriverse, or something altogether unknowable—an agnoverse (to coin a term). Each of the worlds making up this pluriverse, polyverse, or agnoverse situates the bearer within some understanding of that more encompassing reality, a reality that is actively turning (from the Latin *vertere*) in one direction or many. This is what it means to bear a world, to image, and to live and dwell in it.

That we bear and share worlds with other dwellers, and other kinds of dwellers, is the starting point for any philosophy worth promoting today. The fruit of that philosophy will be a contribution to the task of living with those others.

# PART I

...

# Images and Ecologies

## FROM THE BEGINNING TO THE DIGITAL

# One
# THE IMAGE

*The image is present to our gaze, certainly. But that presence, or visibility, relies on the medium in which the image appears, whether on a monitor or embodied in an old statue. In their own right, images testify to the absence of that which they make present. [. . .] In this lies the paradox of images—in the fact that they are or mean the presence of an absence—and this paradox is in part the result of our capacity to distinguish image and medium. [. . .] They need a presence as medium in order to symbolize the absence of what they represent.*

—*HANS BELTING*, An Anthropology of Images: Picture, Medium, Body[1]

*[I]mages are not as limpid as concepts; they do not follow the mind's activity with the same flexibility; they can only be governed indirectly; they maintain a certain opacity, like a foreign population in the midst of an orderly state. Displaying, to a degree, will, appetite and motion, images almost seem to be secondary organisms within the thinking being.*

—*GILBERT SIMONDON*, Imagination and Invention[2]

*Every image is in some way a "portrait," not in that it would reproduce the traits of a person, but in that it pulls and* draws *(this is the semantic and etymological sense of the word), in that it extracts something, an intimacy, a force. And, to extract it, it subtracts or removes it from homogeneity, it distracts it from it, distinguishes it, detaches it and casts it forth. It throws it in front of us, and this throwing [jet], this projection, makes its mark, its very trait and its* stigma*: its tracing, its line, its style, its incision, its scar, its signature, all of this at once.*

—*JEAN-LUC NANCY*, The Ground of the Image[3]

• • • Images surround us on all sides. They decorate the walls of our homes and are displayed on our clothes, our vehicles, and signs that mark our roadsides and fill our cities. We see them, admire them, puzzle over them, and glean information from them at every significant site of our everyday lives: our schools, gyms, doctor's offices, stores and businesses, government facilities, churches and temples. We store them in our wallets, for occasional sharing with friends, and tattoo them in ink into the skin of our bodies. They fill books and magazines and radiate from (and move across) our smartphones, computer screens, and media devices. Some of these images we interact with daily, internalizing them so that they appear in our dreams, our reveries, and our imaginings, in our mind's eyes and mind's ears (and this book will define images to include not just the visual but the auditory, olfactory, tactile, kinesthetic, interoceptive, and other kinds). Some of these images—for instance, of police violence directed at individuals like George Floyd and Breonna Taylor, or of protester violence directed at symbols of the state, or of flags, religious prophets, or symbolically significant buildings being burned, desecrated, or attacked—become the fulcrums around which history turns.

This image richness of our world is the first of two facts that ought to frame any discussion of images today. Not only is our world full of images, but new ones are coming into being every day, with all of them disseminated along technical networks and hardware and software platforms—from YouTube, Instagram, and TikTok to media outlets and databases of many kinds—which are evolving so rapidly that few of us can keep up.

The second fact is that images feature at the center of so many of the cultural, political, and religious conflicts found in the world today. Such conflicts—around the "truth" or "fakeness" of images, around how different groups of people (or deities) are depicted in them, how they react to them, and around their qualities, significance, and sacredness or profanity—can only be expected to intensify with every passing year, with every billion humans added (to a number that has surpassed eight billion as I write this), and with every degree of temperature rise forecasted by climate scientists. The role of images both in raising the climate of politics and in navigating the climate of Earth has become incontrovertible.

These two facts make the study of images an increasingly important part of understanding today's world. This book proposes a broad and encompassing way of thinking about images. Its focus is not so much the images themselves as it is the relationship we humans have had, continue to have, and will likely have in the future with images—our images, other people's images, and images whose authorship and provenance are uncertain. It presents, in its first half, a typology of six distinctive "regimes" by which those relationships are and have been organized. Understanding the differences between these regimes and something of their history will help us see how our own understanding of images is not the only one, nor necessarily the correct one; images might be made to work very differently than they do for us. It also helps us to get a better handle on the image-rich world of today, an image-world that surrounds us, immerses us, captivates us, and shapes our lives in ways we may barely understand.

In its second half, the book presents interpretations of several sets of images—"image formations" that arise within "image ecologies"—in light of the typology presented here. The first of these sets are images depicting the present as a time of crisis—a time called by some the Anthropocene, though the emphasis here is not so much on the triumph of humanity (the Anthropos) over the world as on the perils exhibited in that triumph. The second consists of works in our digital image-world that seemingly animate the world by depicting animals (of the nonhuman kind) interacting with each other and with humans in unexpected, sometimes transgressive, and instructive ways. The third concerns a set of strategies pursued by some artists and image-makers to access a "higher" (or "deeper") world even in the midst of a tacit denial of the existence of any world beyond that of modern humanity. The chapters probe the tensions between different kinds of image relations: for instance, between the regime of the "expression-image," for which images are valued as works of artistic expression; the regime of the "world-picture," which values images as accurate duplicates of sensible reality; and the regime of the "ideal-image," for which they are valued as windows into an otherwise inaccessible, transcendent world (one that reappears throughout modernity in the guise of "the sublime"). Each of these readings highlights ways in which different ways of relating to images combine with new technological capacities to create new potentials for working with images in the complicated image-world we inhabit.

The book, then, proposes something like a diagnostic toolkit for understanding the work that images do, and can do, for us today. Its goal is not to be thorough and comprehensive about any of the specific regimes it analyzes. That goes as well for the digital image-world, as I will call it—the thickly mediatized world in which images flow, connect, modulate, and otherwise shape the larger world of people, bodies, and "nature" in novel and barely mapped ways. The book does not aim to get into the weeds of debates and rival perspectives on today's image-rich world. It aims instead to provide something like a global overview of things many of us may already intuit, and then to apply that overview to some interesting phenomena that populate both the boundaries between image regimes and the connections that relate humans to the more-than-human world today. The book will have done its work if its insights—its categories and classifications—are found to be helpful in interpreting the work that images do today, and if it sheds light on the relationship between an image-equipped humanity and the Earth within which that humanity makes its dwelling.

## WHAT IS AN IMAGE?

Before we venture further, we need to define what we mean by the word. Images have been considered and studied in a wide range of fields: by philosophers, psychologists, anthropologists, historians and archaeologists, artists and photographers, architects and designers, geographers and cartographers, neurobiologists and animal scientists, roboticists and engineers, and scholars of art and media studies, religion, and science and technology.[4] Vigorous debates about images and about seeing have raged for decades among art historians and scholars of culture and media.[5] Following what philosopher Richard Rorty influentially called the "linguistic turn" among intellectuals,[6] scholars on both sides of the Atlantic identified a "pictorial" or "iconic turn," which redirected attention from textual and discursive representation to the materiality, affectivity, and effectivity of images and pictures, what they mean, and even what they "want."[7] While some have continued to focus on decoding the meanings and unveiling the political and ideological uses of images,[8] others have advocated a more iconophilic recognition of the power and even agency of images, which are variously said to mediate, transform, and enchant their viewers, stirring them to tears, passions, "image wars," and "iconoclashes."[9]

One typology of images, which restricts itself to the visual, includes the following categories: solid (or three-dimensional) images, pictorial images, arrested images, mirror images, projected camera images, photographic camera images, retinal images, optical after-images, memory images, and mental images.[10] W. J. T. Mitchell in his straightforwardly titled essay "What Is an Image?" notes another typology: "We speak of pictures, statues, optical illusions, maps, diagrams, dreams, hallucinations, spectacles, projections, poems, patterns, memories, and even ideas as images." Images, he adds, can be graphic, optical, perceptual, mental, and verbal.[11] If we were to add to this the full array of nonvisual images—auditory (from recorded sounds to hallucinated voices), olfactory, tactile, kinesthetic, and other kinds—we would have a tremendous array of data to work with.

Most work on images proposes some way of simplifying what it is that makes an image distinct from other things. In a synoptic overview of contemporary philosophical approaches to images, John Kulvicki succinctly defines images as "likenesses made to present things," arguing that images are one of two main ways of presenting, or representing things, the other being verbal and/or textual.[12] The definition of the image I will follow in this book builds on this notion that the image *presents* things by referring to those things, at least in part, through likeness or resemblance. More precisely, I will define an image as a *perceptible form that produces an effect in an observer in part through its resemblance to something else.*

There is a lot to unpack in this definition, and this book will take some time in doing that. But as a first stab, this definition will be helpful for us in its emphasis on four things.

(1) *An image is a form that is sensed or perceived.* It need not be a visual form (as mentioned). And let us not trouble ourselves with whether an image must really be there in front of us or if it could also be in our minds, or somewhere in the relationship between the two. We still call "mental images" images, and they could not exist in our minds without being the sort of thing we could perceive with our senses; the two share that quality, but their relationship can be left aside for now.

(2) *An image produces an effect.* By this I mean that it is active—it is an image by virtue of its imaging, and not simply in its being there to be perceived if a perceiver happens to come along. Our working rule will be this: if a tree falls in the forest and there is no one there to hear it, then it does not make a sound. This is not because sound waves are not produced by it (they are), but because there is no organism nearby to turn those sound waves into perceived sounds. That's a highly unlikely scenario (as with many thought exercises), but the point is that the image *is* what it *does*. The image, as defined here, will not be the sound waves themselves which may or may not be turned into a "sound." It will be the sound as it is perceived, which is always already meaningful, or feelingful, or meaning- and feeling-inducing and -provoking. This will be the pragmatic and processual part of our definition; more on that momentarily.

(3) *The effect it produces is in or on an observer, and it is in relationship to a "something else" that is not directly present to the observer.* This means that the image is not *equivalent* to the effect it has on an observer, nor is it equivalent to the something else that the image points to, reminds one of, or otherwise refers to for that observer. The image understood completely—which we can more technically call the "image relation" or "image event"—is inclusive of these two relationships. The image, in other words, includes three elements: there is the image itself, the perceivable form; there is the thing it refers to, which is its object or referent; and there is the effect that it has, an effect which could be a meaning, a feeling, or something of both. The second of these—the thing being referred to by an image—is not directly present but is *made* present by the image. It is presented, represented, indicated, or otherwise brought to presence in and through the image. We could depict this relationship as a triangle, one that shows a movement, a shift, or a connection made between the something that is there (the image) and the something that is not there (the referent), and another one from those two to the someone for whom the two are brought together in the effect—the meaning, the feeling, the significance—they produce. Without the image, the referent and the effect are unrelated; the image is their mediator.

To speak of the "effect" that an image produces is not meant to suggest a causal arrow moving from the image (or the referent via the

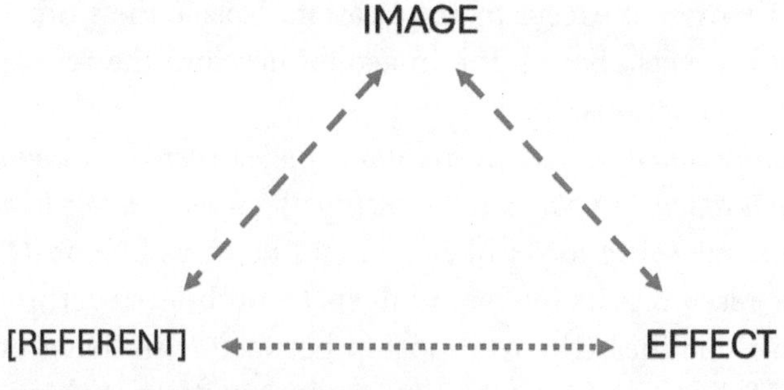


**FIGURE 1.1.** The image relation/event.

image) to its recipient, as if the recipient were passive. It is better to think of the effect as something produced in and through the entire relation. The "imaging event" encompasses all three points of the triangle: the image itself, its referent, and its registration, or its bearing, in a beholder. The image could have arisen as a result of a triggering event in the world outside the observer (which would make this more of a *perceptual* image), or it could have arisen purely as a result of the neurophysical activity of the observer (which would make this more of a *mental* event, such as one based in the memory of a perceptual encounter). But its arising is triadic, with the "image itself" mediating between its referent and the meaning it bears for the observer. (By "the observer" I simply mean the bearer of the image and the recipient of its effect.)

Moreover, the correspondences between the referent and the registered image, and between the referent and the meaning or effect, are never complete. There is always a shift, a movement, or a slippage that leaves behind an elusive remainder that cannot be contained, encompassed, or even measured in the imaging event. The point is that a presence is established. As Hans Belting puts it in *An Anthropology of Images* (cited in the opening quote to this chapter), the "paradox of images" is "that they *are* or *mean* the presence of an absence."[13] An image combines this presence (of an absence) with meaning: it produces meaning (which may also be feeling), and in this lies its eventness, but it does this through its presence, without which it could not function. It *makes* something (else) present through its own presence. The "something else" is made present through the image, but its (presumed) existence elsewhere or elsewhen is part of the relationship. (Because it is not directly present except by implication, I place the word "referent" in square brackets above.) The image is therefore the real and active mediator of a relationship.

(4) *Finally, and crucially, the relationship between the image and what it refers to is at least in part a relationship of resemblance or likeness.* The image in some sense looks like, sounds like, feels like, tastes like, or otherwise resembles its referent in its form, outline, structure, or other perceivable qualities. The relationship between them need not be entirely and fully that of resemblance—indeed it may not always be clear what makes it a resemblance or how much of a resemblance is needed to qualify as a resemblance—but it is this "being like" that makes something an image as opposed to, say, a word, a clue, or another kind of sign. (More on signs in a moment.) An image, in this sense, always has a secondarity to it; it is always a reminder, even as it *adds to* or *builds on* whatever it may be reminding of. It is always an echo of something, a repetition, even as it opens onto difference, transformation, or novelty. (More on repetition and difference in a moment.)

A simple example of an image is that of a human face, such as the one pictured in figure 1.2. When you look at this face, you are aware that

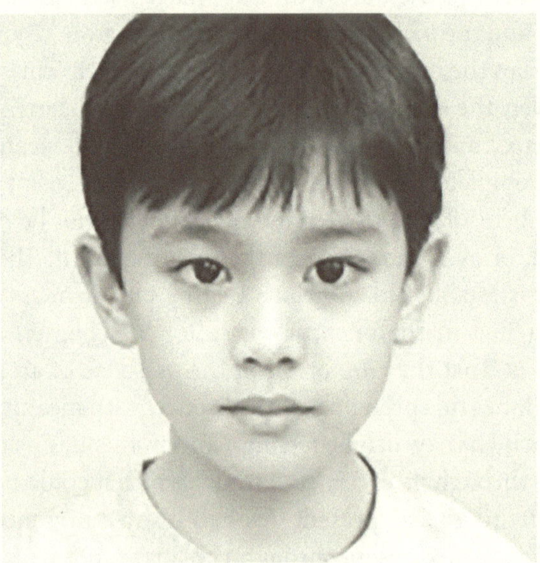

**FIGURE 1.2.** Image of a human face.

it looks like the face of a real person, but also that it is *not* that face. If it were, that face would be attached to a body and a consciousness that would see you. It would not be a square surrounded by white space on a leaf of paper (if you are holding a book in your hands) or on the screen version of a page. Assuming you do not actually believe that the eyes on this face see you the same way that you see them, this qualifies as a sign whose meaning depends on its resemblance to something that is not present. Whether in fact there is a person whose face this represents—a person whose facial profile was captured by camera at some previous point in time—or if it is a composite image created by artificial intelligence from myriad data it has processed, we are not sure. But while that may complexify its meaning, it does not prevent it from meaning what it does: *the image of a face of someone who may have existed in reality.* More specifically, that someone seems to be young, a boy, and vaguely "Asian" in appearance. That person may stand beside you as you gaze at their image, or they may not exist at all. The image is not them, but it brings their absence into presence for you at this moment that you gaze at it. Its imaging is an occurrence here and now, for you, even as it connects you to a *there* and a *then*, when the picture may have been taken of a person who may have gazed into a camera, or, alternatively, to a more ambiguous act of image-creation by human-prompted AI. It is a sign that signifies in large part through resemblance to something that exists, in some sense, elsewhere and elsewhen.

My reference to signs brings us to the most important theoretical source informing this inquiry. This is the work of American philosopher and logician Charles Sanders Peirce (pronounced "purse"). Peirce founded the field now called semiotics, or the study of signs, which is devoted to how things come to *mean* anything. Unlike the other major strand of semiotics, founded on the work of French linguist Ferdinand de Saussure, Peirce was not only interested in the meanings themselves. He was also centrally concerned with the process by which meaning occurs for anything or anyone, and therefore in how meaning itself is even possible. Signs, for Peirce, are the basic units of meaning. Their signness lies in their signification, or their production of meaning; it is their action as such that is their essence. And signs are the basis of all life, and indeed of all things.

Peirce conceived of three basic kinds of signs.[14] First, there are those that take their meaning from the resemblance or likeness between the sign or "sign-vehicle," the thing that carries meaning, and its referent. They look, sound, smell, taste, or feel like the thing that they refer to. These he called *icons.* Second, there are those that take their meaning from the directly physical, causal, or "existential" connection between the sign and its referent—in the way that a weathervane indicates the direction of the wind, or that smoke on the horizon indicates a likely fire somewhere below. These he called *indexes* or *indices.* And finally there are those that take their meaning from convention, rule, or habit, which he called *symbols.* These mean what they mean because they are part of a larger system of meanings, one whose basic rules must be learned before the individual meanings can be understood or used. Words are generally this third kind of sign. And while these three forms of signification are not always, nor even usually, easily separable, the difference is significant for reasons that should become clear soon. The image, as I use the word, is that for which the primary basis of meaning, its center of gravity so to speak, is the first of these (the iconic) rather than the second (indexical) or third (symbolic).[15]

Unlike images, language works mostly through the symbolic or conventional register. Words mean things only because they are part of vast, interconnected networks of other words, meanings, and operational rules, which in their combination we call languages. The exceptions are mainly onomatopoeic words that sound like what they mean (which are therefore iconic) and deictic words that take their meaning entirely from their contexts (which are therefore indexical). For humans, linguistic communication is especially important; we rely on words, texts, and stories to a degree that is unmatched among creatures we know. Understanding these requires understanding the logic of language, which means the interrelation of words and concepts within systems that both connect and differentiate concepts with and from each other. Understanding words requires understanding the language they are part of.

But the iconic and the indexical are also present in the ways we communicate and make sense of the world. The iconic even weaves its way into language, so that the most powerful uses of language are those that include clear and resonant images: metaphors that suggest likeness between things we know are different, for instance, between body parts and social or political units (head of state, head of the family, body politic, underbelly, having a leg to stand on, hitting below the belt), between social classes and spatial or temporal categories (higher authorities, upper and lower classes, vanguard, and retrograde), or between mental states and sensory phenomena (darkness and enlightenment). These are more complex forms of signs, which will not be the focus of this book, but they help to demonstrate how images are indeed everywhere.

As sensorially perceptible forms, images include formal qualities that are capable of being maintained across contexts. This makes images sharable between people and contexts, which in turn connects them to networks of meaning, use, production, and interpretation. This is true even while their uses remain negotiable, contestable, and unique to any specific image-event. There is a necessary ambiguity in my description here: I say that an image is sharable, but I have also just claimed that the image is an image only in its imaging—which means that the image I perceive today cannot be the same as the image you or I will perceive tomorrow, no matter if it is the same photo shared on a different computer, or the same road sign, poster, billboard, or cell phone ringtone. There is something shared, and there is something different—just as there is something the image resembles (which makes of it an image) and there is some way in which the resemblance is never complete. The image *differs* even as it *repeats*.

My choice of words here is partly informed by the title of Gilles Deleuze's metaphysical treatise *Difference and Repetition*, in which Deleuze argues that "difference" is not secondary to "identity" or sameness—there are not things that maintain their identities and, only secondarily, things that happen to make those identities change. Rather, for Deleuze, difference is more like the primary fact of the universe: there is something at all only because there is differentiation.[16] Change, transformation, and movement are at the core of all things. The image, in this sense, *differs* in at least two primary ways: it differs from the thing that it refers to, which makes of it an image; and it differs in that its particular instantiation as an image-event is always different from any other. These two differences, or deferrals—between the image and its referent, and between the image and its effect—are the two "movements," "shifts," or "spans" that make of it a *sign*. And the likeness that is carried across these "spans," which is always a repetition with a difference, is what makes of it the kind of sign that we are calling an *image*.

An image, then, is something that means, or that makes meaning, that carries a "force" (to use Jean-Luc Nancy's evocative language, cited in the epigraph to this chapter), by reference to something else—an elsewhere, an elsewhen, or both. Imaging is a making of meaning through reference, which means through connection. It is the kind of connection that, when multiplied and cross-referenced, weaves worlds. Imagination, then, is the bearing (and ongoing production) of the images that constitute worlds for living in. Meaning is not solely made through images; it can also be made through direct reference—by the kind of sign called an index (as when a clap of thunder means, or indicates, an electrical storm)—and through the complex and more arbitrary system of meanings shaped by language. But images are inherent to the making of meaningful worlds, for humans and for other image-bearing creatures.

This definition of an image is somewhat idiosyncratic. Like other everyday words—mind, nature, thought, self, spirit, world, and so on—"image" is used in a multitude of ways, and my use of the word will hardly be able to avoid all the connotations suggested by other uses. For that matter, it is not necessarily a word that travels well across cultural contexts. In German, for instance, there are no separate words for "image" and for "picture"; both are translated as *Bild*. Given the German language's proximity to English, one can see how complicated this might get. For all its messiness, I am hoping that my definition will provide us an adequate place to start.

## PROCESS SEMIOTICS

There is an ontological ambiguity at the heart of my definition of the image. If the image necessarily *repeats* while producing, or at least enabling, *difference*, how far back does the repetition go? If everything repeats something that came before it, and that in turn repeats something that came before *it*, what is the original, to which all repetitions trace back their lineage and from which all are derived?

My short answer to this question is: the repetition goes *all* the way back, and so does the creativity. This may not literally mean "back to the Big Bang" or to the original creative act that begat the universe. But if it did, I would add "but that was also a creative repetition of what preceded it"—a previous big bang, or whatever else we might imagine, wherein the constraints on our ability to imagine become evident. The point is that both repetition and creativity are built into the understanding of the sort of thing that we, and the universe, are.

In another sense, we might say that the original image was the first echo, or the first image seen in a mirror, such as a pool of still water. Before there was water, there was a substance that allowed for something to be echoed back. Imaging begins with echoability. Once something—the first form, a visage of some sort, or a sound (such as the sound of "the Big Bang," and without a substance for it to resonate within, there could have been no bang)—is capable of being echoed, and once there is someone or something capable of perceiving that echo, there is imaging.[17] Imaging therefore begins as "thirdness," which is a word that plays a key role for Peirce, who distinguishes between "firstness," or a thing in and of itself without reference to anything else; "secondness," or a direct and causal relation between two things; and "thirdness," or the mediation or generalization of a direct relation. Imaging is in this sense the first form of thirdness: the perception of a relationship between a thing and its repetition, its echo. Imagination, in turn, builds upon imaging; it is *ongoing thirdness* made or built from this most basic form of thirdness.

Lest it sound as if I am speaking mythologically, this is the point at which I should articulate the ontological core of my argument. The definition I am proposing of the image and of imagination draws in part on the work of image theorists whose names will be referenced in the footnotes throughout this book, but it also emerges from my previous work on images, and on moving images in particular.[18] In that work, I developed a process-relational (or process-semiotic) conception of images drawn from the process metaphysics of Alfred North Whitehead, the processual semiotics of Charles Sanders Peirce, and a range of other thinkers loosely allied around the following three understandings:

1) Reality is most fruitfully understood as consisting not of objects or substances, but of events, occasions of experience, acts of existence, or becomings.

2) Within these events, subjectivity and objectivity, or the mental and the material, in some sense co-arise; they do this as "a response

to what it given." The response is possible because of a creative openness inherent to things; "what is given" is there because of the conditions shaped by what came before. The response, in turn, determines the next set of conditions for the next set of responses; and so on down the ever-branching stream. Determination and openness (to some degree, even if infinitesimal) are conjoined in every event that makes up the universe.

3) These events act and build on each other dynamically and systemically, historically and ecologically, to create the complex worlds in which we live.[19]

If we take something like "relational process" to be central to all life (if not all things), with "process" considered something like the act of processing—the act of "taking up" things perceived and consequently "bringing forth" further things—then it is fair to say that the world is both consumed and produced through the acts of its constituent agents.[20] Whitehead coined the word "prehension" for precisely this kind of "taking up," that is, for taking account of and responding to things given in experience. Prehension, for Whitehead, is analytically distinguishable into a "subjective pole," a component involving the arising, formation, or consolidation of a subjective perception, a becoming-subject; an "objective pole," or the becoming-object of those elements, factors, or perceived things that served in this way for the becoming-subject; and a specific way in which the two are actively and creatively constituted, which is the form taken by the prehension.[21]

Peirce spoke of the same kind of act or event as "semeiotic" and emphasized its triadic character, wherein something (the "representamen" or "sign-itself") is taken as standing for something else (the "object") for a third (the "interpretant").[22] As an example, hearing a phrase of birdsong could evoke a certain set of meanings in the mind of a bird, a predatory animal, or a human who hears it. Analogously, the phrase "I hear a bird" can evoke a certain type of auditory and/or visual image for a human listener. Both of these is the production of a sign (or several), even if the latter involves language and the former does not. Signs, for Peirce, exist in their production: if no one hears a tree fall, then it has not made a sound—which means that the air wave contractions resulting from the fall have not been interpreted acoustically by an organism capable of hearing them because no such organism is in its proximity.

For Peirce and the semioticists who followed in his wake—including the entire fields of biosemiotics, ecosemiotics, zoosemiotics, phytosemiotics, and others—life itself occurs and unfolds through distinctly semiotic acts.[23] A process-semiotic approach understands the world, or at least the living world, to consist of events of semiosis, which are events of relational process, events of mediation resulting in novelty. Such semiosis is not at all restricted to human beings—far from it, in fact—but humans draw upon a complicated array of meaning-making forms, including the iconic (which are based on resemblance between objects and their referents), the indexical (based on causal relationship between objects and their referents), and the symbolic (based on habit or convention), and understanding our world today requires grasping this full complexity of semiotic modalities.

If images are a form of signification, and if signification is always active and relational, always an *act* rather than a *thing*, then the world, or at least a meaningfully lived world, consists at least in part of *acts of imaging*. How we *image* the world, and how we take up and transform those images in our acts of imaging, is both how we add to the world and how we constitute ourselves in the process. Imaging, by this definition, represents a form of accessing, or, in Whitehead's terms, prehending. As Whitehead once put it, "mind is inside its images, not its images inside the mind."[24] The image is the form or vehicle facilitating an act of accessing; because it mediates, the role of the image is active.[25] The capacity to form images—not from scratch, but from the world—and to then inhabit those images, is a precondition for any knowledge of the world.[26]

Defining the imagination in this way, as a capacity or faculty that is a precondition for any knowledge of the world, brings my theory close to the philosophy of Immanuel Kant, who presented imagination more or less like this in his 1787 *Critique of Pure Reason*.[27] And indeed, Kant's notion of the imagination as both reproductive and productive, and as a synthetic activity encompassing both the sensible (that which is known through the senses) and the intelligible or conceptual, is central to how I am using this word. But what is a "faculty," and who possesses it? A process-semiotic account of imagination does not dwell on establishing preconditions, capacities, or limitations to what a human (or nonhuman) might be able to do with images or the imagination. It focuses on the activity of imaging—of creating, inhabiting, and transforming images—and on the relations they enable with the world itself. For that reason, I do not much dwell on the philosophy of imagination in this book; there are other places to look for that.[28] I dwell instead on the relations we make with our images and how that shapes the capacity *for* imagination. I take "imagination" to be a kind of cumulative stand-in for the activity of imaging, which is the activity of making the world through the creation of meaning by resemblance.

Images, I will insist, are not merely visual. They are perceptual, which means that they are based in the possibility of perception. As such, they could be auditory, olfactory, tactile, kinesthetic, gustatory, or of another sensorial mode or combination of perceptual modes that a given organism might have access to. Imaging serves as medium of our experience of the world, a world that, in psychologist James Hillman's words, affords "imagistic intelligibility."[29] The images are, in this sense, not in our heads nor in the world (out there); they are in between. They *are* the between, and they (along with other kinds of signification) are the constituents of the world(s) we live. We take up images selectively, allowing them to take and carry us, to hold and possess us, or to otherwise facilitate our movement in and through the world as we make sense of that world for ourselves and for others.[30]

## MULTISENSORIALIZING THE IMAGE

To say that images can be auditory, olfactory, tactile, kinesthetic, interoceptive, or some other kind may seem radical in a context where images are taken to be primarily, if not exclusively, visual. The habit of thinking of images as always visual is a deeply ingrained one, and it shapes some, but not all, of the literature on the topic. This book rejects that habit, and it does so because it seeks a more coherent understanding of imaging as a specific kind of meaning-making activity, one that is grounded in resemblance.

Let me introduce a more precise vocabulary for analyzing sensory experience. We live in a world whose changing forms and processes come to us through sensory perception. Going back at least to Aristotle, the senses have traditionally been enumerated as five: visual (seeing), auditory (hearing), olfactory (smelling), gustatory (tasting), and tactile (touching). But this conception is consistent neither across western scientific domains nor cross-culturally. Sometimes the list is extended to the proprioceptive (body awareness) and the vestibular or equilibrioceptive (movement and balance); less frequently it includes the interoceptive (senses related to internal organs, which enable perception of heart rate, hunger, chemicals in the bloodstream, spinal and cranial nerves, nervous "butterflies," and the like). Other senses have been proposed, including the vomeronasal, which perceives pheromones separately from the nasal, and specific senses to distinguish pain, temperature, pressure, and other features of experience. Folk taxonomies frequently refer to more mysterious forms of perception, such as intuition, a sixth sense, or x-ray vision, alongside more (apparently) metaphorical usages such as sense of humor, sense of duty, sense of rhythm, and so on.[31] Once we begin to include non-western discourses about sensory experience, things get even murkier, as some cultures do not distinguish at all between physical senses and affects, feelings, or emotions.[32] Expanding to other species makes things even more challenging: there is the echolocation of bats, the ultraviolet vision and infrared perception of many species, an electric sense in fish, and magnetic field sensitivity in many species.

All of that said, speaking of five senses is understandable insofar as these relate directly to a recognizable organ of perception—eyes (sight), ears (hearing), nose (smell), tongue (taste), and skin (touch)—while the others do not. But delineating precise locations for each of these (retina, cochlea, taste buds, and so on) becomes challenging: where, for instance, are the skin receptors, and which ones count? I propose that we begin instead with an understanding of some broad generalities of sensory perception. Each of the five "traditional" senses has the capacity to sense a more general perceptual "field" and, in contrast, a more specific and delineated array of perceptual "objects." We can speak of a visual field and of visual objects; a sonic or auditory field and of auditory objects; an olfactory field and of olfactory objects; a tactile field and tactile objects; and, at least hypothetically, a gustatory field and gustatory objects. Insofar as specific objects take on specific meanings, they become signs: this is where we get visual images, auditory images, olfactory images, tactile images, and gustatory images. The imagined smell of roses is an olfactory image (icon) of roses; the imagined taste of lemon is a gustatory image of lemon; and so on. In the same sense, we could speak of visual or auditory indexes and symbols: the sensation of being tickled by one's lover, for instance, is an index of her touch, though it may also be a symbol of her love. The stars on the U.S. flag, on the other hand, take their meaning neither from any resemblance (iconic) to particular stars in the sky nor from the activity of those stars (indexical), but only from the symbolic understanding that they represent states that collectively made the United States of America.

A fully fledged analysis of all the senses, even one that restricted itself to the traditional five, would take us too far afield for the purposes of this book. Instead, I will delve more deeply here into the world of sound, or what François Bonnet in his wonderful meditation on *The Order of Sounds* calls the "regime of audibility."[33] The sonic, audiovisual, and poetic-literary will return in later parts of this book, but the assumption throughout will be the definition of the image provided in the previous pages.

Bonnet's *The Order of Sounds* begins with the image of a seashell which, when we hold an ear to it, resounds with the sound of the sea. Applying a Peircian analysis to this, we can ask: is this a trace of the actual sea we hear (an index), our own memory of the sea (an icon), or a convention understood from hearing and reading about seashells taken to "contain" the "sound of the sea" (a symbol)? When the sound of a bullroarer is taken to be the voice of a god or a lake-monster, or when church bells are taken to signify the arrival of sacred or divine time, is that sound iconic because it is *like* the object, indexical because it is *of* the object, or symbolic because it is taken as such within the system of cultural meanings in which that is possible? Would a Kaspar Hauser, a feral child who had never previously experienced church bells, know anything of their intent or significance? When the sound of a thunderbird or of sirens is heard, is this a matter of pure and direct hearing (indexicality), of resemblance (iconicity), or of interpretation (symbolicity)?

Any interpretive framework that renders such sounds meaningful—that takes the bullroarer to be the correct god and not another one, or the sound of thunder to be a thunderbird rather than a raven or the meaningless discharge of electricity—eludes full arbitrarity, to one extent or another. That is, to the degree that the thunderbird in fact sounds like thunder, or that ambulance sirens sound oceanic, powerful, alluring, and "sirenic"—their perception transcends the merely arbitrary, conventional, and symbolic (in Peirce's sense). Whatever else we may say about these signs, they are not entirely arbitrary; at some point in their evolution (so to speak) they either resembled a source (iconically) or issued directly from it (indexically), and their meanings continue to harbor at least a trace of those significances. So the question here may ultimately be a matter of distinguishing the iconic from the indexical.

The technological reproduction of prerecorded sounds is literally iconic—they sound like the originals. But is it so only when the hearer knows it is a recording and not the real thing? When the musical tritone, or augmented fourth interval, is taken to be the sound of the devil (as it may have been in certain medieval European contexts), or the tonal drone of the Indian raga (or the meditative *Aum*) is taken to be the foundational ground of the cosmos, is its performance iconic (yes, indeed!) or indexical (yes, but for whom)? Is the repeatedly insistent tritone at the center of proto-heavy metal band Black Sabbath's eponymous song "Black Sabbath" the mark of the devil (an index), or is it merely a likeness of that mark (an icon)? It is also of course a winking nod to the tradition that, for whatever reason, took that interval to be the devil's, which means that it is therefore also a symbol. But in each of these cases one could argue that it is in the blurring of the icon and the index that we come to participate in the world: that the world comes to be a place in which sounds—and images, smells, and tastes—*can* be reproduced because they point back to an original, and in which the tension between the originality and the reproduction becomes a lively and negotiable space for determining what is what.

What this implies for our definition of the image, as a sign incorporating likeness or resemblance, is that the degree of likeness to an original is a variable that may remain to some extent unresolvable. There may, in other words, be regimes within which an image is taken to be not an image but the original, the thing itself (Black Sabbath's tritone *is* the devil); and in this case our calling it an image becomes an etic, or outsider's, strategy of interpretation that differs from the emic (insider's) reality it is interpreting. This is an ontological risk we should be prepared to account for as we move forward. In key respects, it will remain at the heart of our understanding of images and imagining, because it in fact prefigures one of the image regimes to be examined in the following chapter, that of the "animate-image."

To the extent that we recognize the Black Sabbath song as music, however, we are recognizing it as participating in a language akin not only to other arts but also to language itself, and consisting of iconic, indexical, and symbolic forms in varying degrees. If music, as Whiteheadian philosopher Suzanne Langer called it, is an "occurrent" art of "virtual time" determined "by the movement of audible forms,"[34] some of those forms will be recognized in their relationship with each other—as elements of a symbolic language that is a language like language itself, whose elements refer to their relationships with each other (the note G sounds different in the context of a C major scale than that of an E minor scale). Others will be recognized for their resemblance to extra-musical things: to upward or downward movement, quickening pulses, birdsong, flowing water, steam trains, crashing metal, and devils. With aural images, no matter how connotatively symbolic they get (opera, hip-hop, and black metal all connote quite different sensibilities and cultures), they remain always already iconic in reference to what they sound like, and indexical in reference to their methods of production (the plucking of strings, the banging of metal, the fluttering of vocal chords).

As with music, so with dance, theatre, poetry, and other forms of creative expression: each generates meaning through culturally, and sometimes subculturally, specific systems of difference which, like much of language, seem arbitrary; but also through its simulation of things known from non-artistic contexts—say, those of politics, sexuality, bodily experience, nature, and so on. Teasing these apart is analytically feasible only up to a point. Even with visuality, this "always already ambiguity" can never be entirely eliminated. When I look outside my window and see a view of a lake and of mountains I know to actually be there, they are, for me, the things themselves: the mountains, the lake (in this case it is the Adirondacks on the opposite side of Lake Champlain, which I can see from the window of my Vermont home; for you of course mentioning these may conjure images from physical memory, or from photographs, travel brochures, or tourist geographies). I also recognize the lake as a lake because it shares in the character of lakeness—it is in this sense iconic of something I know to transcend this particular lake. But still I know that it is there to be touched and waded in if I were to walk down toward it. And yet, a moment's thought will remind me that what I see is an image reconstructed by my brain from electromagnetic waves perceived by my optical receptors. The relationship here is indexical and somewhat complicated, based in evolutionary strategies underpinning the sensory apparatus by which I receive and interpret my world, with that interpretation always being somewhat predetermined through a set of algorithms that my nervous system (and yours) have found to be functional for our type of human living.[35] I see the lake as "blue" because of a shared understanding that that is what it is, and even if its color is closer to those I would in other circumstances call "green" or "gray," I will still see it as blue as a matter of neuro-culturally determined habit.

My habits in this sense may not be as arbitrary as those making up language, but language is itself never quite arbitrary either, as its development is thoroughly historical and thereby causal: today's languages are the results of historical networks of indexical determination that have resulted in what today may be both commonsensical and seemingly arbitrary. The word "lake" bears no resemblance to the appearance, sound, or smell of any actual lake; in its synchronic context, it appears perfectly arbitrary. But considered diachronically, its arbitrariness could be thoroughly deconstructed through a systematic and historical reconstruction of the evolution of the English language, of its predecessors (Old English, Old French, Latin, and so on), and of the speakers who enunciated it along the way.

The point here is that the very distinction between icon, index, and symbol breaks down when submitted to sufficient scrutiny. This breaking down—the elusiveness of reality in the face of our attempts to parse it—is something we will also see when we begin to distinguish different types of image regimes. Reality is a flux that submits to generalization only at the cost of its own messy detail. The best we can say is that, in an ultimate sense, the world is what Buddhists describe in their concept of *Pratītyasamutpāda*: it is a systemic network of dependently arisen phenomena, with each phenomenon being determined by multiple causes without which it could not be what it is. In this sense, a "fully Buddhist" analysis—which happens to be congruent with a "fully scientific" analysis—would take causality to be fundamental to the world's functioning, which suggests that it is the *index*, the sign of causality, that most accurately presents that world to us. But causalities will always remain somewhat elusive to living beings, who are reliant on noting resemblances and, in the human case at least, on denotative systems of meaning (such as language), for interpreting the world. In a dynamic world, it is actually imperative to learn to read signs quickly: to note resemblances and to act on expectations derived from prior experience. This is how cognition works, according to neurocognitive scientists, for whom experience is a construction derived from the interaction of sensory input with a complex architecture of responses and expectations built from previous experience.[36] Iconic, and thus imagistic, thinking is therefore central to everything we humans do; and there is little reason to believe that this is not the case for every other life form as well.

My attempt in this book to distinguish the icon—the likeness and resemblance incorporated into a sign—from the index and the symbol is therefore an exercise of abstraction by which I am choosing to inflect my interpretation of things. In this sense the entire interpretive edifice of this book, with its focus on images as at least partly iconic, is an active, and ultimately contestable, choice: it is a way of participating in the world and never only a way of observing that world. Its goal is to see what this form of interpretive participation may bring—what its emphasis on *knowing by resemblance* adds to our understanding of the world. That is the journey on which I invite you to follow me. And all of that suggests that images are always already ensconced within networks or ecologies of relations.

## IMAGE ECOLOGIES AND IMAGE REGIMES

Closing her influential 1977 essay entitled "The Image-World," American cultural critic Susan Sontag proposed that "if there can be a better way for the real world to include the one of images, it will require an ecology not only of real things but of images as well."[37] While her essay was nuanced and complex, the wording here is unfortunate if it suggests that the image world and the real world are distinct and separate, or that the distinction between "real" things and their representation as "images" is what counts. In what follows, I argue instead that an "ecology of images" is already built into the world—that the world is configured along more than one such ecology—and that our task is to better understand how these ecologies have worked in the past and how they are working today, so as to inhabit them more ethically and responsibly.

In the years since Sontag's intervention, scholars of cultural and visual studies, film and media studies, science and technology studies, art history, and related areas have grappled with the proliferation of images and image media, as well as with the question of how this proliferation is connected to longer-term trends in technology, economy, ecology, and society.[38] Scholars of religion have attempted to understand the role of images, visuality, and sensory cultures in the spread, transformation, and maintenance of religious ideas and practices.[39] Scholars of media have developed novel approaches to understand the mediation of images, texts, and practices not only by human-made systems for recording, storing, transmitting, and processing information, but also by "natural" forms of mediation, and some have developed provocative ecological models for media and culture more broadly.[40] Finally, scholarship associated with the so-called ontological turn has made it impossible to ignore that previously taken-for-granted assumptions about reality, including the reality of images and of the things they refer to, may not be universal nor even widely shared by many societies today and in the past that do not fall into the category of "modern."[41] Their views are in some ways met by the views of those approaching these questions from very different directions: namely, from those of Indigenous, traditional, and non-western worlds. All these trends are relevant to the proposals that follow.

"Ecologies" can loosely be taken to mean the networks of consumption, production, and circulation that organize and embed the relations between organisms and other entities. To reduce our reliance on the metaphorics of capitalist production, these can also be described as networks of relational interdependence, by which organisms "take up" and "bring forth" their worlds, alongside the circulatory networks enabling these processes through which circulates agency, or the power to do.[42] In his recent work on the ecology of images, David Morgan proposes:

> The ecology of an image consists of those artifacts and forces with which it comes into connection—viewers, certainly, and image makers, but also the availability and chemistry of pig-

> ments, the trees, lumber industry, and market that provide the panels on which images are made. The panels are shaped by weather and worms that besiege wooden supports or stretcher bars over time; the sunlight that fades pigments; the fashion of framing and displaying images; the commerce of taste; the long, dense histories of genre, theme, and subject matter; style, paint medium, and technique; and the cascade of images from which pictures emerge and into which they vanish in endless acts of homage, comparison, emulation, and rivalry. This assemblage of human and nonhuman actors is the matrix for understanding any given image. [. . .] Images are instruments or technologies that connect bodies to places and to one another, productively integrating humans into their physical and social ecologies.[43]

Drawing on the triadic "ecologies" of Gregory Bateson, Félix Guattari, and C. S. Peirce, I have elsewhere distinguished between three forms or registers of ecology.[44] In the scientific sense of the term, ecology consists of the study of the relationships between organisms and objects studied scientifically, which means as they are seen, measured, and analyzed. This includes the pigments, trees, lumber industries, panels, and so on mentioned by Morgan, and it spans the entire production-consumption cycle, from the extraction of resources to their deposition as waste. I call this *material ecology* in that it focuses on matter, the substance of things seen from their "outside."

The study of relationships between the experienced "interiorities" of things—the subjective "you" and "I" who experience things, and all the other entities that do so in one way or another—can in turn be called *social* or *political ecology* in that its focus is intersubjectivity, or the ascription of agency to oneself and to others and the relations that arise from that ascription. I see you seeing me, hearing me, making sense of me; you see me making sense of you; we respond to each other in ways that may be inflected by "the commerce of taste," the "histories of genre, theme, and subject matter," and so on (as suggested by Morgan), but with an eye toward acknowledging each other's agency. How we carve up that acknowledgment of agency—who or what is included in it, who has a "voice" or a "seat at the table," and what expectations and obligations those relations carry—makes up the sociopolitics of the given situation.

Finally, the study of relationships between the perceptual or prehensive dynamics that constitute things—the ways in which the "taking up" and the "bringing forth" of our experience are effected, the chiasmic intertwinement (as Maurice Merleau-Ponty referred to it)[45] of bodily, sensorial, perceptual, and medial entanglements—these are identifiable as a third kind of ecology, which I call *perceptual* or *medial ecology.*[46] If perception is taken as a matter of material substances, including sensory organs and their extensions or modifications, mediating what is seen, heard, felt, and understood, then it is a matter of mediation. I therefore use the terms "perceptual" and "medial" interchangeably, in part to underline the point that perception *is* mediation and that media, including the novel kinds found in our world today, are forms of and for perception. It is here, in the perceptual entanglement, that the parsing of the social and the material—of what will count as subject and what as object—takes place. The latter two are effects, so to speak, of the first; they constitute the two ends of a kind of oscillatory continuum along which the social and the material get negotiated.

These three ecologies are a way to indicate the variegated nature of the relations that make up the world. Some of them can be studied scientifically (as would a natural scientist). Others require methods that are hermeneutic, or interpretive, and require talking about things and reflecting on them philosophically. The claim that underlies my triadic parsing of this territory is that neither a materialist nor an idealist or interpretive description of the world ultimately suffices; mind and matter, objectivity and subjectivity, are intertwined in ways that must be understood dynamically, and the process by which they emerge, moment to moment, is central to that dynamism. That is where the act of accessing the world figures in; and central to that act (and to all such acts) are the images and signs that support and shape that access. It is important to reiterate that these three sets of ecologies are not separate: neither the social nor the material can exist without the subject-object forming activity of prehension, and in a certain sense only the latter is "ultimately real." Recognizing these as three analytical categories or registers, however, is helpful insofar as these are attended to for the experiential realities they signify.

If images are the perceivable forms that mediate our relationship with ourselves and with others (including nonhuman others), then there have certainly been a variety of ways in which that mediation has occurred and a variety of beliefs about the nature of that mediation and of the reality that is being mediated. In the remainder of this book, I propose and develop a typology of image-relations, or what I call *image regimes*. These are not *types* of images per se; rather, they are types of relations that humans have had with their images, relations that have established themselves through particular traditions of thinking about images, reality, and humanity. The distinctions between these regimes are schematic and heuristic. They are intended not as exclusionary categories nor as chronologically developed modes (though at least a few of them depend on specific historical developments that are important to understand); and they are certainly not an exhaustive list. Rather, they are meant to provide a loosely phenomenological typology of tendencies or orientations, some or all of which might be found in any particular image practice.

To be coherent, a typology of "image relations" or "image regimes" should be based on clear principles. A typology could, for instance, be grounded in diachronic, historical, or developmental criteria, which could involve asking: how have people's relations to images evolved over time, and what factors have conditioned the most obvious shifts between one orientation and the next? Or it could be grounded in structural or ideal-typical principles, which would ask: how does a particular kind of image-relation conceive of the world and humans' place in it? Is there some key variable (or two or three) along which such conceptions can be distinguished, such that we could map out a set of possible image types? Does one image regime, for instance, rely on a conception of reality as a unified field in which humans act in ways similar to other entities, and another on a conception of the human world as being fundamentally different from another world—whether it be the "natural" world, accessible to scientists, or the "supernatural" world accessible to religion? Does an image regime situate humans midway between the animals (and plants and rocks) and the gods? And whatever the imagined structure it relies on, does it perceive agency as moving in one direction only (from the gods, or from natural laws, to the human realm) or in both or all directions at once? Asking such a question will elicit a range of possible answers, and mapping out the full range along a limited set of axes would result in a possible typology.

These kinds of distinctions play a role in the typology I will present, but my goal is not to offer a comprehensive account of responses people have had to images.[47] Nor is it to shed light on historical developments framing the human relationship with images, or on cross-cultural differences in those relations. Each of these will figure somewhere or other: there will be some relationship between historical and technological developments with at least a few of the six image regimes to be presented here. As a taxonomy, however, the foundation for what I offer will be fluid and pragmatic. It is an attempt to distinguish six of the most prominent forms of image-relations based on a mix of rules applied promiscuously in order to help us navigate the world of images today. Even the very task of mapping them out could be taken as privileging a particular image regime—one that considers the mapping of such relationships fundamental. This is in itself an exercise of power. The question of the cross-cultural validity of these categories will thus remain unclear. I present these six regimes as a starting point for comparative and empirical elaboration, but do not attempt to defend them in the face of the wealth of ethnographic and historical evidence that could be brought to bear on them. Furthermore, these categories are in no way intended as mutually exclusive. The actual use of images partakes of whatever regime is at hand. Ultimately, it is not the regime that matters, but the image: in any particular instance, it is the specific image that counts. The regimes remain abstractions that are useful to think with.

I would even go so far as to say that not only is the idea of an image regime an abstraction from a much more complex reality; so is the very category of "image" itself. To understand how images work, it is important to understand something of what they may be in aggregate, and something of how they interact within systems, networks, and regimes that themselves are changeable and negotiable. But ultimately it is the image in its specificity that matters. An image of Jesus is not an image of Krishna. For devotees of one or the other, it is not the image that matters—it is the being it embodies: the Messiah, Lord Krishna, Quan Yin, Nuestra Señora de Guadalupe, Yemayá, Elvis, Beyoncé, Lionel Messi, Batman. The believer's ontology is defined by the other, the deity, the force in whose gravitational field we orbit. By the same token, a screensaver image of the rock face of El Capitan in Yosemite National Park is not equivalent to a screensaver image of one's child, grandchild, lover, or cat. An image of a sports car in a magazine advertisement is not the image of that car being driven out of the driveway by one's wealthy neighbor (or the sound that it makes as the neighbor revs its engine conspicuously). Each of these is a different image, different in its contexts and its meanings. And contrary to what Marshall McLuhan famously quipped, the medium in which an image is presented is not its message, though it may alter, condition, and contain that message. The thing itself will always still count for more than the system of interpretation being applied to it, whether consciously or unconsciously; and that thing itself will always be more than something that we might generically describe as an image. It is in this sense that an image has an "opacity," if not a "will, appetite, and motion," as Gilbert Simondon describes it, an irreducibility that makes it distinctively its own (this is something we will examine especially in chapter 4).

All that said, it is useful to consider how images function in these multiple ways, and how their functioning in a new and increasingly dominant regime—that of the digital image-world—may be describable as an ontology that includes and subsumes all of the others to varying degrees. Shedding light on the novelty of the regime of the digital image-world is the prime objective of this book. But that regime cannot be understood without understanding some of its main predecessors, because those continue to work in and through the novel and reshaped terrain of images, image-events, and imagescapes within which we find ourselves. The new lives of images are therefore always a recapitulation of their old lives, but today they are also much more than those.

Two

# FIVE IMAGE REGIMES

*Images—in all their aggregate conditions, as sign, work of art, inscription, or picture that acts as a mediation to access something else; as social representations, symbols, schemes; from their role in cognition, the sensuous body and mimetic exchange, to the image as an object that, as a mediator, acquires an agency of its own—are what any relation presupposes, since we have no direct access to the world. Images, whether merely mental or materialized, are, by definition, boundaries: conjunction and disjunction at the same time, creation of a difference, and creation of a relation. They organize, uphold, cross, transgress, affirm, or undermine boundaries.*

—ANSELM FRANKE, *"Much Trouble in the Transportation of Souls, or the Sudden Disorganization of Boundaries"*[1]

*[T]he human understanding is an "image-needing one" [. . .] the human spirit needs images which it uses symbolically to disclose meaning beyond them. There is no leaping clean out of an image-world so that spirit knows ultimately itself.*

—CHARLES W. HENDEL, *"Introduction" to Ernst Cassirer,* The Philosophy of Symbolic Forms[2]

• • • Images, as Anselm Franke suggests, are hardly one thing, and they are relational in their nature—"conjunction and disjunction"—rather than anything that can be isolated. And because they are what we do—we image—we can hardly know them, "leaping clean out of an image-world," in Hendel's words, apart from knowing ourselves.

The task of identifying different kinds of relations with images--the kinds of things I am calling image regimes--is complicated by the fact that the world does not have a singular history, no matter how many historians have tried to narrate it as such. Historical research and archaeological findings guarantee that we continue to learn about the past, to such a degree that our efforts undermine themselves in the process. Many of the histories that have been told in languages familiar to westerners are histories that posit "the West" as a kind of single organism, evolving from its own internal dynamics. Other histories—Chinese, Indian, Aztec, and so on—may parallel that history or counteract it, evolving autonomously, but in the end they are typically considered to have met on the grounds of modernity, at which point the history of the West becomes the history of the world.

Such Eurocentric histories are insufficient today for a host of reasons. One is that they are retrospective, or what historians call presentist: in their thinking about the past, they assume what we know today. There was in fact no "West" in Greco-Roman times, and whatever carryover there was from those times to the European Renaissance can hardly be understood apart from the Muslim world that (largely) carried it, yet which has not been written in as central to it. Another reason is that they are simply inaccurate, with history being much more global and crisscrossed than such histories suggest. Histories of the image have nevertheless been molded on these kinds of narratives, and while their insights require broader contextualization today, those insights can sometimes be profound. I will refer to some of these in what follows.

Capturing the entire history of images in a single narrative, however, risks far too much damage to the empirical details. French philosopher and mediologist Régis Debray, for instance, has attempted to capture the history of images in a threefold model that resonates with models we are familiar with from other contexts.[3] Debray names the "three ages of looking" the "era of idols," the "era of art," and the "era of the visual," with each corresponding to certain sources of authority (respectively, the supernatural, natural, and performative/machinic), temporal horizons (eternity, tradition, innovation), modes of attribution (collective/autonomous, individual/artistic, spectacular), norms (celebration, creation, production), governmental structures (curial-ecclesiastic, monarchical-bourgeois, media-market), pathological tendencies (paranoia, obsession, schizophrenia), and so on.[4] Viewed from a certain height over the earth it surveys, this loose progression captures a great many historical generalities. But both above and below that height, it comes to feel like a formula into which facts are slotted irrespective of their details.

The typology I present in this chapter will be no more exhaustive nor systematic than Debray's, and its scope will hopefully be more humble. (That said, for those who like a certain typological neatness, I provide a distillation of the six image regimes in graphic form at the end of chapter 4. It should be taken with the grain-of-salt knowledge that in their reality images are always slipping and sliding from one type to another. The world's recalcitrance against categorization is in this sense a feature and not a bug, and I fully admit that my efforts to rein it into a conceptual system are always bound to fail.)[5] To be more specific, the distinctions that follow are based in part on historical configurations that have shaped the present—which makes it somewhat genealogical—and in part on where each regime locates agency. Specifically, if images mediate relations between humans and something that is beyond the human—whether this be considered nature, divinity, or some more specific referent—the question becomes: is agency primarily located on the side of the human, the beyond-human, the image itself, or somewhere else, such as in the circulation between them?

The six image regimes identified here—five in this chapter and the sixth in the next—are in this sense constellations identified for convenience. Our exploration of them will be based on a loosely historical sense of how these emerged into wider acceptance, to the point that they served as a somewhat hegemonic formation within certain cultural arenas. The first three have arguably been much more widely established around the world than the last three, whose historical emergence is largely traceable over the past few hundred years. The first serves loosely as a kind of baseline from which the second and third deviate. They are ideal-typical, not actual, but defining them as regimes will allow us to assess them in terms of their similarities, differences, and potentialities for interaction within the use of images today.

## ANIMATE-IMAGE: THE IMAGE THAT ACTS AND AFFECTS

Images take us. They beckon to us, lure us, captivate us, and move us. They transport us, carrying us from a "here" to a "there" that renders us changed in the process.

Some of us speak of images this way today even while we acknowledge that we are speaking metaphorically. An image, after all, does not act; it is a human product and its action is only what was imparted into it by its maker. Or so it is said. But is the latter merely a modern conceit, one that most people in the world, if measured over centuries, have not really followed? Do images live? Do they exist as sovereign actors, vehicles or agents of a dynamic reality with which we communicate, negotiate, and interact? The regime of the animate-image may be furthest from the publicly acknowledged norm within educated strata of industrialized societies, but it has featured in so many cultural contexts, including but certainly not restricted to those we call "indigenous" or "traditional," as to be almost a baseline norm for human relations with images. For millennia, humans have shaped images that were used to accomplish things, to transport their beholders into a world of meanings signifying something far greater than the material itself from which the image—the cave painting, the statue, the amulet, the "idol" and "icon"—was crafted. In the process, the wood, rock, paint, or figure would come alive, becoming the god, the hero, the angel, the ruler, the animal spirit.

An ethnographer's stance requires us to bracket out any questions of the realism, reasonableness, or scientific factuality of this view and accept simply that people have indeed assumed images to be real, active, and agential in relation to us. Understanding the animate-image requires understanding how it could be that everything—or at least any particular thing—could be considered alive and animate. A good summary term for such a perspective may be *animism*, the term introduced in 1871 by Edward Tylor in his book *Primitive Culture*, ambitiously subtitled *Researches into the Development of Mythology, Philosophy, Religion, Language, Art, and Custom.*[6] While Tylor's work, like that of many nineteenth-century anthropologists, was founded on outdated colonial assumptions, the term "animism" itself has reentered the agenda for an increasing number of cultural anthropologists, scholars of religion, art theorists, and some non-westerners themselves, if only as a gesture toward the reopening of questions raised and inadequately answered by Tylor and his colleagues.[7] Animism in these contemporary renditions has much to do with the effort to reconceptualize agency in the midst of the ontological, new materialist, posthumanist, and decolonial theoretical "turns." (We will discuss this "neo-animism" more directly in chapter 4.)

Accordingly, the animate-image is what Bruno Latour would describe as a *mediator* and not a mere *intermediary*: it not only carries an influence to its human perceiver, but it shapes and contributes to that influence.[8] Its effect on the perceiver is potentially or actually transformative. It is taken to be a social agent that is corporeal and energetic, with which our relationship is not one of contemplation but of engagement and participation, and potentially a relationship of obligation, negotiation, inhabitation, or mutual metamorphosis. Images, if they are animate, oblige us, "hail us," "coax, seduce, or entice us," and when we accept their offer, they have the capability to "take" us, challenge us, and transform us.[9] The image is in this sense as ontologically real as anything else, and therefore potentially *more* real or significant than many things (at least in specific instances, when the image has been properly prepared, understood, or approached), and its impact on beholders is more or less efficacious and transformative. It is taken to have its own agency, its own needs or desires, its own being, presence, and capacities or capabilities.

Examples of the animate-image regime include the use of religious objects as carriers of divine or spiritual energy or force—as in the treatment of an icon or statue as the eyes or presence of a divinity, a spirit, an entity that both exceeds the image and inhabits it. This "force that exceeds" can be personal, as with deities, or impersonal, as with the energies or qualities known as *qi* (in China), *prana* (India), *mana* (Melanesia and Polynesia), or *àshe* (Yoruba), which suffuse or circulate through the world but get particularly concentrated in specific objects, people, animals, or phenomena. The purpose of artistic images in the Igbo world of West Africa, according to Chinua Achebe, is "to channel a spiritual force into an aesthetically satisfying physical form that captures the presumed attributes of that force." As evident in Igbo arts such as dance and masquerade, this channeling is less a simple act than a continuous process: "It stands to reason," Achebe writes, "that new forms must stand ready to be called into being as often as new (threatening) forces appear on the scene. It is like 'earthing' an electrical charge to ensure communal safety."[10]

Such objects make present what would otherwise be absent. As

Diana Eck writes in her analysis of the divine image in India, the "central act of Hindu worship" is "to stand in the presence of the deity and to behold the image with one's own eyes, to see and be seen by the deity."[11] The image is the place where the gaze of the deity meets the gaze of the devotee. As such, the image mediates. This is not to say that humans are not active in relation to it; most such images are shaped in some way, prepared, and taken care of. In numerous East Asian contexts, as Lauren Kendall describes, statues, paintings, and masks are "made by skilled artisans according to strict protocols" in "workshops dedicated to this purpose" and it is "through appropriate procedures" that "the statue body becomes the body casing of a socially present god, spirit, buddha, or *nat*."[12] These images must be cleaned, kept pure, and consecrated, with their treatment being instrumental to their efficacy.

In Andean religious festivals today, as Nico Tassi recounts, worshippers "act" upon images, "not only by dancing for them, looking at them, and praying to them, but also by dressing them, adding and removing decorations, fitting photographs between the canvas and the frame, donating hair, gold teeth, and garments to be fitted onto the image, or simply lighting a candle, decorating them with flowers, or offering them drink and food. Images [are] 'looked after,' 'reproached,' 'bribed,' and 'danced.'"[13] Tassi describes images in these contexts as "corporeal agents" that "sensually engage people *and* spirits and 'attract' them into relationships and exchange."[14] Inca cosmology, still resonant in the practices of urbanized indigenous Catholic *cholo-mestizos* in Bolivia, is woven around "a system of reciprocity reproduced by the sensorial relations and interchange of perceptions between the human body, the huacas," or "idols," and the body of the Inca king, substituted today by the Christian God(s) and saints.[15]

"The case from West Africa," David Freedberg writes, "is the same as the case from Byzantium. The image, once properly prepared, set up, adorned, and decorated, becomes the locus of the spirit. It becomes what it is taken to represent."[16] It is this "becoming" that enables the Orthodox Christian to kiss the icon as if it is the face of the saint or messiah. As Freedberg notes, there is some measure of this kind of "becoming" in the treatment of the art object by educated westerners today: "We too feel a 'vague awe' at the creative skills of the artist; we too fear the power of the images he makes and their uncanny abilities both to elevate us and to disturb us. They put us in touch with truths about ourselves in a way that can only be described as magical, or they deceive us as if by witchcraft."[17] It is only our education that has taught us *not* to speak of images this way.

I would like to propose that the animacy of images can be considered primordial.[18] It is there as a result of what an image is—its evocation of something that is not there. The viewer is required for the image to act, and that viewer is always shaped by the expectations and habits he or she has accrued through a lifetime of dwelling within a specific cultural milieu. But, as David Morgan says, "Even if we as viewers are complicit in its construction [. . .], the image returns our look with a power that affects us."[19] The image attracts the human eye because of its likeness or resemblance to other things that we, on some level, understand and respond to. The slab of rock shaped in the form of a human face, or the pattern of sand dunes that resembles waves on an ocean, is recognized as such whether it was intended and shaped to be so or not. In this sense, Morgan is correct to describe images as "technologies that act on human beings, as well as on others—gods, the dead, the living, malignant forces, animals, and the world around us. Scarecrows frighten birds; icons are conduits to the saints they depict, and they have often been used in processions to fight the plague or protect cities from invaders; works of art are devices for moving us, refining our sensibilities, enlightening our minds and spirits."[20] Drawing on actor-network theory, Morgan describes this way of conceiving of images as a form of "Enchantment Network Theory."[21] Images, in this view, act by enchanting their beholders within webs or "spells" of commonality and difference and the relations of obligation that ensue from these.

Enchantment has long been a theme within certain streams of critical and environmental theory. Drawing upon Max Weber's work on the disenchanting consequences of modernity and Max Horkheimer and Theodor Adorno's theorization of the ambivalent "dialectic of enlightenment," a line of thinkers has either argued that modernity has had its own enchantments all along or has explicitly proposed the virtues of *re*-enchantment.[22] Like some of the former authors, David Morgan rightly asserts that enchantment and disenchantment need not be thought of in civilizational terms, as if the western world took a detour through a grand disenchantment, a fall from the grace within which other societies found themselves. Processes of enchantment and disenchantment occur side by side, not unlike Foucauldian power relations; their effects emerge at the local scale at which they are applied. Disenchantment, Morgan writes, "can be a useful means of opposing other people's enchantment and securing one's own."[23] The iconoclasm of one set of disenchantments—for instance, in a Protestant missionary's debunking of his subjects' "idolatry"—are intended not just to displace those subjects from their cultural and religious coordinates, but also to make them available to another, rival set of enchanting coordinates—the One God, the Holy Spirit, the promise of western civilization, and so on.

Images thus facilitate networks of enchantment; they mediate processes by which social actors align themselves within broader networks of power and agency. Images take on a life within ecologies that, as Morgan writes, enchant them by enveloping them in an "extended social apparatus."[24] "The power of the saint acts through a meandering confluence of dreams, relics, a devotee's pain and desire, the stories of the saint's life and death, institutional rites, processions into the countryside, and the testimony of fellow pilgrims,"[25] to all of which we can add economic and property relations, webs of pilgrimage routes, and political machinations. This power of the saintly image reappears today as the power of the musical idol, the political hero, the porn star, and the eco-graphic, whose images connect their devotees and followers into relational networks by which desires (political, sexual, cultural, environmental) are rekindled, dance moves are imitated, and donations are elicited and made. The image of President Trump on a sign on one's lawn, the porn star poster on one's wall, the crucifix waved at visitors to an abortion clinic, the raised Black Lives Matter fist—these all not only speak but act: they bind, protect, pollute, offend, cast away, or inflame.

Examining the neurological underpinnings of mind, emotion, and belief, philosopher Stephen Asma and psychologist Rami Gabriel define animism as "the belief that there are many kinds of persons in this world, only some of whom are human," adding that "one's task, as an animist, is to placate and honor these other spirit-persons."[26] Perhaps only a little contentiously, they add that "most people in the world are best characterized as animists." "Almost all of Africa," they assert, and "Southeast Asia, rural China, Tibet, Japan, rural South and Central America, and the indigenous Pacific Islands—pretty much everywhere except Western Europe, the Middle East, and North America—are all dominated by animistic beliefs. Even places where later religions like Buddhism and Catholicism enjoy *formal* recognition as national faiths, much older forms of animism comprise the daily concerns and rituals of the people."[27]

If this pervasiveness of the animate-image sounds surprising, or seems a bold claim to make, it is fair to ask if the ocularcentrism of image theory contributes to this situation. As mentioned in the previous chapter, music does not lend itself to an easy distribution in the semiotics of icons, indexes, and symbols. If the tritone served as our example of a musical image that was at once index (the sound *of* the devil), icon (sounding *like* the sound the devil makes), and symbol ("the sound of the devil"), something like this could be said for almost any element of music. The rhythmic "groove" of jazz or hip-hop music both embodies and reflects a certain sensibility—a way of moving through the world (related, some have argued, to African deities)—that makes it different from European folk song or Western classical meter. Sonata form embodies a sensibility of tension and release that arguably sublimates sexuality within culturally "refined," upper-class bodies; heavy metal propels a similar energy into a more direct and bodily viscerality; funk and related dance musics mobilize this viscerality into dance; and the music accompanying a voodoo ceremony takes this viscerality to the next level, that of possession by a deity. In another register, Javanese gamelan music reflects an understanding of cosmic rhythms and harmonies, and classical Indian ragas envelop listeners within a particular sensibility, a *rasa* or "taste," that cultivates attunement to the emotional qualities it is meant to convey.

A casual listener may think of all of these as interesting connotations or as by-products of music. In some cases, as with the Indian and Javanese, they could even play the part of didactic tools (which points toward the next image regime). But a "true believer" (even in the European classical mode), for whom music is an emotionally powerful force, knows that music enters into and changes a performer, a listener, a dancer. It may remind a listener of something heard or felt before, or of stories and histories, spaces and places, myths and enchantments, but it can also bring these alive into listeners' bodies, feelings, and minds. The power of music is in this sense the best evidence for the animate-image regime—or, more accurately, for multiple animate-image regimes, since these are rarely singular regimes. As music can come to inhabit a body, the animacy of the image (including the optical, sonic, or even textual image) is something that can become embodied in people, individually and collectively. We will return to this embodied multiplicity of the animate-image following a journey through other image-regimes.

It is in the rivalry between image-laden enchantments that the *next* image regime emerges. The claim, with the ideal-image, is that *our* image and our set of relations is not just like yours, but that ours accesses reality in a way that yours does not. From within one set of image relations, another is seen not only as an alternative enchantment but as

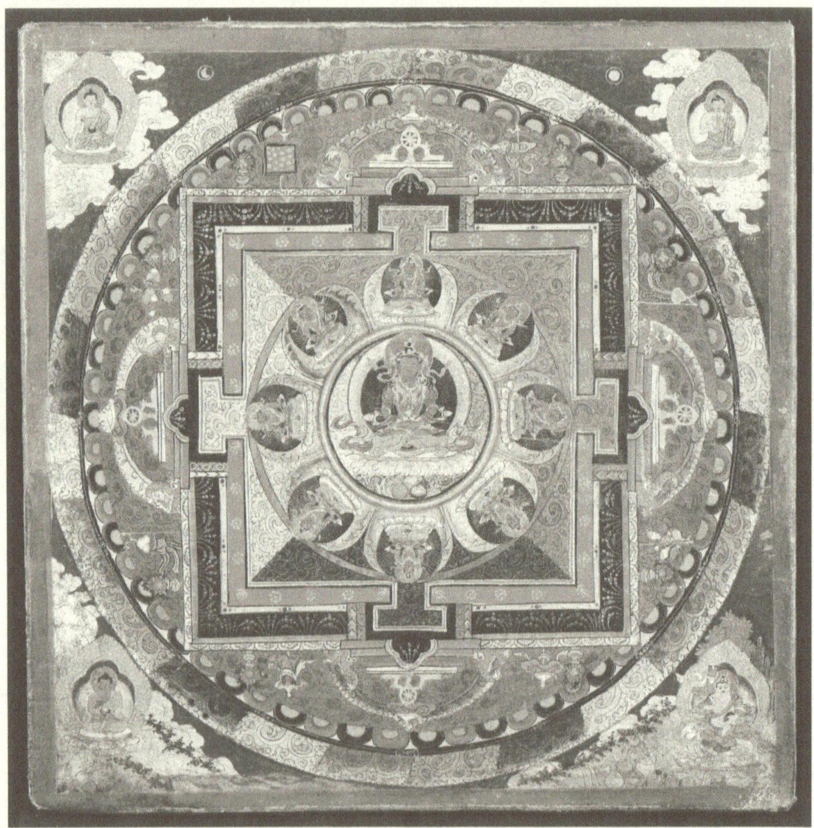

**FIGURE 2.1.** Mandala of Amitayus, paint on wood, nineteenth-century Tibetan school. Rubin Museum of Art. Public domain.

a *misleading* and even *dangerous* one. Some images connect with the ideal; others distract, conceal, and steal their beholders away from that ideal. To do this, the image has to be seen as functioning not within a horizontal landscape of distributed agency, but as operative at the interface of a human reality and a reality that is vertically transcendent and ontologically superior to that one, and that remains unaffected by the machinations of human image-making. The ideal-image regime is possible because the ideal has now been removed from the world that follows from it.

## IDEAL-IMAGE: THE IMAGE THAT REVEALS

If the image is sometimes taken to be alive and possessed of its own authority, in some contexts the power of the image is withheld from us. The image becomes not a mediating ground but a window onto a place or realm of power, a realm that is removed from our direct access and to which the image provides our only access point. The power of the image is not its own, but belongs to something beyond it: a divine or transcendent sphere, a causal realm, a place of ideals of which we perceive only their semblances, their echoes, their pale reflections.

What the ideal-image reveals or displays is something like the ordering of the world, and the relations, principles, forces, beings, or powers that are responsible (so it is claimed) for that ordering. The image functions as a symbolic representation, a stand-in and an intermediary, a symbol by which one can comprehend and contemplate the reality to which it points, but which does not itself affect that intermediary such that we, in engaging with it, might have a power over it. The image is in this sense transparent, not adding to the ideal that it reveals. The ideal is not to be confused with the image; the latter points to the former and renders it accessible, but it is the former that is of paramount significance. The ideal-image represents an ideal that is beyond the image itself.

This term "ideal" is intended to remind us of Plato's distinction between the world of images and the world of Ideas, with the latter being the "real" world and the former being but a pale and distorted reflection of it. The relationship between the two thus becomes an issue for those who accept the distinction. There is a long tradition in the Christian world of taking the images of the world as gateways to the *more* real world of the divine (and a long tradition of Neoplatonism that reproduced this notion well beyond Christianity). Bonaventure's *Journey of the Mind Towards God*, a thirteenth-century treatise that synthesized Christian thinking on images, put it this way:

> All created things of the sensible world lead the mind of the contemplator and wise man to eternal God. [. . .] They are the shades, the resonances, the pictures of that efficient, exemplifying, and ordering art; they are the tracks, simulacra, and spectacles; they are divinely given signs set before us for the purpose of seeing God. They are examples, or rather exemplifications [*exemplaria vel potius exemplata*] set before our still unrefined and sense-oriented minds, so that by the sensible things which they see they might be transferred to the intelligible which they cannot see, as if by signs to the signified [*tamquam per signa ad signata*].[28]

As Freedberg explains, this came to constitute a "general theory of signs" whereby the visible and cognizable world was a way for humans to grasp the divine world. The first was a means to the second; the earthly was relative, while the divine was eternal, transcendent, and ultimate.

Bonaventure, like his contemporary Aquinas, expressed the iconophilic position whereby images were valued and treasured, though not as ends in themselves. Their value was threefold: to instruct the unlettered; to render the mysteries of the Incarnation and the examples of the saints more visualizable and therefore more memorable for their beholders; and to excite the emotions toward the goals of a Christian life. The images of the saints are in this sense models for human behavior, but as imaged visages, with eyes that might in turn see us, they also act upon us and interact with us, imposing judgment on our action and providing impetus for appropriate behavior. Images of saints act within a network that thereby combines the animate-image and the ideal-image. They become "focal objects" and "interfaces" that contribute to the dynamic array of social (and socializing) forces, provide means for obligating people in relation to them, and connect people to the heavenly abode that is *both* elsewhere and infuses and interpenetrates this worldly realm.

This seemingly smooth movement between the *animacy* of images and their *ideality* can be found in many cultural settings. Anthropologist Susanne Küchler describes Australian Aboriginal societies as "image-based polities" in which images functioned to "model the cognitive basis on which relations can be understood recursively, and thus predicted. Seemingly small-scale, yet distributed," she continues, Aboriginal polities "model productive social relations via a grid-based, generative, and transformational image system that ingeniously permits relations to be understood and predicted," independently of the social position one may inhabit within the given polity.[29] As with images of the saints, images here function as a system that encodes ideals and coordinates human action. Images provide models of "how to be 'in relation,'"[30] yet they are not only of a didactic nature; interaction with the images serves to enact and potentially alter the relations they depict.

The valuing of images as means to an end—that, for instance, of ensuring appropriate behavior in relation to a transcendent deity—is precisely what made it possible for others to judge the means as utterly inadequate to the ends. In other words, it opens up the path for an iconophobia, and ultimately an iconoclasm, or at least an "aniconism," which reflects a disillusionment with images, representations, or replicas. The latter, in this mode, can only ever fall short of the ideal that is the ultimate goal: divinity, or the "supernature" of God. For some iconoclasts, images are not only judged as better or worse depictions of the ideal; they can in fact present the grave danger of being mistaken *for* those ideals, and this perceived danger becomes the fulcrum for a generalized critique of images. Wars have been fought over this difference between the image and the ideal: as when the iconoclasts of eighth- and ninth-century Byzantium declared the iconophiles "idolators" for their heresy of rendering images of that which cannot and must not be pictured; or when Protestant reformers decried images as insults to God, attempts to replace the divine visage which could not be humanly seen with pale reflections that could only, at best, be projections of our own longing (and, at worst, instruments of power or terror wielded by all-too-human agencies).

Another way of saying this is that images have different roles vis-à-vis the imaged referent—a referent that may be a deity, a spirit, an ideal, an absent beloved, a memorialized past event, a royal or significant individual, and so on—than they do vis-à-vis their social functions and the functions of the images of others. When it comes to the latter, they may elicit conflicts, clashes, and image wars. But iconoclasm in its most general guise—as aniconism—represents the strongest critique, even a denunciation, of the image as an ontological entity. The desire to access the (presumed) highest reality directly, apart from any image or representation thereof, or to grant that highest reality its own arena, a space that is undefiled by any image—this desire can be found in many forms even today. It is not only evident in well-known Islamist critiques of the profane depiction of Mohammed. As I will argue later in this book, contemporary seekers of "direct experience" with wild animals aim for a kind of transcendence of the world of images, even when they bring their cameras along to provide evidence that they have actually witnessed those animals in the flesh. The assumption here is that the image is secondary, a mere support, evidential statement, or promissory note for the reality of the directly experienced thing, which is primary. This is not so much an aniconism as it is an *idealism*, a "denigration of vision," as Martin Jay called it,[31] with its complementary assumption that the reality that precedes the image is higher, more primary, or of greater value than anything capturable as an image.

Iconoclasm, then, can be a general aniconism, which tolerates no graven images that would compete with the unimageable Ideal (as in Taliban-controlled Afghanistan, where images of the Buddha or other deities are only fit to be demolished), or it can be more specific, that is, an attempt to eliminate certain networks of images, or, in Jacques Rancière's terms, certain "distributions of the sensible": Christian images in Muslim Cappadocia, capitalist images in the communist USSR or China, Soviet monuments in the post-Soviet republics of the 1990s, Saddamist monuments in post-Saddam Iraq, and so on.[32] These take the image (the statue, the monument, the anthem, the specific dance) as a powerful indicator of a rival and rejected Ideal, a post-Ideal or false Ideal/idol, or a visualized affront to the non-visualizable Ideal. Where aniconism is explicit about its goals (to eliminate the icon), the regime of the world-picture will come in under the pretense of harboring no such goals; but that is getting ahead of ourselves.

Aniconism aside, three exemplary forms of the ideal-image can be identified.[33] The first is the *cosmogram*, which depicts key principles or structuring relationships making up the universe. John Tresch provides a generous suite of examples of such "depictions of the elements of the cosmos and the connections among them":

> Lucretius's epic of the things of nature; Tibetan mandalas, at once temple blueprints, metaphysical maps, and meditation aids; mosques that unite God with creation beneath their domes without directly representing him; cathedrals' pictorial narratives of creation and salvation and the labyrinths that lead the pilgrim into their hidden meaning; Dogon rites that wrap a cube crowned by a cone in a blanket to enact the fusion of heaven and earth; Hindu palaces situating the King precisely amidst people, government, and gods; Newton's *Principia*; Bacon's high-tech reinvention of Solomon's Temple in *New Atlantis*; encyclopedias, maps, and trees of knowledge of all kinds; university ground plans; information architectures and search engines; Joyce's *Ulysses*; Darwin's *Origin*; Charles and Ray Eames's *Powers of Ten*; Philip K. Dick's "How to Build a Universe That Won't Fall Apart Two Days Later."[34]

The status of these varies in terms of whether and how accurately they are held to "depict the elements of the cosmos," but that is part of Tresch's point. "Because they present a totality yet," as material objects, "remain firmly within the local and the empirical, cosmograms raise the possibility of an *open holism*. They offer proposals of unification without requiring uniformity." And they are always subject "to contestations, additions, deletions, and replacements."[35]

Cosmograms can be complex, as with Tibetan Buddhist mandalas or the mandala-modeled architecture found in temples like Borobudur in Indonesia or the Meenakshi and Koodal Azhagar temples in Madurai, India. Or they can be simple, though any simplicity is likely to mask an extensive character that is nevertheless all-encompassing. The Kongo cruciform may be a simple cross marked on the ground, at which a person stands to make an oath. Its one line, in Wyatt MacGaffey's words, "represents the boundary; the other is both the path leading across the boundary, as to the cemetery; *and* the vertical path of power linking 'the above' with 'the below.' [. . .] The person taking the oath stands upon the cross, situating himself between life and death, and invokes the judgement of God and the dead upon himself." The totality, writes Robert Farris Thompson, signifies the "compelling vision of the circular motion of human souls about the circumference of its intersecting lines. The Kongo cross refers therefore to the everlasting continuity of *all* righteous men and women."[36] A version of it (see image) shows a horizontal line dividing the world of the living from that of the dead, with water in between, four cardinal points representing elements and seasons of the day and of life, and the arrowed circumference denoting the round of reincarnation.[37]

A cosmogram need not be visual; it can equally be a sound, a phrase, or a performative sequence of some kind. The Sanskrit mantra "Om mani padme hum" is a simple phrase whose multiple levels of meaning, expounded in books and discourses and used for ritual and meditative purposes for centuries, are said to contain the condensed essence of Buddhist philosophy and cosmology.[38]

Historically, cosmograms have been especially notable in temple cultures, state societies (especially those of revolutionary states), and empires, whereby ordering principles are taken to precede and transcend the human social world, which is considered to be secondary to the ontological primacy of the sacred or ideal world. In these contexts, they frequently take on a less open form. Ideal-images have a useful-

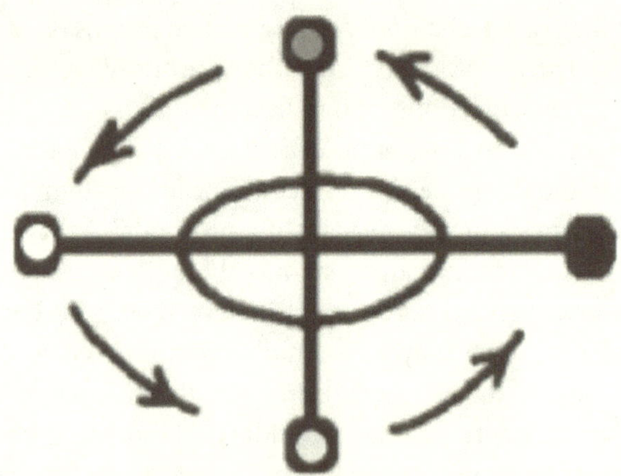

**FIGURE 2.2.** The Kongo Cosmogram – Yowa, Kongo sign of the cosmos and continuity of human life. CC BY-SA 4.0.

ness in facilitating the Durkheimian functions of religion and politics, whereby social systems are managed over large temporal and spatial scales.[39] That cosmograms play a role in ordering society is recognized by institutions and groups aiming to replace old orders with new ones. It is something like this that Hans Belting has in mind in saying that it was the "adoption of images" that enabled Christendom to "assert" its "claims to universality in the context of Greco-Roman culture," which enabled its imperial spread.[40] As Halbertal and Margalit demonstrate in their study of idolatry, the Jewish commandment against "graven images" is not just a religious mandate but also a "territorial mandate," "a way of controlling a place and conquering a territory."[41] This function becomes secularized within the revolutionary state iconographies of the Soviet Union, Nazi Germany, Maoist China, the Kampuchea of the Khmer Rouge, and other states that seek to establish their own visual and narrative regimes by overturning, and often erasing, those they have overcome. Cosmograms can be produced democratically as well. Tresch describes the first half of the nineteenth century in France, when in a

> time of ceaseless upheaval, a call for a new doctrine to unite society was answered in an explosion of representations of the cosmos. Many of these panoramic diagrams, creation narratives, rallying slogans, and crystalline fragments reached their publics as unprecedented technological objects: journals, *feuilletons*, and books mass-produced by steam presses. Other cosmograms took nonverbal forms: Charles Dupin's charts and maps of productive forces; Charles Fourier's phalanastery; the hall built at the Paris Observatory for Arago's *Popular Astronomy*; Humboldt's *Views of Nature*; the colossal woman-temples designed by the Saint-Simonians; or the Religion of Humanity's guiding *imago mundi,* Auguste Comte's Positivist Calendar.[42]

The relation between some of these and the Enlightenment worldview will be explored below. As the list suggests, however, some ideal-images come with a force of certitude, whereas others must work to establish themselves as such. In the gap between the two, their *making* becomes visible; we will turn to that in the next section.

All propaganda art is in this sense a form of the cosmogram, though it can be found in partial or muted forms in any national context. It is worth recognizing, as contemporary "propaganda artist" Jonas Staal reminds us, that all art can function as propaganda, that is, as the visual and narrative enactment of power in the service of one or another vision of society or the cosmos. Staal distinguishes the "elite propaganda" of authoritarian states from the "popular" and "emancipatory propaganda" that might contest it.[43] In a sense, the propaganda role of images can be seen in a broad spectrum of visual and sensorial objects, from full-scale depictions of entire universes (as with Tibetan Buddhist mandalas or building-sized Communist murals) to the more distributed forms by which a system of objects functions to encode meanings across time and space (as found, for example, in Australian Aboriginal societies).

The second form of the ideal-image is a more democratized, or at least decentralized, version of the first. If the cosmogram depicts the entirety of the cosmos in some aspect or another, the more typical ideal-image depicts something specific in that cosmos, highlighting the qualities depicted *as* their ideal form. Portraiture, especially of royalty and culture heroes or leaders, epitomizes this category. Pedagogical illustration accompanying depictions of the narrative history of a people or other elements of the world—for instance, medieval bestiaries, illustrations accompanying historical manuscripts and codices, magical or alchemical treatises, Tarot cards in their esoteric usage, and so on—frequently partake of both the cosmogrammatic and the portraiture functions of images. The depicted ideal is understood as partaking of the qualities of something that is beyond its representation, but ultimately it is "only" an image, a representation, whereas what it represents is real and meaningful. Something like this could be said of landscape paintings, visual or sculptural depictions of animals, and related depictions to the extent that they portray something that is understood to be real, powerful, and significant, yet transcendent of the depiction itself. The popularity of the selfie in social media today adopts this perspective of personal portraiture as an act of self-assertion and idealization, whilst overlapping with the next regime to be examined below. With this kind of "cosmographic portraiture," there is always the possibility of asking whether the image in fact *harbors* the power of its referent or merely *represents* it: the slippage between the ideal-image and the animate-image remains ever present as a possibility, even a threat.

A third exemplary form of the ideal-image takes its force from the tension between what can be depicted and what cannot, that is, from the representable and the fundamentally aniconizable, which eludes or exceeds the capacity of representation. If the ideal is taken to be inexpressible and beyond encompassment, then the image can at best only hint at its existence. The concept of the *sublime* has become a repository for this relationship between what can and what cannot be encompassed in imagistic depiction. In western history the sublime has become entwined with the shifting understanding of divinity and the sacred. For modern nonbelievers, divinity may no longer be there, but the place of divinity may remain as a kind of emptied yet lingering space that is gestured at and, by implication, substituted for by another, more tangible ideal. For instance, in the landscape paintings of the Hudson River School or Ansel Adams's photographs of nature, what is being substituted for divinity is the nation, or nature itself, or a kind of mutual infusion of the two. In other forms of sublime imagery—the industrial or technological sublime, the nuclear sublime, the toxic sublime, and so on—other qualities and characteristics are depicted as similarly embodying a kind of transcendent ideal, even as it shows the absence of what it knows to be no longer transcendent (divinity, nature, etc.). Abstract art can itself come to take the place of the sublime: as W. J. T. Mitchell notes (and as we will see in chapter 7 of this study), "The colored daubs and streaks on the canvas" of an abstract expressionist painting can "become, in the proper context—that is, in the presence of the proper ventriloquist—statements about the nature of space, perception, and representation." They are in this sense "contaminated" both "by language," as Mitchell acknowledges, and by the aniconic—by the referent of a reality itself that eludes representational art but makes itself felt within the abstract and *non*representational.[44]

The sublime, in this sense, has allowed for a continually shifting displacement of what constitutes ideality, without ever eradicating or fully emptying ideality itself.[45] In the second half of this book, we will refer to the ways in which images of the Earth, of animals, and of modern divinities partake of the sublime even as its status remains unstable. With the transition to modern experiences of the sublime, however, we can no longer avoid the topic of the modern art object. The primary paradigm for thinking of this object is as a production of expression by its artist-creator.

## EXPRESSION-IMAGE: THE IMAGE THAT EXPRESSES

If the power of the image can be removed from us by claiming a transcendent field in which that power originates—the image being a window onto, or a representation of, a reality that exceeds, precedes, or supersedes our own—then the most direct way to reclaim that power is to deny the existence of that transcendent field altogether. There are two ways to do this, each with gentler and more aggressive variants. In this section we consider the first, according to which the power of the image comes neither from itself nor from what it represents, but from its maker (who usually happens to be human). The next section concerns the second, wherein the power of the transcendent is replaced (ostensibly) by the world, but a world as mediated in very specific, and often unacknowledged, ways.

With the expression-image, power is conceived of as moving in the opposite direction from that of the ideal-image. It is not withheld from us but is, instead, the property of the artist who shapes the image. It is a human power, though some of us are better than others in drawing that power out of ourselves. The reality expressed in the artistic image is not considered transcendent or separate from the observer, even if the artist's insight *into* that reality may be granted a special status.

This image regime is of course most characteristic of the contemporary category of the art object. While it can be found in many times and places, it has arguably flourished most forcefully in the western world since the European Renaissance, a period in which the devotional "cult images" of medieval Europe had been supplanted, if at least partially, by a "cult of images" and its corresponding "cult of artists."[46] The expression-image is valued for its expressivity, the virtuosity of its craft, style, beauty, novelty, insight into some feature of the world, or the creative or artistic genius it reflects and embodies. As described in Hans Belting's paradigmatic art-historical work *Likeness and Presence* (*Bild und Kult*), art as the modern world has known it is "invented by a famous artist," "defined by a proper theory," and "acknowledged for its own sake."[47] Elements of "art for art's sake" have been present long before the Renaissance (for instance, in post-iconoclastic Byzantium),[48] but in its complete form, the modern art object comes into full presence in the nineteenth century, when it becomes "oriented around individual achievement, monetary value, and detachment from everyday life."[49] (The addition of monetary value makes this also a "capital-image," but that brings in complications we won't get into here.)

The expression-image regime has resulted in a focus on style, a pluralization of styles, and the competition among artists and movements that has flourished under artistic modernism. Unlike the ideal-image, which is taken to represent an ideal that *transcends* the merely human or worldly realm, the expression-image is taken to represent or provide glimpses of an ideal that is very much "of the world" or that presumes no ontological distinction between the human world and any other. To the extent that an arrow of agency can be established in the workings of the image, the power of the expression-image comes from its human maker, not from any force beyond the human world.

One could say that today's entire contemporary art world—the galleries and museums, studios and schools, catalogs and magazines and biennales, departments of art-historical scholarship and schools of art-critical journalism—is founded on the expression-image regime, where it is the artist whose skill, expertise, and genius is valued above all. We go to galleries to see exhibitions of specific artists; we study their lives, their personal struggles and achievements; we celebrate them and pay great sums to hang their work on our walls. We develop "taste cultures" marking an identification with specific artists and art movements, internalizing their perspectives on the world as our own. An entire criminal industry has emerged to steal the works of famous artists and resell them on the black market.

But when examined more closely, even this regime begins to come apart. What to make of the throngs of pilgrims who line up daily to view the *Mona Lisa* at the Louvre in Paris? (Some 22,500 do so on average, and over eight million annually.) Is this to admire a painting, or to stand (and be photographed) in the presence of a magical object, itself barely visible behind a crowd of flash cameras and whose movement is continual in order that a maximum number of visitors may flow through the museum? It is the expressiveness of the image—the enigmatic smile, in particular—that is most frequently commented upon, but the fascination the painting has evoked over the centuries is not only a fascination with Leonardo's achievement in it, but also a fascination with the enigma of the woman who was its subject, of what her smile may reveal, of the value of the painting itself, and of an elusive and "magical" quality that reflects a kind of object-centered sublimity—which therefore implies an ideality and a certain animacy.

This example shows us how it is that any particular image may partake of multiple image-regimes: how the animate-image can infuse the expression-image, how the ideal-image reflects a play of power within each of the others, and so on. And, at the same time, how the image as an expression of the artist—as a fully human act, a creative act, an act that itself reveals something essential about what humans are capable of—may be an ineradicable element in the making of any image. As a particular relationship between a thing or form, a referent (a *second* thing pointed to by that thing or form), and an effect or meaning that is emergent within the image-event, the expression-image suggests that the hidden hand of artistry or creative agency is always present within *any* image. In some ways of conceiving images this agency is highlighted, while in others it is occluded, but this always remains an option to be activated or not.

Pushed even further, the question of creative agency is not even necessarily subsumable within the question of *human* agency: it may be the agency of nature, of divinity, or of the cosmos that is at work in an image. In her evolutionary account of art-making, Ellen Dissanayake suggests that an active, intentional creativity—"artifying" is her word for it—is present in the activities of other species of organism as well: in "play, mark-making, self-adornment, and ritual/ceremony," what we see is animals "intentionally making parts of the natural and manmade environment (shelters, tools, utensils, weapons, clothing, bodies, surroundings, and other paraphernalia) extraordinary or special by marking, shaping, and embellishing them beyond their ordinary functional appearance" through "formalization [. . .], repetition, exaggeration, elaboration, and—in some instances—manipulation of the perceiver's expectation."[50]

In this sense, it is perhaps necessary to state that what we are calling the "expression-image regime" is a specific relationship wherein a *human* artist or artists are taken to be active and agential in the relationship between form, referent, and effect. In all the situations where this regime makes itself felt, it is the human maker that is considered active, agential, and notable. In the relationship between human, image, and world, the expression-image names the situation in which the arrow of agency is considered to point from the first toward the second term of the triad.

As mentioned earlier, these first three image regimes, between them, account for a great variety of the ways humans have interacted with images prior to the modern era. Consider a complicated cultural phenomenon that takes place at regular intervals, perhaps seasonally or annually, in different forms around the world: a ritual procession involving masks, mobile sculptures, flags or banners, music, and dance-like movement. We may call it theatre, while scholars of religion may consider it ritual or religious festival. Some of the images are known to represent known entities—spirits, saints, political figures, or ideas. To the extent that they represent ideals and serve as reminders of their importance, they are ideal-images. To the extent that they are embodied in individuals, or in objects, and transport those individuals or objects into other forms of existence, other perceptual states or modes of consciousness known or believed to be temporarily accessible, they are animate-images. And to the extent that they are known and appreciated by their users to be made, shaped, and crafted by human hands for the purpose of the quality of the craft that went into their creation, these images are expression-images. The locus of agency can therefore be multiple and can circulate from one place to another: from the artist to the object, from the object to the user or participant, and from all of these to the idea embodied in it. The more it circulates, the better its craft; or at least that may be one particular understanding of this interplay of image regimes.

## WORLD-PICTURE: THE IMAGE THAT COPIES

The historical reality, of course, is more complex. The latter regime, the expression-image, became more widely established during the European Renaissance in part as a response to the perceived power of the ideal-image regime of its time. If it was a way of reclaiming some of the power of the image from its displacement by the transcendent field within the ideal-image, a second way to do that emerged. This was to deny the agency, efficacy, power, or reality of that field by replacing it with a new one. The ideal was after all neither visible nor measurable outside of the image; it was a matter of "faith" and of "custom" to take it as actually existing.

In the regime of the world-picture, this denial became definitive and effective because it presented a new regime in its place, subtended by a new technological apparatus—one of visibility, measurability, and fidelity. The visibility of the world-picture depended on its technical infrastructure, which itself was ideally rendered invisible, moved to the background, and forgotten; but its capacity to produce such visibility was central to its power.

The term "world picture" is taken from Martin Heidegger's profoundly influential essay "The Age of the World Picture" ("Die Zeit des Weltbildes," 1938), where Heidegger claims that the "fundamental event of modernity" is the "conquest of the world *as picture*." By the latter he meant a "'structured image" (*Gebild*) that is "the creature or image of man's production" (*das Gebild des vorstellenden Herstellens*) "which represents and sets before" and thereby facilitates mastery or dominion over the world.[51] In other words, in contrast to a world ordered according to values provided in an ontological dispensation delivered by a divinity or some other ontological authority—such as the Olympian gods, for the ancient Greeks whom Heidegger admired, or by Jesus of Nazareth and the Church instituted in his name—the "age of the world picture" has come to be ordered according to how things are seen and measured: as "standing reserve," or as objects in space meant to be calculated, recorded, assessed, analyzed, and put to use. The world-picture is a way of understanding the world via its picturing and recording—through mechanical science, photographic (and audiographic, cinematographic, and other) techniques, and more recently through informational and data systems, with humans, in time, also becoming mutually produced as subjects and objects of this picturing, scientific gaze. The image is treated, then, as a more or less accurate copy of the world as it is in its "objective" reality, which is assumed to be its character as object (not subject), a physical and material reality that can be known as such, measured, and set to work.

Presented this way, the world-picture regime would seem to have arrived as an invading army onto the territory held by the ideal-image. But history is more nuanced, its rough edges smoothened by the meandering turbulence of centuries. In the history of images, perceptual faithfulness to the object has arguably been there all along, even as it was woven into the animate subjectness of the image. If we focus on the history of western painting, we find the shift to visually "realistic" representation took a few centuries to establish itself as central to the picture-making art. In the paintings of the Florentine Giotto di Bondone (1267–1337), interior light and real-world space bring a warm realism to the bodies and scenes of the Virgin, the Messiah, and the angels and demons of the Late Medieval imagination. "Otherworldly" ideas, as Gosetti-Ferencei notes (and as they seem to us today), come to be "anchored in this-worldly space and time" in ways that were utterly novel at the time.[52] If these are the first hints (in Europe) of the world-picture regime, they come gently, even before the expression-image regime's cult of the artist has even been felt. It took another century for linear perspective, with its rationalization of sight, to be mastered by Brunelleschi, Raphael, and others, and another three or four centuries before the habit of verisimilar representation became so widely established as to constitute a regime.[53] Moreover, the question of verisimilitude is never entirely settled: while the pictorial realism of post-Renaissance art is hardly in dispute,[54] the dialectic between perception (the world-picture), artistry (the expression-image), and the world (as animate and as ideal) continues to generate novel contenders for perceptual realism—in Impressionists' heightened attention to the "lived intimacy of the perceived,"[55] in post-Impressionists' focus on the geometricity of the object (Cézanne) or the optical multiplicity of visual perception (from Cubism to Op Art), and in the quests for an innocence of "direct perception" in the films of Stan Brakhage and others.[56]

If the world-picture regime represents a realism, however, it can also be seen as continuous in key respects with the understanding of the world as a systemically relational or networked cosmos patterned by similarities and resemblances, correspondences and analogies, "signatures" and "sympathies" between things at all scales. This is more or less the world-picture developed by an array of Neoplatonically influenced "natural philosophers" during the European Renaissance of the fifteenth and sixteenth centuries. These included Paracelsus, Marsilio Ficino, Bernardino Telesio, Pico della Mirandola, Francesco Patrizi, Tomasso Campanella, and Giordano Bruno. While this cosmology may have never entirely established itself as hegemonic, numerous thinkers from Eustace Tillyard and C. S. Lewis to Michel Foucault and Frances Yates have highlighted its significance in reordering conceptions of the cosmos between the medieval and early modern eras, attaining a particular force in Elizabethan England.[57] (We'll come back to this magical cosmology in chapter 7.) Encyclopedic pictures of the world can be found in multiple historical contexts and were favored especially by imperial centers, as seen, for instance, in Ming Dynasty China's *Yongle Encyclopedia* of 1408. Assessing the understanding of images found within them is complicated, but the general conception of an ordered anthropocosmic world—with humanity poised somewhere on a hierarchic or multileveled "chain of being" between earth and heaven—falls broadly into the conception of the cosmogram, described above in relation to the ideal-image.[58] The question, then, becomes: how did the modern world-picture emerge from these others, and what was its innovation?

Given the ideals of fidelity and verisimilitude underpinning the world-picture regime, let us consider how the world-picture regime differs from that of the ideal-image. Does the assumption that the world literally *is* as it is measured—as science reveals it to be—not put it into the same category of image-relation as that which sees the world as *literally divine*, or literally the domain of a transcendent God or pantheon, whose own histories both precede, preempt, and overshadow anything that humans might themselves aspire to? Is the difference not simply that in place of a divinely ordered universe we have a universe of laws as revealed by science—which, after all, is still a universe of truth-claims, of faith in those claims, and of reliance on authority, though in this case it is the authority of the new priesthood of scientists? The world-picture, in this reading, is a variation on the ideal-image. It just happens to be the one that scientifically informed modern people take to be true, or to at least approximate truth in a way that the others apparently do not.

In other words, by assuming that the regime of the world-picture is more accurate than one or another regime of the ideal-image, are we not failing to see that the means of establishing it are no different in principle than the means of establishing the Latinate Christian, Tibetan Buddhist, Classic Mayan, or Ming Dynasty world-pictures? To get at these kinds of differences, Bruno Latour wrote in his provocative tract *We Have Never Been Modern*:

> All natures-cultures are similar in that they simultaneously construct humans, divinities and nonhumans. [. . .] All of them sort out what will bear signs and what will not. If there is one thing we all do, it is surely that we construct both our human collectives and the nonhumans that surround them. In constituting their collectives, some mobilize ancestors, lions, fixed stars, and the coagulated blood of sacrifice; in constructing ours, we mobilize genetics, zoology, cosmology and hæmatology.[59]

By substituting the more common word "cultures" with "natures-cultures," Latour is suggesting that there is no "objective nature" we can ultimately appeal to, since our sciences are merely one particular way of constituting a "collective," one that happens to impact that collective quite radically. Rather than seeing the shift from an outdated ideal-image to a scientific world-picture as a liberation from superstition into the clear light of objective reality, Latour is arguing that what distinguishes so-called modern society is simply that it "translates, crosses over, enrolls, and mobilizes more elements which are more intimately connected, with a more finely woven social fabric" and with "a deepened intimacy, a more intricate mesh" between society and technology.[60] In other words, there is a distinction, but it is not found in the distinction of truth from falsity, but in the size, scale, length, and complexity of the networks that are fabricated in and through the practices of Latour's "we," the "moderns." Science *works*, in ways that previous truth-systems may not have, because its imbrication with the world is more intricate, more intensive, and more self-correcting and verifiable. But it is still fallible and contingent, and still dependent on a range of mediations, methods, and practices that, at times, seem no less ritualistic and faith-filled than the practices of the pre-moderns. When Latour claims that "we have never been modern," he is pointing to the fact that it is the practices that determine the outcome, and that these will always remain negotiable with an incredibly broad range of players. (Among them, in Latour's later writing, is the "massively distributed" player, or ensemble of players, he cautiously names "Gaia.")

But this difference between science and religion, for many in our world at least, remains substantial. Once causality has been defined in scientific terms, the world comes to be produced in those terms as well.

The image is effective in that its impacts are real and undeniable. This does not mean that things could not have always been otherwise. If we lived not in a world transformed by science and technology—a world of factories, electricity, oil-burning vehicles, chemically enhanced foods and medicines, and all the rest—if we lived instead in a world where shamanic spirit-world journeying answered all of our questions to the point that its efficacy was irrefutable, then we would simply have taken a different turn, whose modus operandi was defined differently. We would be partaking not in a world-picture regime, but in a regime in which distinctions between animate spirits or forces were so thoroughly established they would have taken on their own trajectories of quantum developments, with distinctions perhaps between a spirit-image regime and a soul-image regime, or something else unimaginable and unnameable from within our terminological universe.

The real novelty with the world-picture regime is that the image as icon and likeness becomes strengthened and supported by the image as index and trace. The world that is captured in a picture is a world that is causally incorporated into that picture through the indexicality of its presence—an indexicality achieved through photography or some other technique of direct translation.[61] As Susan Sontag writes in "The Image-World," a photograph is not just a depiction; it is also a "trace" and the direct "registering of an emanation" of its object. Something like this occurs not only with photography, but with telescopy and micrography, crystallography, photogrammetry, cinematography, phonographic audio recordings, and with informational systems of all kinds: each registers direct traces of what they represent.[62] With this indexicality of all of these mechanisms comes a tremendous power—the power of the image as material evidence of the real. It is as evidence that photographs, audio and video recordings, and other forms of material documentation come to adjudicate what happened or did not happen at the scene of a crime, which team member was responsible for the infraction resulting in a penalty kick, and what my social media feed says that I saw or did last night. Evidence-making tools become powerful, and to the extent that they are distributed within a population, that power comes to be dispersed. The capacity to control what counts as evidence, and who has the ability to provide and define it, becomes an arena of contestation. If in earlier decades it was the "fourth estate" of journalists who claimed the capacity to document, share, and voice critiques of the powerful, today that power is claimed by anyone with a smartphone, a laptop, and the ability to use it politically.

Sontag spends a sizable chunk of her "Image-World" essay discussing the reaction of the Chinese Communist government to Michelangelo Antonioni's 1972 documentary *Chung Kuo*, in which Antonioni's method clearly follows the expressive documentarian ideal—a mixture of the world-picture, which assumes that reality can be captured "as it is," and the expression-image, which celebrates the keen insight and observational genius of the artist. For Antonioni, it was the candid photograph that counted—"the beauty of the cracked peeling door, the picturesqueness of disorder, the force of the odd angle and the significant detail, the poetry of the turned back."[63] In Antonioni's hands, photography was able to "capture" and "reveal" reality in all its nuances, paradoxes, variegated features, and elusive dynamism. The Chinese government, by contrast, decried Antonioni's neglect of the "moral order of space," the idealized portraiture that would capture Communist China at its well-dressed Sunday best.[64] "The Chinese," Sontag writes, "resist the photographic dismemberment of reality" in favor of a portraiture that captures the object "straight on, centered, evenly lit, and in its entirety," a reality that must be posed if it is to express the "correct" view.[65] As with all forms of government or religious propaganda, the image, for the Communist Chinese government of the time, was intended to didactically convey an ideal. It was to be "constructed around a single, ideal observer" and aimed to perpetuate a "Great Monologue."[66]

One could say that a central goal of both the expression-image and the world-picture regimes has been to destroy the ability of human institutions to perpetuate such power-laden monologues. The first did this by displacing authority from the ideal *beyond* the image to the artist and maker of the image; the second, from human institutions to the "world as it is," that is, as revealed to be self-evident by the scientific methodologies that established it as such. In combination, the world-picture and the expression-image have produced perhaps the most powerful image-making technology the world has seen in that its impact includes the dissolution of authority for "traditions" and moral orders that have emerged over centuries around the planet. The irony is that both the world-picture and the expression-image replace those dissolved ideals with their own—ideals that are captured in what might be called the regime of the modern, liberal order, with its twin foci of scientific modernism (world-picture) and individualism (expression-image, with its romance of artistic expressivism).

If the world-picture regime tends toward a dismissal and denigration of the ontological claims embedded within the animate-image and ideal-image regimes, the world-picture also carries socially generative tendencies of its own. One emerges when the world-picture comes to function as a replacement of the ideal-image regime. When the image of the world becomes its own ideal, a projection of what science, modernity, humanity, or some such assumed agent is capable of, it becomes *spectacle*: the globe as a great unifier, the epitome of technological progress, the image of the future, the ideal world to come. This is why so many global corporations and entities have taken the image of the globe as their iconic signifier. This in turn becomes a simulation among simulations: the image of totality as a composite reproduction of many reproductions. The exhibitionary complex of colonial modernity grows into Google Earth. (But we are getting ahead of ourselves again.)

A second tendency, this one potentially more troubling, arises from the indexicality from which the world-picture is built. When images are causally connected to their sources, it does not take much to trace those sources in ways that can themselves be operationalized. The "picturing" of individuals, groups, and the world in general enables the gathering of those pictures into a database by which they can in turn be analyzed and incorporated into systems of regulation and control. As Sontag writes, "Through being photographed, something becomes part of a system of information, fitted into schemes of classification and storage which range from the crudely chronological order of snapshot sequences pasted in family albums to the dogged accumulations and meticulous filing needed for photography's uses in weather forecasting, astronomy, microbiology, geology, police work, medical training and diagnosis, military reconnaissance, and art history." Photography "redefines" reality "as an item for exhibition, as a record for scrutiny, as a target for surveillance"; it "fragments continuities and feeds the pieces into an interminable dossier, thereby providing possibility of control."[67] Indexicality makes it possible to bring the world *into* our imaging of that world so that the two become intertwined and mutually correlated. World-pictures in their aggregate build up a database that provides an ever more complete picture of the world. They enable an instrumentalization of the world, a "challenging forth" and "setting upon" the world, as Heidegger puts it, so that it is "enframed" as a "standing reserve" of extractable resources ready to be put to use. As Max Horkheimer and Theodor Adorno wrote some years before Heidegger addressed the same topic of technology, the Earth itself has become "wholly grasped and mathematized" and thus "fully enlightened," for good *and* for ill.[68]

This becomes the panoptic function of the world-picture, which enables the management of organizations and societies, including the "disciplinary society" described by Michel Foucault and the "society of control" described by Gilles Deleuze.[69] Such management is possible because the world-picture in all its forms, from photographs and sound recordings to satellite images and X-rays, facilitates not only the observation of reality, but its direct manipulation. This manipulation can be for good or ill: as Sontag writes, "military reconnaissance photographs help snuff out lives, X-rays help save them."[70] Google Earth helps us (and governments, and crime syndicates) find places and people we are

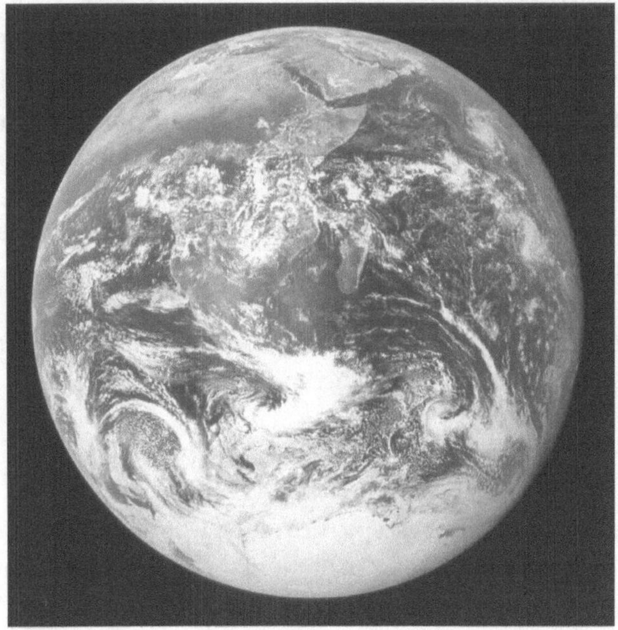

**FIGURE 2.3.** Apollo 17 "Blue Marble" image. NASA, 1973. Public domain.

looking for. Surgical devices help doctors find cancerous growths we (or they) wish to eliminate. The world-picture orders the world instrumentally, making it ever more available to technical manipulation for any ends. This, combined with its way of insinuating itself into our very understanding of reality, is what Heidegger, Foucault, and other critics most lament about it. If this was the case in the analog era, it is multiplied and thickened in the digital era, when data-images come already subsumed within metadata that can be read by algorithmic programs even if they are opaque or unknown to their viewers.

By enabling a quantification and modeling of the world in its extractable components, then, images can be *operationalized* as a diagrammatic interface for modifying the world. Operational images, as Jussi Parikka argues, act within functional apparatuses that "operationalize terrains and targets," and that in effect transform the world into a terrain for operations, and the world's constituents into targets for action and modification (all of which becomes much more the case with the moving-image regime).[71] The political question to be asked about the world-picture, then, is *whose ends will it serve?*

Photographic and audiographic technologies carry this twin capacity: "On the one hand, cameras [and microphones] arm vision in the service of power—of the state, of industry, of science. On the other hand, cameras make vision expressive in that mythical space known as private life."[72] The two potentials represent distinct image regimes, and the tension between them is one that has marked modernity in its alternations between classical and objective norms of science and government, on one hand, and the romantic-expressivist ideals of its recurrent countercultures on the other. Heidegger identified the world-picture as an "age," but it is better considered a mode, one that comes to the fore under specific conditions but that nevertheless remains supplemented, complemented, or haunted by other modes.[73]

## MOVING-IMAGE: THE IMAGE IN MOTION

If the world-picture presents a picture of the world "as it is," and if that world is itself understood to be in motion, then its picture ought to also be in motion: it must be a motion-picture, a moving-image. It must, in other words, be cinematic—a product of the kinematograph which reproduces the motion (*kinema*, *kinesis*) of the world itself.

The capacity to photographically reproduce the movement of the world emerged in a world that had itself been mobilized into greater, faster, and more expansive motion. The rapid industrialization of Europe and North America in the nineteenth century, with its mobilization of energy drawn from coal and oil reserves that had been collecting and compounding in the earth for millennia, dramatically increased the geographic movement of raw materials, manufactured goods, and people. If the historical breeding ground of the world-picture regime had been that of early modern and Enlightenment Europe, then that of the moving image, and specifically of the cinematic image, was the late nineteenth century, in the midst of this growing mobilization of social and technological forces. Among these forces was the production of photographic imagery that, in time, came to more or less accurately reflect the kinetic nature of life itself.

Since musical, theatrical, and performative arts had long produced images that were thought to move as and with life—these were moving-image regimes in their own right—it was the visual production of movement, in a form aimed to reproduce the movement of the world with indexical accuracy, that was novel at this time. The cinematic moving-image regime is in this sense a fusion of the world-picture regime with previous moving-image regimes, such as theatre and ritual drama. Its technical basis could allow us to call it a "world-*motion*-picture," with its history best considered transitional in that it enhanced the capacities for (re)presenting motion, but otherwise built on existing forms of imagery.

But the cinematic moving-image was not just a mobilization of the world-picture regime. It unleashed a powerful combination of image regimes that together resulted in a heightened capacity for spectacle, enchantment, and affective engagement in motion-picture worlds. Early cinema, as historians like Tom Gunning have shown, was marked by its capacity to captivate and enchant its viewers. The early "cinema of attractions," as Gunning named it, harnessed visibility in order to draw viewers into the motion it depicted.[74] Among its goals was to astonish and hold its viewers rapt. One of its greatest powers, according to early French filmmaker Jean Epstein, was its "animism," a capacity to provide "a semblance of life to the objects it defines," and through close-ups, temporal manipulations, and other techniques, to restore the world's animacy.[75] Beyond merely animating the objects it showed, through its own movement—slowly, quickly, and in any direction—the motion-picture camera became a mobile, seeing presence, a machinic subjectivity that sees differently from us whilst allowing us to see through its eye(s). The camera took viewers on "phantom rides"; it "wandered" voyeuristically, "probed" and "investigated" what it showed us, selectively revealing a world even as it concealed what it kept out of the frame. Cinema's animatedness became its primal pleasure, even as viewers understood that it was technologically conjured. Its calling card became a mixture of the animate-image, with its capacity to hold and to carry viewers along on a "ride"; the expression-image, understood to reside in the artistry behind its fashioning; and the realism of its world-picture technology, that is, of the indexicality of its being built from fragments—photographic replicas—of the world itself.

Film theorists have alternately stressed the realism of the cinematic arts (André Bazin, Siegfried Kracauer, Stanley Cavell) and its aesthetic expressivism (Tom Gunning, auteur theory, Jean Epstein, Béla Balász, Gilles Deleuze), couching these within debates over "realism" and "anti-realism," "representationalism" versus "presentationalism," "illusionism," "utopianism," the "impartiality" of camera vision, and a host of other concepts.[76] The cinematic fusion of lifelike animacy, documentary realism, and authorial expressivism became especially potent when cinema showed human characters acting and responding to all-too-imaginable situations, such that their ways of action—of walking, talking, and projecting themselves into the world—became possible for viewers to model, emulate, and come to inhabit. In this spectacular combination of image regimes, films over the past century and a quarter have profoundly affected their viewers and participants, taking them on cognitive and affective journeys that, at their most compelling, changed both viewers and worlds.

Led by Hollywood and followed by those who copied and, in various ways, contested it, cinema disseminated ways of being and concepts of the world—resonant images and affectively powerful representations of cities, nations, histories, territories, life-worlds, socialities, and imaginary worlds—that have shaped the world in their images even as they have made possible new ways of being. All of this was the focus of my previous book *Ecologies of the Moving Image*, where I presented histories by which moving images deployed, recalibrated, and resignified three dimensions of the world of our experience: the social, including the political; the biological or, more broadly, the animate; and the geographical, territorial, or spatial. Cinema reconstructed each of these in multiple directions: in some hands, it solidified national imaginaries (as in the classical Hollywood Western) only to later challenge them; in others, it gave rise to existential modalities of experiencing worlds in crisis, struggles over identities and other social clashes, and worlds of mobility resonant with life in globalizing, neoliberal conditions. It did all this while capturing the events of the world and entertaining its viewers. It is not too much of an overstatement, as Francesco Casetti does, to call cinema the "eye" or "gaze" of the twentieth century. "Not only did it record a large number of its events," Casetti writes, "but—by recording them—it has also been able to structure a reflexive spectatorial experience in which to receive them." Among other things, cinema "constructed new forms of subjectivity, redefined space and time, expressed social, racial, and gender identities," and "contributed to the mass industrialization of culture."[77] Its impact has been such that the world we live in today is a cinematized, or post-cinematic, world; we dwell in, with, and amidst the results of cinema's reshaping of our lives.[78]

Cinema's way of presenting its worlds was very specific in that it involved seated audiences taking in an entire experience of a film-world in one go. In *Ecologies of the Moving Image*, I analyzed this experience as conforming to Peirce's categorization of experience in terms of its firstness, its secondness, and its thirdness. While viewing a film, a viewer entered into a process of negotiation with the world the film presented to him or her. That world consisted of three dimensions. There was the firstness of the film-stuff itself, the audiovisual substance that shimmered and vibrated, displayed and sounded. It was sonic and visual, and it moved. This was the *spectacle* of film, which is what captivated the first audiences of the motion-picture: it revealed a world, and its revelation was simply there, vibrant, in front of us. In the *sequentiality* of what was there came the second dimension: one thing followed another, and so we, viewers, were drawn into that one-thing-after-anotherness that prompted us to wonder: What will come next? How does this relate to what we just saw? What will this character do? But as viewers, we always brought ourselves to the act of viewing, which means we brought our world with us—our knowledge, our expectations, our hopes and fears. This face recalls faces we have seen before; this place looks familiar to us, but with a twist. Film's third dimension was its *referentiality*, its "aboutness" or capacity to represent things of and from the world. In the interplay between its spectacle (a cinematic version of Peircian firstness), its sequentiality (secondness), and its referentiality (thirdness), film invited and engaged us in a process of living through film-worlds as their imaginal participants: observers, voyeurs, but always with cognitive and emotional stakes in the viewing (and hearing) of what films offered.

Cinemas were of course not the only place where audiences could watch images that moved. Moving images were increasingly integrated into other media, such as concert performances, classroom pedagogy, museum displays, and the like. (And cinema had its long prehistory, from shadow puppetry to magic lantern exhibits and peepshows.[79]) In the meantime, however, a second medium emerged that altered the landscape of moving-image consumption for much of the industrial world: television. By 1960, nearly 90% of U.S. households included a television set. From 1970 until the present, that number has remained above 95%, with much of the rest of the world coming to replicate that in the same period.[80] For a broad swath of humanity, television became the "electronic hearth" of the home. It came to provide a continuously available media environment, one that could act as foreground or as background, and that offered a "switchable" interface into a multichannel world that seamlessly mixed information, entertainment, and advertising (and/or propaganda) in an expanding array of time-bounded, rhythmically organized packages.[81] The television set itself was simply a home conduit into a much broader network, one built of electrical grids (power grids, cable systems, and so on), electromagnetic flows of radiation (first mastered by radio broadcasting), production studios and broadcasting streams, and, ultimately, satellite grids situated in the upper atmosphere of the planet. Built onto this infrastructure was an experiential world that allowed viewers to maneuver their way through a multichannel, audiovisual "current of simultaneous event reception."[82]

Among its differences from cinema was its economic model, one that, in the form of network television, came to be experienced as a constant flow of interrupted programming, with regular interruptions allowing for advertisers to market products to audiences that were already there, watching. Advertising in this context became a kind of background hum, the "words from our sponsors" that shaped the experience of television watching whilst providing a rationale for the medium's very existence: these are the things you need to buy in order to *get* by (or to "get ahead"), which in turn is why you (or someone) need to work for the companies that make them. In this way television came to shape a certain temporality of passive participation, one marked by a schedule of distractive entertainments, "consensus news," and even more distracting advertisements that were ignorable but ineradicable. The balance could be different with public-interest (or state-controlled) programming, but the general model that spread most widely was a commercial one.

The growth of television, followed by the innovations of cable and digital television, in many ways paved the way for the internet, which began as a shared informational database but has now come to replicate the continuous and multichannel nature of its media predecessor. In the meantime, the proliferation of video recording in cameras and cell phones, and the interactivity of the latter, contributed to the participatory nature of the emerging medium. As noted by the curators of the Museum of Modern Art's exhibition "Signals: How Video Transformed the World": "Video is everywhere and nowhere at once. It surrounds us as signals and waves and data flows, but it remains ephemeral, shape-shifting, endlessly dispersed and dislocated."[83] This could be a precise description of the internet; but we are getting ahead of ourselves again.

Cinema and television provide two different, but ultimately not incompatible, models of moving-image media. In his cinema books, Gilles Deleuze distinguished between the "movement-image" and the "time-image" as two overarching subregimes of the moving-image, based largely on their presentation of time as either causally connected action (movement-image) or as "time itself," open both in the direction of the future and of the past (time-image).[84] Each of these subregimes presented multiple options for creative experimentation, with new modes of cinematic expression emerging as the medium's technical capacities evolved. Among other things, these modes of moving-image media heightened the possibilities for two forms of image-making that were at least incipiently present in earlier media: those of collage and montage. Techniques of visual montage, photomontage, and musical collage had long been used by artists, but the temporally outstretched nature of the cinematic medium, combined with its possibilities for rapid change via editing, provided the means for a continual montage effect, with heterogeneous materials placed into direct contact with each other so as to produce synthetic meanings. (In chapter 5, we will consider the capacities of cinematic montage, or what I will call the "montage-image," to bring about new relations among types of image including forms of the animate-image, the ideal-image, and the world-picture.) Television in turn provided for a more open-ended engagement with both space and time, one that was instantaneous and synchronous in its reliance on live transmission, multiperspectival in its array of options, and switchable (via remote control) across that proliferating array of options. Media philosopher Lorenz Engell, in this light, refers to televisual imagery as "the switch image," a feature of televisuality that remains central to the experience of digital media today.[85] In contrast to the intentionality of artistic and cinematic montage, television, in its switchability as well as its incorporation of a multiplicity of types of imagery—news programming, serial fictions, the casual entertainment of comedy and game shows, random advertisements and public service announcements, and so on—provided a kind of ongoing collage effect that has arguably also become part of the experience of the internet.[86]

Theorists of digital cinema have reconsidered what constitutes cinema in light of a changing technology: what is the role of indexicality and its "reality-referent" when photo-realism comes to be displaced and ultimately replaced by digital image capture and composition? As Francesco Casetti has argued, cinema has always "vacillated" between the "image-imprint" and the "image-artifice," between "having a grasp on the world, having too much of it, and not having any left at all."[87] Theorists have proposed and debated a series of terms for the novel image forms of the digital era: these include the "neuro-image," the "morph-image," the "liquid-image," the "rhythm-image," the "infographic image," the "softimage," the "networked image," the "algorithmic image," the "discorrelated image," and the "postimage."[88] What these terms indicate is that the transition from a photographic, light- and chemical-based cinematic medium to a digital medium over the past few decades, facilitated by the development of digital television, has been accompanied by an equally remarkable set of shifts in how moving images are created and experienced. If, at the turn of the century, movie theatres almost exclusively showed films using light projected through celluloid (or polyester) onto screens, by 2017, 98% of the world's cinemas were digital.[89] At the same time, the modes of storytelling, editing, camera movement, cinematic time and space, and other elements of the film experience have come to be transformed and multiplied by the capacities of digital technologies, both in their production and in new forms of consumption and viewership. Moving images have become plastic, fluid, infinitely modulable, spatially unmoored and temporally elastic, while viewers' (and listeners') experience of them has become much more open, flexible, interactive, and immersive. The capacities of cinema and of television have in this sense been combined and deepened by the interactive and generative database nature of the internet.

Before we move on to the latter, however, it is worth noting the continuities and the divergences between traditional cinema and the cinematic, or "post-cinematic," forms of the digital era.[90] As Lev Manovich argued in his 2001 assessment of new media, cinema's stamp remains imprinted on new media forms: "Cinematic ways of seeing the world, of structuring time, of narrating a story, of linking one experience to the next, have become the basic means by which computer users access and interact with all cultural data."[91] Cinematic codes—such as one-point linear perspective, conventions of the mobile camera and the rectangular window-like framing of represented reality, and cinematic strategies of connecting space and time, of representing human memory, thinking, and emotion, and of "depictive credibility"[92]—continue to shape online interfaces, computer games, virtual worlds, and other new media forms.[93] At the same time, the integration of these forms into the flow of users' daily media experience continues to soften, smoothen, stretch, and open up the regimen of moving imagery into something much more immersive, connective, and labile. Manovich, in that same volume, proposed that live-action, narrative cinema will one day come to be seen as merely an episode, "an isolated accident in the history of visual representation." Such a history will have brought the moving image back full circle from its earliest forms as animated drawing or painting, through its heyday as live-action narrative representation, to its newly rediscovered form as animated image-interface. "*Born from animation*," he emphasized, "*cinema pushed animation to its periphery, only in the end to become one particular case of animation.*"[94]

It is time now to examine what has become of this newly (re)animated mode of smooth, immersive, connective, and interactive life that constitutes the image-world of digital media.

## Three

# THE DIGITAL IMAGE-WORLD

*[T]he Anthropocene era implies not a new image of the world, but the transformation of the world into images. . . . This alteration is also accompanied by an unprecedented explosion in the circulation of visibilities, which are actually making the outcome of these alterations opaque. [. . .] The fantasy that everything is or can be made visible coexists with the increasing automation of cognition.*

—IRMGARD EMMELHAINZ, "Conditions of Visuality Under the Anthropocene and Images of the Anthropocene to Come"[1]

*Everything happens in the middle, everything passes between the two, everything happens by way of mediation, translation and networks, but this space does not exist, it has no place. It is unthinkable, the unconscious of the moderns.*

—BRUNO LATOUR, We Have Never Been Modern[2]

• • • Today many of us live in a world so rich with images—moving images, expressive images, images that picture and reproduce the world in ever more detail, and (still) the ideal- and animate-images that have long characterized human world-making. All of them move and mix in novel combinations, translations, and mediations (as the quotes above suggest), thanks to technologies that continue to evolve amidst us. In this sense, the world is not only full of images, but the images have come to constitute an image-world: a networked, interconnected synthesis in which separating one image from others, or stabilizing an image, stilling its flow, has become more difficult than ever.

The term "image-world" is Susan Sontag's, and in her eponymous essay she noted that "when the notion of reality changes, so does that of the image, and vice versa."[3] "Through being photographed," she wrote, "something becomes part of a system of information. [. . .] Reality as such is redefined—as an item for exhibition, as a record for scrutiny, as a target for surveillance [. . .] an interminable dossier."[4] In a powerful paragraph summarizing the role of images in modern, industrial, consumer-capitalist society, Sontag wrote:

> A capitalist society requires a culture based on images. It needs to furnish vast amounts of entertainment in order to stimulate buying and anesthetize the injuries of class, race, and sex. And it needs to gather unlimited amounts of information, the better to exploit natural resources, increase productivity, keep order, make war, give jobs to bureaucrats. The camera's twin capacities, to subjectivize reality and to objectify it, ideally serve these needs and strengthen them. Cameras define reality in the two ways essential to the workings of an advanced industrial society: as a spectacle (for masses) and as an object of surveillance (for rulers). The production of images also furnishes a ruling ideology. Social change is replaced by a change in images. The freedom to consume a plurality of images and goods is equated with freedom itself. The narrowing of free political choice to free economic consumption requires the unlimited production and consumption of images.[5]

Sontag's analysis was prescient, yet she could hardly have anticipated the flourishing of so many new forms of image-making as we see in our world today. Her essay ended with a nearly apocalyptic argument about the ultimately "self-devouring" nature of the capitalist project. "Images," she wrote, "are more real than anyone could have supposed" and the ever-increasing rate of production and consumption of images has the result of consuming—which, she reminds us, "means to burn, to use up"—reality itself.[6] At heart, Sontag's was both an *ecological* argument about material production and consumption and an *epistemological* argument about lust and insatiability. But we have had nearly a half century more of images since her essay was published and the world is still here, bruised and beaten perhaps but also enlivened with new technologies and with a few billion more potential users of those technologies. Let us, then, follow the growth of this image-world in a more step-by-step way.

To start with, images in Sontag's day were of many different types, among them printed, photographic, cinematographic, and televisual. Today all of those kinds of images can still be found, but they have also been subsumed into a globally distributed and pervasive system of image production and consumption that is enabled and facilitated by digital technologies. The emergence and growth of these technologies has made possible a dramatic proliferation and increased, and increasingly rapid, dissemination of images, image-making, and image-consumption. It is now possible to watch images being made *as* they are being made—for instance, as they are filmed by live webcams—in many places around the world at once. The infrastructure to facilitate this is made up of cameras and recording devices, sensors and monitors, electronic data storage systems, satellites and on-land reception equipment, networks of cables connecting continents, and much more. All of this constitutes a "ubiquitous photoscape," as Martin Hand calls it, constituted in part by "the visual publicization of ordinary life."[7] But it is also much more: it is now a mediasphere reliant on and essentially contiguous with digital media, which in their nature are networked and interconnected, interactive, hypertextual, hypermediated, databased, and to a large degree automated.[8]

What concerns us here is not their physicality—a physicality that metaphors of "the cloud" conceal, since they require a massive global infrastructure of computer networks, storage systems and data server farms, undersea and overland cables, factories, mines, waste dumps, and much more (which has been well documented elsewhere).[9] Rather, it is the ways in which we, their users and inhabitants, experience them. To most of us, digital media are an integrated feature of our lives: we interact with them through screens, keyboards, and other devices by which we connect ourselves to a larger world of images, texts, ideas, social communities and relations, institutions, and physical environments. Digital media facilitate our public and private lives, enabling a wide range of connections with the world at large, and reshaping that world as they do so. With the presence of cameras, including those on smartphones as well as webcams, so ubiquitous now, and the capacity to view what they capture so readily available (if not as ubiquitous), it is possible to argue, with Paula Albuquerque, that public space has become "cinematized": "The profusion of media that record and transmit imagery over the Internet," Albuquerque writes, "characterizes a contemporary cinematic mode of existence, wherein audiovisual media are a constant and pervasive presence," and individuals are aware of and have internalized this fact, allowing it to shape their behavior, consciously or otherwise.[10] At the very least, we can say that public space has become *mediatized*, and that the distinctions between private and public space have become altered and blurred.

Insofar as this digital image-world builds on the other image regimes we have examined, it has proliferated images to such a degree that they not only *reflect* the world more accurately but come to play the role of *standing in* for it and *shaping* it in dynamic, interactive, and highly automated ways. The construction of reality by images is of course not new. But digital media have enabled new forms of connectivity and participation, whereby previously more stable images, many of them indexically linked to the "real world" via photographic technologies, have become fluid, decentered, mutable, "liquid," "morphing," "modular," "slippery," and "sticky," even as they are increasingly linked into hypermediated networks or "ecologies" of connection, interaction, immersion, responsivity, modulation, community, commerce, programmability, governmentality, and even neurology.[11]

Part of this description—of images as networked, and image use as interactive within immersive ecologies of connection and relationship—echoes the view of the cosmos previously described as the "encyclopedic" world-picture, which I associated with the Renaissance and Elizabethan worlds of relations and signatures described by Michel Foucault, Frances Yates, and others. This is a world whose participants interact with others in and through the relations between images, or between how things *appear* and what they *mean*. There is, as John Lechte argues, a "transparency" between what *can* be designated as an image and what *is* imaged, or made present, or between semiology (the study of signs) and hermeneutics (the study of their meanings).[12] What is different today is the technological reliance of such a networked, patterned system of images on digitality. We live in a networked image-world made possible by the technological world-picture regime: specifically, by the indexicality of photography, audiography, telemetry, and other means of recording, measuring, modeling, and analyzing reality, that has constituted a historical watershed enabling the recording and "datafication" of the world.

The digital image-world is therefore historically dependent on the world-picture regime (and its moving-image aftermath). At the same time, as we will see, the digital image is no longer easily traceable to its indexical sources: once it has become datafied, any discernible link to an original, source, or prior model for any specific image becomes lost within the networks of data and metadata that enable and configure it. As a result, the images we find in the digital image-world become fluid and morphable, with transformation occurring without leaving perceivable traces of its details. Indexicality is not exactly eliminated in digital media, but it is blurred, and effectively lost, within networks in which it has become intangible *except* through further datafication, for instance, through tagging, or at a larger level through machine learning and artificial intelligence.

## THE DATA-IMAGE: THE IMAGE DOUBLED AND OPERATIONALIZED

It is reasonable to ask, then: What happens to images in the world of digital media? Once images have been turned into digital data, are they still even images? Or have they become something else—numerical data sets, number fields, image and data streams, modular flows, combinatory patterns, fields of relations? We may still find distinct images within these flows, still or moving as the case may be, but do the streams that carry them qualify as images under the definition advanced earlier in this book?

I had defined an image as a "perceptible form that produces an effect in an observer in part through its resemblance to something else." The internet and the technologies and experiences connected to it, from smartphones to conferencing apps, organizing platforms, and interactive virtual environments, certainly include images within them. Some of these are static visual images, even if they are graphically produced digital composites. Many are moving audiovisual images (or simply auditory images), and some add hapticity to the sensorial mix; many are time-based and experienced as part of a televisual flow. Images, Jens Eder and Charlotte Klonk write, are used for "representing, illustrating, entertaining, distracting, directing attention, protesting, providing evidence, explaining facts, simulating real-world actions, creating imaginary worlds, symbolising the non-perceptible, changing modes of perception, evoking affects and mobilizing action."[13] To this list we can add Jussi Parikka's list of operations, in which images help to execute and program "material surfaces and events" through "targeting, analyzing, comparing, tracking, navigating, extracting, trapping, projecting, forecasting, measuring, and quantifying."[14] This makes them all "operational images," "pictures that are part of an operation," in Haroun Farocki's words.[15]

A subset of all of these images remain indexically produced in their origins, from light striking photochemical surfaces as it is reflected off the surface of the world, sound waves striking the diaphragm of a microphone, or something analogous. Indexicality remains present both in the origins of some images and in their reception (as sound or light waves, and so on) by users. The environment, however—the medium within which those images have their effects—is different, as it consists of fields or "flows" of data within which images, like other information, are stored, analyzed, circulated, replicated, modulated, and transformed. It becomes possible, then, to speak of digital images as having "a double existence": as viewable visual forms, or displayed images, and as "signalized," "insensible" and "invisual," imageless and nonpictorial "image files," "strings of data," or "datasets."[16] By some accounts, the first is no longer the norm but has become the exception, requiring software to be made viewable by human observers. At the same time, the humanly visible image remains the template and the model for the dataset that renders it "machine-readable" and thereby functional within a digital environment. Together, these two dimensions give the digital image an "operability" or "operationality," and a "programmability" and "processability."[17] This enables images to work within spaces of operation, modulation, and transformation where they sometimes act as carriers and mediators, and sometimes as mere accompaniments to distributed datasets and processes.[18] Operational images "organize the world," Parikka writes: they organize "much of what contemporary culture fundamentally looks at, including figures, graphs, diagrams, trajectories, models, plans, simulations, control screens, spreadsheets, and so on," and in doing so they organize our perceptions, capacities, and limitations.[19]

A single image is, in this environment, no longer singular; its circulations and transformations are no longer fully predictable. When images, as Simon Rothöhler writes, "can no longer be ascribed to a binding media location, a constant materiality, a key actor, a central agency," they "can only ever be understood as both fluid and reversible phenomenalizations of an operatively distributed media logistics."[20] As images circulate—between cameras, screens, servers, and digital processing systems of various kinds—they become part of the ever-thickening mediatory apparatus that *is* the digital image-world, the world of technical and infrastructural relations that renders a certain kind of image-work possible.

One can see in Rothöhler's account the tendency to assume that images once were something and now are not: that they were still, singular, representational, and bound to a location or "constant materiality," but are now set free into fluid circulation. Recall, however, that process-semiotic theory takes images to always be in motion, "in the act" and "on the move." In a world ceaselessly being produced and reproduced, images are never entirely still except in their contrast to things that are less so. Nevertheless, the imaging that occurs within a digital image-world is very different from the imaging that occurs in a purely non-digital environment. The relationship between images, within this operant flow, and their human users has changed. It is not that digital worlds have replaced physical, pre-digital worlds: there are still sensing bodies with palpable organs, rooms in buildings, schools and playgrounds, streets and cars, gardens, forests, and seas. All, or most of them, are connected to the digitally networked image-world, but are not reducible to it. They are supplemented by, intertwined with, and in key respects overtaken by that world, but they also retain their autonomy from it. But our experience of the latter is very different from non-media experience and from our experience of earlier, pre-digital media.

## EXPERIENCING THE DIGITAL IMAGE-WORLD

If cinema provided for a certain kind of experience, one in which a viewing audience sat down in front of what was being offered and then received it—in its spectacle (or firstness, to use Peirce's terms), its sequentiality (or secondness), and its referentiality (or thirdness)—in order to negotiate their own relationship with it, the experience of the digital image-world is substantially different. One may still begin and end that experience, if only temporarily, by turning on one's smartphone or laptop, or logging into one's browser, and at the end by setting them down or closing out of them—to go to the bathroom, take the dog for a walk, feed one's children, bicycle to work, or retire to bed at the end of a day. But the image-world itself has no beginning or end: it is always there and "always on." When I log in, it is in part to see what has happened while I was away: who has sent me emails or commented on my last social media post, what others have been sharing, and the latest news about a war in a faraway country or the trials of a football star or former president. The firstness of the digital image-world experience consists of this "always on" quality. Rather than providing a spectacle to watch as it happens, digital media provide an ongoing hyper-spectacle that continues whether we are there to monitor it or not, with no inherent limit to how much attention we might be willing to give it. As Paul Frosh writes in *The Poetics of Digital Media*,

> Digital mobile devices and their infrastructures have not replaced the "always on" of one-to-many connectivity underpinning twentieth-century broadcasting, or the framework of ambient attendance and companionship that it produced. Rather, they have *thickened* it through their intimate closeness to the individual body, *animated* it through interactive interfaces and *devolved* it to individuals, groups and technical systems through the intensive and extensive complexities of their networks. The multi-sensuous accompaniment of digital devices continually on our persons, the operative restlessness made imperative by user interfaces, the perpetual companionship of more proximate and individuated others (as well as of the apparatus itself) made visible by social media—these all take the unparalleled constancy and readiness of twentieth-century media and simultaneously expand and condense them, making the mediation of the world experientially denser and more intense than in the past.[21]

All of this has instantiated a particular type of media life for users and dwellers within digital media worlds. "In place of the production of an extended lifeworld and its multiple mediated presences (its figures and its ground)," Frosh writes, "we live in an era of the demonstrative performance of mediation as overt, continual activity."[22] This continual activity consists of the many interactions by which we engage with others via screens and gadgets. In this sense, the image-world's firstness and its secondness have become combined: there is no immediate present that is not always lodged within the sense of constant flow. While some of us may still view and admire a still image (say, a screensaver), or for that matter may listen to the radio, watch television, and read books and newspapers, many of us now do these things within a context in which their significance is always imbued with the possibility of doing much more. As we read, listen, or view something, we can always also do other things—we can click, like, tag, link, comment, capture, friend, follow, favorite, select, save, record, post, share, scroll, browse, stream, surf, text, chat, google, zoom, tweet, troll, screenshot, update, upload, download, trash, surf, and navigate.

Some of us create new identities in the process of doing these things; and some come to know ourselves better, such that a Descartes of social media might say, "I surf, click, and link—therefore I am." With our ability to navigate and move proactively and projectively through the many possibilities afforded by digital media, humans have become not so much observers or subjects as we are literal surfers and "swimmers," whose mode of action mixes looking with speaking or texting, linking with liking or commenting, up- and downloading, recording and editing, modulating and remixing, and otherwise interacting with databases layered with possibilities for lateral connectivity and multilocatedness. Unlike cinema, the digital image-world does not produce a singular, consistent object-world and subject-world; rather, it produces an oscillating sense of object-worldness and subjectivation. It is a multiplatformed world, rather like a many-roomed house that we can move through at our leisure, engaging differently with different rooms (platforms), some of which have their own worlds (Instagram world, Twitter/X world, TikTok world), with their own operational rules and affordances (social media apps being different from music or video streaming apps, gaming applications, news browsers, and so on). All of these coexist and potentially overlap, and our engagement with them can be sequential, simultaneous, or a mix of the two. The entire experience has become seamless, integrated, and both continuous and discontinuous—always interruptible, yet continually rejoinable.

In terms of its thirdness, that is, in the ways that our experience of the digital image-world enables a referential and interpretive sensemaking that shapes our sense of the broader world, the digital image-world becomes a kind of kaleidoscope of platformed activities through which the "real world" appears through a patchwork quilt of overlapping perspectives, informational fragments, and continuing, never fully convergent discourses. Our digital activities, which may be work-related, news-related, friends-related, or entertainment-related, allow for a more seamless integration of our sense of worldhood, for instance, in which our feelings about climate change, the matter of Black lives, the #MeToo movement, or the abortion debate may affect our social media posts, entertainment choices, and news preferences (in turn enabling algorithmic governance to shape them even more). Our experience becomes interactively cocurated by our actions and the algorithms that mediate them, so that an enhanced sense of worldness might become something like what Steven Colbert meant in coining the word "truthiness": yes, we live in a world, one shared to some degree with friends (or social media "friends"), but it is not necessarily a world shared with *the* world. It is a *worldyness* that consists of varying degrees of *truthiness*, *friendyness*, and lifelikeness. Each of these has become a semi-animate likeness of something that they recall, but never quite bring to fruition.

This raises the question of how the world that has enabled the emergence of the digital image-world has itself changed in ways that facilitate this certain sense of worldyness.

## POLITICAL ECONOMY AND THE REALITY-EFFECT OF DIGITAL MEDIA

Our user experience takes place in the context of structural developments in the political economy of media, and the political economy of capitalism in general, whose importance cannot be overstated. This is the emergence of a digital capitalism that defines the parameters of individual, group, corporate, and state participation within digital media. Analysts of contemporary political economy variously speak of (to quote just one list of designators) "[a]lgorithmic capitalism, cognitive capitalism, communicative capitalism, data capitalism, digital capitalism, frictionless capitalism, informational capitalism, platform capitalism, semiocapitalism, surveillance capitalism and virtual capitalism."[23] Participation in digital media takes place within a "platform ecosystem," an "'appliancized' network of proprietary social network sites"[24] that emerged in the first decade of this century, and that has shaped the infrastructural, economic, and governmental organization of media since then.[25] The browsers, programs, apps, and platforms shaping our experience of these ecosystems are in turn the basis for a new economy of "surveillance capitalism," built from the financialization of the online and offline behavior of internet users, whose clicks, interests, consumption patterns, social media contributions, and other online habits are subjected to machine-learning analysis in order to be sold as predictive tools to third parties. While this may sound like a niche development within the global economy, it has in fact transformed that economy and led to the rise of the largest and most powerful corporations on the planet, including the so-called American Big Five (Google/Alphabet, Apple, Microsoft, Amazon, and Meta) as well as others around the world (such as China's Tencent, Alibaba, Huawei, Baidu, and ByteDance).

In an effort to situate digital media within this political economy, Steven Shaviro builds on Michel Foucault's and Gilles Deleuze's respective arguments about governmentality and the "society of control" to argue that the modus operandi of this neoliberal, networked, and hyperflexible capitalism (three more terms to add to the above list) has become a ceaseless pressure for continual modulation. In this political economy "of crises and convulsions"—a world of "modulation, digitization, financialization, and media transduction" that is "ruthlessly organized" around the relentless logic of commodification and capitalist accumulation—governmentality has shifted from *disciplinary* forms that molded individuals into subjects according to relatively fixed parameters, to a *flexible* society of ongoing, never-resting and never-sated change, where *continuous recombination* is a necessity for survival.[26] There is, in other words, nothing solid left beneath our feet: just as the global financial system sloshes around like a drunken gambler on a storm-tossed ship, so do jobs, careers, personal and collective identities, corporate and national marketing strategies, and values all shift and mutate to keep up with the flow of a fluid and elusive reality. To survive, you must stay continuously on the move; if you stop moving, you will be left behind.

This account of life's high-pressure fluidity is no doubt overgeneralized, as one's life experience will vary depending not only on economic circumstances, but on the existence of community supports, health and social welfare systems, national and local cultural traditions, and the like. And there are movements afoot to *contain* the forces of this globalizing, computational capitalism, or to keep them at bay—movements that include conservative as well as liberal, reactionary as well as revolutionary political inflections, with overlapping goals that include providing a sense of stability amidst the seeming global chaos. But there is no doubt that the ways in which collective life is governed have been affected by the technologies that facilitate that life, and that digital technologies have opened up new possibilities and foreclosed others. The perceived and experienced liquidity of the digital image-world—its unreliable images, rapid transformations (of apps and platforms, regulatory discourses, and political repercussions), and "tribalistic" impacts—have multiple effects both on our experience of that image-world and on the world that remains outside of it. On one side, these lead to a questioning or perceived unreliability of the image (and of political agency, of "truth," and so on). But on the other they can contribute to new connections between images and "realities."

With the first trend, it is the "deepfake" that most epitomizes the liquidity of digital imagery. Deepfakes are a form of what is called synthetic media that use sophisticated data technologies to generate audiovisual representations that, to the untrained eye, appear to have captured physical reality in the same way that a film or video does; in other words, they appear to be "real"—indexically captured bits of reality—when they are in fact manipulated and thus "fake." They do this by employing artificial intelligence and machine learning, which process vast troves of data to render believable facsimiles of physical reality in audiovisual form and, crucially, to make those facsimiles appear to do anything imaginable. The generation of deepfakes can be for any purpose: promotional, pedagogical, creative, entertaining, satirical, deceptive, exploitative, and abusive. Deceptive deepfakes have successfully been used in facilitating heists, mobilizing political movements, and disseminating negative publicity against its targets.[27] It is this category—deepfake manipulations in which politicians appear to say things they have never said, movie stars appear to act in explicit porn videos (when they have not), and activists appear in compromising situations—that has generated the most controversy to date.

The "deeper" point about deepfakes, however, is that the media that viewers have long trusted to be realistic are now capable of creative license beyond their originators' wildest dreams. By playing on the cognitive biases, or "processing fluency," by which humans key in on sensory information that is easily processed—the visual appearance of an expressive face, for instance—deepfakes render audiovisual images utterly unreliable, in the sense that one can never know if they represent something that ever happened or not. "The greatest risk of deepfakes," Graham Meikle writes, is "that they are known to exist: if we know that everything can be faked, we risk losing the capacity to believe in anything."[28] In this sense, the spread of deepfakes and other forms of media manipulation contributes to the erosion of trust that is said to characterize the "post-truth condition."

If the processing power of machine learning and AI can give digital imagery the potential to take us further away from reality as we have known it, the same power can also bring us closer to that reality. Specifically, it can "thicken" and "augment" users' relationships with "geolocated" sites and spaces within the physical world. Apps make it possible to situate oneself in geographic space in much more informed, real-time ways: for instance, to know which cafés are currently open in one's neighborhood, where road traffic is lightest or heaviest, where to find an available car-share or e-scooter, where one's friends are, what sort of bird or mushroom one has just spotted, or how to avoid police barriers during a protest. Smart homes, smart cities, smart farms and forests, and the much heralded Internet of Things all thicken the possibilities for decision-making at every potential data-point within networks of sensing, monitoring, and management that can be top-down, bottom-up, or lateral and multivalent in their uses and configurations.

Indexical technologies, such as those that contributed to the world-picture regime, have always enabled an extension of human perception outside the scope of the unenhanced human sensibility. This was Marshall McLuhan's argument about media. Its extension today is much more systemic, with image-capturing and image-processing technologies becoming interlinked in global networks whose activities proceed according to parameters not subject to individual control, yet which have pronounced effects on human perception and behavior. Some of these activities contribute to a "sensorization" and "smartification" of environments that are enabling the emergence of a globalized "extended sensorium." In a series of books including *Program Earth* and *How to Do Things with Sensors,* Jennifer Gabrys has described the many ways in which this global-scale sensorization has been assembled through cameras, sensors, satellites, and computers so that computational technologies have become "constitutive of environments, have environmental effects, and also inform environmental practices."[29] This is also Mark Hansen's point in his provocative *Feed-Forward: On the Future of Twenty-First Century Media.* Hansen writes:

> in a world linked together by multi-scalar computational networks and increasingly populated with intelligent sensing technologies ranging from environmental sensors to the smart phones and other portable devices we now carry with us as a matter of course, *experience simply is not what it used to be*: far more of what goes on in our daily lives is carried out by machines functioning at their own timescales, meaning outside of our direct perceptual grasp but in ways that do significantly affect our activity.[30]

Like Hansen, Shane Denson points to the transformation of the "anthropotechnical interface," such that human sensation and perception itself are being reconstituted "metabolically" by the "atmospheric" and impersonal environment of ubiquitous computing.[31] Echoing these points, Andrea Pinotti argues that with the growth of immersive and interactive digital environments—those of virtual reality (VR), augmented reality (AR), and mixed reality (MR)—the boundary between representation and reality has become blurred to the point of being an open border for two-way traffic. This, Pinotti argues, renders the image "an-iconic," whereby virtual environments are experienced not as representations of real environments but as *actual* environments of a new kind.[32] How such novel environments evolve is up to us. For Hansen, digital technologies afford the opportunity to enhance the "infra-empirical infrastructure underlying and informing our daily activity."[33] He continues, "With the unprecedented capacities of our digital devices and sensors to gather information about behavior and about the environment, we literally acquire new and alien 'organs' (which must not be confused with prostheses of *our* human sense organs) for excavating extraperceptual dimensions of experience—our own as well as that of other entities." As a result, we could "come to enjoy an expanded sensory contact with worldly sensibility."[34]

Needless to say (as Hansen admits all too briefly), such an optimistic vision would require overcoming "the myriad contemporary entities and institutions that seek to capitalize" on the affordances presented by these technologies.[35] As the digital image-world regime suffuses our everyday lives, its hyperlinked multilocalities and interactivities increase the buy-in of those who come to serve as its image producers, consumers, managers (with social media content moderation outsourced to individuals around the world), and its dwellers. With the internet, the computer terminal, and the cell phone having become second nature to billions of humans, humanity has come increasingly to inhabit, and be inhabited by, a novel neurosensory architecture, with epistemological, political, and ontological implications that are becoming evident as they become unavoidable. Our ways of knowing are shaped by the ability to access information online—information that takes the form of images, narratives, datasets, and platform architectures—but also by the differential ability to sift through and make sense of this information. In the "attentional economy" of computational capital, there are stark differences between those whose attention and online behavior is the resource from which wealth is generated, and those who manage that attention and capitalize on its wealth. Political formations in turn have been modified among certain of these ways of knowing, with new coalitions and alternative understandings and "realities" being built, at the same time as all are shaped by the economics by which these technologies proliferate.

The rise of digital megacorporations—the Amazons, Apples, Google/Alphabets, Facebooks, and Huaweis—is not only a response to the desires of these technologies' users. It is also a response to the possibility for new forms of capital, including that which Shoshana Zuboff has christened "surveillance capitalism," premised on the capturing, collection, analysis, and reselling of the data of its users.[36] The competition for profit from these new data frontiers shapes one side of the digital economy. Another side, meanwhile, is always entangled in other potential uses of data by governments, militaries, political parties, and less visible agents within shadow economies whose boundaries remain elusive. In the midst of this activity, we users are allowed, indeed encouraged, to pursue our own paths and desires. Images, within this flow, have therefore become vessels and carriers of our individual cognitive and affective investments, and of collective currents of energy, affect, attention, and desire. These in turn are shaped and modulated by algorithms that fold our activities into larger, more sweepingly aggregate forms.[37]

Ontologically, then, what sort of world is this world of digital media? To oppose the digital or virtual against the real is hardly helpful at this point. The questions to be raised about the digital, rather, concern the kinds of realities—fictional, indexical, simulated, augmented, hybrid, or layered—made possible by it, their multiple levels of interaction with the physical world (some more visible and others more opaque), and their many ways of reshaping, remediating, and remixing the world that came before digital media.[38] The real-world effects of digital technologies include effects on people—modifications of perception, attention, sociality, memory, and trust[39]—alongside effects on nonhuman and material ecologies, such as the ecological impacts of their manufacturing, their carbon-intensiveness, and so on.[40] Reality itself gets reshaped into something understood to be algorithmic and transactional. So does the capacity for agency, movement, and power within it, all of which are entwined within processes of algorithmic modulation serving the goals of multiple players, from individual users and hacker collectives to corporations, governments, and mutable geopolitical alliances.

There is no guarantee that agency will even be in human hands. As digital artist-activist Trevor Paglen noted in 2016, "The overwhelming majority of images are now made by machines for other machines, with humans rarely in the loop." The machine-readability of images, he argues, carries revolutionary implications. It "allows for the automation of vision on an enormous scale and, along with it, the exercise of power on dramatically larger *and* smaller scales than have ever been possible."[41] "Machine-to-machine seeing apparatuses" range from automatic license plate readers (ALPR) mounted on police cars, buildings, highways, and private vehicles to cameras in malls and department stores that track facial expressions and discern people's moods; and from social media companies' analysis of their users' every move to a global array of sensors tracking the movements of humans (legal and illegal), animals, automobiles, airplanes, satellites, and much more. Machine vision systems, as Antonio Somaini recounts, scan and identify "faces, bodies, gestures, expressions, emotions, objects, movements, places, atmospheres and moods—but also voices and sounds, through technologies of *machine hearing*." These are then

> labelled, stored, organized, retrieved, and processed as data that can be quickly accessed and activated for a wide variety of purposes: from surveillance to policing, from marketing to advertising, from the monitoring of industrial processes to military operations, from the functioning of driverless vehicles to that of drones and robots, from the study of the inside of the human body through the analysis of medical imagining [*sic*] all the way up to the study of the surface of the Earth and of climate change through the analysis of satellite images.[42]

Machine-learning systems, such as generative adversarial networks (GAN) and convolutional neural networks (CNN), work to generate information from information. They work with vast text and image databases on which to train their operational functions for increasing precision and predictive capacity. One such dataset, ImageNet, includes 14 million images organized according to 21,000 categories; another, LAOIN-5B, is made up of five billion images and text-image pairs.[43] As far as images go, the result of all this, Paglen writes, is that images no longer just represent and mediate, but now "intervene in everyday life," operationalizing it by "actively watching us, poking and prodding, guiding our movements, inflicting pain and inducing pleasure." He concludes, "We no longer look at images—images look at us."[44] At the same time, images, texts, and human perceptions have become correlated and discorrelated in complex ways, with the metadata by which images are tagged coming to shape and shift their meanings in unpredictable directions.[45]

This leads, on the one hand, to the stacking of the deck by assumptions loaded into the neural networks and human-designed algorithms—assumptions, for instance, about race and gender, socioeconomic class, geographical location, religious and political persuasions, potential criminality or profitability, and so on, all of which result in what observers call "algorithmic injustice." On the other hand, it gives rise to unpredictable forms of machine-generated creativity. As news reports have told us in the wake of the latest crop of generative AI chatbots like OpenAI's ChatGPT, Microsoft's Copilot, Google's Gemini, and Anthropic's Claude, artificial intelligence can and will "hallucinate." AIs will respond with confidence, but either inaccurately or "inappropriately," to questions outside the range of their training data and allow those hallucinations to shape their further behavior.[46] Questions about the future of artificial intelligence thus revolve around both the likelihood that their immense power will be put to *intentionally* harmful uses and to the likelihood, or perhaps certainty, of *unintentional* consequences.

## THE CONDITIONS OF "TRUTH"

It is easy to experience a sense of exhaustion when confronting this mix of the unreliable, the informationally overwhelming, the agentially indeterminate, and the technologically unpredictable. This is very much a part of the notorious "post-truth" condition, in which all forms of expertise appear discredited, no one can be trusted, and the truth is no longer even considered to be "out there" anymore; or of it is, it is so far "out" that any grounds for commonality in its pursuit are lost. Against this pervasive sense of exhaustion, digital activists like Paglen and the Forensic Architecture group insist that distinctions can still be made, and that the proliferation of data does not exhaust the possibility for making sense, but rather multiplies the possibilities for new ways of sense-making: for collaborative and open-source architectures of engagement and for new modes of "commoning" among newly constituted publics. In a world that seems swamped with data, the tools of artificial intelligence and machine learning are available to render this data meaningful, but they leave open the question of who will control their use and to what ends they will be put. If dominant economic and political forces are already using these tools for their purposes, can sufficient safeguards and institutional controls be put in place to render them open and accessible to widely shared, publicly defined goals?

The politics of digital media are being shaped by decisions being made today, and attending to those decisions and the policies they embody is mandatory if they are to develop ethically and democratically. Among those arguing for a more immanent politics of digital production are media theorist Matthew Fuller and architect Eyal Weizman, who argue that politics in an image- and data-rich world requires an "investigative aesthetics" that counters the "anti-epistemology" of radical doubt by "reveling" in and "struggling" with the world's complexity.[47] It does this by seeking "to integrate (but not homogenise) multiple viewpoints, opening up the circles of investigation, establishing new alignments between different sites, styles and institutions of diverse types and standings," from scientific laboratories and universities to artists' studios, "activist organizations, social groups rejecting the status of victim for that of agency and leadership, national and international legal fora (when they can be effectively used), the media, and cultural institutions." Such an investigative aesthetics, they write, "uses technology, but interrogates the politics of the very technology it uses; it uses multiple platforms to represent things publicly, but queries the limits and politics of these fora of representation; it involves knowledge production while keeping a critical eye on the power-knowledge nexus."[48]

Fuller and Weizman, alongside other researchers, like Paolo Cirio, Kate Crawford, David Houston Jones, Miren Gutiérrez, Antonio Somaini, Erika Balsom, and T. J. Demos, point to the work of artist-activists—including Trevor Paglen, Forensic Architecture (Weizman's group), the Otolith Group, Hito Steyerl, Susan Schuppli, Grégory Chatonsky, Holly Herndon, Refik Anadol, and filmmakers-turned-digital artists like Harun Farocki, Laura Poitras, Arthur Jafa, and John Akomfrah (to be examined later)—as demonstrating the power of digital tools to challenge the dominant political tendencies of digitality.[49] The work of Holly Herndon and Matthew Dryhurst, who use artificial neural networks and text-to-image generators like Dall-E, Midjourney, and Stable Diffusion, but also work to develop a "consent layer" that would allow artists to trace their own data through its digital uses and appropriations, suggests that individual artists can both *take* control and *democratize* control of the images a digital, algorithmically modified, AI-generated world makes possible. Herndon and Dryhurst posit a world of "infinite media," in which anyone can responsibly "adjust, adapt, or iterate on the work, talents, and traits of others," making creative expression a kind of collaborative commons of "spontaneous generation and transformation."[50] Truth, in such an infinitely mediatic, creative sphere is less about accuracy in representation, and more about free expression accompanied by political and economic accountability.

But asking individual artists and activists to take on the challenges of image accountability is hardly a solution to the vexing problems raised by digital technologies in a world of "infinite media." Countering their more pernicious tendencies requires systemic policies by which democratic oversight can shape and manage the development of those technologies. Whether and how a more diverse, democratically rooted, and multisited politics can be integrated into media today is a question that will loom in the background of the studies in part 2 of this book. We can, in any case, refer loosely to two schools of thought. One sees digital technology as fundamentally intertwined with capitalist economics, such that its developmental trajectory appears all but unstoppable (despite calls for political intervention). The second is more promising in that it sees the technology as at least potentially neutral and its ends as open and modifiable.

Cognizant of the critiques but arguing for a more open understanding of digital systems, Jonathan Bratton sees digital technologies as an interacting set of communicative, mediative, and operational systems, a "network of networks" he calls "the Stack." Bratton describes it as the "accidental megastructure" formed by "various types of planetary-scale computation (e.g., smart grids, cloud computing, mobile and urban-scale software, universal addressing systems, ubiquitous computing, and robotics, and so on) not as isolated, unrelated types of computation but as forming a larger, coherent whole."[51] This megastructure has an architecture that Bratton delineates into six layers: those of the user, the interface, the address, the city, the cloud, and the earth. This description suggests that the world itself has transformed into a unified, architecturally coherent and technologically structured field. Other observers note the many gaps between the layers and within them—for instance, between producers, consumers, investors, users, and regulators, with their various, often competing social locations and interests.

Before looking at the specifics of image regimes, we will need to deal with a few more overarching questions: of how image regimes interact with language and textuality, how they come to be embodied in specific but different materialities, how they generate different psychodynamic propensities, and how they interact with each other. In the following chapter, which serves as a theoretical recapitulation and synthesis preceding the empirical studies of part 2, I will try to show that in the real world of humans living meaningful lives amidst more-than-human relations, image regimes do not usually show up *as* distinctive regimes. This is not how they are typically perceived, even if a dramatic change of regime may be perceivable to observers. Rather, they show up as specific image constellations—ecologies of images and meanings by which worlds are organized, which are perceived as distinctive because of the images themselves that feature as central within them. These "imaginaries" interact among each other in various ways. Sometimes they erupt in clashes—*iconoclashes*, to use the resonant word suggested in Latour and Weibel's comprehensive collection of materials on that topic. But more often they connect in more peaceable relations, as sparring partners, for instance, or as sporting associates, whose tensions produce novel relations and hybrids. Sometimes they genuinely couple, producing offspring that account for what historical retrospect might even demarcate as genuine developmental progress. I will suggest a few of these, which I will call the "creative-image" and the "montage-image," in part 2. I hope, in any case, to show that the relationship between image ecologies and image regimes remains today the most complex question facing humanity.

Four

# THE PLAY OF IMAGINARIES

*Images, too, must take sides: as neutral windows adequately representing the objective world (by way of divine or machinic inscription producing an uncontaminated mimetic accuracy that reduces the deceptive to a minimum), or as mere subjective representations, with no claim to an objective world; that is, in the last instance, as an animistic mirror of sorts, a projection of interiority onto the outer world, reduced to the picture plane. The status of photography provides perfect evidence of this ever-shifting status: Either the photograph is seen as a merely machinic product, over which consequently no right of authorship can be claimed [. . .], or it is seen as the expression of a subject [. . .]. In each case, the turning point, the infrastructure of a complex chain of mediations, is blended out.*

—ANSELM FRANKE, *"Much Trouble in the Transportation of Souls, or the Sudden Disorganization of Boundaries"*[1]

*Part of the reality of groups is made of images, materialized as drawings, statues, monuments, garments, tools, and machines, as well as turns of phrase, formulas like proverbs that are true verbal images (akin to slogans). Such images ensure the cultural continuity of groups and are constant intermediaries between their past and future: they are both vehicles of experiences and knowledge as well as specific modes of waiting.*

—GILBERT SIMONDON, Imagination and Invention[2]

• • • It is precisely the "turning point, the infrastructure of a complex chain of mediations," in Anselm Franke's words, that our theory of images aims to get at. How is this infrastructure materialized, and how does it become part of the "cultural continuity" of collective formations of humans engaged in more-than-human worlds? This chapter hopes to show some ways in which this occurs and to elucidate and distinguish the tendencies of the six image regimes identified thus far.

The six regimes, as mentioned, follow a not entirely commensurate set of distinguishing criteria. They are not pieces on a chessboard, whose underlying "operating table" of structuring parameters is clearly defined and unchanging.[3] They are more like the list of animals from Borges's "famous Chinese encyclopaedia," cited by Michel Foucault at the beginning of his study of the ordering of the modern episteme, *The Order of Things* (*Les mots et les choses*), in which "animals are divided into: (a) belonging to the Emperor, (b) embalmed, (c) tame, (d) suckling pigs, (e) sirens, (f) fabulous, (g) stray dogs, (h) included in the present classification, (i) frenzied, (j) innumerable, (k) drawn with a very fine camelhair brush, (l) *et cetera*, (m) having just broken the water pitcher, (n) that from a long way off look like flies." The ordering of the six regimes is not so much structural as it is genealogical. I intend for it to make sense when looking backward from within our current time and space, one that may be *between* configurations, but which is actively being reshaped by the spread of digital media.

Roughly, however, we can distinguish them by focusing on their respective understandings of reality and of agency. The first regime, that of the *animate-image*, takes the image to be an active mediator within a relational network. It supposes that agency flows bidirectionally, or multidirectionally, within an interactive, ontologically differential realm that includes the human and the extra-human, however the latter be conceived. We could call this an "immanent transcendent" conception of the image in that it considers humans to be part of a larger world that includes images and other kinds of things—things that may be transcendent of us, but that we participate in. The transcendence of things is therefore local, empirical, and subject to negotiation.[4]

The second regime, that of the *ideal-image*, supposes a separation between two realms: a worldly, mundane, or merely human one and an ontologically superior, transcendent, or ideal one. Images, for their part, act as stand-ins or representations of the latter to the former. It takes the image to be passive in relation to the reality that is beyond it, which acts or expresses itself through the image. Transcendence, in the ideal-image regime, becomes generalized and ascribed to that which is *beyond* the world, the local, and the empirical; transcendence here takes precedence over immanence.

The third model, the *expression-image* regime, sees agency working in more or less the opposite direction to the second: it reclaims power for the immanent, and specifically for human agency. It takes the human creator, the artist or producer, to be instrumental in shaping the effect and power of the image, even while that agency takes its impetus from the world itself, a world the artist skillfully and insightfully captures in some form, character, or quality. The image is in this sense passive in relation to its human creator. The ideal world that had been presumed to lurk beyond the image is here decentered, if not entirely eliminated from the picture.

The *world-picture* regime, in turn, presents a variation of the ideal-image in which the distinct and transcendent reality-referent has been jettisoned altogether. In its place stands the indexicality of direct, causal connection between the image and its origin. The image now represents, with greater or lesser fidelity, a reality that is inclusive of, and of the same ontological substance as, humans; we are all part of a world of indicators translating previous indicators, signs transducing signs. There is nothing beyond the meshwork of signification. An image is a copy or representation, successful or unsuccessful as it were, of the real world, and that world is ontologically singular in that it places humans and other things on the same level of operation, a level that renders all things interoperable. Agency here is no longer ascribable to an outside, though it may be ascribed to immanent laws or forces, such as the "laws of nature."

With its photographic roots, the *moving-image* builds on the latter, but multiplies opportunities for hybrid forms of engagement, which come to be reintegrated in variable ways. Those new opportunities in turn facilitate the emergence of the *digital image-world* of our contemporary hypermediated culture. The image now becomes fully lodged within a relational network that is materially embodied, digitally enabled, and maximally interoperable, and that allows for and includes all of the other types of images. (See table 4.1 at the end of this chapter.)

The Franke quote that opened this chapter gets at the opposition between, on one side, the ideal-image regime and its technological "bastard cousin," as it were, the world-picture regime, both of which ascribe an objectivity and ideality to the world beyond the image (which the image aims to capture) and, on the other side, the subjectivism of the expression-image regime. As Franke writes, the "infrastructure" of the "complex chain of mediations" that constitutes image-making is "blended out." While this may be the case once an image regime becomes a regime, taken for granted by those who participate in it, I will suggest in this chapter that this infrastructure is most evident—least "blended out"—in the case of the animate-image regime insofar as the mediations the infrastructure enables are acknowledged as agential.

The actual use of images, however, can be complex, promiscuously partaking of several regimes at once, even as it need not recognize its own economies of agency. When an icon or statue of Shiva or of the Virgin Mary is treated as sovereign, appropriately decorated and carried in a procession, it is both animate—real and sacred in and of itself, with the capacity to communicate and transform its worshippers—and ideal, representing a higher reality that may be responsive but is not dependent on our participation. Modern photo imagery is replete with images that combine ideality, animacy, and sometimes other regimes. Capitalism, through its advertising and marketing arms, could be said to produce "desire-images," which are intended to elicit an affective relationship to an object depicted; in this, it presents an ideal (the object referred to) as well as a relationship to that ideal (the consumer as needing and potentially obtaining that object), and it works "animately" by eliciting an affective movement toward that ideal. By a similar token, the nation-state and the nationalisms that undergird it, in their many variants—liberal, socialist, fascist, corporatist—produce "allegiance-images" intended to create a sense of identity with depicted ideals.

Images also allow for ideals to be criticized. With political satire, assumed ideals are subjected to other ideals: propaganda to its critical unveiling, "image" to "substance," and so on. In the image-rich world of the internet, the combinations become endless. If I were to go online to seek images of a divinity or of a musical or entertainment idol in order to then model my behavior on that divine or human being, I could be engaging with an ideal-image (represented by the idol), an animate-image (to the extent that I am interacting with it), an expression-image (if I am critical of imperfect depictions of that being, but appreciative of more faithful and expressive depictions), a moving-image (if there are videos involved), a world-picture (if there are maps of places I might visit, for instance, associated with that idol), and weaving it all together, the datafied image-world of the internet.

In what follows, I will resituate the work of the image within the networks in which it functions. These include language, alongside embodied and material practices of various kinds. The latter involve affective relationships between images and their users, and to get at the dynamic and coproduced, or co-agential, nature of these relationships, I will draw upon religion scholar and art historian David Morgan's "enchantment theory" of images. This in turn will lead into a consideration of the psychological dynamics infusing our interaction with images. I will end with a series of propositions, or "rules of thumb," for understanding the operation of images and image regimes. These loose rules are rooted in a kind of as-if story about the evolution of image regimes, a story not intended to be taken literally, but intended to help us better understand the relationships between images, image regimes, and image ecologies. I will conclude the chapter with a thought exercise responding to a similar exercise first presented some years ago by image theorist W. J. T. Mitchell.

## IMAGINARIES AND LANGUAGE

I have defined images as perceptible forms that produce effects in observers in significant part through their resemblance to something else. This definition highlights the iconicity, or Peircian firstness, within the signness of images. In contrast, language is symbolic, in Peirce's terms: it signifies through a set of relationships that is arbitrary in the way it creates meaning, even if its arbitrariness might disappear when subjected to an exhaustive history of its own construction. The relationship between a word and what it signifies is different from the relationship between an *image* and what it signifies because the word signifies not directly, but as part of a system of differentiated yet interdependent signs, or what archaeologist David Lewis-Williams calls "an already-existing mental symbology."[5] Language makes meaning not through individual words, but through the entirety of its relational, differential matrix.

So, for example, the word "cat" designates a furry, four-legged creature not because there is a direct relationship between the word (or its sound) and the animal, but because the word has come to denote that for speakers of English. Abstracted from the context of the English language (or its Germanic or Latin roots), neither the sound associated with the word "cat" nor its three sequential letters mean anything furry, four-legged, or alive. Even within those linguistic contexts, the word in itself is insufficient for indicating whether its referent is a wild cat or a domestic cat, a specific cat or catness in general, a comic-book Cat in the Hat or a person taken to be catlike in one feature or another ("catty," a "cool cat"). It is only in the context of speaking or writing that its meaning comes to be attached to something specific and material, yet that meaning is always dependent on the other words that accompany it. To the extent that they are dependent on other words, words can never serve as final arbiters of meaning. For instance, "yes" will likely not mean "no," but what it *does* mean depends on the indications that precede, accompany, and follow it.

In the context of speaking, the meanings of words also depend on nonlinguistic things such as intonations, gestures, hesitations, and manners of speaking. To the extent that physical gestures contribute to the meaning of words, and to the extent that such gestures are imagistic—nods of the head indicating acknowledgment, waves of the hand indicating magnitude or direction, and so on—language comes to be shaped and inhabited by images. In yet another sense, images inhabit words in that words themselves include a metaphorical dimension—the word "dimension" (from the Latin *dis-metiri*, meaning "to measure out" or "to measure apart") being as good an example of that as any. Metaphorically speaking, images serve as the glue that binds the materials of language, helping words to cohere to each other and to the world, even if they always do this only partially and elusively.

Words, one might posit, begin as images: they are categorical distinctions named into existence by drawing together other named distinctions. As an example, let us take an invented word: "bluesable." From what I can tell, as I write, the word doesn't exist yet; I have never heard it before, and a web search shows scant evidence for its use (only a single Instagram site, apparently). Yet its existence is plausible: it consists of the word "blues" and the suffix "-able," suggesting that something designated "bluesable" is capable of being turned into "blues." We understand the latter not simply as a color, but as a metaphor for a certain feeling or style of expression, a metaphor that has become a literal denotation of a recognizable style of music, *the blues*, which emerged at a specific time and place (the U.S. Deep South in the mid to late 1800s) and has come to shape musical forms much more broadly since then. The reference to the color blue makes the concept "the blues" imagistic: it evokes a picture of blueness, alongside images of those thought to be its musical creators or conveyers (who might be imagined as enslaved Africans or their descendants, utilizing specific kinds of vocal inflection and the like). The suffix "-able" adds to this new word the sense of a potential in things or in experiences: something that can be turned into the blues. If I were to use the word in a poem, it would be taken as an image or metaphor. If it should over time enter the lexicon of common English usage, the metaphor would become "tamed" (another metaphor), but would retain a metaphoric quality, its capacity to "transfer" (*metapherein*, Greek, meaning, to "bear" or "carry" [*pherein*] something "over" or "across" [*meta*)]) from a different or higher level to the one of its present use. As this discussion suggests, the concept of metaphor is itself metaphoric in its origin. This is the case with most words: the only question is whether the metaphor remains evocative and open in its capacity to suggest a multiplicity of meanings, or if it has become tamed or deadened (which are also metaphors) into literalism (another metaphor). The meanings suggested by "bluesable" include or evoke imagistic content, both visual and aural.

This excursion into word-making suggests that words and language are forms of semiotic thirdness; they are productive generalizations from experience, which only mean anything by virtue of their distinction from other generalizations. (For linguists, here is where Saussurean semiotics meets Peircean semiotics.) Let's take the following passage: "'Oh!' I said, pointing to the bowl of milk. 'It's for the cat.'" "Cat" distinguishes a particular kind of creature from others (dogs, unicorns). "For" distinguishes a particular relation that is different from "against," "to," "with," or "about." "Said" distinguishes a form of speaking that, in having happened in a particular way, is different both from "did not say" and "might say," from "is saying" or "will say," and from specific manners of saying, such as "narrated," "exhorted," or "whispered."

"Oh!" distinguishes a sound indicating surprise from sounds indicating other feelings or emotions. Each word provides further capacity for distinctions in use: a soft, questioning "oh?" is different from a long, declamatory "Oh!!" And so on. The full passage fixes the meanings of each of these words in ways that the words themselves could never do. The action of the speaker pointing to the bowl, gesturing with her face to the questioner (who had asked, "Why is that bowl there?"), and everything else preceding the exchange, give it more fixity. The quotation marks place the entirety within a kind of thought bubble, making this an episodic moment in imagined time.

Words, in other words, do not mean anything on their own; their meaning is part of the system of language, which includes words, syntactical rules, communicative understandings, and social and historical practices. Even if the entirety of their context of speaking is shared by their listener, their meaning can still be elusive. This is something that Jacques Derrida's painstaking deconstructions of philosophical concepts and terms showed, at least about textuality, or the "writtenness" of words.[6] Derrida's analyses highlighted the differential systematicity of language—the way in which the meanings of words depend on distinctions between opposed terms, all of which connect with other terms similarly distinguished in differential ways, and all of which can slip away into other potential readings and interpretations. It is this ultimate indeterminacy of language, the absence of a "transcendental signified" to anchor the "play of differences," that enables language to function as a deeply layered, finely tuned, yet always negotiable and never entirely fixable mechanism for distinguishing things in the world of human experience.

This in turn allows it to serve for the kinds of mental or representational, and ultimately physical, manipulation of things that humans have come to excel at. In situations that entail relations between people and their more-than-human environments, language has come to enable a detailed knowledge of those surroundings, including the kind that anthropologists have called "traditional ecological knowledge."[7] The cliché that Inuit people have a hundred different words for snow may not be literally accurate, but the principle—that detailed knowledge arises from contextual practice—is correct. While each of the words describes a different kind of snow—fresh snow, fine snow, crusty snow, muddy snow, a snowy blizzard, and so on—and therefore brings to its users a different image of snow, the ability to use them in narratives or in directives for action would not exist without language. Images and words in this sense coevolve through their usage. And at some point in their coevolution, forms of script, including glyphs, diagrams, notational icons, and full-fledged hieroglyphic systems, evolve as hybrids of the two, beginning as image and turning into the complex coding mechanism that is writing.[8]

With the development of technical means of reproducing both images (through photography, videography, and the like) and words (through typewriters and computers), it has become possible for words and images to generate each other in practices that do not necessarily involve human agency. In the previous chapter I described Trevor Paglen's observation that machine-readable images today generate more and more novel images without human participation, except at the outset of the process. To be machine-readable, however, the images require text, if only to provide the metadata that allows them to be digitally analyzed. Neither images nor texts can proliferate without the technical practices that connect them together.

Images and words thus coevolve with practices. And when it comes to practices that matter most to people—which in many contexts has meant practices taken to be either religious or ideological—the work of images becomes particularly important insofar as it connects different spheres of those people's lives, including their emotional lives, motivations, and relations with others.

## IMAGES, MATERIALITIES, AND ENCHANTMENT NETWORKS

The relationship between images and religion has been studied extensively. In the previous chapter I noted this relationship in reference to the animate-image and the ideal-image. Here I want to consider it in its ecological contexts. For this I turn to scholarship that takes human cognition, or mind, to be not merely mental, but embodied, situated, and distributed in social and material relations. In cognitive science, the latter view has come to be known as 4E, as it takes cognition to be materially *embodied*, socially and environmentally *embedded*, technically *extended*, and *enacted* in practices. To these four E's others have added an A for *affective* (4EA); my own preference is 6E, to include *emergent* in time and in process, and *experienced* situationally, affectively, and imaginally.[9] Variations include the material-engagement theory of cognitive archaeologist Lambros Malafouris, the study of material religion, and related "new materialist" approaches to the study of religion.[10] Malafouris's summary of his approach provides a helpful starting point for understanding all of this work: "Things mediate, actively shape, and constitute our ways of being in the world and of making sense of the world. Things also bring people together and provide channels of interaction. Things envelop our minds; they become us."[11]

Some of those things serve as the material embodiments of images. The relationship between religion, images, and the work of imagination—the concerted production of imaginal realms and imaginaries—is not a new topic; at least one scholar of religion has even proposed that we redefine religion itself as "imaginative formations."[12] I have elsewhere argued that what is essential in understanding religion is that it deals not with matters of fact, but with what Bruno Latour has called "matters of concern."[13] Religion may be about God or gods, spirits, beliefs in what happens after death, and other apparently empirically unprovable concepts; I will come back to some of these topics in chapter 7. But religion is at least as importantly about how (and why) to live, how meaning is given or ascribed to activities, and how to evaluate and account for one's life choices. The beliefs that, for many, constitute the fabric of religious reality are in this sense less important for their empirical significance ("Does God exist?") and more for how they are made operant within a social, emotional, and relational context ("Why do I feel bad about what I have done? Will I be judged for it? How will my peers and relations think of me if I fail to appropriately conduct a reparative action or ceremony to atone for it?").

In a series of works including *Visual Piety* (1998), *The Sacred Gaze* (2005), *The Lure of Images* (2007), and *Images at Work* (2018), art historian and religion scholar David Morgan has provided a most detailed analysis of the "material culture of enchantment."[14] For religious realities, or any realities, to "work" for people, they need to be lodged within a coherent network of activities, commitments, and enchantments, as Morgan describes them. And the efficacy of that network is real because it is coordinated, maintained, and kept in place by the world around us—a world of buildings, tools, structural arrangements, relevant images and designs, and other material presences. I previously described Morgan's "Enchantment Network Theory," which sees images as "technologies that act on human beings" and on "gods, the dead, the living, malignant forces, animals, and the world around us. Scarecrows," he wrote, "frighten birds; icons are conduits to the saints they depict, and they have often been used in processions to fight the plague or protect cities from invaders; works of art are devices for moving us, refining our sensibilities, enlightening our minds and spirits."[15] The scarecrows, icons, and works of art—or political posters, internet graphics, national anthems, and dance moves—are material phenomena connected together in relational webs. They work when they bind us within an "extended social apparatus," a network that allows agency to flow and circulate between humans, nonhumans, transhumans, and whatever else, real or imagined, in an efficacious way.[16]

Morgan's *Images at Work* provides a detailed analysis of such extended networks and ecologies of material and nonmaterial forces. Its understanding of enchantment as something that may "precede religion, magic, science, and art" and that "is located *both* in the mind *and* in the world," with belief and practice being co-constitutive in its production, helps us understand the role of material objects, including their imagistic qualities, in the maintenance of worlds and meanings.[17] Morgan examines the interplay of belief and "make-believe," the enchantments of *artifice* and of *artifact*, across a range of examples: from ancient Greek narrative, Roman divination, Orthodox Christian icons, amulets and votive figures, ritual sacrifices, saints' relics, and divination practices to Pacific coast tribal masks, early modern manuscript illustrations, spirit photographs and portraits of deceased family members, table manners, fairy tales, war postcards, celebrity photographs, personification in the naming of NASA spacecraft, automobility and its fetishization, subway turnstiles, meanings found in slabs of rock, and the *Wizard of Oz*. The work of the material world is central to all of these examples. For instance, in the case of religious images that "exhibit the features of having been made by human beings *and* having made themselves," this dual nature makes them products of culture and nature, "metamorphosing" from "one to the other" and thereby "exert[ing] power over us."[18]

Far from being located merely "in the head," then, belief, in Morgan's analysis, is a "condensed" and "sedimented practice" that "stabilizes experience" by engaging people "with those who taught them, those with whom they practice, and those who benefit or suffer from the practice."[19] "The world builds us and we build it, or rather the life-world that feels and appears to us as the *real* world."[20] Enchantment, he argues, is both "an engine of human culture" and its "glue."[21] It encompasses sedimented practices incorporating "[w]ords, actions, objects, occasions, forces, gods, and people" in dense networks of operational engagement, such that the world comes to be made up of alternate possibilities for network-building.[22] Consequently, when the agency of saints, icons, incense, chanting, and pilgrimage is replaced by that of sanitation, pasteurization, molecular biology, or the rapid manufacturing of vaccines, it is not because the latter are easier to believe or to "make real" than the former (as might be suggested in some analyses of religion).[23] It is because the networks of enchantment that bind people into compelling worlds have frayed to the point where new networks might now be established. Both are forms of enchantment that occur side by side, and they are sometimes in conflict with each other. Their effects emerge at the local scale at which they are applied, and when one set of enchantments is in crisis—due perhaps to colonization, genocide, civilizational collapse, or other causes—and another set presents itself, what happens is best seen not as secularization but as a changing of the guard.

Disenchantment, in this sense, "can be a useful means of opposing other people's enchantment and securing one's own."[24] The iconoclasm of one set of disenchantments—as when a Protestant missionary actively debunks the purported idolatry of his subjects—is intended not just to displace those subjects from their cultural and religious coordinates, but also to make them available to another, rival set of enchanting coordinates—the One God, for instance, or the promise of western civilization. The same can be said of science (in its many forms), conspiracy theory, populist politics, or whatever else. The sacred canopy, as sociologist of religion Peter Berger famously called it,[25] which provides an overarching set of beliefs and commitments for a people, is built of connections and material relations; it gains its sanctity from the buy-in of those it brings together. Which of them are "religious" and which are "secular" or "scientific" (or seemingly "obvious") is a question one particular culture has come up with to distinguish itself from others, but it may not be the pertinent one for the world at large. When enchantment is understood to be the "nonrational work toward making a home in the universe" and "the embodied search for a world that works in one's favor," as Morgan puts it, then it is something we are all fated to do for as long as that universe is there for us.[26]

What does vary across imaginaries, however, is the relationship to images. More thickly enchanted cultures enchant in and through their images, which also means through the material embodiments of those images, which are taken to represent ideals—that is, they are ideal-images—but also act upon people, that is, as animate-images. This combination of animate-image and ideal-image regimes has shaped many of the kinds of cultures we would today call "religious." Science-based cultures, on the other hand, replace much of that imagistic ideality with the indexicality of the world-picture regime, that is, with images that function as instrumentally useful *duplicates* of the sensible world itself rather than as revelations of a world beyond the sensible. Unlike the ideal-image, the world-picture regime asserts no behavioral norms for relating to the world; if anything, it disavows such normativity. Historically, the scientific community grew in stature by distinguishing itself from the theological and religious spheres, to which it relegated questions of moral judgment in favor of the judgment of empirical fact. The images produced within the scientific world-picture regime were, in this sense, disenchanted, freed of the "superstitious" attachments of religion, even if they served to enchant science's own capacity to produce a new kind of "literal," "sensible" truth.

Modernity, however, as many critics have shown, has never been truly disenchanted. It has had its own enchantments: scientific and technological enchantments, from wondrous discoveries to race cars and space travel; religious and "post-religious" enchantments, from evangelical revivals and spiritualist séances to UFOs and sundry esoteric or magical fads; political enchantments, from nationalisms and fascisms to communist and other utopian efforts; and an ongoing production of popular enchantments in the form of theme parks, extravagant shopping malls, celebrity pop stars, sports fanaticism, interactive gaming worlds, and more. Since the beginning of the motion-picture industry, images have multiplied the enchantments of a technologically connected world, with the digital image-world being a kind of logical evolution from the enchantments of previous decades.[27] As images and image regimes enchant and disenchant, they inform and enfold us, their bearers, in ways that alter our relationships with ourselves and with others. They are, in other words, psychodynamic. Let us examine this more closely.

## PSYCHODYNAMICS OF IMAGE RELATIONS

Images make present what is otherwise absent; they connect an (absent) *object* to the (receiving) *interpretant* by way of the (mediating) *sign*. The interpretant is the "translation" or "understanding" of the sign. It is a sign-function; it should not be mistaken for an interpret*er*. Where, then, is the *self* or *agent* of interpretation? Peirce's semiotic theory is sometimes misunderstood to be a theory without a psychology. In a characteristically oblique statement taken from a 1908 letter written to semioticist and friend Victoria Lady Welby, Peirce wrote, "I define a Sign as anything which is so determined by something else, called its Object, and so determines an effect upon a person, which effect I call its Interpretant, that the latter is thereby mediated by the former. My insertion of 'upon a person' is a sop to Cerberus, because I despair of making my own broader conception understood." This "sop to Cerberus" is uncharacteristic for Peirce, since he more often defines the sign as something universal, not necessarily human or personal in any way.

Yet there is a psychology to Peirce's processual semiotics. It is anti-Cartesian; it does not assume the existence of a continuous mind, consciousness, or "I." It is pragmatic and processual in seeing any sense of self as itself a sign, a subject and product of semiosis. As with Whitehead's notion of prehension, Peirce's sign is atomic and singular; it is an event among events. The sense of self, on the other hand—which is analogous to Whitehead's notion of a "society," a coordinated collectivity of prehensions—is cumulative, relying upon a complex set of continuities across significations. Philosopher Charles Hartshorne, who studied with Whitehead and edited and maintained Peirce's archive at Harvard, notes in his discussion of Whitehead's theory of prehension that "to be *influenced* by something is to *prehend* that something." He continues, "The whole microstructure of the world, its pervasive structure," including all the cellular, nerve, and bodily functions that keep each of us alive, may be "given to us only in a blurred manner," but they are part of the causality of each prehension, each signification, that underlies whatever continuity makes up the sense of selfhood of an individual person.[28] In other words, the cognitive, emotional, and physical components of selfhood are causally given and passed on in every moment in which "the self" is active. Which features are recognized, which are heightened or emphasized, and which are assumed, backgrounded, or temporarily forgotten, may vary, but they are carried over in the process by which the self is signified. The self, as Vincent Colapietro puts it, is for Peirce a "continuity of reactions" (which are semioses) embodied within "an enduring network of interpenetrating habits" (the human organism).[29] For Peirce, "signs are not to be explained by reference to some occult and intrinsically private power called 'mind,' but the mind itself is to be explained in terms of those manifest and inherently intersubjective processes called semioses."[30] The upshot of Peirce's processual-semiotic theory is that "to be a self is to be in process of becoming a self, a process that is never complete."[31] In contrast to more privative notions of selfhood such as that of Peirce's friend William James, "the individual self," for Peirce, "is in its innermost being, not a private sphere but a communicative agent," one that unfolds through the ongoing production of signs and meanings that are always relational.[32] "The person," Peirce wrote, "is not absolutely an individual," since "his thoughts are what he is saying to himself" or "what [he] is saying to that other self that is just coming into life in the flow of time."[33] The thoughts that make the self constitute a running dialogue, an inferential set of operations of "indexical self-reference."[34]

In this sense, each image we bear—each sign-relation involving resemblance—is a confirmation of our relationship to what is imaged. To bear an image is to receive it, absorb it, accept it, submit to it, take it in. The activity of bearing signs is ongoing, and it is cumulative in the sense that signs build upon other signs. Insofar as the image has a bearing on how we make ourselves, on how it contributes to the making of the "I" who is in the place of, or causally connected to, the interpretant of the given sign, that image participates in our self-making. What we moderns call the self is the vessel for that which accumulates, dynamically and interactively, through the semiotic encounters by which we participate in our worlds. Our sense of self develops itself cognitively, affectively, bodily, and socially in relationship to the absences—the theres and thens—that are brought to presence in signification.

If subjectivity is always semiotic and relational, different kinds of signs, and perhaps especially different kinds of images, shape it in different ways. Animate-images involve subjectivity in an open, dynamic interaction with them, an interaction in which the sense of self spills over or is carried into the image and is liable to be changed in the process. "Animate-image subjectivity" is what philosopher Charles Taylor has attempted to describe in his concept of the "porous" self, one that is "open" and "vulnerable" to "spirits, demons, cosmic forces," with any "boundary between agents and forces" and between "mind and world" being "fuzzy" and indistinct.[35] In his influential books *Sources of the Self* and *A Secular Age*, Taylor describes such a porous self as being relatively universal up until modern times, at which point it comes to be replaced by a "buffered self," one that is "bounded," "autonomous," and potentially "master of the meanings of things for it." For the buffered, modern self, demons, spirits, and magic forces "no longer impinge"; desires may do that, but they are "de facto inclinations," "solicitations" that are "deprived of any higher meaning or aura," and disengagement from them becomes not only possible but normative.[36]

Taylor's dichotomy is overgeneralized and has been critiqued as such; our analysis can get more precise than that.[37] If the animate-image produces a porous self, the spread and acceptance of an ideal-image regime shifts this porosity into a more unified sense of directionality, a social and transcendent contract by which society is organized in relation to the ideals that constitute and coordinate it. Selfhood comes to be *subjected* to those ideals in a relationship of unequal dependency. As Judith Butler observes, subjection consists in "the simultaneous *forming* and *regulating* of the subject" through a "fundamental dependency on a discourse we never chose but that, paradoxically, initiates and sustains our agency."[38] This is the kind of subjectivity modern theorists have variously tried to critically assess: Hegel with his account of the master/slave dialectic, Freud with his model of the psychic apparatus, Althusser with his notion of the subject's "interpellation" into ideology, and others probing the relationship between subjectivity and modern regulative "governmentality." The ideal-image regime is in this sense an *ideological* regime, where ideology "confers upon the individual the capacity to recognize himself in a social identity," but one that is always subordinate to the ideal.[39] As Foucault and Deleuze have argued, subjecthood and subjectivity are intimately related and always somewhat negotiated, but when coordinated to a high degree can lead to the development of a "fascist self," one for which public and private life come to be fused in totalistic "communities of feeling."[40]

There are many forms of ideality, however, and the ways they interpellate, "hail," or "coax" us into our subjectivation are rarely entirely successful. Other possibilities for subjectivity remain available, even if obscured: there is the kind of dyadic exchange offered by the animate-image, and the expression-image's capacity for self-determination. With its reversal of the presumed line of agency, the expression-image regime affords new lines of agency for subjectivity that, in their effect, raise the question of what it is that *can* or *should* be expressed. Who or what is "the self"? What is its natural condition, its pure desire? Who am I that can express myself in the objects I make? Even as the expression-image regime celebrates a democratization of agency, it paradoxically results in an objectification of the self *as* its images: the subject becomes identified with, and objectified in, its objects, products, and possessions. As the subject is driven to create *out* of itself, the place of subjectivity becomes emptied, a lack (in Jacques Lacan's terms) that may be intolerable and that therefore comes to be a site of moving, partial, and unreliable self-ideals: the *narcissistic* self, with its continual reflection upon itself as self-generative, or the *modular* self, experimenting with ideals that never quite establish themselves.

The world-picture regime, on the other hand, imposes an objectification of the self—analogously to the *subjection* imposed by the ideal-image regime, this might be called an *objection*—by which the self would take its place alongside an objectification of the world at large. It is here that Charles Taylor's "buffered" self becomes bounded and neutered, objectified within the discourses and practices that aim for a representational transparency whereby the world is fully known, measured, and accounted for. Science's indexical chains of reference become the standard for assessing the truth of any statement or claim: the mind *becomes* its matter, the self becomes its brain, and humans become a species among others, reducible to their genes or the evolutionary programs that play themselves out through us. Much of modern art has vacillated within the interplay between the world-picture and the expression-image regimes—between the professed rationalism of "Apollo's eye" and the self-expression, Dionysian at its extreme, of romantic individualism. With its expansion of options for experiential mobility, the moving-image regime has in turn enabled a multiplication and dispersal of subjectivity; and the digital image-world continues this mobilization and operationalization, with the digital self becoming ever more modular, recombinant, and dispersive.

History unfolds, we might say, in the tension and historical movement between regimes. When an ideal-image regime is challenged, punctured, and finally defeated, there will be a gap in its subjects that begs to be filled, perhaps through religious conversion of one sort or another. If the challenge comes from the world-picture regime, the filling will never be complete, as the world-picture offers little experiential solidity to the subject. Subjectivity becomes thinner and at the same time more bounded, more individual, more "modern." European colonization of the Americas might be best understood as a defeat of social orders made up of varying degrees of animate-image and ideal-image regimes, in which embodied imagination served to maintain relations with land (space) and with ancestors (time) that persisted in the background of social life. What the colonizers offered in the place of these relations could never satisfy, and the resultant trauma has continued for generations. For "moderns," and especially late-modern neoliberal subjects, the affordances of selfhood come with a range of anxieties and neuroses that leave its subjects both too "empty" and too "full": full of lures for subjectivation—all of the seeming options for individualization, for status, for accumulation, and so on, that are available to most citizens of modern, industrial societies—but against the background of a felt vacancy, an absence of the reciprocal relations that would ensure the stability, security, and viability of their realization. When this emptiness comes to the fore, late capitalist subjectivities become vulnerable to the appeal of latter-day fascisms, with their fantasies of the revival of national greatness, of closed borders and the extirpation of difference, and of authoritarian leaders who embody these fantasies.

Much more can be said on the capacity of image regimes to enchant, disenchant, and contest the possibilities for subjectivation and objectivation, which, according to the process-semiotic model, are how imagination works. I will propose to summarize these in a set of rules of thumb that will help us in our examination of specific imaginaries in part 2 of this book.

## FIVE PROPOSITIONS, OR RULES OF THUMB

### 1. Image regimes and image ecologies are materially embodied

Images, as I have argued, connect: they mediate, establishing a relationship between something here, in the direct experience of a person, organism, or life-form, with something *there* or *then*—before, beyond, remembered, projected, or otherwise in the realm of the thinkable but not directly sensible. And when they do that with a particular force and a seemingly agential power, and perhaps with a certain ambiguity, they come to embody that power. The animate-image regime, as such, evolved to build networks, with images serving as mediators to make connections possible. Communities and societies could now be built.

All images, and all image regimes, function within and through the mediation of networked assemblages of agents and actants, not all of which are human. (Sometimes none of them are human.) This is because images, as perceivable forms, require materiality, and semiotically function within extended networks of meaning and practice. If we posit a "just-so story" of the evolution of image regimes that would parallel the evolution of human societies, we could imagine the materialities enabling the building of image-based networks, or imaginaries, becoming more complex and mobile as societies became more complex and mobile.

The requirement of materiality brings with it distinct possibilities of indexicality. While the previous chapter described the world-picture regime as the regime in which indexicality was definitive, conferring authority upon the images that constitute it, indexicality in fact figures in each image regime in one way or another. Insofar as animate-images serve as vehicles for imagistic expression or "inhabitation," their action is visible, audible, or otherwise perceivable to others; it is therefore taken to be indexical of the interpreted meanings these images bear. For instance, when a Voudou priestess becomes possessed by the *orisha* known as Erzulie, it is evident to observers, within the community of believer-practitioners, that this has happened. The evidence is in the dance of the priestess.

Ideal-images in turn produce their own indexicalities as material evidence of what they point toward. Aztec bloodletting rituals display the circulation of blood between humans and divinities. Bones and relics of Christian saints are, or were (in medieval times), visible signs of the power they embody and confer. Icons, buildings (such as temple architecture), and even the design of cities can follow principles articulating the ideals of an ideal-image regime. In this sense, the ancient Chinese imperial city, with its formal, cardinally oriented axiality, is not so different in principle from the modern metropolis, with its looming bank towers marking the composite center of capitalist power.[41] The difference is in the ideals represented by each.

Questions of literal causality—signs and traces of the powers signified by an image—are thus not new to the world-picture regime. Each image functions within an ecology of practices and material connections, and insofar as a certain material circumstance is taken as evidence of a process understood to be occurring, it is indexical of that process. Indexicality is, in this sense, the materialization of something known or interpreted as occurring. Whether it is in fact occurring, or is a misunderstanding of something else—for instance, whether it is the goddess Erzulie who possesses an individual, or a neurological state triggered by rhythmic dancing and drumming that is responsible for that person's behavior—is a question that arises between rival imaginaries. Where one perspective, that of the Voudou practitioner, interprets the materiality in one way, another, that of an ostensibly scientific observer, interprets it another way. But the material embodiment is there for both to see; the only question is *what* it is an index of.

With the world-picture regime, infrastructural materialities come to play a more directly causal role, rather than an associational or correlational one, in supporting the claims made for images. Technological infrastructures become all the more detailed as the infrastructure scales up toward the global level, and at the same time scales down into more refined digital modulation, with the development and growth of digital data systems. In part 2 of this book, we will examine instances of this global scaling, by which the indexicality of photo-documentation is used to make a case about the human relationship with the Earth as a whole. At the same time, we will note how the reliance on digital data systems opens up new potentialities for communication (and for miscommunication) even as it changes the ways in which images are received, translated, and interpreted.

Alongside this scaling up, there has also been a speeding up and multiplication of image materialities. I referred to mobilization in my discussion of the moving-image regime, and to the vastly increased circulation of images in discussing the digital image-world. In part this is a result of technologies of reproduction, which have made it possible to copy and distribute images on scales previously unknown. The mass production of print in the sixteenth and seventeenth centuries contributed to a colossal spread of the expression-image and world-picture regimes, even as the actual functioning of images retained their "animacy" and "ideality" in specific situations. The circulation of images takes many forms: as Olga Moskatova writes, "Images travel as engravings, postcards, banknotes, postage stamps, carpets, advertisements, flyers, or passport portraits. They are transported by mail, ship, or plane and disseminated in telecommunication networks, magazines, or newspapers. Images are carried in envelopes, intimate jewelry, boxes, albums, frames, or reels."[42] Electronic circulation launched this spread into an ever higher orbit, and digital media enable a kind of multivectoral "spreadability" alongside the "softening" or "fluidization" of images already described.

For all their fluidity, digital images cannot exist without the complex material infrastructures that enable them to be produced, disseminated, interpreted, reproduced, and reprocessed.

### 2. Image regimes and image ecologies enable the formation of nodes, access points, and regulatory formations or priesthoods

Since they function within networks of enchantment, image ecologies enable constellations of agency to form at crucial link points, which serve as the hubs and spokes of those networks. To the extent that these come to be embodied within or mediated by specific figures, human or other kinds, they enable the production of priesthoods and other regulatory formations for managing access to the power, glamor, charisma, potency, or agency facilitated by or associated with the networks.[43]

Different image regimes do this in different ways. In an animate-image regime, glamor or charisma tends to focus on the image itself. There may be charismatic individuals who facilitate access to the power of the image, but their role is typically either modest or relatively direct. A shamanic healer chanting the sound of a deity, in order to literally or figuratively enter the body of an ill individual and remove a blockage to its healthy functioning, may require the individual's belief, or at least the suspension of disbelief, in the power of the shaman to accomplish that act. Tribal societies frequently include subtribal organizations or social groups with their own protocols for who can access which kinds of knowledge, for what purposes, and so on. Images, in these situations, can function both to represent ideals (sacred or esoteric knowledge, for instance) and to carry or mediate the power conferred within those ideals. The use of images could therefore combine elements of animate- and ideal-image regimes.

At a certain point in our just-so story, the rules of a specific animate-image regime (that of Tribe A, let us say) might come to conflict with the rules of another (Tribe B). And so it becomes possible and perhaps necessary to establish transcendental or vertical coordinates for a regime that could surmount the horizontal traffic. The ideal-image regime per se developed as a way of jumping levels, but first it had to establish the higher level. Alternative image networks could thereby become "idolatrous," or false, in that they lead not toward but away from that "higher level." Boundaries between one image-regime (or image-culture) and another could be established through a preferential hierarchy by which the ideals of the first came to defend themselves against the ideals of another. With ideal-image regimes, then, especially as found in vertically concentrated power structures, charisma and glamor becomes more broadly organized, with priestly castes—Hindu Brahmins, Catholic male priesthoods, the Communist Party apparat, and so on—developing to control access to the power believed to be available. As such societies become more complex, the bureaucracy of access becomes more stratified and specialized.

As ideal-image regimes come themselves to be criticized, their critics could appeal to new openings, but they could also push further with the ideality itself. One new opening was that of the expression-image, which opened up the possibility of new resources *within* the maker or fashioner of the image. ("But your gods are just idols, fabrications, figments of your collective imagination! Look, here is the wizard behind the mask!") Charisma, in the expression-image regime, becomes individualized and, in effect, democratized among the individuals perceived to be most capable in their expressive artistry. In time, of course, a "star system" may develop around key artistic or creative individuals, with a class of interpreters—scholars, art critics, wealthy patrons, or grant-disbursing bureaucrats—coming to play an intercessory or brokerage role even as that status is understood to be secondary to that of the artists themselves.

Another opening of the ideal-image regime, that of the world-picture, created the possibility of "truth" being found in the copy of the world itself, even as it denied any possibility of transcending that world. ("Our map, unlike yours, is real—trust your very eyes!") In time, as technology has come to take greater prominence within world-picture, moving-image, and digital image-world regimes, its champions, governors, and intermediaries have come to play the role of a new priesthood. In the digital world, every software app and platform maintains its own protocols and access rules, algorithmic control systems, and management layers, with minimal transparency to most users.

Meanwhile, reversions to alternative ideal-image regimes always remain possible. Fundamentalist religious movements, communist and fascist revolutionary utopias, and other efforts to challenge or escape modernity have proliferated as modernity (and hypermodern digitality) has come to be ever more encompassing. Relying on a similar denunciation of "unreal" ideals to deny the possibility of transcendence, propaganda regimes have presented their new world-pictures as immanent forces embodied in their own ideals (the Party, the Hero, QAnon's mythical "Q"). Soviet or Chinese Communist propaganda posters established this-worldly ideals, which in effect acted as parodies of the religious ideals they replaced. Religious icons, meanwhile, were taken out of the churches where they conducted their mediatory work and placed into museums of atheism, as tokens for demonstrating how the church misled and "vampirized" the citizenry. This was iconoclasm in the service of a new iconography, whose virtues were rooted not in any transcendent world but in the immanent force of humanity—a humanity guided by the Party of the Revolutionary Vanguard acting in accordance with the dialectical materialist nature of history itself.

As we will see in part 2 of this study, ideal-image regimes develop to challenge the disenchantment that has been ostensibly produced by the world-picture regime. At the same time, they can be easily challenged for their seeming naïveté, their anti-modern romanticism, their repetition of colonial tropes (as with the animal photography of Gregory Colbert, to be described in chapter 6), and their questionable politics. In a rather parallel way, the world-picture regime has developed its own forms of self-parody: "Look, the power of science!" it says—as it destroys worlds by smashing atoms, and exhausts ecosystems with its intensive deployments of synthetic chemicals and industrialized methods of soil-depleting farming, rapacious overfishing, tropical deforestation, and so on. (We will discuss *The Anthropocene Project*'s ambivalent reliance on photo-documentation in this light.) In this way, we might add a subproposition: *image regimes begin as openings and end as parody.* But that progress need not be inevitable either.

### 3. Some image regimes mix better (and in this lies their power); others mix less well (and in that lies their threat)

The first three image regimes we examined, in particular, have been found in countless variations and combinations over time. Much of what is today considered religion consists in part of ideal-images: understandings of a hierarchy of gods or spiritual forces, whose accessibility to humans is constrained and channeled into ritualized practices, such as confession and communion for Catholics, or other rules of appropriate conduct, penalties for witchery, and so on. Yet these ideal-images do not hold much power or even interest among people unless they can be made to *move*, that is, unless they can be *animated* within people's lives. Festivals, processions, and ceremonies that engage the senses and emotions, facilitating altered states of consciousness, render the ideal-images alive for devotees. The Marxist idea that religions act as a kind of opium by which authority is kept in place can hardly account for their persuasiveness and the undying commitment of the opium eaters.

Ideal-image and animate-image regimes may mix well, but where the ideals of different imaginaries fail to find agreement, ideal-image regimes, with their vertical power structures, can become potent sources of conflict. Christian and Muslim imaginaries produced centuries of warfare over the land idealized by both as their holy land of origins and sacred memories. Ideologies, that is, ideal-image regimes, have served as the rallying points for conflagrations throughout history when their material embodiments have come to entangle each other in competition over space, place, and time.

At the same time, mechanisms can develop for cohabitation and synthesis between different ideal-image regimes. Traditions of interpretation—such as the so-called *interpretatio graeca* and *interpretatio Romana* developed by Herodotus, Plutarch, Pliny the Elder, and others going back to ancient Mesopotamia, Sumeria, and Egypt—enabled what historian Jan Assmann has called the "major cultural achievement" of polytheism, wherein "cross-cultural translation" allows for the "articulation of a common semantic universe."[44] "By disarticulating the sphere of the numinous into distinct roles and functions, it converts the divine world of a particular group into a format that makes it compatible with the divine worlds of other groups and cultures."[45] In this way, Osiris (Egyptian) became interchangeable with Dionysus (Greek) and Bacchus (Roman), Ra became Helios and Sol, Isis and Hathor were equated (in different contexts) with Aphrodite and Venus, and various deities took on local personages (as have the Virgin Mary and Guanyin, in later settings). This convertibility, Assmann argues, "expresses a general conviction in late antiquity about the universality of religious truth and the relativity of religious institutions and denominations and the conventionality of divine names."[46] This tradition of comparison and translatability has remained an option, finding followers among scholars of comparative religion and in the ecumenical pursuit of interdenominational and interreligious, as well as religio-scientific, collaboration. It is also visible in the ways in which enslaved and diasporic Africans retained their traditional deities by blending them with Roman Catholic saints in Cuba, Haiti, Brazil, and elsewhere.

As noted in chapter 2, the spread of the world-picture regime came as a threat with deeply subversive implications for ideal-image regimes insofar as it presented new mechanisms for establishing evidence-based truth upon indexical principles. The history of science is not a singular history, however; previous periods can be found in which empirical arguments countered theological arguments. Assmann, for instance, identifies an early version of this in the "revolutionary monotheism" of Egyptian pharaoh Akhenaten (ca. 1360–1340 BCE), who deemed the traditional pantheon of deities superfluous when it was discovered that the sun generated "not only light and warmth, but also time." He proceeded to close temples, abolish cults, destroy images, and erase the names of gods (thereby demonstrating that empires could be established with whatever tools were available).[47] Similar instances of "natural philosophy"—from astronomy to the physical sciences—finding both agreement and disagreement with "religious philosophy" can be found in ancient Greece, India, China, Mesoamerica, and elsewhere.

But the institutionalization and internationalization of scientific labor in the early modern period created a situation where science's instrumental reason posed a daunting and ultimately unassailable challenge to religious authorities. Arguably, the only ideal-image regimes that have flourished for any length of time since then have been those, like liberal humanism or its religiously tinted relatives (such as Christian humanism), that have developed conceptual ideals that find viable coexistence with scientific ideals and practices. Exemplary historical examples of this mixture can indeed be found: Enlightenment philosopher and mathematician Auguste Comte worked to establish science not only as a method for gaining truth, but as the basis for a utopian society with its "Religion of Humanity," its *Positivist Catechism*, and its prayers, spiritual exercises, priestly hierarchy, and temples. While this fusion of ideal-image and world-picture regimes did not achieve any fruition within his lifetime, its vision served as the inspirational basis for the Templo da Humanidade in Rio de Janeiro, Brazil, a building whose architectural detail reflects both Comte's anthropocentric "planetary imperialism," as John Tresch calls it, and his humanistic goal of urging "gratitude, care, and above all love for the planet and its inhabitants."[48]

Meanwhile, the expression-image regime that developed in modern Europe is paralleled by long-standing traditions that recognize the artistry and craft of image makers throughout history. Shamans and healers are valued, after all, not only for the way they passively embody divine or cosmic forces, but for their skillful agency as individual mediators, wonder workers, and bringers of health, wealth, or desirable change. The cult of the artist may be at its maximum today in the cults of artists like Taylor Swift and Beyoncé, but it is not only their genius that is celebrated; it is the ideals they stand for (freedom, womanhood, Blackness, and so on). In the same way, the political murals of Diego Rivera are celebrated both as expressions of an individual creative genius and as representing the ideals of the Mexican Revolution; in them, the expression-image meets the ideal-image. Similarly, Caspar David Friedrich's 1817 painting *Wanderer Above the Sea of Fog* expresses Friedrich's artistic sensibility and is taken to represent the sublimity of nature and of the human capacity to grasp it intellectually (in the Kantian reading).

All of this shows the historically complicated terrain we get into when teasing apart "actually existing image regimes." It is enough to conclude, however, that iconoclashes as well as icono-couplings remain possible within and between imaginaries. We will examine instances of these in part 2 of this book.

### 4. Each image regime is an amplification, a restructuring, or a folding and channeling of the original, animate-image regime

Because images serve to mediate, the question is whether all images will mediate in all possible directions, or what sorts of circulations will be set up, within which mediation may move at the expense of other possibilities.

The animate-image is alive because of its capacity to mediate; the more it mediates, the more it is alive. The risk is that its many animations produce competing and conflicting networks. The ideal-image aims to monopolize imagistic agency by setting up a separate domain that is rendered safe from infiltration and severing alternative channels for mediacy. The risk is that its monopoly fails or that it becomes oppressive. The expression-image regime returns agency to human image-makers, but it can only do this if the transcendence of the ideal is denied or if there is some kind of symbiosis established, a link connecting the agency of the artist to the agency of the ideal (for instance, of God, saints, spirits, the nation, Nature, and the like). And to the extent that the denial of transcendence is successful, to that extent the expression-image limits its own capacity for agency: artists are admired, but only as special cases of what we can all do.

The world-picture regime, in turn, denies the transcendence of the ideal-image but attempts to establish a new set of possibilities by which collective human agency—a collective agency that soon becomes that of its new spokespeople, the priestly caste of scientists and technologists—can manage and control a tamed "nature." Mediation in the direction of an outside becomes impossible or illegitimate. Religion is simply a matter of personal belief, not a real connection to real agential forces. The world-picture, however, never fully eradicates its rivals. Expression-images, ideal-images (especially in their sublime-image form, as we will see in part 2), and even animate-images continue to move viewers and audiences, and when moving-image media have become widely established, they take on the functions of all of these regimes. The same can be said for the regime of the digital image-world, except that now the movement of agents becomes so fluid and dissembled that it can hardly be known or controlled at all, except in automated, mass-managed forms.

What underlies each regime, then, is the *movement* of images. Images are, at their very basis, a form of connective movement: movement from one place to another (between what is there, present in the image, and that which is absent but *made* present in and through it) and movement involving the bearer of the image, who is beheld or moved by the image, and who may in turn be capable of shaping and moving *with* the image. In this sense, image regimes differ only in how they attempt to channel or constrain the movement that is inherent to images. Will it be in one direction only and, if so, which one? From the ideal (which is transcendent) to the image? From the maker (artist) to the image? From the world (as revealed through technology) to the image? Will the movement be kept in check by a priesthood of one kind or another? Will the recipient of the image be passive or actively involved in engaging with and potentially changing the image? Even if the movement of any particular image can always be contained, the nature of image *as* movement will never go away.

### 5. We should therefore value the original image regime

I have suggested, at multiple points now, that the animate-image is a kind of "original" image regime; that it came first and that the others are variations of it. It is time to put a little thought into how this may be so and what it may mean for us today.[49]

If images mediate, and if some images (at least) mediate between humans and a more-than-human world, then it is important to take account of the differential between the two sides of this relationship.

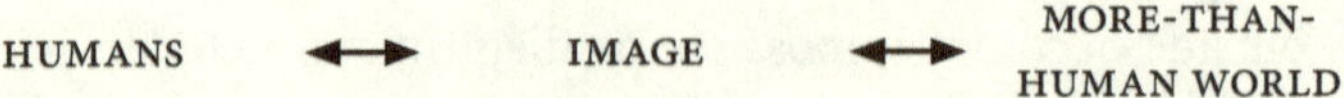


The last few hundred years have firmly established one way of looking at this relationship, which skews leftward in the above equation. This is the view that it is humans who are active makers and shapers of the world, and who are the relevant agents, while the others—a category that includes not just the obvious others (animals, insects, birds, trees, and so on) but also less obvious ones (gods, spirits, inanimate forces) and, among them, material objects such as constructed images—are at best only in a position to respond to us. To the extent that we must respond to them—for instance, when "acts of nature" like hurricanes and earthquakes force us to do that—it is not *their* interests that matter, but ours.

There are two versions of this argument, an ethical one and an epistemological one. The ethical version, which asserts that it is human rights and interests that count and not anything else's, is widespread today; we can loosely call it *humanism* (though that's a more ambiguous term) or *anthropocentrism* (which is more precise). The epistemological version is less widely shared, but has nevertheless influenced the social sciences, which inform many understandings of the human. We can call this version *social constructionism* in that it asserts that, for all that nature or reality may offer us, the human hand (or mind) is ever present and ineradicable in shaping what we know of nature or reality. It therefore makes sense to focus our gaze on the human and not so much on the materials or other "others" we might share the universe with.

Both of these views have had their share of critics in recent years, and I will not belabor these critiques except to articulate the most influential accounts that focus on the other end of the above diagram. The first is an ecological or environmentalist perspective, which argues that ignoring the more-than-human world makes little sense today, and that this could in fact make all the difference between survival and a terminal, apocalyptic end of the human experiment. While it may be possible to "save the Earth" without taking human interests into account, the opposite strategy—of not taking the living world's interests into account—could only amount to failure. A subsidiary argument focuses on the rights and needs of nonhuman animals, but this view is best seen as a form of moral extensionism, which moves the boundaries toward the right side of the above equation, but does not attempt to eliminate them altogether or to rebalance both sides. The second dominant form of the critique of humanism is theocentric, or otherwise religious: this is that human needs and interests are secondary to the divine, that some forms of culture (such as those represented by some notion of "traditional values") grounded in "revealed truths" should therefore trump the pursuit of human interests, and that the apparent disarray of the contemporary world provides suitable evidence that the latter pursuit has failed to produce the general happiness and well-being it has promised.

What these alternatives leave untouched is the image itself, which remains a mere channel for the movement of agency, from one side to the other or vice versa. If the nonhuman world, conceived as materiality, is agential, then by definition the image will also be agential. But what I want to argue is not only that the image retains a *residual* agency—either because of the human agency and intentionality that shaped it or because of the nonhuman agency that extends in its direction—but that the image is agential in its nature because it is at the center of the image-relation. It is an active mediator. Agency is not something the image (or the human, or the nonhuman) *has*. It is something that occurs, and that circulates, in and by way of the image. In a process-semiotic view of reality, agency *is* circulation, movement, and the responsive shaping of "things given." The image-relation is an image-event, which could not arise without the image. The image-event marks a triadic relationship, with the image-form itself (the sign that is taken to be iconic in reference to a referent) facilitating, shaping, and enfolding the connection between referent and interpretant. Image regimes can obscure the active role of the image by ascribing its agency to its human creator alone (as in the expression-image) or to the transcendental world beyond (the ideal-image, the world-picture), but these are obscurations that end up misunderstanding the nature of images, and therefore of reality.

This distributed and circulatory notion of agency resonates with some media theorists' arguments about the networked and "atmospheric" nature of digital media. Mark Hansen, for instance, advocates a "radically environmental perspective" that takes human agency to be one form among others that are "internally differentiated, dispersed across various scales and operational divisions, and implicated in and immanent to a total, multi-scalar cosmological situation" in which "human agency operates as a configuration of the elemental," that is, at an "ambient" level that is "'above' and 'below' that of the human subject."[50] I want to resist the notion that this "ambient elementality" is new and specific to digital media systems, though I recognize that it is materially reconfigured, and therefore potentially thickened and deepened, in in these systems.

These assumptions will be presumed in my readings of image formations in the second part of this book. To flesh out what they mean, I wish to return to a question raised some years ago by visual historian W. J. T. Mitchell. In 1996, Mitchell penned an article whose title provocatively asked, "What Do Pictures Want?"[51] The article opened with a series of caveats and hesitations that today might seem superfluous to some; its premise that pictures might "want" anything would find sympathetic recipients among followers of the ontological, object-oriented, speculative realist, and new materialist turns. Despite some provocative conclusions, however, Mitchell's real goal was not to make pictures come alive, but simply to acknowledge that for many people they already *are* alive and that this may never be eradicated, as modernists once had assumed or hoped would happen. "In short," he wrote, "we are stuck with our magical, premodern attitudes toward objects, especially pictures, and our task is not to overcome these attitudes but to understand them, to work through their symptomatology."[52]

My goal here is neither to follow nor to disavow Mitchell's method, though I would aver that his assumptions about "magical, premodern attitudes" are an unnecessary and perhaps anachronistic constraint on our thinking. (In this I tend to agree with Bruno Latour's questioning of whether we have ever "been modern."[53] If Latour provocatively answered "no," I would at least let the case remain open.) Mitchell's ultimate question, however—what do pictures want *from us?*—remains a useful one. If we changed his "pictures" to our own "images" and reframed the question within the context I have been proposing, we would have to at least acknowledge the following three facts: (1) that images are shaped by agency, that is, that they are *made*; (2) that images are conduits and mediators for the workings of agency, that is, that they in turn *make*—they shape and modify how agency proceeds through them; and (3) that images are haunted by the reality of agency's dislocation, deferral, indetermination, and dissipation—which means that they, in their very materiality, harbor their own, always somewhat unknowable agency. Images are made, they make, and they unmake.

If images connect and mediate relations—for instance, relations between two people, or between a priestly elite and a social community, or between people and animals, gods, or geographically specific more-than-human worlds—they always do that in ways that are partially but never fully determined by whoever or whatever makes them; by their receivers and interpreters; and by their own substantial reality, consisting of their materiality, their appearance, their presentation, and so on. So there is an indeterminacy at each of the three points of our triadic definition of the image: with respect to the intended referent (what does the image *want to refer to?*), the intended interpretant (what does the image *want to be taken for?*), and the intended image itself (what does the image *want from itself?*). The first two of these points are generally known; the latter is more troubling, but only if we see the "intent" of the image as something like a conscious intent or hope. If we consider it as the kind of thing phenomenological philosophers call intentionality—a kind of systemic "orientation towards," which may be conscious, unconscious, habitual, enfolded, or algorithmic—then it is no longer a problem to consider "what the image wants" even from itself.

The remainder of this book will take seriously that images *may* want something, but also that the ways they come to us—their arrangements, environments, and relational entanglements—make a difference to how it is that they can want anything. In the multilayered, engrossing, networked, and increasingly automated image-world of digital media, what an image is *changes*, and in the process so do we and so does the world. That images both harbor and facilitate agency is part of their power or magic; it is what gives them agency. That images are doing that differently and, in many ways, more powerfully makes them all the more important to understand today.

This view of images as powerful and agential comes closest to the regime I have defined as that of the animate-image, The animacy, or indeed the animism, of images is best thought of not in the sense that Edward Tylor considered animism a misguided belief that lifeless things are alive, but in the sense evoked by philosopher of science Isabelle Stengers's "reclaimed" animism. For Stengers, reclaiming animism "means not *returning* to a more authentic or 'true' state of being before the advent of modern technology, but rather *reactivating*, in a pragmatic manner, the potentiality of a 'more than human world.'" It is, she writes, "a matter of recovering the capacity to honor experience, any experience we care for, as 'not ours' but rather as 'animating' us, making us witness to what is not us" and thereby affirming that we humans "are not alone in this world."[54] We are not alone because we share our world with all of the others with which we are interdependent. Animism recognizes that humans are not the only subjects in the world, and that the world is not bifurcated into subjects and objects, but that, as Whitehead described it, subjectivity arises wherever objectivity arises—the two co-arise within relational action. This means that, as philosopher-anthropologists Déborah Danowski and Eduardo Viveiros de Castro put it, "every trans-specific interaction in Amerindian worlds is an international intrigue, a diplomatic negotiation," a form of "cosmopolitics."[55] The growing movement of "earth jurisprudence," which has succeeded in ascribing legal personhood to rivers such as the Whanganui in New Zealand, the Ganges and Yamuna in India, Ecuador's Vilcabamba, and Colombia's Atrato and Amazon—long after the courts of the world recognized the "personhood" of corporations—is intended to follow through on the implications of this animist sense of shared, relational personhood.[56] This not-aloneness in the world is what I will probe in the second half of this book. In its seeking to identify the animacy of and within images—so as to better relate to those images, aesthetically, ethically, ecologically, and politically—mine could be called a *neo-animist* conception of the image.

A return to animism, however, is not necessarily an entirely positive development. We humans are "not alone" also because we have added *new* others, or new relations—technical relations—to the always already not-aloneness of our worlds, and we are still in the process of determining the status of these new relations. As Achille Mbembe points out, there is an animism in the ways that digital technologies, with their electronic and algorithmic reason, enable an exchange of properties between humanity and objects, leading to a “knot of paradoxes” that risks a desiccation of life.[57] Working through this knot of paradoxes is essential at a time when animism of one kind or another not only suggests itself as an option, but presses in on us in less desirable forms. If, as I have been suggesting, images do harbor this power to make and unmake the world, how can we best work with that power to shape worlds that are ethically, politically, and ecologically more viable than the ones most readily on offer in our Anthropocenic predicament? That will be my starting point for the studies featured in the second half of this volume.

TABLE 4.1. The six image regimes

| | 1 | 2 | 3 |
|---|---|---|---|
| ***Image regime*** | **Animate-image** | **Ideal-image** | **Expression-image** |
| ***Action of image*** | Sovereign agent (corporeal, energetic), mediator | Symbol, representation (mimetic), intermediary, didactic instrument | Expression (of artist's "creativity" or creative response to world) |
| ***Response to image*** | Active, fluid, participatory (to engage, inhabit, be moved by, be obliged to) | Contemplative (to see through to the divine or cosmic reality beyond) | Critical, appreciative (of the artist's craft, style, novelty, insight) |
| ***Relationship to reality*** | Embodiment, manifestation (and medium) of reality | Representation, symbol (associative) | Expression of human insight into reality and/or human creativity or spirit |
| ***Nature of (ultimate) reality*** | Fluid, energetic, relational | Ideal, Platonic (transcendent) | Mostly passive, except for human action |
| ***Evaluative claim*** | Some images are more alive than others | Some images are more real (ideal, true) than others | Some humans are better artists than others |
| ***Relationship between image and text*** | None (text is image) | Text is image; text supplements or undergirds image | Text supplements image |
| ***Priesthood tendency*** | Direct facilitation | Hierarchic, secretive, bureaucratic | "Star system," interpretive elite |
| ***Psycho-dynamics*** | Dynamic, diverse subject-object relations; "porous self" | "Subjection," interpellation, unequal vertical porosity | Individualization (democratization of agency), "outward" objectification |

| 4 | 5 | 6 |
|---|---|---|
| **World-picture** | **Moving-image** | **Digital image-world** |
| Representation / copy of reality (mimesis) | Representation / copy and synthesis of previous modes | Hybrid; synthesis, modulation |
| Critical (assessed in relation to corresponding physical reality), exhibitionary / spectacular | Hybrid / synthetic (critical / appreciative, contemplative, exhibitionary / spectacular, active) | Fluid, participatory, preferential, contested, algorithmic |
| Representation, correspondence, more or less accurate; index of reality | Hybrid | Connected, networked |
| Material, indexical, mathematical, informational | Material, dynamic, in motion | Fluid, energetic, informational, algorithmic, fungible, modular |
| Images can approximate reality, derive their truth from direct / causal relationship to reality | (All of the above) | (All of the above?) |
| New textual systems supplement image | Text is part of image | Text is mixed with image; image-world organized by binary text |
| Scientific priesthood | "Star system" | All of the above; algorithmic governance |
| "Objection," objectification in a world of objects | Subjective options, mobilization, dispersion | Modular, recombinant, dispersive subjectivity |

# PART II

## We Are Not Alone

### (POST-) HUMAN BECOMINGS IN THE IMAGE-WORLD

Considered ecologically, all life on this planet is the product of one or another permutation of the interaction of energy, in the form of light and heat originating from the sun, with the surface of the Earth that it strikes. Everything we know is an evolved permutation of that open-endedly differentiating process. All forms of life, at least as we know it, are active transducers of the world around them—all "process" their environments, which means that they engage in semiotic and material relations with them. Action, relational response, transformation, and novelty are built into the system.

Humans are one species among many that have developed specific forms of signification to communicate and intersubjectively process the world. Of the communicative forms humans rely on, language is distinct in its complexity, flexibility, and richness. But images, which mediate relations based partly or largely on iconic signs, remain both primary and essential. And among the material and energetic forms of processing that contemporary humans have developed is the transformation of petrochemicals into energy and into novel materialities such as plastics, industrial chemicals, and nanomaterials. It is these petrochemical technologies that are taken by many as a key indicator and cause of the Anthropocene, the Era of the Human, where global climatological and ecological systems are being forced into new and unpredictable systemic realignments. But the specific political-economic arrangements that have accompanied the growth of these technologies are also important to consider for their causal role.

This Anthropocene "condition" or "predicament" has been accompanied by a global proliferation of image technologies that increasingly take the form I am describing as the digital image-world.[1] Most of these image technologies are thoroughly inscribed and embedded within the political ecology of petrochemical civilization, which means that their political-ecological basis is not sustainable over the long term. But they have also become the way we Anthropocenic humans communicate, translate, incorporate, and engage with the world. That suggests that if they are part of the problem, they must also be part of the solution.

With that in mind, what questions could help us understand the capacities of images to enable engagements that are more appropriate—more ethical, just, responsible, and cohabitably effective—with and in relation to the Anthropocenic situation? The three ecologies articulated in chapter 1 help us distinguish between three registers by which images today are produced, consumed, and circulated. Each suggests a set of questions, which could be summarized as follows:[2]

1) *Questions of materiality, or material ecology*: What makes this image, with and from what or whom, at what cost, and with what material impacts?

2) *Questions of effectivity, or medial-perceptual ecology*: How does this image work? How does it mediate, transport, carry, and modify what it makes and shapes in its action (including its bearers, deliverers, and transmitters)?

3) *Questions of representation, or social ecology*: Who and what does this image stand for, to whom, and at whose expense? How and for whom does it facilitate and reconfigure agency?[3]

The studies that follow will refer to one or another of these questions as they arise, though not in any systematic fashion.

More importantly, however, my analyses begin from a premise that I have suggested, but not clearly articulated yet. This premise takes imaging to be a form of world-making. This is not peculiar to humans. In a process-semiotic view, the universe is a communicative universe, made up of relations always in process between subjects-in-the-making and objects-given-to-that-making, with the two exchanging roles every step of the way. The universe is biosemiotic; it brims with the making of meaning. And among the meanings that are made for creatures like us are meanings of worldness, in which possibilities for future worlds are entertained, thought and felt, played and worked with, responded to and realized. Imaging is the making of worlds and the taking on of those worlds, in ways that allow us to change the shared worlds we create together.

Each of the six image regimes I have identified—animate-image, ideal-image, expression-image, world-picture, moving-image, and digital image-world—is with us today in multiple variations, and for each of them images matter in different ways. Moreover, for some of them, the acknowledged role granted to the image may fall short in one respect or another when judged against the process-relational, neo-animist conception articulated in chapter 4. The ideal-image, for instance, in ascribing a certain untouchability to the sources of meaning taken to undergird the value and potency of images, neglects to account for the responsibility of the human perceiver (as well as the human maker) in shaping the image-relation. If the ideals are pre-given, then they may be taken to be nonnegotiable. How then can we adjudicate between competing ideals—competing claims and beliefs about divinely ordained ultimates, such as are readily found in today's global world? Unless it is acknowledged that ideals may change or be renegotiated, there would appear to be little role for human modification of ideals toward coexistence with others. Ideals may be necessary insofar as they grant a vision forward, but they may also be imprisoning (and sources of conflict) if they cannot adequately contend with competing ideals in culturally pluralistic worlds.

By the opposite token, the expression-image may overemphasize the agency of the artist at the expense of the world beyond the image. In isolation from ideals, which might elucidate what *should* be depicted in a given time or place, the "genius" of the artist could be applied to depicting anything at all. Because of the opposed directionality of agency in the two image regimes, there is a kind of dialectic between ideal-image and expression-image regimes that reflects the relationship between what Morgan calls the "enchantment of belief" and the "enchantment of make-believe."[4] The first takes its power from claims about truth, while the second takes its power from our willingness to go along with fictional, as-if narratives. To the extent that the ideal-image enchants and holds power over us, it is because of our unavowed submission to its animacy, its capacity to take us in its thrall. We ascribe its power not to the image, but to the transcendent reality that ostensibly undergirds it. As for fiction, on the other hand, to the extent that it enchants us, its power is one that comes from our *avowed* submission to its animacy. We go along for the ride knowing full well that it is a ride. In recognizing and celebrating the power of the artist or creator of the ride, however, it is the maker rather than the thing made that becomes the agent. This ignores not only the power of the world beyond the image (the ideal) but also the power of the image itself in its objective presence and obduracy.

In practice, however, as Morgan argues (drawing on Bruno Latour's work on "factishes"), these two forms of enchantment—of belief and of make-believe, of artifact and of artifice—tend to commingle, with fiction ultimately transmuting into fact and vice versa.[5] The risks of these two image regimes are therefore complementary. In some sense, their mediation is found in the animate-image, which recognizes that the image itself is the site of an active negotiation between the image-bearer and the image-borne. At the same time, the agency of the artist may be *under*accounted for when it is the image itself that is taken to be the location of agency. (In practice, animate-image cultures tend to be quite aware of the importance of image-making, that is, of crafting the image to required standards.)

The world-picture, in its turn, carries a risk that has long been identified by its philosophical critics, including the Frankfurt School theorists, Heidegger, Foucault, and more recent ecological critics of technology.[6] In ascribing ultimate reality (if not necessarily agency) to what is "picturable" from measurable and directly transferable indices of the world, the world-picture seemingly denies reality to all else—to feeling, subjectivity, experience, agency, and all the things that make our lives feel real and meaningful. The moving-image builds on and accentuates the capacities of the world-picture, but its main effect is to intensify, multiply, and mobilize images themselves, leading to the growth of the image-world in which we find ourselves today. In this brave new digital world, imaging has become corpuscular, microbial, and micro-biosemiotic. Once we have entered the world of algorithms and artificial intelligence, imaging comes to make up a semiotic microbiome whose inner workings can no longer be known. Moving images today, at least in our experience, are in some sense returning us to the regime of the animate-image, but the risk now is of oversaturation, where the distinctiveness of the image is being lost in an imagistic flow that is bound to the prerogatives of the multipolar corporate-state nexus that manages and algorithmically enables that flow. Thus, any critique of images today must also be a critique of image culture and of the political economy that shapes it.

That said, it is possible to identify more promising forms of image production amidst the many available. In the next three chapters, I will examine three key sites of image production found within artistic, documentary, and media cultures today. The first of these sites addresses, accounts for, or warns about the altered relationship between human society writ large and the Earth on which it has extended itself. "The Anthropocene" is an attempt to name something so large that its humanity is somewhat uncertain—it is industrial-scale humanity, industrial not only in scale but also in method. It reflects what Lewis Mumford once called "the Megamachine," which has achieved a new criticality and precarity in its relationship with the Earth's ecological processes.[7] The second site consists of depictions of unusual transspecies encounters between animals, or between humans and nonhuman animals, as shared in online social media. If the first focuses on the achievements and impacts of industrial humanity (writ large) in relation to the nonhuman world (also writ large), the second concerns the boundary encounters between specific humans and specific denizens of its "outside"—the wild spaces that remain, intangibly and somewhat mysteriously, in our midst. The third site takes us to a different "outside"—a wilderness that is as mysterious as it is open-ended. If the very concept of the Anthropocene centers humanity as its lead actor, the unstated question that has accompanied this centering, or "anthropocentering," of the last few hundred years, is the question "Are we alone?" Chapter 7 will take up this question by looking at a few key nodes of cultural production that answer the question negatively. In its better known manifestations, this consists of the religious expressions and practices of humanity, but careful study reveals the question to embody a great range of creative and sometimes utopian impulses.

With the first of these sites of image-production, I focus on two projects, the multimedia *Anthropocene Project* and the ecologically themed multichannel video works of Ghanaian-British artist John Akomfrah. With the second, I shift my gaze to a range of videos that emerge not from a single artist or group of artists, but rather from direct interactions between people and animals. Since this topic of humans and animals is somewhat easier to identify as a theme in social media than the focus of either chapter 5 or chapter 7, this chapter will also serve as a case study of one of the prime social media sites, YouTube. And with the third, my initial focus will be the art of Hilma af Klint, an artist who died several decades ago but whose art was only discovered by the broader art-going public in the last decade or so. From there I move to the work of African-American artists who have grappled both with more traditional forms of immanent transcendence, focused on the ancestral genealogies that underpin human time, and on the current possibilities for a kind of technical or technological "not-aloneness" represented by the incipient potentials for a more open future. In my reading, the work of these artists, including composer-bandleader Sun Ra and poet Alexis Pauline Gumbs, suggests that creativity may be connected to the action of an expansive array of forces or beings including those marked "transcendent" or "spiritual," which ground their efforts in an understanding of the past and, at the same time, prompt them forward into exploration of novel futures.

These three empirical chapters are not intended to be exhaustive studies of these respective boundaries between humans and the Earth, humans and other animals, and humans and our divinities. They are intended more as preliminary mappings, with a focus on a set of exemplary cases. My goal with each study is not so much to understand what the artists themselves are attempting to do, though this will of course be important. It is, rather, to think about how these image formations figure into our own consumption of images today and what sorts of questions they raise for us. My hope is to elucidate how images—including but not limited to those that circulate in today's digital image-world—are not merely communicative of information (about their subjects) and expressive of subjectivity (that of their audiences, users, sharers, and appreciators), but how they embody affective, emotional, and even spiritual perceptions and dimensions of our relationship with the more-than-human worlds we live in. These, I will show, are linked to specific ways of combining image regimes outlined earlier in this book. I will also attempt to indicate some limitations of thinking generically about humans, animals, and spirits, gods, or whatever we might make of the transhuman and transanimal. Each of the categories represented by these three formations—Anthroposcene, Therioscene, Theoscene—is a blurred mixture that is troubled by variations, both internal and external, and by the multiple boundary relations that ensue from them.

In this sense, my goal is to represent an open array of "posthuman becomings." The literature on posthumanism and the posthumanities is extensive and contentious, a little bit like the literature on the naming of the Anthropocene. I have previously argued against the designation of a "post-" in relation to a humanity that has hardly reached any completion, synthesis, or culmination.[8] If anything, humanity has barely begun to emerge into anything resembling a unified species-being, and to posit a "posthuman" situation is at best a strategy to critique certain definitions of the human in relation to others. We are of course biologically specific. Whatever our past relations with Neanderthals, Denisovans, Florensiensis, and other hominids, the species that designates itself *Homo sapiens sapiens*, the self-proclaimed "wisest of the wise" among hominids, today shares a genetic identity that makes us distinct from other species, not least in our mutual interbreedability with others of our own kind, a category that includes all humans and, to the best of our knowledge, excludes all nonhumans.

That aside, humans have emerged and *become* all manner of things in the time we have lived on this Earth. We have formed tribal affiliations and constructed empires. We have lived frugally in small territories, and transformed, or terraformed, vast ecosystems. We have rarely acted as a singular "we" except in global, statistical terms. We have more commonly defined our "we-ness" not as a unified species but as something else: as collectives whose relations with animals, with deities, and with all manner of other things have been central to those definitions. Today we face a parallel situation, as we continue to work out our relations with (or without) animals, with or without deities, and with (and without) various other things including our common humanity. The Anthropo(s)cene can in this sense be taken as a call to the possible formation of a collective humanity, a call that raises questions about what this would mean. The Therioscene is, analogously, a call to the possible formation of a collective animality; and the Theoscene, to a collective divinity, or at least a collectivity underpinned by a sense of divinity that is both ancestral, or related to the past, and anticipatory, or related to the future.

What are our specific relations with each of these projects, multiple and incoherent as they may be? Each of them relies today on images, yet it is not clear that we understand what these images are or what they may do to us. Whatever it is that we are becoming, we are certain to engage with questions of what it is that we are, as humans; what our relations are to be with other animals that are still with and around us today; and what else there may be for us to relate to, with the kind of deference and respectful coaffiliation once reserved for gods. Who is it that *we* may *become*?

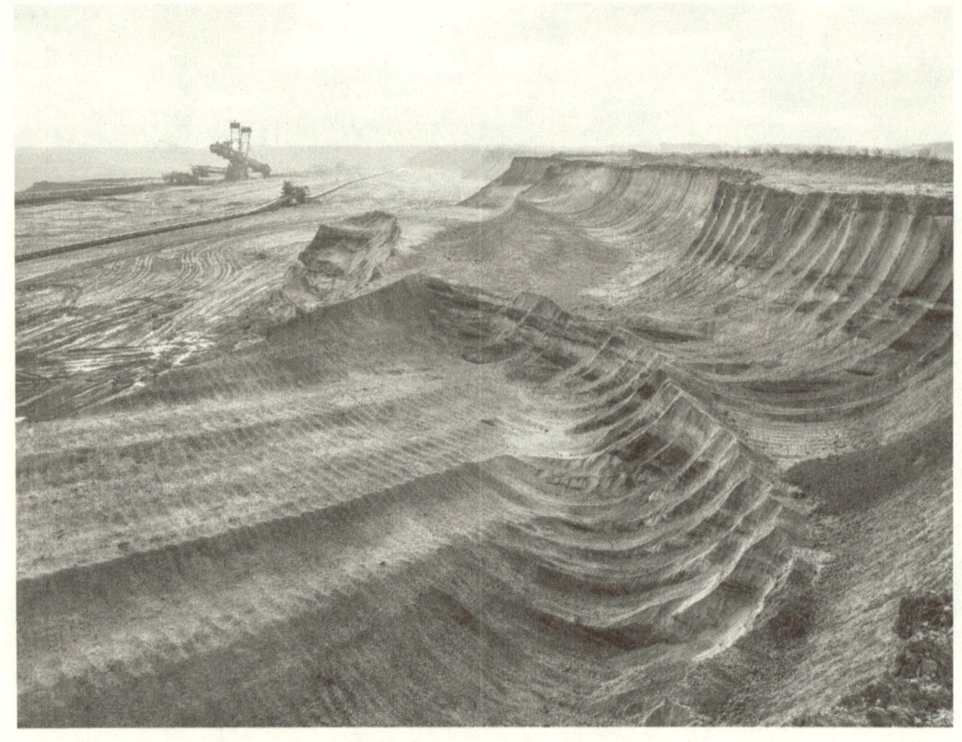

**FIGURE 5.1.** Edward Burtynsky, *Coal Mine #1, North Rhine, Westphalia, Germany* (detail), 2015. Photo © Edward Burtynsky, courtesy of Nicholas Metivier Gallery, Toronto.

## Five

# ANTHROPOSCENE

*The Anthropocene is an event, a point of bifurcation in the history of the Earth, life and humans. It overturns our representations of the world.*

—*CHRISTOPHE BONNEUIL AND JEAN-BAPTISTE FRESSOZ,* The Shock of the Anthropocene: The Earth, History and Us[1]

*[T]he Anthropocene is more a boundary event than an epoch. [. . .] our job is to make the Anthropocene as short/thin as possible and to cultivate with each other in every way imaginable epochs to come that can replenish refuge.*

—*DONNA HARAWAY,* Staying with the Trouble: Making Kin in the Chthulucene[2]

• • • The proposed geological epoch known as the Anthropocene has come to be configured within three or four predominant value orientations. The first is the one intended by the scientists who came up with the term: in their hands, it is a neutral, presumably objective description of how humanity has become the dominant species on the planet, altering its geological surface in unmistakable ways. This variation of the narrative is significant enough to warrant popular interest, but in itself is not likely to captivate and motivate much of an audience beyond that of scientists, popular science buffs, and intellectuals interested in understanding the world. That it has recently been rebuffed, somewhat contentiously, by a subcommittee of geologists tasked with determining whether or not to reclassify our current epoch as "the Anthropocene" is an indication that the scientific world works by rules that are opaque to the broader public. Both of our opening epigraphs speak to this development rather presciently, as I will detail shortly.

So the term has become contested between several other, more value-laden perspectives. One of these sees in the Anthropocene a critical, even desperate, call for change. In the hands of those commonly called environmentalists, the term is a clarion call, a jeremiad, even as it generates debates over whether it is too anthropocentric and celebratory. If the Anthropocene marks an event, then for the scientists, it is a mystery to be solved (when did it begin? what accounts for it?), while for the environmentalists, it is more akin to a crime to be adjudicated and expiated. The Anthropocene marks the human transformation of the Earth to the point where the planet's habitability, for us and other species, has been seriously jeopardized. This first of our case studies will therefore be an exploration of a crime scene: the Anthropo*scene*.[3]

A related perspective shares with environmentalism the desire to formulate tools for redirecting society, but finds the overarching singularity of the Anthropocene narrative too problematic. If the Anthroposcene is a crime scene for holders of this view, it is not a new one, but continuous with at least five centuries of criminal activity. Instead, proponents of this set of critiques reject the term in favor of others: Capitalocene, Eurocene, Technocene, Petrocene, Homogenocene, Urbanocene, Manthropocene, Econocene, Plantationocene, Wasteocene, Plasticene, Thanatocene, Necrocene, Negrocene, Anthrobscene, Anthropo-not-seen, Eremocene (Age of Loneliness), and others that variously name the factor most indicative of, or culprit most responsible for, the current state of geophysical affairs (capitalism, European colonialism, transatlantic imperialism, technology, patriarchy, etc.).[4] Taking a set of these as more or less unified and rigorously theorized, I will refer in what follows to the "left-decolonial" perspective. Its key insight is summarized by Brazilian philosophers Déborah Danowski and Eduardo Viveiros de Castro, who write that "the genocide of Amerindian peoples—the end of the world for them—was the beginning of the modern world for Europe: without the despoiling of the Americas, Europe would have never become more than the backyard of Eurasia [. . ..]. No pillage of the Americas, no capitalism, no Industrial Revolution, thus perhaps no Anthropocene either."[5] Cameroonian philosopher Achille Mbembe complements this view by distinguishing between the "megaprocesses" causing "long-term planetary environmental changes" and the *specific* constellation of power that drives them, the "contemporary process whereby power is constituted, expressed, and reconfigured, and acts and reproduces itself as a geomorphic [earth-shaping] force." Borrowing a term from a mid-twentieth century architectural movement, he labels this process "brutalism" (and so we could add the Brutocene).[6]

A somewhat contrary perspective comes at the Anthropocene from a more hopeful tangent. Proponents of a "good Anthropocene," often labeled "ecomodernists," see the term as indicating and even celebrating both what humanity has achieved and the promise that it could do even better—to overcome its current challenges and create a livable relationship between humanity and nature. Some of the latter go further and see the Anthropocene as a station on the way toward something even more glorious, a "singularity" of some kind within which humans are a mere precursor, but without whom the further achievement would not be possible. I will largely set this perspective aside, but it is important to acknowledge its influence among powerful proponents of digital technology.[7]

Public communication about the Anthropocene tends to fall into one or more of these perspectives. As an outcome of scientific research and deliberation, news of the Anthropocene has been shared by science journalists across the full range of journalistic media. By the middle of the second decade of the current century, the term's use in popular media had attained a certain critical mass of respectability. One study counted over three hundred separate newspaper articles in the U.K. and U.S. press in the years 2014 through 2016;[8] and the use of the term has only multiplied since then. The authors note that this growing "Anthropocene Corpus" has tended toward a largely "negative" vision, "with a prevalence of terms pointing to an unfavorable outcome, e.g., 'catastrophe,' 'crises,' 'collapse,' 'irreversible' and 'extinction.' "[9]

Meanwhile, the growing field of environmental humanities has taken up the term both as a useful shorthand for the confluence of issues examined in the field—from climate change, biodiversity loss, and species extinction to environmental justice and eco-political contestation—and as a target of sustained critical analysis. In popularizing the term, environmental humanists have aimed to provoke conversation, debate, and sometimes activism through strategies that engage audiences in multiple ways. The Anthropocene has been the focus of books and articles, conferences and symposia, museum and multimedia arts exhibitions, storytelling festivals and poetry slams, interdisciplinary workshops, biennales, and other hybrid-format and "post-disciplinary" initiatives.[10] Examining a variety of these, Ritts and Bakker propose the term "Anthropocene festivals" to capture the way in which these events manifest a "collective desire to explore humanity's geological condition as interactive relation."[11] They discuss examples under titles including "Welcome to the End of the World/Welcome to the Anthropocene" (Ushuaia, Argentina), "Arts in the Anthropocene" (Mexico), "Eco-Visionaries: Art and Architecture After the Anthropocene" (Lisbon, Portugal), "Earth Lab" (London), "Deep Time" (Chicago), and numerous others. Among the largest of such efforts, the "Anthropocene Curriculum," "Anthropocene Campus," and "Anthropocene Project" initiatives, all developed by the Berlin-based Haus der Kulturen der Welt (HKW, or House of World Cultures) in collaboration with the Max Planck Institute for the History of Science, have managed to successfully create cross-disciplinary international networks of natural scientists, social scientists, humanists, artists, designers, and educators.[12] At their best, these events manifest what Ritts and Bakker call an "aspirational culture" that "collectively model[s] novel forms of environmental governance" and that, in its effects, can enable "new ways of addressing collective response to ecological breakdown, uncertainty, and disaster."[13]

Reaching the broader public through such transdisciplinary approaches, however, has arguably proved a more elusive goal. Since my interest is in the popular uptake of Anthropocene ideas and images, I wish to examine a project whose scope and scale are equally ambitious as these, but whose form is more traditional—primarily that of documentary visuality—and whose impact has arguably been broader as a result. Also called *The Anthropocene Project*, though unrelated to the two-year Berlin-based project of the same name, this multidisciplinary effort is aimed at a broad cross-section of audiences, including attendees at popular museums, school groups that have made the exhibition part of their curriculum, and film-viewing audiences both in theatres and at home.

My analysis of *The Anthropocene Project* will be informed by the environmentalist and left-decolonial perspectives mentioned above. While the latter pursues multiple lines of critical inquiry, Stefania Barca's 2020 book *Forces of Reproduction: Notes for a Counter-Hegemonic Anthropocene* can be taken as a helpful synthesis of these into a powerful critical apparatus, which I will introduce here briefly.[14] In laying out her argument, Barca wields this critique against a three-minute video entitled *Welcome to the Anthropocene*, which was presented at the opening plenary of the 2012 Rio+20 Earth Summit. In Barca's analysis, the video epitomizes the "hegemonic" or "master narrative" of the Anthropocene, which focuses on capitalist-industrial modernity as a kind of tragic but worthy hero that is responsible for our current challenges, but that is equally capable of solving them. Drawing on feminist, historical-materialist, anti-racist, decolonial, and anti-speciesist perspectives, Barca weaves together a counternarrative of "other-than-master subjects" who collectively make up the "forces of reproduction," that is, who are collectively responsible for "the work of sustaining life in its material and immaterial needs."[15] The "narrative violence of the official Anthropocene storyline," she writes, "transpires from the fact that it systematically silences both the structural inequalities of modern economic growth and the non-capitalist alternatives to it."[16] The crime scene, in this reading, has a more specific suspect than all of humanity. It has specific causes (colonialism, capitalism, masculinism, and anthropocentrism) and victims (the colonized, the proletariat, women and nonbinary people, and the nonhuman life of the planet), and potential solutions rooted in ways of being that have been and remain alternative to those causes.

Barca's multipronged critique of *Welcome to the Anthropocene* can similarly be applied to *The Anthropocene Project*, and my analysis will compare the latter to another multimedia project whose contours take more complete account of the "other-than-master subjects" and "forces of reproduction" Barca names. But first I will treat the scientific project of delineating and communicating the Anthropocene, in order to see how a concept intended to be applied methodically and understood in an indexical relationship to the world has become transformed. I first examine the ways that the Anthropocene has been imaged (and imagined) by geologists, and how it came to be that the proposed Anthropocene epoch has been formally rejected, at least for the moment, by that community of specialists. Next, I examine the multimedia *Anthropocene Project* in detail to show its reliance on visuality, and especially on the mixture of the indexical and the ideal known as the *sublime*. The chapter concludes with a study of John Akomfrah's multimedia installations *Vertigo Sea* and *Purple*, both of which treat the Anthropocene within a deeper set of historical processes and reference points. In their method they also depart from the primarily indexical mode of imaging the Anthropocene to one that makes full use of the montage capacities of moving-image media, presenting a form of image I will call the *montage-image*. Together, these readings will probe the ways in which the Anthropocene does or does not "overturn our representations of the world," as Christophe Bonneuil and Jean-Baptiste Fressoz suggest in this chapter's opening quote, and whether any of these mediations might prepare us to cultivate the "imaginable epochs to come" that Donna Haraway proposes for taking us beyond the Anthropo(s)cene.

## -*CENE* OR NOT -*CENE*? INDEXING THE SCIENTISTS' ANTHROPOCENE

While it had some forerunners, the concept of the Anthropocene as a geological epoch was first proposed by atmospheric chemist Paul Crutzen in the year 2000, with an earlier use of the term by limnologist Eugene Stoermer. Within a few years of Crutzen's blurting it out at an earth science meeting, geologists were taking the concept as a serious proposal to mark a new epoch in the history of planet Earth, an epoch brought about by human activities.[17] For geologists, an epoch is not just any time period; it is part of a nested set of delineations: from smallest to largest and most encompassing, these are known as *ages*, *epochs*, *periods*, *eras*, and *eons*. Each is a geochronological unit, that is, a unit of time as marked by Earth history (geology) and determined through the practice of chronostratigraphy, or the reading and writing (-*graphy*) of layers of rock (*strata*) marking time (*chronos*). The entirety is based on the long verified observation that the remnants of the earth's surface lay themselves down in horizontal layers, with the more recent laid on top of the less recent. The smaller chronostratigraphic units denote smaller levels of change over time; these combine to make up the larger ones, which denote larger changes.

The geologic time scale provides a kind of chronostratigraphic "address" for anything in the geologic record. We who live today are said to find ourselves "in" the Holocene or—if it should come to be accepted—the Anthropocene epoch, which are respectively the second and potentially third epochs of the third period (Quaternary) of the third era (Cenozoic) of the fourth eon (Phanerozoic) since the formation of the Earth. The Holocene, which began some 11,700 years ago, is roughly the thirty-eighth epoch in Earth's history. To say that we are *in* it, however, or in the Anthropocene, is to presume that we, or someone, could step out of time and see ourselves inside it. We cannot: we are at the leading edge (one of an infinity of leading edges) of a set of dynamic processes that unfolds not with the flatness of unrolling a roll of paper, but with noticeable folds, twists, and lumps. Whether today's present will one day appear smooth or lumpy, or form a dramatic twist in the geochronological fabric, cannot possibly be known until that present has become past. It will take additional layering on top of it—further epochs or ages at the very least—to see what it will look like once it is laid down. Geology is after all, at least in its stratigraphic form, a reading of the past in the rockscape of the present. Its ability to read the present is constrained by the fact that the present is not yet past. Its layering can only be predicted or, perhaps, divined. (More on the latter in chapter 7.)

Like other natural scientists, geologists work through the production and analysis of indexical signs.[18] Using physical instruments, they collect empirical observations of traces marking causal relationships. They measure, collate, compare, compress, and connect these to reveal causal trends and patterns in the world around us. They represent these graphically and interpret them in writing, which is published, distributed, read, discussed, debated, refined (or rejected), and projected into further research. Empirical evidence, which is always evidence *of* something (and therefore *of theory*), in this way fuels theory-building, which gives rise to further evidence gathering, with representation and interpretation being a central part of the process. The indexical in this way becomes discursive, and vice versa. The work of science involves the production of what Bruno Latour calls a "reversible chain of transformations," a chain in which "indexicality is produced and sustained in circulation by scientists laboring to maintain the stability of indexical referents as they move from context to context."[19]

The idea of a new epoch, and its proposed name, the Anthropocene, are both discursive constructs—theoretical concepts developed to make sense of phenomena that can be measured empirically and assessed in reference to what is known. For those concepts to serve science, they must be able to operationalize indexicality. And for the Anthropocene epoch proposal to be accepted by geologists, it must follow criteria developed by the geological community for identifying other epochs. The first such criterion, which led to the first challenge for proponents of the theory, was clear definition, including a precise starting point (since the epoch would have only just begun). Proposals for marking the beginning of the Anthropocene have ranged far and wide: they include the extinction of mammoths through human predation some 14,000 years ago; forest clearances and rice cultivation occurring five to eight thousand years ago; the year 1610, as marking the Columbian Exchange, which resulted not only in the decimation of the majority of North and South America's Indigenous populations, but also a profound alteration of ecosystems including a noticeable dip in atmospheric carbon dioxide concentrations; the onset of the Industrial Revolution, especially with the development of the steam engine; and the so-called Great Acceleration of the mid-twentieth century, with its introduction of radionuclides from hydrogen bomb tests alongside the deposits of plastics, concrete, and other technogenic substances across the world.

As with other steps in the process of identifying a geological epoch, the trajectory taken by the international geological community in articulating the Anthropocene has involved identifying clear and measurable demarcation criteria, reducing them to the clearest stratigraphic signal possible, and then identifying a site, a so-called golden spike, that reflects this signal especially well. Selection and reduction has in effect occurred at multiple stages of the process. The geological community is as "nested" as its time scales, and within the International Union of Geological Sciences' (IUGS, the top level) International Commission on Stratigraphy (ICS, the next level down), it is the Subcommission of Quaternary Stratigraphy (SQS, the third level, for our purposes) that has taken responsibility for the Anthropocene epoch proposal, which it delegated to a group formed in 2009 called the Anthropocene Working Group (AWG, level four).

The AWG worked persistently since then to "assess the Anthropocene as a formal strato-chronographic unit defined by a GSSP," or Global Boundary Stratotype Section and Point delineating the "lower" (beginning) boundary of the unit. (GSSP are the points known informally as golden spikes.) As documented in the "Earth Indices" exhibition, held at Berlin's Haus der Kulturen der Welt (HKW) and curated by artists Giulia Bruno and Armin Linke, who followed and worked alongside the AWG for a ten-year period, the process of determining whether and how to make the case for the Anthropocene epoch relied on a complex suite of instruments, procedures, and practices for documenting, analyzing, and evaluating the most recent layers of Earth's geological archive, or "core." Bruno and Linke relate the process of geological data gathering to the reading and interpreting of a musical score: "The materiality of the [geological] core describes time, technology, climate change, changes to Earth—it partitions these changes into something a bit like a musical score. To read and interpret this score, you need different media technologies, photographs and chemical processes, which are transformed into data and then analyzed again."[20] An image in the exhibition, provided by a geological team from Poland, includes the caption "Every slice is like a CD with different environmental signal [*sic*]."[21] As with most physical sciences, images and imaging technologies are central to the process of data gathering and analysis. "A graph," Bruno and Linke note, "is an image, and so too is a core sample, since often it is not the material core that is analyzed but rather images of it. In science, you cannot see something without relating it to context: an image without the metadata and the source is nothing."[22] The metadata is, in effect, the indexical signature evidencing the causal relationship between the image and what it signifies.

In 2016, the AWG "decided by a majority vote that the Anthropocene possesses geological reality, that it is best considered at epoch/series level, that it is best defined beginning in the mid-twentieth century with the 'Great Acceleration,' and that it should be defined by a Global Stratotype Section and Point (GSSP)."[23] Following extensive reviews of geological literature, consultation with myriad teams of scientists, and analyses by multiple laboratories, the AWG developed a short list of proposed sites around the world, one of which would be chosen as the golden spike, the single location that best records it in the geological record. By 2019, twelve sites had been identified, located in lakes, seas, reservoirs, caves, peatlands, and ocean reefs around the world. Core samples taken from them ranged from a mere 45 centimeters in length to a mammoth 133 meters. What united them, according to the "Earth Indices" exhibition, "is that they constitute high-resolution archives of at least the last century and record global as well as local anthropogenic signals, including traces of mid-century nuclear bomb testing, fossil fuel combustion, industrialization, agriculture and ecosystem change."[24]

By 2022, the AWG was prepared to vote on the site that would be the golden spike, and by 2023 they had selected a small lake in Ontario, Canada, called Crawford Lake. As one journalist summarized it, in Crawford Lake "the waters are so deep that whatever sinks to the floor usually remains without mixing with the upper layers of water, so it stays preserved, offering an amazingly good record of geological change. Since the middle of the 20th century, the sediment there has been inundated by the byproducts of human activity: plutonium isotopes from the nuclear bombs we've detonated, ash from the fossil fuels we've burned, and nitrogen from the fertilizer we've used."[25] The concept had thereby found its image, the ideal carrier of its indexicality, through a process of nomination, study, measurement, comparison, and evaluation.

Reading the notes and publications of the AWG, it is striking how often its members have been asked to vote on something or other, from the precise date of the beginning of the Anthropocene epoch and the candidate sites for the golden spike to much more refined details.[26] The entire process moved, in effect, from a global scale proposal—the Anthropocene as a marker of what makes the present different from the past—to a temporally specific date, which became November 1, 1952, coincident with the detonation of the first thermonuclear device, and finally to a specific site that best encompasses the criteria associated with the latter date. In the process of increasing the specificity of what was being identified, more and more of the richness of the original concept disappeared into the background. This is what led long-time AWG member Erle Ellis to submit a public resignation letter in July 2023. In his letter, Ellis decried the "misleading and regressive perspective on Earth's transformation by human societies" that he saw the AWG "now promoting." Ellis wrote,

> To define the Anthropocene as a shallow band of sediment in a single lake is an esoteric academic matter. But dividing Earth's human transformation into two parts, pre- and post- 1950, does real damage by denying the deeper history and the ultimate causes of Earth's unfolding social-environmental crisis. Are the planetary changes wrought by industrial and colonial nations before 1950 not significant enough to transform the planet? The political ramifications of such a misleading and scientifically inaccurate portrayal are clearly profound and regressive.

"The AWG's choice," he continued, "to systematically ignore overwhelming evidence of Earth's long-term anthropogenic transformation is not just bad science, it's bad for public understanding and action on global change."[27] Calling it "bad science," however, implicates the process for delineating other geological epochs and temporal units as well, all of which have followed more or less the same procedures, but with much lower political stakes.

Ellis's complaints did not take place in a vacuum. By late 2023, the AWG had concluded its work and forwarded its proposal—for a "Crawfordian era" of an "Anthropocene epoch"—to the Subcommission on Quaternary Stratigraphy (the next level up). When, in March of 2024, the SQS voted against the proposal by a vote of 12 to 4 (with two formal abstentions and three other non-votes), AWG chair Colin Waters voiced his unhappiness. In a newsletter editorial, he complained of IUGS pressure to rush the vote, the ICS "breaching their own statutes and rules," and the existence of a "catalogue of complaints about unethical behavior by those in high-office over the past decade who have aimed at preventing fair assessment of any proposal."[28] The chair and vice-chair of the SQS committee responsible for the vote claimed it was conducted illegitimately, with "procedural irregularities" including that several members were past their term limits. The chair, Jan Zalasiewicz, announced that he had been asked to step down from his role on the committee.[29] The vote was nevertheless unanimously approved on March 20, 2024, by the IUGS executive committee (the highest level), which then announced that the Anthropocene epoch proposal was thus rejected. The comments of some of those who voted against the proposal indicate that it was not necessarily a rejection of the Anthropocene idea, but that it was in part a rejection of its becoming an *epoch*. Some have proposed that it instead be considered an *event*, along the lines of mass extinctions or oxygenation of the Earth's atmosphere, which may have catastrophic impacts but do not attain the status of an epoch.

As it happens, then, the international geological community rejected the idea of an Anthropocene epoch at least in part because its own criteria had become too specific to reflect the concept's original purposes. To put it in Latourian terms, the series of transformations failed to preserve the "reversible indexicalities" it called for. The motivation for delineating a new temporal unit had been to point to the overwhelming and multiple points of evidence that human activities had altered the planet's surface. But by 2024, the process by which an epochal proposal gets vetted had reduced its own criteria to both a single start date and a single location on Earth to represent the change. One might be forgiven for thinking that science was, in this respect, a victim of its own tendency to reduce its own claims to the most indexically clear image, which in this case became a lake in Ontario. Science was also arguably "contaminated" here (I use the word without judgment) by politics, that is, by some scientists' understandable desire to have an effect in the world.

The result marks an important ambiguity in the very idea that geologists can speak of the present in the epochal terms by which they organize the past. To name the last 75 years the beginning of an "epoch" is to state that we have entered something definable and knowable. If instead the Anthropocene is simply the current name for an *event* or a *condition* that, in fact, defines the global situation today, then it need not have geologists' imprimatur at all. Perhaps it is not the study of the past—through its indexical traces in the layers of the earth—but the study of the present that should be guiding our collective response to the global situation. The IUGS executive committee suggested as much in its statement announcing the decision: "Despite its rejection as a formal unit of the Geologic Time Scale," they wrote, "the Anthropocene will nevertheless continue to be used not only by Earth and environmental scientists, but also by social scientists, politicians and economists, as well as by the public at large. It will remain an invaluable descriptor of human impact on the earth system."[30]

What is arguably at stake between the framing of the Anthropocene as a new epoch into which we have entered and, alternatively, as an event and a condition to which we must respond, is the capacity to act. Framing the Anthropocene as an epoch, Matthias Grotkopp writes, "tips the scales towards the illusion of a new normal, instead of framing it as a succession of crossed thresholds into the unknowable and unforeseeable."[31] The remainder of this chapter will examine two large-scale efforts to address the event and condition of the Anthropocene—this crossing "into the unknowable and unforeseeable"—using the tools of visual or audiovisual media.

## ANTHROPOCENE SEEN: *THE ANTHROPOCENE PROJECT*

If the scientists' Anthropocene is determined through a chain of indexical references collected and analyzed on a planetary scale, the environmental artists' Anthropocene draws upon the indexicality of the same world-picture regime, but adds to it the sense of an ideal, though a threatened and destabilized one: that of harmonious human relations with the Earth. Insofar as that ideal is not precisely delimitable, it draws its power from the imagery of the sublime. That is, it is an ideal that is perceived to be withdrawn or withdrawing, ineffable yet somehow felt and expressible. In one sense the ideal is the grandeur of nature, the cosmos, the immensity within which we humans dwell; it is the sublime of capital-*n* Nature. In another sense, it is the immensity of the human hand in things, which has come to replace the divine hand once perceived to have guided or undergirded the world that exceeds us; it is the anthropic and/or technological sublime. In this shared ground between the indexicality of the world-picture regime and a kind of polyvalent and underdetermined ideal-image is where we find the power of *The Anthropocene Project,* a massive documentary project led by photographer Edward Burtynsky and filmmakers Jennifer Baichwal and Nicholas de Pencier.

Among the many art and media projects on the Anthropocene, *The Anthropocene Project* stands out as much in its ambition and scope as in the precision of its message. The project consists of a touring multimedia art exhibition encompassing several dozen large-scale photographs (some of them displayed on ceiling-to-floor banners), high-resolution murals, several videos, a set of augmented reality (AR) installations, gigapixel essays, 360° virtual reality films, and interactive, educational tableaux; a feature-length documentary film; two books; and an extensive web site. Each of the media brings a different set of strategies to the artists' key concern, which is "how to give compelling aesthetic form to the evidence that has aggregated in the geological record through persistent and globally interconnected human activity."[32]

In conceiving the project, the three artists found themselves united by "the sense that documentary images—be they photographs, films, or augmented reality installations—can reveal the extent and character of some of the most affected places in the world."[33] In this goal, *The Anthropocene Project* straddles the boundary between the neutral/scientific and critical-environmental uses of the term "Anthropocene." With their interest in the documentary image, the artists are drawing on the indexical power of the world-picture regime, the tradition of accumulating and exhibiting visual evidence of what the world looks like, with a focus on the "sheer scale" of the human impact on that world.[34] In the case of Burtynsky, the best known of the exhibition's three cocreators, this desire to visually capture the monumentality of "large-scale systems" has been a lifelong preoccupation. In an essay in the book that accompanies the project, Burtynsky describes how his pursuit of wider "vantage points" and "elevated spots" was strengthened by remotely controlled digital technology (including drones, airplanes, helicopters, and a "forty-foot pneumatic monopod"), satellite images, and "specialized 3D software" that allowed him "to capture and stitch together thousands of images of an object or a place, and render such scenes in full detail—as images that may be experienced in all their dimensionality."[35]

In all of this, the artists are subjecting themselves to a conundrum, which is that Anthropocene visuality, with its aerial views from above, "enforces the authority of a Western aesthetic mode rooted in imperialism [. . .] and the conquest of nature."[36] This is something that critics of Burtynsky's work have noted before.[37] The trade-off, as Kelly Oliver puts it, is that the "fantasy of the whole earth allows us to continue with illusions of mastery and globalism, but now in the service of saving, rather than destroying, the planet."[38] The hope with such documentary photography is typically that once people see the physical evidence—and once they are shocked by its inhuman scale—they will act appropriately in response to it. Audience response research, however, has shown this relationship to be rather more complex.[39] At the same time, Burtynsky's photographs have sometimes been taken as emblematic of a "toxic sublime" that both draws attention to the toxicity it depicts and, at the same time, aestheticizes it, without enabling the kind of comprehension of its causes that might motivate action toward mitigating or obviating those causes.[40] Insofar as Burtynsky is documenting the world's environmental "crisis hotspots," he is arguably following the masculinist "heroics" and "techno-imperialist logistics" of what Donna Haraway has called the "god trick," the disembodied, positivist view that sees "everything from nowhere."[41]

With *The Anthropocene Project*, however, Burtynsky's monumental photographs are supplemented not only with highly informative captions, but also with Baichwal's and de Pencier's video vignettes and, for those who read the book or listen to the guided tour, with a more detailed textual apparatus bringing the whole into a comprehensive interpretive framework. Baichwal relates, in an exhibition panel, that the project "is a culmination of all the conversations we have ever had about art's capacity to provoke change, as well as the merits and drawbacks of doing this experientially: to not preach, harangue or blame, but to witness, and in that witnessing, try to shift consciousness."[42] She writes that "Burtynsky's photographs take people to places they are connected to or responsible for but would never normally see, and he finds the wide view that communicates them in one frame." Baichwal's and de Pencier's films, on the other hand, "try to explore and extend the narratives of place by deepening understanding of context and detail, then reflecting this back onto ourselves."[43] Baichwal relates, in a different context, that Burtynsky's aerial views are set into dialogue with the filmmakers' more grounded documentary ethic, whereby "you can only understand scale when you are constantly pairing it with detail, and where you're above but you're down on the ground [. . .] saturated in a place."[44] This interest in deepening understandings of specific places and situations to which audiences may be "connected to or responsible for" in order "to shift consciousness" captures the artists' motivation. The responsibility for the Anthropocene predicament is, in this account, shared, and addressing it requires the kind of "deepened" understanding enabled by effectively rendered and carefully curated images.

Between them, the several dozen, mostly wall-sized photographic panels and short videos of *The Anthropocene Project* cover a tremendous range of topics, including geology, climate change, species extinction, landfills, coral bleaching, burning rainforests, population growth, energy consumption, industrial farming, plastics manufacturing, clear-cut logging, aquifer pumping, monocultural palm plantations, and extraction (and refinement) of oil, coal, fracked natural gas, lithium, copper, phosphate, potash, and other minerals. Locations depicted cover the world, from Lagos, Nigeria, to Norilsk in the Arctic Circle, and from the deserts of Saudi Arabia to coral reefs off the coast of Australia. The documentary film, in turn, is divided into seven sections: "Extraction," "Terraforming," "Technofossils," "Anthroturbation," "Boundary Limits," "Climate Change," and "Extinction."

The experience of taking in the entire project can be overwhelming, as attested by visitor comments. This appears to be an intended effect, whose lingering results could be expected to generate conversations and shape feelings for days or weeks afterward. A section of the exhibition gauges viewers' emotional responses to the exhibition, providing visual graphs of their answers to the question "How does what you've seen here today make you feel?" On the day I visited the exhibition, at Toronto's Art Gallery of Ontario in November of 2018,[45] the majority of responses fell into a negative but not "politically activated" set of categories: in order, these were "worried" (22.9%), "sad" (19.1%), and "angry" (16.6%), with the remainder consisting of "informed" (14.1%), "motivated" (9.8%), "unconcerned" (8.8%), and "suspicious" (8.7%). (Impressed with the interactivity of the questionnaire, a few boys were pressing buttons repeatedly to see if they could alter the response curve. "We need to make 'unconcerned' go up," said one, in an apparent desire to see a more equitable distribution of responses.) To the extent that the questionnaire can be trusted, then, it reflects the nature of the Anthropocene predicament, and in particular the *scope* and *scale* of human technological impacts on the Earth, which the exhibition succeeds at capturing exceedingly well. That these succeeded in eliciting emotional responses—particularly "worried," "sad," and "angry"—without the accompanying motivation to do anything with those emotions, is an important indicator for us to keep in mind.

Returning to the ecocritical questions I posed above—of materiality, representation, and effectivity—the makers of *The Anthropocene Project,* in their comments, show a genuine awareness of the project's materiality. These artists travel the world and expend tremendous effort and resources to produce a product that will be seen by audiences around the world. The impacts of their travels, photography, and technology, while not minimal, are of course much less ecologically damaging than most of the industrial activities they document. With respect to representation, while there is some effort to contextualize specific issues in their local settings, what is represented is broadly pan-human: it is the agency of technological humanity that is responsible for the extraction, pollution, waste, and ecological disruption of the activities portrayed. The exhibition makes no effort to parse the causes or responsible parties, which means it also makes no effort to suggest alternatives or counter-hegemonic narratives. The question of people's responses to these images is posed, but there is no commensurate depiction of possible forms of action, resolution, or indeed collective agency in addressing the challenges of the Anthropocene. Their goal is to make the challenges real and tangible; the organization of any social movement to exert pressure or agency toward remedying them is outside their purview.

While Baichwal refers in an interview to the possibility of an "authentic exchange of vulnerability with the people, or indeed other species in some way, who are in those contexts," it is not clear to what extent this "exchange of vulnerability" is evident in the final products of the documentarians' travels.[46] Among the more poignant parts of the exhibition is the 3-D virtual-reality installation of burning mounds of thousands of elephant tusks, stockpiled by the Kenyan government as a disincentive to poachers and ceremonially burned at the prompting of Kenyan wildlife biologist Winnie Kiiru. De Pencier describes the scene's "apocalyptic beauty" as "like something ripped from the pages of the Bible."[47] The ivory burn, which occurred in Nairobi National Park in 2016, serves as the framing device for the film *Anthropocene: The Human Epoch*, in scenes described by Robert Enright as an "elemental Dantesque inferno."[48] The effect is to witness a catastrophe. The vulnerability, it is clear, is that of the elephants, or that of the last surviving male northern white rhino, whose 2018 death is documented in the film. But it is not clear how and which human hands are involved in any part of this equation: the poachers (or indeed the poor of Kenya and surrounding countries), the biologists and government scientists, the westerners whose environmental and biological assumptions play an outsized role in local settings, or any others. The result is that the filmmakers have shared with us the privilege of witnessing the crime scene, even as the criminals run free and unidentified—or, little better, are all of us.

Enright captures the filmmakers' strategy of shifting between vista, panorama, and intense close-ups, a strategy the exhibition seems to be trying to duplicate in its alternation of aerial images, close-ups, VR installations, and texts. The prerequisite that the scale of the "crime scene" be adequately documented meant that

> whatever the filmmakers looked at, whether activity or site or consequence, had to be the largest of its kind. So the Gotthard Base Tunnel in Switzerland is the world's longest railway tunnel; the Atacama solar project is set in the driest desert in the world; the Hambach coal mine in Westphalia is the largest open-pit mine in Germany and uses the largest land machines ever made by humans; and the Dandora landfill in Nairobi is among the biggest in the world. Each of these projects is extreme and exceeds anything we could have imagined. The scale of what we're seeing, and the skill of its cinematic delivery, beggars belief. How are we to process machines that can carve out 240,000 cubic metres of earth every day; or conceive of 10,000 kilometres of potash tunnels under the town of Berezniki, Russia; or measure what the daily emission of 16 million tons of CO2 actually means?[49]

In all of this, *The Anthropocene Project* could be said to duplicate the scalar requirements of what it is documenting; in aiming for maximum impact through spectacle, it is using the "master's tools" to "dismantle the master's house," a task that Audre Lorde famously argued was impossible.[50] In this, it can hardly hope to succeed against the challenges announced by Stefania Barca's "counter-hegemonic Anthropocene." If matching the scale of the "crime" with the scale of its depiction is a limitation of the project, there are moments that transgress this scalar correlation and that follow a more "productive clash of scales," as Matthias Grotkopp calls it, leading to a sense of irony and incongruence.[51] Grotkopp describes "moments when the shift from abstraction to concreteness lingers on the threshold, when it is unclear, at which scale and from what perspective we are looking," when we recognize we may be making an error of judgment, for instance, mistaking "destruction for beauty and vice versa." "These structures of clashing scales, of incongruence and bewilderment," he writes, "have the potential to let us feel the entanglement of the many worlds of human cultures and nonhuman agents with the life-giving earth."[52]

But the moments are too few, Grotkopp concludes, and are subsumed within a more general move to abstraction and distance. Instead of facilitating any detailed understanding of the multiple processes that have contributed to the Anthropocene—from colonialism and capitalism to specific policies, industrial processes, and corporate or political actors—the project tends to abstract and aestheticize what it depicts.[53] As Shannon Stevens and Richard Wainwright point out in a review of the film (to be discussed shortly), the filmmakers render bureaucratic and corporate structures anonymous, even obscuring corporate logos "by light, fog, distance, or absence," which they take to be akin to "showing the enormity of Hiroshima without mentioning Ameri-

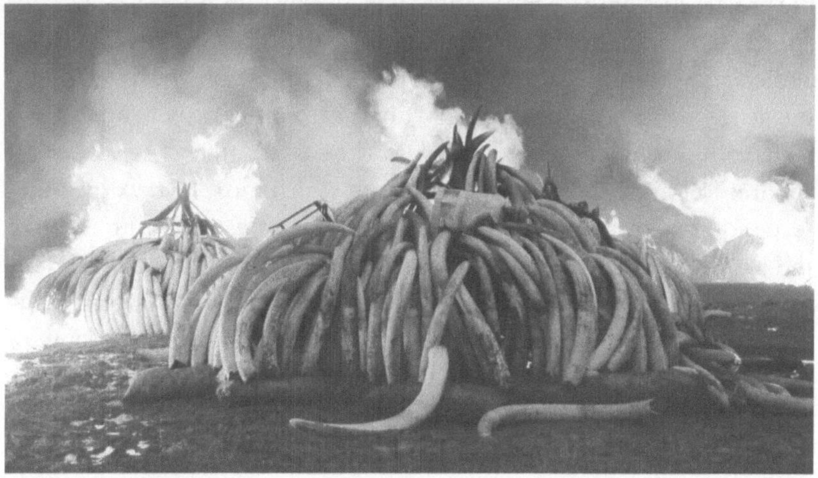

**FIGURE 5.2. Production still from *Ivory Burn*, Nairobi National Park, Kenya. Nicholas de Pencier, Producer. Photo courtesy of Anthropocene Films Inc. © 2018.**

ca's development of nuclear technology and its willingness to deploy it."[54] And while there is evidence of the distinctive social ecology of the Anthropocene—for instance, in the massive images of an "overpopulated" Nairobi—the voice of those who are part of these images is limited (about which I'll speak in a moment), and there is no indication of the causal connections between the economic and societal factors underlying them, or of the sense that there may be alternatives available. The audience for *The Anthropocene Project* is similarly a generic "first world" audience—those who (the film suggests) are indirectly responsible for the crisis—and the goal is to rouse that audience into awareness of the scope and scale of the crisis, but not into any obvious kind of action. In this, the project may be seen as a kind of necessary first step, though even that leaves open the question of whether the step is a forward step or a side-step.

## EXTENDING THE AUDIENCE FOR ANTHROPO-SEEING

Since *The Anthropocene Project's* launching, the touring exhibition has been shown at museums and galleries in Toronto and Ottawa, Canada; Bologna, Italy; Malmö and Stockholm, Sweden; Helmond, Netherlands; Buenos Aires, Argentina; and Kaohsiung City, Taiwan. The audience for the entire project is thus limited geographically, but parts of the project disseminate much more widely. The film *Anthropocene: The Human Epoch* is the major part that is likely to be seen by the widest audience around the world. It is a film that most obviously falls into the genre of the eco-documentary, and much of its cachet comes from its devotion to documenting images of the Earth today. As viewer responses to it have shown, however (about which more below), the film's reception has overlapped with that of other genres including those of the art film and fictional depictions of dystopian futures. Like Godfrey Reggio's 1982 film *Koyaanisqatsi*, for instance, which launched the genre of big-budget, nonnarrative features highlighting the beauty of the Earth and humanity's conflicted place within it, *Anthropocene* falls into a genre of visual essays depicting what can now be called the "Anthropocenic sublime." In its particular case, it depicts the workings of the techno-industrial machine, or what urban sociologist Lewis Mumford called the Megamachine, a machine that extracts, manufactures, moves, consumes, and excretes, but without ever closing the loop to render it assimilable by its environment. It depicts this as a sublime object, a toxic and industrial sublime, but also an anthropic sublime, with scenes that remind one of fictional films such as *Blade Runner* (the oil refineries in Los Angeles) and the massive earth-moving machines from Hayao Miyazaki's animations (the coal excavator in northern Germany).[55]

Despite this tendency to play into megamachinic tropes, however, the film avoids reducing humanity to the generic, insect-like mass so prevalent in Reggio's "*Qatsi* trilogy." It does this by in fact placing human labor at the center of its narrative vignettes. Practically every geographic episode in the film—from the vast mining sites in Siberia, the Ural mountains, northern Germany, and South America to a massive landfill in Nairobi and the world's longest underground tunnel in Switzerland—features an interview with a worker or two involved in these scenes of what might be called "productive destruction." Even as their work appears as a kind of indentured servitude to a massive industrial machinery, several of the workers express pride in their roles. Acting as stand-ins for us—Virgil-like guides to these infernos (to draw on the Dantesque metaphor mentioned earlier)—the film seems to suggest that humanity has been reduced here to the level of a handmaiden to technology, and that there is a certain ambivalent pride that could be taken in this role.

The film's voiceover narrative, however, complicates this. Alicia Vikander's voice, while infrequent, manages to lucidly convey the basic data points of the Anthropocene in ways reflective of the scale of the challenge humanity faces: "We now dominate over 73% of ice-free land because of mining, agriculture, industrialization and urban growth"; every year "humans extract between 60 to 100 billion tons of material from the earth and remove more sediment than all the rivers of the earth combined"; carbon monoxide levels have risen to a higher point than any time in the last 66 million years; and so on. At the film's conclusion, Vikander offers a glimmer of hope: "The Earth is 4.5 billion years old, and its history can be read in the rocks," she intones before informing us that "the tenacity and ingenuity that helped us thrive can also help us pull these systems back to a safe place for all life on Earth." Kenyan conservationist Winnie Kiiru, whose words punctuate the film's opening and closing scenes of the burning rhinoceros tusks, makes this hope, as well as its urgency, more specific: "I was not able to stop this elephant from dying," she says, "but I am certainly able to stop it from being desecrated further"—which becomes a kind of metaphor for the whole film. In the film's final scene, she concludes, "Let's kill this trade. The opposite is unimaginable."

There are risks, however, to taking the rhino tusk industry as a stand-in for all Anthropocenic industrial activity. Earlier, an armed Kenyan anti-poaching officer had said, "We are protecting wildlife, but at the same time we feel we are the enemies because we are human, and humans are the poachers." The implication is that humans are complicit in nature's demise, and that we are in fact on both sides of the problem, with an ambiguity that cannot be wished away. Moreover, the decisions driving our complicity are hardly reducible to shadowy "poachers." The economic system that drives it is much larger, more entrenched, and more politically empowered than this. And with the ambiguities surrounding the individual sites of Anthropocenic magnitude—the lithium pools of Chile's Atacama desert, needed for the electric batteries that would power humanity's renewable energy future, are no less massive than the coal, potash, or marble mines, and the Nigerian megachurch "built for a million worshippers" in which devotees sway and dance to a joyful live band suggests nothing more than ambiguity—it is not even clear whether it is scale that is the enemy, or who or what is. The cause of the Anthropocene predicament remains unnamed and faceless except as a generic Anthropos.

Some five years after its initial release, the feature film *Anthropocene: The Human Epoch* has had a limited run at festivals and first-run cinemas, won several awards (8 wins and 14 nominations according to the Internet Movie Database), and was readily available for viewing in multiple digital venues. As of May, 2023, it had an 89% positive rating (of 46 critics) at Rotten Tomatoes (62% audience score of 50+ ratings) and 71/100 score (of 7 reviews) at Metacritic; 7.2 out of 10 from over 1,900 ratings at the Internet Movie Database; and 4.4 out of 5 on Amazon (with 69% 5-star reviews out of 295 global ratings). On YouTube, the most popular site discussing the film by far was the Official U.S. Trailer site, which at the time of writing had 6,800 thumbs up, 481 thumbs down, and 807 comments.[56] I analyzed the comments on June 18, 2021, by examining all of those with 20 or more thumbs-up votes ("likes") or 10 or more follow-up comments (22 comment threads in total). Keeping in mind the culture of YouTube commenting—it is a venue dominated by opinionated, tech- and pop-culture savvy users, often with an ironic sense of humor—the comments are nevertheless revealing. (See table 5.1 for the most "liked" and most engaged comments.)

The most common types of commentary at the time of analysis fell into two categories: the first is focused on media references, with a strong tendency toward the knowingly ironic (comparisons to "alien," "horror," and "monster movies" making up nearly four-fifths of these in popularity, and references to *Koyaanisqatsi*, *The Matrix*, *Blade Runner*, Grimes's album *Misanthropocene*, etc. making up the remainder); the second could be called "human-critical environmental laments," with a subcategory of "eco-irony" (see table 5.1). While the popularity of media-referencing comments was much higher than that of environment-referencing comments (1,963 to 1,146 total likes), the engagement with the second category far exceeded that of the first (161 to 63 follow-up replies). The highest-engaging of the environmental comments involved critical discussion of the role of capitalism ("you can't eat money," which is a quote from a popular song by Aurora; and "There's no species-wide 'we' who are responsible for environmental destruction. Rather, capitalism . . . enables and necessitates destruction"). The total number of likes for the capitalist-critical comments well exceeded those for the overpopulation-critical comments. The latter echoes what can be observed on the YouTube site for the trailer announcing the film's original September 2018 premiere at the Toronto International Film Festival, where the most popular comment by far asked "why Canadian filmmakers on their search for manmade natural disasters have traveled all the way to communist countries such as China and Russia and managed to shoot in restricted areas where in their door step lays Alberta's oil sand industry." (The Alberta Tar Sands oil project is infamous among Canadian environmental and social justice activists for having decimated a vast territory of northern Alberta.)

What all of this shows is that YouTube commenters on the *Anthropocene* film trailer, while predictably media-savvy, showed a high capacity for engagement with the film's critical message about humanity, industrialism, and to a more limited extent the economic causes of the "destruction" portrayed. While there were, unsurprisingly, some trolling comments critical of the film's environmentalist message, these did not attain much popularity or engagement. (Only one received over 20 likes, though barely. Replies to trolling comments also did not show much popularity.) At the same time, however, while there was discussion of the film's cinematographic attributes, there was little engagement with issues of "what to do" in response to the complex problems depicted. Awareness, as mentioned earlier, does not easily translate into action or even awareness of what action is available. Environmental doom, as earlier analyses of eco-documentaries have shown, is much easier to grasp and to relate to than is social movement organizing and capacity-building.[57]

It is important to mention that the YouTube data does not indicate whether commenters had seen the actual film or only the trailer. This relates to another important point: that while the filmmakers' goal is to have a singular and dramatic impact on audiences, most of the public engages with images like these not by attending individual art exhibitions or even films shown in their entirety at cinemas, but by encountering them disseminated within more daily and mixed interactions with images. The audiences for *The Anthropocene Project* exhibition, film, and books are necessarily limited when compared to the audiences that receive countless images each day on their computer screens, smartphones, and other image devices. That larger audience, if and when it receives such images, encounters them amidst the continuous flow of their digital image consumption. This means that their intended effects—including those of producing or depicting "truths" about the world (a premise of the world-picture image regime)—will usually come already attenuated by the oversaturated yet participatory environment within which dwellers of the digital image-world find themselves.

In that visual and sensory ecology, images that do not provoke much reaction will tend to fade into the background. Those that do will tend to be linked with forms of sharing and community-building that draw upon existing narrative and interpretive frameworks. As can be seen in the YouTube commentary for the *Anthropocene: The Human Epoch* trailer, for YouTube viewers these frameworks typically include mediatic reference points—including fictionalized depictions of the future (horror movies, monster movies, alien movies, *Blade Runner*, *The*

*Matrix*) as well as aestheticized portrayals of human-environment relations (*Koyaanisqatsi*, Grimes's *Misanthropocene*). Frequently this shows an ironic acknowledgment of the multitude of image-relations within which the new imagery of a film like this is interpreted. This makes its imagery never quite "new," but always already an echo of what has been seen before. Recalling the response to the 9/11 imagery of planes hitting the World Trade Center, which commentators found to be resonant of Hollywood disaster movies, eco-apocalypse has already been witnessed in fictionalized Hollywood forms, and so the presentation of documentary evidence is always already redolent of what we see and know to be not only *possible* but also *entertaining*. It is after all much easier, as Fredric Jameson famously quipped, to imagine the end of the world than the end of capitalism; and when the latter is imagined, it takes forms like the *Mad Max* series, which, after all, is not capitalism's end so much as its reduction to its bare essence.[58]

In the YouTube commentary, the reference to "alien movies"—by far the most liked comment on the U.S. trailer site (with 844 likes)—resonates both with viewers' awareness of Hollywood's horror movie promotion history *and* with the eco-critical view that humanity is acting like an alien species on the Earth. The latter is evident in some of the responses to that comment, such as the much "liked" reply, "In a sense it is. We are the aliens on a planet on which we did not evolve." Such replies indicate that this comment blurs the two analytical categories of "media-referenced" and "eco-referenced" commentary. Similarly, the eco-ironic comments referencing the cinematography that "makes the earths [*sic*] destruction look incredibly beautiful" and proposing the alternative title "Humanity Was a Mistake: The Movie" both highlight the mediatic nature of the imagery in the film. This is not to suggest that viewers of *The Anthropocene Project* exhibition do not walk away from it having been impacted by what they have seen. But it is to say that the more ensconced those viewers are in the world of digital media, the more those images resonate with and amplify the mix of image-relations and sensibilities that are already there. This is a mix in which documentary reality is always already entwined with various genres of fiction (horror, environmental collapse, and so on), and in which the world-picture is never fully dissociated from the expression-image and the animate-image (horror being the ultimate form of ani-

**TABLE 5.1.** Most popular and most engaged comments on YouTube U.S. trailer site for *Anthropocene: The Human Epoch*

| Likes | Replies | Comment text |
|---|---|---|
| | | **Category 1a: Media Irony** |
| 844 | 31 | From the thumbnail, I thought it's an alien movie. |
| (50) | | • *Reply: Are you a scientologist or something?* |
| (30) | | • *Reply to reply: don't correspond with it. It'll lure you into conversion. You've been warned!* |
| 480 | 9 | I thought it was a horror movie but close enough. |
| 134 | 2 | Thought this was gonna be a monster movie. I wasn't wrong. |
| 91 | 8 | I thought it was a monster movie |
| **1549** | **50** | **Media Irony Subtotal** |
| | | **Category 1b: Media References** |
| 244 | 11 | Add some Philipp Glass music and make it a Koyanisquatsi sequel |
| 44 | 2 | "Told you so"—Agent Smith |
| 39 | 0 | That's sad . . . Alexa, play Anthropacito. |
| 37 | 0 | The year is 2019 no more need for CGI and model for Blade Runner, everything did come true |
| 29 | 0 | Great Ad for the new Grimes album! |
| 21 | 0 | Remember Smith's speech to Morpheus in the first Matrix? |
| **414** | **13** | **Media References Subtotal** |
| **1963** | **63** | **TOTAL MEDIA-REFERENCED COMMENTS** (categories 1a + 1b) |
| | | **Category 2a: Human-Critical Environmental Lament** |
| 370 | 30 | People will definitely watch it but still don't care. |
| 241 | 36 | How do you explain to a higher lifeform that you knew what you were doing was destructive, but you wouldn't stop because it was worth sacrificing the environment for a made up concept (money)? It's like we thought we could just eat the money once the earth was destroyed. |
| (32) | | • *Reply: When the last tree is cut, the last fish is caught, and the last river is polluted; when to breathe the air is sickening, you will realize, too late, that wealth is not in bank accounts and that you can't eat money.* |

| Likes | Replies | Comment text |
|---|---|---|
| (25) | | • *Reply: Destructivity isn't a function of some sort of collective human agency. Obviously people are aware that they can't eat money, and the majority of people in the world would, if properly informed, support aggressively green policies; so why are you blaming what must be a political problem on humanity as a whole? There's no species-wide "we" who are responsible for environmental destruction. Rather, capitalism, a system which concentrates power into the hands of a wealthy few, enables and necessitates destruction; the culpable party here isn't humanity per se but the ruling class, the 1%, who call most of the economic shots in the world. Our responsibility, as the ruled class, is to undermine or dismantle that system in order to reclaim power and to protect the environment.* |
| 61 | 6 | The planet will never die, but we will . . . |
| 60 | 16 | We will destroy this planet unless we change. Period. |
| 40 | 1 | Slated to be the shortest geologic epoch of them all . . . |
| 22 | 4 | "Everything that has a beginning has an end." We are too many! |
| 7 | 15 | We deserve whatever punishment nature gives us. |
| 11 | 10 | I still don't understand how there isn't any serious talk about controlling human population. |
| 4 | 13 | Think of the countless atrocities we would have been spared had the human race never existed. |
| **816** | **131** | **Human-Critical Environmental Lament Subtotal** |
| | | **Category 2b: Eco-Irony** |
| 246 | 25 | great cinematography, really makes the earths destruction look incredibly beautiful |
| 84 | 5 | Humanity Was a Mistake: The Movie |
| **330** | **30** | **Eco-Irony Subtotal** |
| **1146** | **161** | **TOTAL ECO-REFERENCED COMMENTS (categories 2a + 2b)** |
| | | **Category 3: Anti-Environmental Cynicism** |
| 21 | 7 | I love it when people try to financially capitalize on ecological issues. What are the odds that they take private jets to all of the press junket events? Do as I say, not as I do. . . . |

matedly affecting imagery). Images providing "evidence" of humanity's "flawed" relationship with the Earth are thus difficult to dissociate from images of science fiction dystopias, monstrous sublimes, and other long-trodden visual media tropes.

The task of communicating the Anthropocene predicament, and of doing it in ways that enable cultural and ecological change, is therefore a task that is imbricated in, and complicated by, the multiple image ecologies already circulating in the world. As far back as 1992, Andrew Ross characterized "images of ecology" as coming in two predominant valences: "On the one hand, belching smokestacks, seabirds mired in petrochemical sludge, fish floating belly up, traffic jams in Los Angeles and Mexico City, and clearcut forests; on the other hand, the redemptive repertoire of pastoral imagery, crowned by the ultimate global spectacle, the fragile, vulnerable ball of spaceship earth."[59] These images come to take on an ideality of "good" and "bad" ecology, with the question for environmental artists and activists being how to display them in novel and surprising ways. To the extent that scientific images, which attempt to portray measurable "truths" about the world, are always technico-aesthetic constructs, they risk falling into the gap that separates the world-picture regime from the ideal-image regime. For instance, when global climate maps depict rising surface air temperatures in red colors, they take indexically arrived at "facts"—mean temperature statistics—and apply emotionally impactful aesthetic decisions to them. As Birgit Schneider has argued, this turns them into "cosmograms," schematic pictures presenting a cosmology in which humanity is moving inexorably toward a "burning world."[60]

*The Anthropocene Project* exemplifies the power, but also the limitations, of the documentary, evidentiary mode of the world-picture regime. In its compilation and presentation of images documenting crisis points of a world that is, at least metaphorically, on fire, it is intended to display the truth of a world that can only be communicated through scientific and empirical research and the evidential communication that results from it. This has been by far the dominant mode of presenting environmental "bad news" to the public within mainstream media.

Where Burtynsky's imagery consist of photographic documents of the Anthropocene, others present even more direct forms of indexical evidence. Olafur Eliasson's twelve blocks of glacial ice (weighing over 90 tons), found broken off Greenland's Nuuk Fjord and brought into a circular arrangement to melt outside Paris's Place de Panthéon during the COP21 UN Climate Summit of 2015, were exactly this: an *index* of climate change that, by standing in for glaciers melting around the globe, became symbolic, indexical, and iconic all at once. Eliasson's piece elicited a wide public response not only because he is an internationally recognized artist, but also because of this surprising mixture: this was evidence brought from the "crime scene" (off the coast of Greenland) to the "court" where the scene was being judged (the climate summit), in a way that was topical, timely—even demanding rapid acknowledgment as the ice melted—and visually arresting. But it, too, showed only an effect of the changing climate, not its causes.

The rise of the climate justice movement is an indication that the causes are not escaping scrutiny. Calls for climate justice make clear

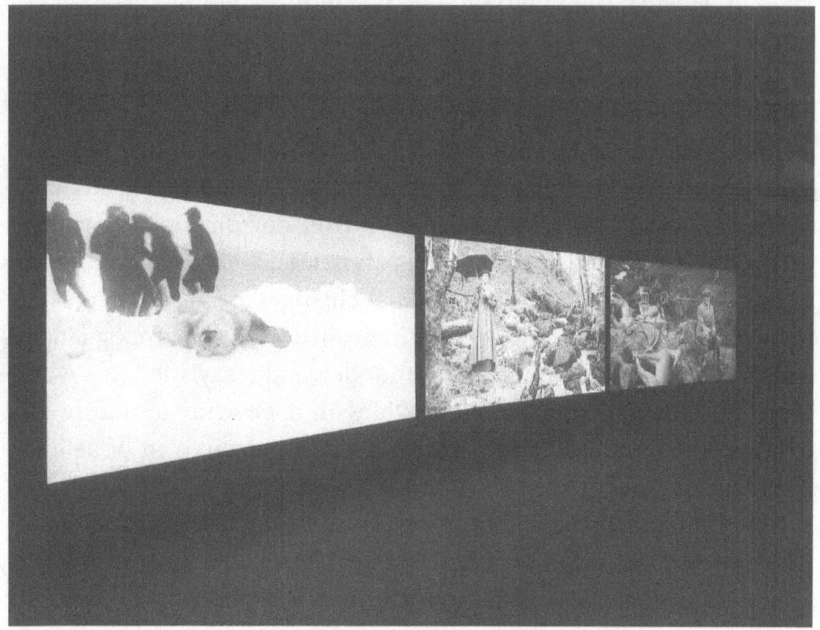

**FIGURE 5.3. John Akomfrah, *Vertigo Sea*, 2015, view of the installation. Three-channel HD color video installation, 7.1 sound, 48 minutes 30 seconds *(AKOM150001)*. © Smoking Dogs Films; Courtesy Smoking Dogs Films and Lisson Gallery.**

that there is perceived injustice. Other slogans of the movement—"System change, not climate change," "Planet over profit," "Divest now," "Corporate greed is destroying the planet," "People power not corporate power"—similarly point to the gap between political-economic power and grassroots interests. It is the link between images and activism that prevents the images from getting lost in the din of an already oversaturated image-world.[61] In the next section, I examine the work of an artist whose interest in climate change and environmental issues emerged from a much longer engagement with the politics of race and the global history of colonialism. It is the montage-like mix of these topics that makes John Akomfrah's work a suitable counterpoint of analysis as an instance of a "counter-Anthropocene."

## ANTHROPOCENE DISSEMBLED AND DISCORRELATED: AKOMFRAH'S MONTAGE-IMAGE

Just as there are images of ecology that have become overused to the point of banality, the same could be said of images of race, coloniality, or working class struggle. Filmmakers who have sought to avoid cliché in addressing politics have found the strategy of essayistic montage to be particularly attractive. Nonfiction film has undergone something of a renaissance in the last few decades as documentarists have deployed creative and hybrid strategies of representation including reenactment, reflexivity, essayistic first-person narrative, docufiction, digital animation, and various defamiliarizing strategies, even as they continue to draw on the power of observational cinema's lens-based capture of the world.[62] There is a long and distinguished tradition among cinema artists of creating polyphonic, multimodal, and essayistic films whose visual and textual composition provides an open array of interpretive options. The term "essayistic" suggests a first-person form of delivery, wherein an actual or implied narrator presents a set of facts and visual evidence documenting an argument. In some documentarians' hands (Michael Moore comes to mind), this has taken the form of a quasi-legal case being made, which can sometimes be entertaining (especially if you agree with the filmmaker), but is almost always polemical. In others' hands, however, essayistic cinema makes use of videographic experimentation—including formal hybridity, visual metaphor, and juxtaposition of voices and perspectives—to challenge viewers not only to think critically about a given topic, but even to question the possibility of film offering answers on it.[63] It is this tradition of openly experimental and self-reflexive "essay film" that offers an apt conjuncture from which to consider the image-world of the "Anthroposcene." The space between filmmaking and video installation art has become an especially active crossroads in recent years. Well known filmmakers like Jean-Luc Godard, Chris Marker, Chantal Akerman, and Harun Farocki have made works intended for multiscreen environments, at the same time as multimedia artists have come to deploy filmmaking techniques, both traditional and digital, in novel ways. A list of artists populating this field of what has been called "post expanded cinema" could include Bill Viola, Bruce Nauman, Isaac Julien, Steve McQueen, Ben Rivers, Yang Fudong, Richard Mosse, Shirin Neshat, Amar Kanwar, Hito Steyerl, Eija-Liisa Ahtila, Kutluğ Ataman, Omer Fast, Lucien Castaing-Taylor, Véréna Paravel, and Angela Melitopoulos.[64]

Among the better known experimental film artists who have approached climate change and the Anthropocene in their recent work, the work of Ghanaian-born British artist John Akomfrah is particularly innovative and interesting. Cofounder in the early 1980s of the Black Audio Film Collective, Akomfrah has gone on to win international accolades for a series of experimental multichannel film works shown primarily in art galleries rather than in film theatres or online formats. Akomfrah's persistent thematic obsession throughout his oeuvre of film, video, and multimedia works is that of migration, movement, displacement, and the cultural memories carried, elicited, unleashed, and rendered possible through that displacement. While the African diasporic experience looms large within this oeuvre, Akomfrah's more recent works take on global contours within which Blackness is a figure against the larger historical canvas of industrial modernity, colonialism, and global cultural and ecological change.

Akomfrah's approach to images is distinctly different from that of *The Anthropocene Project*. Where the latter aimed for a documentary-evidential world-picture, a collection of datagraphic images representing the present at its most compelling scalar magnitude—the Anthropocene as a time of Earth transformation so massive as to attain sublime proportions—Akomfrah digs into the *past* by working with existing image archives—materials produced for various purposes, from historical newsreels and nature documentaries to commercial films and experimental media. He repurposes these images and effectively sets them into motion by historicizing them, counterposing them against each other, and thereby "animating" them for the synthetic thinking of viewers. As a result of their being incorporated into creative arrays of images with multiple origins, their indexicality—their original filming locations, techniques, justifications, relationships with actors or subjects, and so on—can no longer be taken for granted, but rather becomes open to viewers' interpretation. Insofar as Akomfrah's recent films are about the Anthropocene, they are about its historical shaping through multiple, complex, and politically, economically, and ideologically laden currents. Images, for Akomfrah, are not purely evidentiary; instead, they are a way to move from an "is" to a "could be." As Asbjørn Grønstad puts it, for Akomfrah "the cultural archive is neither a static nor transparent compilation of artefacts but an epistemic resource that may be galvanized aesthetically to envision a different future."[65] Akomfrah calls this an "embrace" of the archival material in order to "observe it forensically," in all its "ambiguity in ambitions and intentions," and "to work with it in order to be able to use it in different ways."[66] In interviews he notes the "Janus-faced" and "Proustian possibilities" of the moving image archive, wherein each image "says 'I existed at one point and it's possible that I could exist differently.'" For Akomfrah, it is the philosophy of montage that "allows the possibility of reengagement" with images that serve, on one side, as an open repository of memory, and on the other as images to be worked with today.[67]

Akomfrah's method is synthetic and transversal, with multiple image archives and traditions—effectively, multiple image-regimes—set loose within an intertextual and nonlinear profusion of visual, auditory, musical, and other elements. There is an openness in the result, which requires the viewer to create their own meaning. This can be confusing or frustrating. One commenter, for instance, argues that Akomfrah's montage in his later works "seems merely to accumulate the images, rather than synthesizing them or showing their incommensurability."[68] But this is only so if the viewer is expecting Akomfrah to synthesize them for us, which he refuses to do. Instead, Akomfrah infuses archival and found footage with the capacity to haunt us with its afterlives; this is a use of the past that brings out its ambiguities so as to make them available for a "politics of becoming."[69] As Anthony Downey puts it in a discussion of Akomfrah's ambitious six-channel film *Purple*, the film's multichannel format "enables a decentralization of any singular agency and multiples it, pluralises it, to the extent that the notion of sovereignty itself is what is being broken down: the sovereignty of a singular historical narrative, the sovereignty of a singular subject, and it's being visually and conceptually decentralized."[70]

In their impact, Akomfrah's films *Vertigo Sea* (2015) and *Purple* (2017), in Ian Bourland's words, "offer a complex genealogy of the present" in their visualization and enactment of "a form of multisensory historical essay."[71] *Vertigo Sea* is a 48-minute long, three-channel, high-definition color video installation that premiered at the 2015 Venice Biennale. The work subjects footage from BBC's Natural History Unit, makers of documentaries including *The Blue Planet* (2001), *Planet Earth* (2006), and *Frozen Planet* (2011), to what Jakob Nilsson calls a "semi-repurposing" which doesn't deconstruct or critically negate the originals so much as it "re-imagines" them by recontextualizing them within broader frames of reference.[72] The latter include narratives of colonial travel, the Middle Passage of transatlantic slavery, international shipping, and images of industrial resource extraction including whaling, fishing, and hunting, alongside documentary fragments about today's Mediterranean migrants, some of whom drown while others survive. Among the historical survivors is a key figure, Olaudah Equiano (1745–1797), an Igbo (West African) man enslaved as a boy, who purchased his own freedom at age 21 and became an Arctic explorer and author, and whose autobiography influenced the abolitionist movement that ended the transatlantic slave trade in Britain. This influence was achieved, in part, through Equiano's publicizing of the Zong massacre, depicted in reenacted form in *Vertigo Sea,* in which 133 captives were thrown overboard to satisfy an insurance scheme plotted by their slave traders. Equiano is depicted in *Vertigo Sea,* in several static shots punctuating the film's movement, dressed in period attire looking away, outward to the ocean, pensively as in a romantic painting. His presence adds a sense of witnessing to the historical footage depicted, even as it suggests alternative renderings of the very victims of the slave trade, which runs as an undercurrent through the film's presentation of oceanic history.

Two characteristics are most striking about Akomfrah's cinematic strategy in *Vertigo Sea*. The first is his use of nonlinear and multilayered juxtapositions: this includes juxtapositions between the three screens, and between the images and the soundtrack, but also within the elements of staged scenes (for instance, in the historically referenced tableaux that evoke the work of nineteenth-century artists like Caspar David Friedrich, whilst containing anachronistic elements such as clocks and other flotsam), within the soundtrack (which mixes spoken texts of various kinds—literary-fictional as well as documentary accounts—with instrumental music and atmospheric sounds), and within the film's multiple temporal and spatial reference points. There is constant movement within and between the three screens, with directions, speeds, angles, and momentum also juxtaposed against each other. Movement within the images may feature objects or animals moving leftward, rightward, upward, downward, or in circular or rolling, wavelike motion; speeds of movement include fast and slow as well as sped up and slowed down motion; camera movements include a multiplicity of traveling and tracking shots, revolving camera movements, slow zooms inward and outward; juxtapositions of closeness (in close-up shots) and distance (in wide angle shots); different relationships between the elements of land, air, and water, including underwater shots looking to the ocean's surface, from over the surface looking down, forward motion underwater, and movements toward or away from the surface; and so on. Historical footage, frequently black-and-white, is juxtaposed against historical reenactments, seemingly ahistorical images (of "nature," often sped up or slowed down), and strangely surreal tableaux featuring clocks, historical artifacts, and geological reference points, with the latter, alongside the recurrent sound of a ticking clock, evoking a sense of the multiplicity of time and its measurable attributes. Images, movements, and references echo and reinforce each other even as they set up cross-currents of meanings and interpretations.

All of this contrapuntal movement contributes to the film's second strategy, which is its immersiveness. In this, *Vertigo Sea* evokes a kind of nineteenth-century sublime aesthetic whilst adding elements that counteract it. The use of multiple screens frustrates the viewer's effort to follow a single narrative, such that the images and sounds combine to form a densely unfolding image-soundscape within which one "swims" rather than merely watches or follows (a metaphor I applied, in chapter 2, to active users of digital media). The impact is "oceanic" in the sense that it envelops the viewer within an always somewhat opaque and underdetermined "sea" of images, sounds, texts, and historical reference points, with the beauty of individual shots—of the ocean or nature writ large—thickened by references to histories of racism, slavery, colonialism, and the capitalist extraction of ocean resources, alongside historical counterexamples such as that of Aquiano. There is, in Seph Rodney's words, "too much sea [. . .] too much predacious elegance [. . .] too much gratuitous death," such that the work reminds us "that this world does not belong to me. I belong to it."[73] As another reviewer describes the piece, "Panoramas of crashing waves fill the screen, tidal surges with flocking birds, shoals of fish spiralling upwards in panic, hunted from below by wide-eyed seals. Coiled eels dig into the rotting flesh of drowned whales, grainy black-and-white footage depicts a polar bear being hounded and shot in front of her cubs, all interlaced with footage of slaves being thrown into the Atlantic."[74]

The result is that the viewer is invited to submit to the images: their flow overwhelms our ability to seek narrative connections, instead finding resonances that deepen and cross-signify as the work proceeds. We see the beauty of the sea, and of the world, and its vertiginous circularity and ultimate unencompassability; the pain and the suffering that humans inflict upon it and upon each other, and that the world itself inflicts upon its participants. We see recognizable and sometimes opaque historical references, documentary images of migrants drowning or being rescued from the sea, and scenes of nature at its most untamed. There are storms and shipwrecks, atomic bomb tests, and industrial fishing scenes; whales swimming freely, and whales being hunted by harpoon and harvested in blood-red water; stranded marine animals, and beached artifacts. None of these images come in their own protected space; all flow into each other. In result, the sea is not just sea, but is trade, space, hope and opportunity for some, and imprisonment and death for others. It is repository and archive, ceaseless source of life and swirling attractor of death, beauty suffused with suffering and historical trauma.

If the images come side by side on the three screens, their rhythm is an unpredictable flow. So are the fluid, gradually shifting sonic references—suspended, atmospheric tonal layers overlaid by diegetic sounds and punctuated by short wave radio-like collage elements, and the polyphonic selection of texts that sometimes accompany them, some of them fictional or literary (as with excerpts from Melville's *Moby-Dick*, Virginia Woolf's *To the Lighthouse*, and Heathcote Williams's epic poem *Whale Nation*), others philosophical or documentary testimonies, that make up the soundtrack. All of this is presented as a continual, never resting flow, as if it were life itself flowing, with individual images becoming lost in time as they pass, "like tears in rain" as the replicant Roy Batty put it in Ridley Scott's *Blade Runner. Vertigo Sea* is a moving image of *the* moving image of the world, in all its beauty, terror, human inflicted pain, hope for betterment, and ultimate fleetingness. If it calls to mind the beauty of nature, it does so only to always link it to the history of slavery and colonialism. If it calls to mind the tragedy of migrants, lost and drowning at sea as they are rejected by wealthy European states, it does this whilst reminding us of our own eventual death to come. The work is indexical, iconic, and symbolic all at once. It is spectacular (in the Peircian sense of an unceasing firstness of audiovisual display) and full only of narrative fragments, not of any overarching singular narrative except for the one we may, or may not, piece together from it in our effort to place ourselves into its flow. It is thereby open to interpretation upon interpretation. But the interpretations that suggest themselves are *of* the world we know, which is a world of beauty and of distress, of joy and of injustice, a world where each of these impulses calls to the others without offering any resolution, or indeed any protection.

Jakob Nilsson writes that Akomfrah's cinema no longer presents "a Rational World Picture with beauty and some images of terror added to it, but a complex terror/beauty mixture on all levels," including those of human society, technology, and nature beyond the human.[75] This is all enabled by Akomfrah's philosophy of montage, which, in his own words, elicits "unconscious relations" and "uncanny" affinities "between the subject and historical forces."[76] If earlier cinematic theorists like Sergei Eisenstein and Lev Kuleshov considered montage a tool of the filmmaker whereby disparate shots were combined strategically to create synthetic and predictable effects, Akomfrah's montage is much more open-ended. With its multichannel format, it arguably turns cinema from a linear, time-bound, and sequential art form—characterized by the serial passage from one image or shot to the next—into something that is layered, cross-sectional, and in effect three-dimensional, something that for the first time *frees* montage into its full potential as an open multiplicity of relations, multiple and "heterochronic" in its temporalities. If montage, as filmmaker and theorist Alexander Kluge put it, is the "morphology of relations" that "has as its object something qualitatively quite different" from the "raw material" of the shots it brings together, then montage in Akomfrah's hands aims to open the viewer up to a boundless relay of potential connections across history, geography, and affectivity that its individual images enable in their flowing display across multiple screens.[77] It becomes a form of cinematic animate-image that, far from merely representing the vision of an individual auteur, opens us up to the feeling and flow of the world itself, a world that is layered, dynamic, uncertain, and challenging. (I will come back to this idea of the "flow of the world" in chapter 7.) To indicate the way in which this format enables a coming-to-fruition of cinematic montage, I will call this the *montage-image*.

In a book-length study of Akomfrah's work, James Harvey refers to the "more ecological conception of montage" especially present in his later works, "whereby images and themes endlessly intermingle in restless and spontaneous ways."[78] Guided more by poetic or metonymic association than by instrumental goals, its "ultimate effect is to produce a sense of the interconnectedness of all things and beings as a kind of ambient poetics."[79] If this sounds too unfocused, too "ambient," Anuradha Vikram insists that, for Akomfrah, montage is a revolutionary technique:

> In *Vertigo Sea*, the ocean's power to cajole or terrorize is poetically linked to that of Empire, and the sublime aesthetics of romanticism are put to dramatic effect in the service of that narrative. Simultaneous views of the sea, shown from above and below, across the work's three channels, reinforce the idea that human bodies and those of other mammals, such as whales, seals, and polar bears, are contiguous. The ocean appears as a political and economic space as well as an environmental one, traversed by colonial ships that carry African captives to enslavement, by whal-

> ing ships that strip the sea of life, and by cargo ships powered by fossil fuels that massively deplete the planet's resources. A Black British aesthetic emerges: one that visualizes the earth with the magnitude and sweep of Empire, but absent its callousness, infused instead with concern and compassion for the victimized and exploited. Dark and foreboding images of ships' holds, dismembered creatures, and fragmenting polar sea ice intermingle with effervescent flocks of white birds and hopeful rays of sunlight peeking through storm-wracked sea plants.[80]

All of this is in deep resonance with the work of decolonial theorists like Christina Sharpe, whose *In the Wake: On Blackness and Being* takes the multiple meanings of the word "wake" as a starting point for a philosophy of history in the midst of ongoing Anthropocenic apocalypse. Sharpe writes:

> Wakes are processes; through them we think about the dead and about our relations to them; they are rituals through which to enact grief and memory. Wakes allow those among the living to mourn the passing of the dead through ritual; they are the watching of relatives and friends beside the body of the deceased from death to burial and the accompanying drinking, feasting, and other observances, a watching practiced as a religious observance. But wakes are also "the track left on the water's surface by a ship [. . .]; the disturbance caused by a body swimming, or one that is moved, in water; the air currents behind a body in flight; a region of disturbed flow; in the line of sight of (an observed object); and (something) in the line of recoil of (a gun)"; finally, wake means being awake and, also, consciousness.[81]

Unlike Burtynsky and his colleagues, for whom the Anthropocene marks the culmination of something species-wide, with responsibility for its impacts left unspecified, Akomfrah's layered perception of the Anthropocene takes for granted this "wake work," a kind of living in the wake of ongoing catastrophe. Its analysis, in Akomfrah's reading, requires unpacking the archive of what we know and have seen—the cultural debris that has accompanied the last five hundred years—and reentering it from angles of vision marked by the racial and cultural differences that underlie this history, so as to elicit a more polyphonic profusion of insights and responsibilities. The vertigo of *Vertigo Sea*, as T. J. Demos argues, comes from the loss of "bearings—referentially, philosophically, perceptually" as we confront the "disaster that continues to unfold" between the histories of slavery and colonialism and today's sea level–raising climate change. By, at the same time, showing the "unparalleled splendour of aquatic nature," Akomfrah, Demos argues, is courageously "refusing contemporary cynicism" and recognizing that beauty is part of the world that is at stake in our relationship to systems of exploitation that have benefited some at the expense of others.[82]

## THE OCEAN OF *PURPLE*

With the 2017 installation *Purple*, three oversized screens become six massive ones positioned lengthwise in a gentle arc toward the viewer, creating an arguably even more immersive flow of images. Curatorial notes inform us that purple is the color of mourning in Ghana, Akomfrah's country of origin, and it is the color of floor and wall carpeting (with dirty plastic containers hanging from the ceiling) that greets us as we walk through a tunnel-like corridor to get to the screening space, and its rich, deep hue surrounds us as we watch. (This is in part what makes *Purple* a gallery work rather than anything that could be viewed on six television monitors.) Akomfrah himself has spoken of the title as an homage to Prince's song "Purple Rain," with its "idea of the space of elegy and regret," and of purple as an "inter-zone colour."[83] Purple is the combination of blue, a warm color but also the color of "the blues," and red, which is both lively and the color of blood, of heat, and of alarm (as climate scientists recognize with their global heat maps).[84] The allusive title of the 62-minute work, with its suggestion of an emotional hue within which to contemplate the images as they unfold in front of us, is in fact as close as Akomfrah gets to didacticism (which is to say, not at all). Occasional intertitles are similarly poetic: "The Gift of the Deep Water" (in the birth-themed first movement), "O Earth What Changes Hast Thou Seen!," "Into the Petrified Waters," "The Toxic Body and a Story of Love," "The Winter of Our Discontents," "The Liquid Spirit of Things," "Unforgiving Waters and the Vengeful Memory," "The Alien in the Body" (with its reference to coal miners' black lung disease), and the final movement's "The Vitality of Things." The recurrence of water references connects this piece to *Vertigo Sea*, but also to the very idea of a connective flow between lives past and lives yet to be lived. Montage, in this piece, is not a matter of images generating meanings through their chronological sequencing, but of a set of multilayered flows that connect, echo, reflect, refract, overlap, and interrogate each other, generating allusions and lyrical juxtapositions in a kind of fugal counterpoint.[85]

If one could distinguish a primary juxtaposition in *Purple*, it is between a world in living motion and the still witnessing of it. Motion comes in many forms: there are documentary and archival images going back decades, with a preponderance of black-and-white BBC newsreel footage of coal miners and other working-class communities from the 1950s and 1960s. Much of the imagery reflects the Industrial Revolution and mid-twentieth century datings of the beginning of the Anthropocene: from coal mining and its lung-damaged victims, to nuclear bomb tests and their measurable aftermath, with oil spills, reports of acid rain, smokestacks, hydroelectric towers, and other impacts of industrial activity, alongside images of storms, floods, and the people caught up in them. Judgment for these is reserved as we are provided documentary footage of their justifications: "Alaska will be utopia," a politician intones as bidding for the state's oil stocks begins at the outset of Alaska's entry into oil production, and an English woman declines to respond, when asked by an interviewer whether she could do without laundry detergent. There are moving landscapes—train images, toy trains, automobile test crashes, pesticides being sprayed, farm animals cavorting, dog sleds, bird migrations, and so on—but also footage of dancers in studios and in ballrooms, schoolchildren playing, images of leisure activities, and audio and video recordings of Welsh or Gaelic singers, all of which both comment on and exemplify the movement shown elsewhere. There is repurposed and recontextualized newsreel and movie footage: people being born, walking and cycling, working in factories, going off to war and returning, grooming themselves, dreaming and (in one case) being hypnotized, dying and attending funerals, all woven into a loose arc from birth to death through the film's five "movements" and epilogue. The living human past is recontextualized within a global array of images from around the world: these include images of relatively wild landscapes in Alaska, Greenland, Tahiti, the Marquesas islands, and the Scottish Isle of Skye, that present a certain timelessness under pressure from Anthropocenic activities, but also images that remind us of the political configurations of the late industrial world (including documentary clips of leaders of the Global South's Non-Aligned Movement such as India's Jawaharlal Nehru, Egypt's Gamal Abdul Nasser, Ghana's Kwame Nkrumah, and Yugoslavia's Josip Broz Tito). Nature imagery aside, industrial activity is in this sense both humanized—in Akomfrah's depiction of human lives lived within its contours, for good and for ill—and contextualized in its political-economic conditions.

And throughout there are still figures—looking at the world (seen from their back), looking at us, and looking to the side in seeming contemplation. Where traditional documentary footage shows us the world in motion, Akomfrah shows us not only that world, in multiple simultaneous rhythms of its motion, but the gaze by which that world is seen. His regularly repeated images of a lone figure looking out at the world—a *rückenfigur*, or "figure from the back" as it was known in the context of German Romantic landscape painting—is intended to place us alongside this witnessing figure. In an interview with Ekow Eshun, who calls this still human figure a "bridging point for ellipses across time," Akomfrah acknowledges that this figure is "the quintessential romantic subject, made most famous by the German painter Caspar David Friedrich," and that his importance, for Akomfrah, lies in its representing the Romanticist "project that said that Man—with a capital 'M'—had the ability to access the world in the absence of The Almighty." Akomfrah expands the figure of "Man" from Friedrich's lone white "mastering gaze" to a historically situated, often (though not always) Black person (though most often still male), and expands what is seen through cinematic montage, but the effect is intended to be connective: when we face the thing being viewed with this figure, Akomfrah says, "we do it together."[86] In *Purple*, we are offered images of contemplation alongside images of what is being contemplated: some are still, but most are in motion, weaving their rhythms around us as they do in life itself.

A third, repeated element is that of photographs of people and events being washed over by water. The flow of images here is supplemented by the flow of water over the imaged lives captured in photographs, setting up a Deleuzian juxtaposition of forking, intersected temporalities: there is the lived present, captured as an image of motion; lived pasts, captured as still images, audio documents, old movie footage; the flow of time (depicted as water) washing over them; and the still moment of witnessing amidst it all. In the space of contemplation set up by the video, we see something like T. S. Eliot's "Time present and time past [. . .] both perhaps present in time future, And time future contained in time past. If all time is eternally present All time is unredeemable."[87] Finally, the ceaseless flow of the images is supplemented by an enveloping, constantly shifting soundscape. The soundtrack, scored by Akomfrah collaborator Tandis Jenhudson, consists of a smoothly shaped movement of diegetic sounds, from rainfall and church bells to train whistles, car honks, and industrial machinery; music, from recognizable melodies to sonic washes, contemplative chordal sequences, and Philip Glass–like rhythmic progressions; and a variety of voices and archival audio recordings of interviews, speeches, and the like, together making up a kind of thought-space of Anthropocenic humanity.

This thought-space is one that deserves further consideration. We began this examination of the Anthropocene by looking at the work of geologists, who seek indexical evidence—"Earth indices," to use Giulia Bruno's and Armin Linke's felicitous term—of the shift from a deep past to a notably altered present. They do this by digging into the earth and comparing their findings across locations; the story they tell of a changed Earth is cumulative, made up of the many points of evidence collated, compared, and analyzed. We then examined the ways in which the artists of *The Anthropocene Project* have similarly sought evidence across the earth's surface, but of a different nature—powerful images that would tell the tale directly: of massive human transformation of the landscape, repeated over and over and over again. The strategy is similarly cumulative and comparative: here is what we, humans, have done to the Earth, and it is this situation—the Anthropocene—that it has given us today.

It is notable that Akomfrah's strategy focuses less on the earth than on the water that covers more than half of its surface, and I wish to suggest that there may be a lesson in this elemental choice. Where with the earth we start, seemingly, from the stability of a place—of rock, soil, and the ground into which we burrow to find deep foundations—with water our bodies find no such foundation at all. The ocean is all ceaseless movement and boundless mystery. Burtynsky and other land-focused eco-documentarians tend to present ecological change as historically unilinear, pressed upon the world through the narrative arc of a human species-wide industrialization. In many respects, Akomfrah's work is not that different from Burtynsky's in presenting what Jakob Nilsson calls a "complex terror/beauty mixture on all levels."[88] But the width and depth of the angle of vision mark it as different: where Burtynsky focuses on the results of the Anthropocenic project, Akomfrah includes an array of connective relays—between colonialism, slavery, racism, industrialism, and the feedback of the world itself, with its climate-changing impacts on human communities. Since the connections between these are neither direct nor transparent, but rather are layered and multidirectional, Akomfrah's method is layered, multidirectional, and contrapuntal. Its strategy of layered montage places images that are commonly seen as unrelated in relation to each other to generate an associative synthesis of meaning. And where other collage films—one thinks of the genre of experimental "global travelogue" documentaries initiated by Godfrey Reggio's *Koyaanisqatsi* (1982), which includes other films by Reggio (*Powaqqatsi,* 1988; *Naqoyqatsi,* 2002) and his original cinematographer Ron Fricke (*Baraka,* 1992; *Samsara,* 2011)—subject their imagery to narratives suggesting a fall of humanity from "good" traditional and Indigenous cultures to the industrial Anthropocene with its jarringly inhuman technological speeds and scales, Akomfrah equally avoids such simplistic dichotomies. Instead, we are presented with a world of ambiguous complexities, within which a sense of horror is mixed with a sense of responsibility and resolute self-recognition. This is us and our world, *Purple* seems to say, and the first step toward taking responsibility for it is to allow ourselves to *feel* it. And in that feeling of it, the watery world overflows the banks that would contain it.

Akomfrah leaves a large part of the sense-making to viewers, which can enrich their experiences even as it results in a slipperiness and uncontainability that is "oceanic" in its sensibility. (I will return to this oceanic elementality in chapter 7.) Where Anthropocene scientists *and* visual artists like Burtynsky both focus on the stratified and measurable transformation of land, then, Akomfrah offers a more immersive and "tidal" recognition of historical connections, a perspective shared by other artists of the Black Atlantic. That even Akomfrah's static *rückenfigur* gazes out at the ever changing ocean, an ocean that brings what is neither linear nor measurable nor stratifiable, is significant.

A related difference is in the nature of the seeing itself. For Burtynsky, we, the seers, remain mostly on the outside of what is shown; for Akomfrah, we are invited in, to witness along with the shown witnesses. In this sense, however, while Akomfrah works with a relationally expanded conception of the Anthropocene, it is arguably still an *Anthropo*cene, with the figure of the observing human Anthropos, like the *rückenfigur* he repeatedly employs, remaining central. Akomfrah describes his intention with *Purple* as "clear[ing] the stage" so that there is no longer "a central sovereign subject" nor "climate change as such," but an invitation to "all the actors and then mediating between them through the elemental, vital components that you see in the film—the wind, the rain, the snow, the air we breathe—and those very things that animate the stage of being."[89] That said, the presence of the human subject, depicted as an observing witness, is evident in the film in ways that other-than-human witnesses are not.[90]

The next two chapters propose to build upon this foundation of a "complicated Anthroposcene" in order to suggest some means by which the subjectivity of the others-to-the-Anthropos might also be included: in chapter 6 these will be nonhuman animals, and in chapter 7 non- or transhumans of a more elusive nature. In doing this, we will also interrogate the seeing itself by raising questions about how seeing today is not only a seeing *of*, but a seeing *with*, a seeing *through*, and a seeing *as*. This will allow us to move beyond the world of the exhibited image, and especially that exhibited in galleries, with the elite audiences they tend to cater to. *Purple,* for instance, to date has shown in London, Madrid, Umeå (Sweden), Lisbon, Boston, Moscow, Paris, Kleve (Germany), Miami, and Washington. The exhibitionary requirements of these multichannel works make them much less mobile, but they can also lend a certain site-specificity. For instance, in the case of *Vertigo Sea*'s initial exhibition at the Venice Biennale, the work operated, as James Harvey puts it, "on several intersecting planes of reality, including the transnational and transhistorical subject of the profilmic space; the three-dimensional montage of the spectator's viewing; the communality and interactivity of the museum; and the city outside [Venice] as a space for asylum," with its long maritime history of commercial as well as imperial connections.[91] This site-specificity is arguably lost when the exhibition moves to another city (which Harvey acknowledges), though it might also find new specificities as it moves.

Its availability nevertheless remains limited to a site that can exhibit a work on such a scale. At least with today's technology, it will never quite make it "at scale" to the internet. What difference this makes will become evident in the next chapter, which delves head first into the exhibitionary potentials of the internet's most widely used site for sharing and watching videos (a veritable sea of images): YouTube.

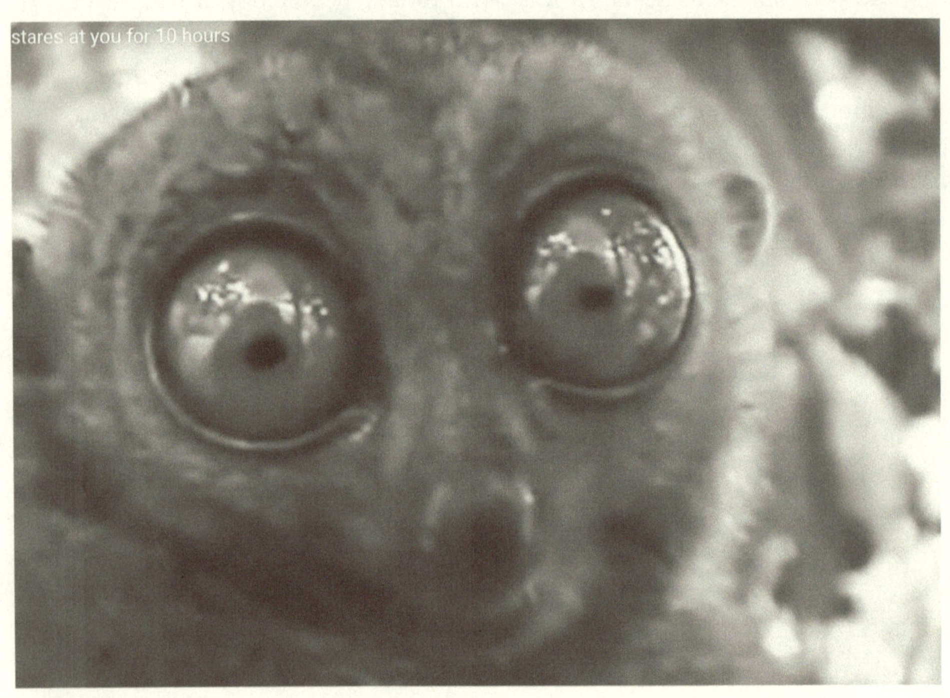


**FIGURE 6.1.** Screenshot from "Dramatic Tarsier Stares at You for 10 Hours," e7magic, YouTube, 2012.

Six

# THERIOSCENE

*Everywhere animals disappear.*

—JOHN BERGER, *"Why Look at Animals,"* 1977[1]

*Today nearly fifty thousand wild, largely migratory animals are equipped with GPS units that transmit a constant stream of wide-ranging data. New animals are hooked up to the circuit every day. [. . .] Animals are now joining humans in the glass house.*

—ALEXANDER PSCHERA, Animal Internet: Nature and the Digital Revolution[2]

• • • Do animals everywhere disappear, as John Berger claimed in his poignant 1977 lament of how they have diminished as a real presence in modern human lives, even as they come to be increasingly caricatured in zoos and in graphic and cinematic depictions? Or are they somehow reappearing in unlikely places, including as part of "the glass house," the digital image-world in which we humans increasingly find ourselves?

With these prompts we move from the self-conscious, politically and artistically motivated production of Anthropocene-focused imagery to something that arises more "from the ground up" and is haphazard in its guiding motivations: the ongoing social media production and dissemination of materials depicting animals, sometimes with humans, engaged in activities that transgress boundaries and confound expectations. Here our purview will be more exclusively defined by the world's most influential video-watching web site, and second most visited web site (with 2.6 billion monthly active users), the platform that has become much of the world's go-to place for finding videos on almost any topic, and for many, for sharing videos, both self-produced and not.[3] I am referring, of course, to YouTube.[4]

As some media observers have argued, digital media are rekindling some of the characteristics of the earliest forms of cinema—notably those qualities that made it most "animated"—but are presenting them in a very different environment, which itself can be considered animated at the level of its pixelated microphysics, or what we might call its microbiology, and not merely in its effects. On the one hand, the public and participatory nature of YouTube makes it an ideal site to study how image production and consumption has become much more hybrid and open-ended, rather like a constant and ongoing montage or collage of images, all of which stretch and spill between the categories outlined in the first part of this book: animate, ideal, expressive, indexical, moving, and digital. On the other hand, the sharing of a wide variety of videos featuring nonhuman animals, including home videos, surveillance videos, comedic montages of the real and the fantastic, and more, makes YouTube an ideal venue for considering how the boundaries between the human and the nonhuman are also being reconfigured in and through digital media.

The boundary between humans and nonhuman animals is not a neatly demarcated line, with fences, border crossings, and passport controls. It is a shifting set of discourses and practices which is as much internalized as externally manifest, which appear in some places and not in others, and which crosscut against a multitude of other differentiations. Ecocriticism and animal studies scholarship has paid attention to some of the ways in which the two sides are mirrored and crossed in literature and the visual arts: for example, utilizing "crude" or "critical" forms of anthropomorphism (depiction of animals in humanlike terms for various ends) and zoomorphism (the opposite), reductionist or "mechanomorphic" depictions of animals as opposed to romantic portrayals of their "allomorphism" (valued otherness), and so on.[5] In *Ecologies of the Moving Image*, I developed an interpretive framework that took those boundaries to be more like shifting magnetic fields, energized by the actions and compulsions of those who value them for the possibilities they offer and the risks they embody. This results in a set of intersecting axes indicating how films or artworks allow viewers to project themselves across those boundaries according to three criteria: perceptions of similarity and difference between humans and nonhuman animals, valences ascribed to either side (positive or negative, attractive versus threatening or repulsive), and the stability of the boundary and possibilities for movement across it (designated in figure 6.2 as "system/order" versus "flux," with "kinesis" indicating the possibility of movement between the two ends).

In what follows, I begin by examining some of the ways in which the digital image-world of YouTube adds to and alters our relationships with the denizens of a "nature" we know to be "out there," even if we are not certain of how and where it is, how it is organized, and how it intersects with our lives. The mediasphere of "animal attractions" is one place where these questions get raised today. We will return to a consideration of the "boundary movements" and relations between animals and humans following an exploration of some of the subgenres found within this growing database of animal-focused videos and online activities.

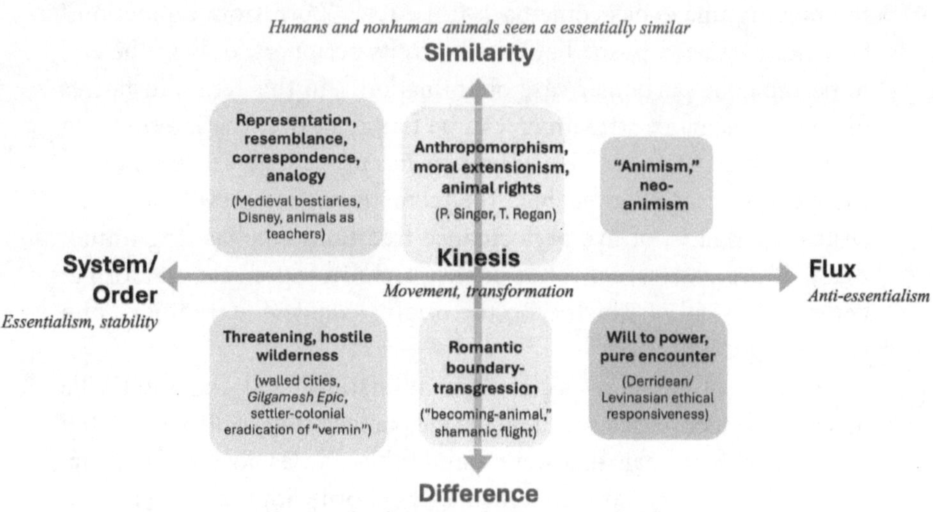


**FIGURE 6.2.** **The human-animal boundary. Adapted from Adrian Ivakhiv, *Ecologies of the Moving Image: Cinema, Affect, Nature* (Wilfrid Laurier University Press).**

## POST-CINEMAS OF ANIMAL ATTRACTIONS

As part of the broader landscape of what some have called "post-cinema,"[6] YouTube and user-generated databases like it have fueled a revival, in a new and very different era, of the kind of "cinema of attractions" that was popular at the origins of the moving-image era. In film historian Thom Gunning's analysis, cinema before about 1906 was devoted exclusively to the "harnessing of visibility," the "act of showing and exhibition" that presented the world through the eye of the motion-picture camera. Early cinema was about spectacle in its purity: the fascination, joy, and exhilaration of seeing and feeling the movement of the world as captured and displayed in this new medium.

Even as a set of conventions developed to turn cinema into a much more narrative medium, spectacle continued to mark certain forms of it, including many that continue to elicit audience exhilaration today—from high speed car chases and crashes to the many special effects found in horror, disaster, science-fiction, and avant-garde film genres. With the emergence of digital cinema, the spectacular and "animated" features of cinema have become foregrounded once again and in new ways facilitated by the medium. Lev Manovich has argued that the moving image has come back full circle: "Born from animation," he writes, "cinema pushed animation to its periphery, only in the end to become one particular case of animation."[7] In this sense, instances of a new cinema of attractions can be found all over the internet. On YouTube specifically, as Henry Jenkins has argued, new forms such as the videoblog (or vlog) enabled the reemergence of a new "vaudeville aesthetic," that is, of live performance traditions emphasizing immediacy, direct address, conversationality, technical spectacle, and formal compactness, all of which echo the original vaudeville traditions of a century ago.[8]

In both of these respects—"neo-animation" and the vaudeville aesthetic—video-based social media enable the kinds of displays of *and relations* with animals that were found in the earliest forms of cinema. As Paul Sheehan has argued, cinema was "born with the movement of animals—a horse jumping, a seagull in flight, some fish swimming in a tank, a cat licking its paws and drinking from a bowl."[9] In the early films and pre-cinematic moving images of Eadweard Muybridge, scientist and "chronophotographer" Étienne-Jules Marey, August and Louis Lumière, and Thomas Edison, animals like these embodied the very kineticism that the moving image was intended to capture. Animal motility served to underwrite the cinematic medium, lending evidential support to its reality claims, in part because we viewers understand that, unlike humans, animals are *not* actors; they are always and ever only "being themselves."

But there is another echo in contemporary animal videos that deserves mention: that of the earliest art, found in caves around the world, which prominently featured wild animals. The latter is sometimes called "theriomorphic" or "therianthropic," depending on whether or not the depictions hybridized human with nonhuman representation. (*Therion*, θηρίον, is the Greek word for wild animal.) What I will examine in this chapter is the diverse range of videographic materials making up what James Leo Cahill has called the "post-cinema of animal attractions," a growing database of cinematic contributions that highlight the strange relations of our own cinematically and mediatically equipped humanity with the nonhuman others that share our lives, and those that live almost entirely outside of our lives.[10] Together these constitute fragments—often unexpected and unsolicited, but contingently captured bits—of a larger, theriological reality that surrounds human sociality and that on occasion interrupts or breaks into it, bursting its sentimental enclosures and leaving several sets of boundaries blurred and uncertain: between the human and the nonhuman, between the real and the unbelievable, and between the urban, domestic, and known, and the wild unknown.

Cahill's 2015 article "A YouTube Bestiary: Twenty-Six Theses on a Post-Cinema of Animal Attractions" provided a tremendously insightful compendium of the ways in which YouTube animals have recapitulated and anachronistically revisited the modes of *actualités* and attractions, two forms of early cinema that respectively aimed for a topicality (*actualité*) and an exhibitionistic display (attractions) of the sort that is widely found in social media today. If, for Cahill, YouTube presented the elements of a "bestiary" of such animal attractions, I want to argue that it also presents the beginnings of a global archive or scrapbook of animal encounters—a database of attractions that, mixed into its multiple corridors with their many references to the human worlds of politics, domesticity, and entertainment culture, hints at the existence of another world that exists alongside ours, but which is typically forgotten, ignored, or assumed to be disappearing. In this respect, wild animal attractions often feature both as spectacles and as a form of "ethnographic taxidermy" which preserves for us what we suspect is being lost for good.[11] In their aggregate, however, they also document animal worlds that intersect with ours in a variety of ways, some of them novel. In Belgian philosopher of science Vinciane Despret's words, "the proliferation of these videos attests not only to new habits but to the creation of a new interspecific ethos, of new relational modalities, that at the same time construct knowledge."[12] At least there is a potential for new relational modalities and new constructions of knowledge to emerge; whether and how they do that is something I wish to probe.

Any discussion of the "post-cinema of attractions" must begin by recognizing that the technological foundations for this cinema have become ubiquitous. Smartphones are everywhere, GoPro cameras are light and dexterous (microphones even more so), and there is an infrastructure of ubiquitous surveillance—from urban and industrial surveillance cameras to wildlife "crittercams"—that supplies the eyes and ears by which such boundary incursions can be witnessed. Indeed, the monitoring of animals, birds, bats, insects, fish, and cetaceans for scientific and other purposes constitutes an increasingly global technological program. Since 2021, the ICARUS project, short for International Cooperation for Animal Research Using Space, has been using a network of satellites and ultralightweight radio tags to track the movements of an increasing number of species globally, with the goal of building up an "internet of animals" to aid in the monitoring of biodiversity change and to "pinpoint areas for conservation intervention."[13] The online tracking database MoveBank, as of early 2025, hosts data from 7.5 billion locations and 7.4 billion other sensor records of nearly 1,500 different animal taxa.[14] Other "dataveillance" initiatives include the BirdVision, Elephant Listening, and Rainforest Connection projects, all of which equip objects and/or creatures with a variety of sensors for the purposes of ecological monitoring, conservation, and what some call "edutainment." Pushing for a more utopian vision, the Animal Internet project (animalinternet.earth) proclaims its goal as "mov[ing] Earth towards a zoocratic future through a vision where the animals are active users and builders of the internet," connecting "to neural interfaces and interpretive A.I. algorithms to build new network frontiers that will shape the future of Earth" in ways that empower animals and animal life.[15] More prosaically, with dogs wearing "smart vests" to patrol neighborhoods in Bangkok, and gulls and vultures equipped with GPS and GoPro cameras to find illegal waste dump sites in Spain and Peru, "mobile photographic devices and animals," in Marek Jancovic's words, have clearly "coemerged" as "technologies of surveillance, governance, policing, reproduction and mourning."[16]

In what follows, I will mostly leave aside discussions of these varied technological systems in order to focus on videos produced for and viewed within social media. I will also largely ignore the many videos of domestic and farm animals—cats (the undisputed leaders in animal videos), dogs, cockatoos, horses, pigs, and the like—except for some instances of wild animals that have been domesticated against the recommendations (or laws) that protect their wild populations. There is a way, however, that domestic surveillance cameras add to our knowledge of animals, as in the "when the dog stays home alone" genre of videos showing dogs violating their owners' rules, getting their own food in the kitchen, knocking things over, or flailing around joyfully on beds they normally aren't allowed to lie on. The boundary between domestic and wild is sometimes transgressed in uncanny encounters as well, such as when a baby rabbit, having been cared for over the period of a week is released "into the wild" only to be "scooped up mid-stride by a bird of prey," as Cahill describes it, in Joey Gore's short 2013 video *Bunnies Can Fly . . . Proof.*[17] In what follows, I will range across multiple environments where wild animals can be found, including zoos, safari parks, accidental encounters at the edges of urban and residential areas, and at other points along the boundaries between wilderness and human captivity.

## EDUCATION AND ENTERTAINMENT ON ZOOTUBE

Cinema has long mixed educational with entertainment functions. While documentary films have always had elements of education and advocacy, art films and international cinema have also enabled viewers to learn about the lives, fictional or real, of people and places around the world. Production costs, however, have necessitated a trade-off between commercial goals and the public interest. Today both of these functions are multiplied, democratized, and opened to the chatter of a billion voices—a skewed sampling of humanity, but a sampling nonetheless.

As with the animal attractions of early cinema, YouTube animals continue to fascinate.[18] It is perhaps emblematic that the very first video uploaded to YouTube, on April 23, 2005, was a 19-second video called *Me at the Zoo*, which featured its protagonist, YouTube cofounder Jawed Karin, standing in front of and describing a group of elephants. The number of YouTube channels catering to animal lovers has since multiplied many times over, with "Animals and Pets" being one of 15 categories that YouTube users can choose from when uploading their videos. (For the record, the vast majority of videos and views fall into the "Music," "Entertainment," "People & Blogs," and "Gaming" categories, but one study showed that cat videos had "more views-per-video than any other category of YouTube content."[19]) Popular YouTube animal channels include Brave Wilderness (which had 21.5 million subscribers in November 2024), The Dodo (16.6 million subscribers), BBC Earth (13 million), Animal Aid Unlimited India (a street animal rescue center, with 7.4 million subscribers), Wilderness TV (7.66 million), Animal Planet (5.65 million), Nat Geo WILD (5.58 million), along with Latest Sightings, Real Wild, iPanda, Animalogic, and many others.[20] Subscribers account for only a fraction of viewers: Yuliya Kisora and Clemens Driessen's analysis of two viral animal videos from the mid 2010s—"Clever Orangutan Makes a Fair Trade with a Human" and "Monkey Sees a Magic Trick"—cited their number of views as, respectively, 25,882,723 and 56,480,311 as of December 2019.[21] Both of the videos had by that time been on YouTube for three to four years. By March 2023, these same videos had racked up at least 51 million and 173 million views, respectively—doubling or more than tripling in just over a three-year period.

While the most popular animal representations on YouTube, by far, fall into the "cute," "funny," and "ridiculous animal" genres, researchers have nevertheless sought to identify more educational potentials. Much of the research to date on animal videos in social media has, in one way or another, probed the question of the digital mediasphere's influence on the understanding and appreciation of animals: do individual videos, or YouTube more generally (or TikTok or other media), positively or negatively influence viewers' awareness and understanding of wild animals? Subsidiary to this are more specific questions, including about the prevalence of information as opposed to disinformation, "infotainment" or "edutainment," and ethical or unethical treatment in relation to the animals depicted; the reality versus stagedness of what is portrayed; and the impacts of social media representations of animals by zoos, conservation organizations, animal rights groups, and others. It is perhaps too early to summarize this research, but, on the positive side, it is evident that "positive framing" of certain species can encourage acceptance of and interest in conservation of those species. On the other hand, there is clear evidence that promotion of certain wild animals as "cute" and "lovable" pets, and staging of interaction with and between wild animals, can have deleterious effects both on the welfare of individual animals and on their species conservation.[22] (More on these issues presently.)

If many urban dwellers' relationships with wild animals are mediated by zoos, it is notable that zoos have long been a popular presence on YouTube, one that researchers have dubbed "the YouTube zoo," or "ZooTube." In an analysis of ZooTube, Andrew Burke presents a history of streaming online zoo animal feeds, or ZooCams, and argues that while these are typically promotional in nature and follow an exhibitionary logic, with their uninterruptedness, unrestrictedness, elusiveness (in that the animals might completely avoid the camera), and "uneventfulness," these streaming videos impact viewers' perception of zoo animal lives. "The streaming live feed," he writes, "is a broadcast form tailor-made for an era defined by 'continuous partial attention,' to use the phrase coined by Internet guru Linda Stone in 1998. The animal cam is perhaps something that is more checked in on than continuously watched."[23] "The logic of the webcam as a surveillance and social technology now structures a mode of existence organized around a more or less constant dissemination of intimate or invasive images shared and uploaded by the very people represented in them."[24] The video feeds further shape viewers' perceptions of the hierarchies of "cuteness," with pandas and penguins emerging above elephants, giraffes, polar bears, and birds, among others.[25]

Kisora and Driessen's analysis of public comments on viral zoo animal videos suggests that aside from merely increasing the "encounter value" with zoo animals, these videos might also elicit a "moral gaze" among some viewers.[26] "Boisterously described by commenters as subjects with biographies and personalities," and with their own "perspectives" and "capabilities," YouTube's zoo animals raise questions about the relationship between humans and nonhuman animals, questions that are not resolved in the comments section of the videos, but that continue as viewers navigate relations with real animals in real zoos and elsewhere.[27]

An instance of a zoo encounter that reflects how this "moral gaze" might operate is a two-minute, 48-second video entitled "Beluga Mesmerized by Violin," uploaded by YouTuber "crystal Pineda" to her personal channel in 2015 and eliciting 5.5 million views and 350,000 comments as of early 2023.[28] In the video, a beluga whale watches with unwavering interest for the video's entire length as a violinist seated in a wheelchair plays a slow and graceful folk melody. The seemingly wide-eyed whale faces the musician throughout the video, planting his forehead against the glass at one point, and appearing to kiss the glass at the end, while a second whale slowly swims and rolls around behind him. The beluga has been identified as Juno, one of two captive bred whales at the Mystic Seaport Aquarium in Connecticut; the second one is Kela,

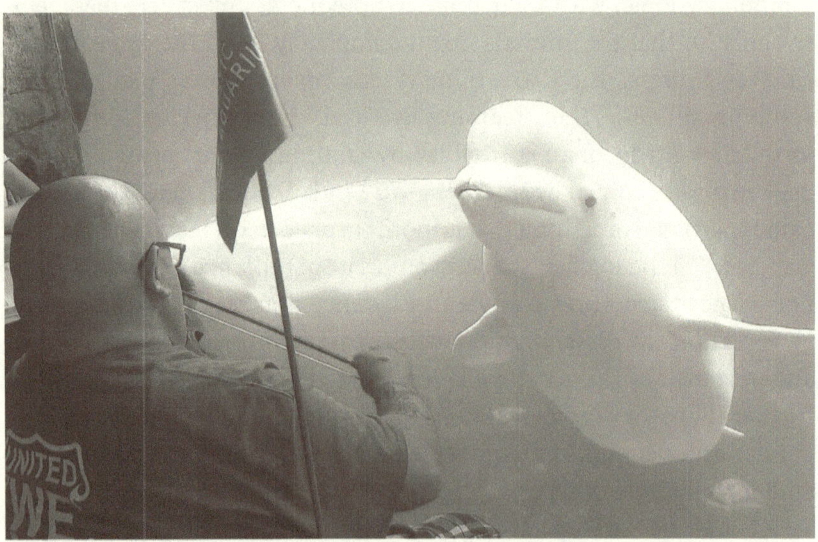

**FIGURE 6.3.** Screenshot from "Beluga Mesmerized by Violin," Crystal, YouTube, 2015.

and the musician is Paul Baker. Public comments on the video include variations on almost every perspective one can take on the scene: delight at the beluga's apparently intent interest in the music; appreciation for the violinist; wonder at the beauty of the encounter, with its tête-à-tête directness (of the bald-headed musician and the hairless listener, as noted by more than one commenter); upset and criticism of zoos and aquariums as inappropriate enclosures for animals; broader critiques of humanity, capitalism, governments, or modernity at large; and humorous, ironic, or sarcastic quips about people, whales, history, and more. The 15 most popular comments in table 6.1, ordered by number of likes, indicate some of the diversity of moral perspectives and attitudes elicited.

While it is not likely that new viewers would read through all the comments—so the identity of the whales, the musician, and the aquarium, along with the latter's "defense," articulated in the lengthy comment by Cyra Niccals, might not be known to most—it is evident that many of those who spend any time with the video are likely to experience an emotional reaction that includes some reflection on the relationship between humans and nonhuman animals. Among the more popular comments (2,100 likes, 78 replies, from 2021) is this one: "Is anyone else so moved to tears by this? I cannot contain this level of emotion I'm experiencing. Two souls of vastly different worlds and consciousness strung together in one shared interaction. I am utterly unable to rightfully put the beauty into words." Sympathy for belugas, whether encountered in zoos or in the wild, is in fact not unusual. One 20-second-long video of a beluga apparently retrieving a girl's cell phone, has now attained a kind of "classic" status with 45 million views and 26,500 comments accrued within four years of its uploading.[29] Other popular favorites include "Mariachi Connecticut Serenades a Beluga Whale" (captainkickstand, 2011), in which a beluga seems to dance along to Mariachi musicians, and "Man's Funny Beluga Song Attracts Beluga Whales Who Sing Back" (The Dodo, 2017, with 11 million views).

When direct encounters with captive animals become impossible, as happened during the early phase of the COVID-19 pandemic, some captive animal facilities decided to stage more open, improvisatory video dramas featuring some of their more charismatic inhabitants.

**TABLE 6.1.** Public comments on "Beluga Mesmerized by Violin"

| Commenter | # likes | # replies | Years ago posted | Comment |
|---|---|---|---|---|
| John Moore | 34K | 205 | 3 | The beluga is probably like: "My great grandmother told me about this sound when she was watching the Titanic sink." |
| CrNessata | 17K | 87 | 3 | The upside down baluga floating around in the background is a mood. |
| Walurus Walurus | 16K | 87 | 3 | Man: wow he's fascinated by my violin<br>Beluga: nice forehead, same |
| Byron R | 11K | 36 | 2 | Beluga in front: emotional<br>Beluga in back: [cartwheels image] |
| R H | 10K | 72 | 2 | Belugas and dolphins don't usually stay in one place like that. Truly interested in the man and his music. Touching, yet somewhat sad. |
| MeJustAimy | 9.9K | 93 | 2 | I once played guitar to a group of cows in the countryside, they all ran up and listened it was lovely <3 |
| Edward Solaire | 9.5K | 38 | 2 | Plot twist: Beluga is looking at a human zoo. He's in the musicians section. |
| templar 1138 | 9.3K | 24 | 3 | Beluga be like, "I'm still listening, just need to breathe."<br>EDIT: Holy shit, how did this comment get so many likes?! |
| Pham Van Hoe | 8K | 75 | 2 | Two people without hair, passionate about music. |
| jp_:D | 8K | 24 | 3 | Can we appreciate the other whale serving as background dancer? |
| Cyra Niccals | 7.3K | 161 | 2 | I know these whales! The one watching the violinist is Juno (the silly in the background is Kela). I had the privilege of getting to meet Juno up close and pet him, learn about him, and even take part in his enrichment. He absolutely loves humans and is completely fascinated by us, perhaps as much as we are by him. He's incredibly playful and curious and loves when musicians visit or anyone else he thinks particularly interesting. He's an amazing creature and I miss him very much, it's so wonderful to see |

| | | | | |
|---|---|---|---|---|
| | | | | these videos of him and his friends in mystic. Also for anyone complaining, he and Kela were captive bred. They can't live in the wild. Mystic Aquarium is not only a haven for captive bred or rescued animals but a research center - the workers will document his health and behavior as well as Kela's and use it to help understand and save their wild counterparts. It was also requested that the whale facility become part of the aquarium as Mystic has a rich history with whaling, and because the local Native tribe (the Mashantucket Pequot people) have a love and admiration for whales - whales are sacred to many tribes. |
| Zarasha1 | 7.3K | 59 | 2 | Just like people have different interest, animals have different interest. The others animals were not interested, but look how focused this cute pie was. I was expecting him to move along, but even after the music stopped he stood there. I really love animals. They are so precious and innocent like children. |
| joan baczek | 6K | 150 | 2 | Two souls speak one held in a wheelchair one held in a tank. Limited in freedom but not limited in love |
| YouLube | 5.8K | 148 | 2 | Everybody talking about the Whale but can we just take a minute to appreciate how good this guy is on the violin |
| Father Gabriel Stokes | 5.6K | 35 | 3 | Then, the Beluga Whale pulls out a Violin of its own and starts playing as well |
| Tranquil Rabies | 5.6K | 27 | 3 | "I approve of the sounds of this land dweller. He shall be spared after our takeover." |

These differ from the beluga video in that they are staged by the facility, yet responses to them reflect a similar range of perspectives. Perhaps the best known of these was Chicago's Shedd Aquarium's videos of penguins being released to explore the aquarium's facilities. Videos of Wellington the rockhopper penguin encountering beluga whales, visiting a local television station, and, with his mates Edward and Annie, going on "field trips" through the aquarium and to the Field Museum and Chicago's Museum of Contemporary Art, mesmerized viewers with the penguins' charm and evident curiosity as they scrambled about, hesitating here, enthusiastically cavorting toward something there, and eagerly exploring their unexpected surroundings.[30]

This pandemic genre of institutional videos became popular, with copycat videos sprouting from other locations featuring penguins (Monterey Bay Aquarium), an armadillo visiting otters (Woodland Park Zoo), a sloth encountering dolphins (Texas State Aquarium), and others. As described by Benjamin Schultz-Figueroa, videos like these "capitalize on the viewer's desire for a potential world where the old architectures of mastery are repurposed towards other forms of being with and alongside animals." Describing the video of Wellington encountering belugas, Schultz-Figueroa notes, "The belugas' interest in the penguin combines with the alien beauty of their floating bodies and the otherworldly lighting of the hall to create a fascinating spectacle of nonhuman interaction." As a result, "After generations of evoking a timeless or cyclical past, animal images now remind us of our uncertain future," a future that is troubling for many, yet which includes the presence of nonhuman animals even as that presence reflects their increasing absence.[31]

## BATTLES AT KRUGER

If zoos are one place where urban humans have typically encountered wild animals, another, less frequented and thus more elite location for such encounters has been conserved areas, such as national parks and wildlife refuges. The politics of conservation retains aspects of colonialism, especially in the Global South, where the world's most charismatic mega-fauna tend to be found. In *The Truth About Nature: Environmentalism in the Era of Post-truth Politics and Platform Capitalism*, political geographer Bram Büscher examines the ways in which online communities have changed the politics of nature surrounding national parks and other sites of nature preservation and consumption.[32] One such hotspot is South Africa's Kruger National Park, where the politics of conservation involve historical relationships to the apartheid political economy within which the park was established in the early decades of the twentieth century. For white South Africans, Kruger provided a means "to bond with an Edenic Africa, filled with 'unspoiled' nature and wildlife, and [to] simultaneously control African peoples," who were thereby denied access to large parts of the South African Transvaal.[33]

While the tendencies toward perceiving Kruger as part of a "fortress Africa," especially prominent among white Afrikaner nationalists, has receded since the downfall of apartheid in 1994, Büscher finds some of its tendencies reemerging as a result of the "new mediation" of what he calls "Kruger 2.0." Like "nature 2.0," Büscher's term for the discursive and representational forms taken by "nature" in the world of digital media ("web 2.0"), Kruger National Park, Büscher writes, "is cocreated through many online forums, including Facebook groups, Twitter, tourism websites, discussion groups, YouTube channels, wildlife-cams, mobile apps, and more."[34] Büscher focuses particularly on wildlife cams, Kruger appreciation Facebook groups, official forums of the South African National Parks web site, and a smartphone app called Latest Sightings, begun by a teenager who "was bored driving around the park 'seeing nothing'" and wanted to be able to collect real-time data about wildlife sightings that would inform the movement and ability of park visitors to witness exciting wildlife encounters.[35] All of these have served to "spectacularize" the park by intensifying a "politics of distinction" oriented toward the sighting of spectacular animals doing spectacular things. Notably, the "first and main distinction for every tourist" visiting South African nature parks is to see the so-called Big Five: lions, elephants, leopards, rhinos, and buffalo.

Part of Büscher's analysis is a video made by a visiting American tourist in 2004 and shared publicly on YouTube in 2008. The 8-minute, 24-second video, known as "Battle at Kruger," portrays a fight between a small pride of lions and a buffalo herd, with a crocodile cameo, on the opposite side of a watering hole from where the tourist's safari vehicle had pulled up. The video won the 2008 YouTube Video Award in the "Eyewitness" category, became the subject of a 2008 National Geographic Channel documentary entitled "Caught on Safari: Battle at Kruger," and by 2023 had accrued over 90 million views on YouTube. A few features of the video make it especially relevant to our analysis, and while they echo points I have made earlier, it is helpful for us to recapitulate them here.

First is the way in which it reflects social media's upending of the conventions of the political economy of cinema, whereby images were made and circulated by a professional industry to a receiving public. This was all the more so with wildlife filmmaking, an industry that required significant capital to support filmmaking crews traveling to special places (typically, national parks and other conserved areas, with the permits and allowances these require), spending lengthy periods of time there collecting wildlife footage, skillfully editing that footage according to extant narrative formulas (such as focusing on exciting and dramatic predator-prey encounters, not on long periods of waiting, hiding, and sleeping), and distributing the results within media networks shaped at least as much by commercial expectations as by public or educational interests. By the time "Battle at Kruger" exploded into the universe of YouTube, this was all turned upside down. With its shaky camerawork and low resolution, the video exudes an authenticity that comes from its being captured by a "casual" visitor, Texan tourist David Budzinski, who had elected on a whim to bring along a new digital camcorder while holidaying in South Africa. The video sat on a shelf for two years, seen only by the families of Budzinski and fellow safari-goer Jason Schlosberg, until the latter decided to share it with a friend by uploading it to YouTube on May 3, 2007. Within weeks it became a video sensation, accruing 3.8 million views in the first month and attracting as many as 200,000 views in a single day.[36] Within three months its views had reached 10 million and it had become the subject of a *Time* magazine article and of ABC News' short-lived televised newsmagazine *i-Caught*.[37] Just over a year later National Geographic Channel aired its documentary—likely the first hour-long television documentary to be inspired by a YouTube clip.[38] Ironically, Budzinski had earlier tried to sell the video to National Geographic and Animal Planet, but neither had been interested.

The second feature, related to the first, is the fact that the relations depicted among the animals "in the wild"—it is of course a tourist encounter in a highly regulated nature reserve—are not pre-interpreted according to standard narrative formulas of, for instance, predator-prey interactions, the social bonds among animals, and so on. The video features four safari-goers and their guide voicing their astonished, often half-whispered observations: "They're crouching"; "Oh-oh, what's the bull gonna do?"; "She's going for him, she's going for him . . . she got him!"; "They're draggin' him out"; "There's a crocodile!"; and so on. But unlike blue-chip wildlife documentaries of decades past, the video lacks any voice-of-God narrator interpreting the action within the broader context of "wild nature." The relations between animals are striking: the lions suddenly run after the buffalo herd and capture one calf, dragging it down to the water; then, as they are working on it, a crocodile emerges and grabs a large part of the calf's torso with its mouth, tugging it toward the water as the lions pull away at the other end. Sometime after the lions pull it away from the crocodile, the buffalo herd returns in much larger numbers, harass and chase after individual lions, and ultimately retrieve the calf, which stands up and walks toward them as if its limbs were fully intact. The buffalos continue to harass the lions, who gradually disappear. The entire interaction is the kind it would have taken several days of filming for a professional crew to capture *if* it would have been captured at all. That lucky day's safari guide, Frank Watts, claimed he didn't "know of anybody who's ever seen anything like this before."[39]

Where a traditional wildlife documentary would have included interpretive commentary, here the raw data is thrown open for YouTube viewers to make sense of for themselves. The comments on YouTube—around 37,000 in mid-2023—demonstrate a kind of interpretive creativity one could scarcely have imagined in the world of cinema and television viewing 50 years earlier. The video is interpreted by way of multiple metaphors: it represents "survival of the fittest," "majority rule," or survival of the most cooperative; the lions represent "government" and "the rich" while the buffalo represent "the working class"; the lions are "the unions" and the buffalo are "american [*sic*] taxpayers"; "Dad goes back for his son and the rest of the herd got his back"; and so on. More recent comments show an increasing self-reflexivity about the video's place within the YouTube universe: it is called "a YouTube classic"; "after almost 10 years, still the most epic video on youtube"; "Battle at Kruger has become legendary!"; "This is actually the video that made me discover YouTube," one viewer writes, as others say, "I remember watching this epic video way back in 2007"; "been watching battle at Kruger for 15 yrs."; and "This is not just the greatest wildlife video of all time but also one of the greatest videos of all time. Imagine all the moments like this that went un-captured in the history of earth." Finally, it is precisely this activity of viewers—the liking, clicking, commenting, upvoting, and sharing—that has made the video go viral. Without the interactive capacities of social media, it would not exist as such.

What the video does for Kruger, or for people's understanding of lions, buffalos, and other creatures, is not as easy to assess. But it is clear from the comments that the greatest appreciation is directed not at the filmmaker or the safari guide (effectively, the film crew), but at the place itself, its animals (especially the buffalo herd), or "nature" writ large. The video is taken to be a snapshot, if an unusual and privileged one, of a world that exists out there on the peripheries of the human world. And where in the past one would have to decide to watch a wildlife documentary, a product that generally carried with it a certain style and sensibility, to see wild animals facing off against each other, today it is more frequent that one will simply come across a video clip being shared on one's social media feed. Another video from the Greater Kruger area that has gone somewhat viral (with close to 50 million views by 2023) is a 13-minute video from 2016 documenting a safari group's close-up view of a male leopard attacking, killing, and casually eating a warthog. Like "Battle at Kruger," "Leopard's Deadly Precision: Warthog's Fateful Encounter" comes largely unadorned by commentary or postproduction. The video, like others of its kind, is a graphic document, a piece of evidence of a different world.

## ATTACKS, RESCUES, AND OTHER CLOSE ENCOUNTERS

Videos like "Battle at Kruger" and "Leopard's Deadly Precision" are no longer rare. Within the mix of online animal imagery, there is a growing subset of videos sourced in individuals' excursions into theriological worlds: "What my smartphone (or webcam) caught these animals doing." Unlike videos intended for scientific use, these are commonly shared—and then linked to, reshared, commented on, remixed, and so forth—either for their revelatory qualities or their entertainment value, or both. They are most often amateur videos and carry a presumption of unstaged authenticity in their amateurishness. Some researchers have argued that such raw footage of animal behavior captured and uploaded to YouTube can have educational value that eludes more professional productions, such as wildlife documentaries, which manipulate footage through sophisticated postproduction techniques. Focusing on understudied play behavior including interspecies interactions and interaction with objects, Nelson and Fijn show that some such videos are not only as popular (if not more), but can be more educationally reliable than wildlife documentaries.[40]

Vinciane Despret, whose book *What Would Animals Say If We Asked the Right Questions?* offers intriguing suggestions toward a "new interspecific ethos," suggests that YouTube videos are "a vector for a previously unseen production of new forms of subjectivity—of new ways of being, of thinking oneself, presenting oneself, and knowing oneself" that, when they involve animals, can present "new relational modalities."[41] Just as earlier animal documentaries introduced "new habits" with respect to animals, who are "bestowed with 'personalities' and emotions" and "become characters" (in turn influencing scientists, like Jane Goodall, who go out into the field with new expectations), so do online videos make animals "part of the cast": "They are talented beings, remarkable for their heroism, sociality, cognitive and relational intelligence, humor, unpredictability, and inventiveness, and they are now part of everyday life."[42] Many things seen in pet videos display a "common work between a human and an animal," showing "a productive complicity" and "mutual learning": "a dog and his owner on top of a skateboard, a cat who learns how to surprise his owner who is himself hiding; we learn what *we* are capable of with them."[43] Other videos exhibit strange or unexpected encounters that, in turn, raise questions about what might be possible in interspecies relations. Anne MacConnell's list of "the kinds of videos that can pop up on YouTube" is a good starting point for considering this growing "repository of anecdotal knowledge," as she calls it: "a monkey sharing a bunch of grapes with a goat; a dog darting through traffic in order to rescue a kitten that somehow found itself in the middle of the freeway; a parrot singing Christmas carols as its human companion provides the accompaniment on the piano." While many of these border on the ridiculous, they also add to the archive of "ways that human and nonhuman animals 'become with' one another."[44]

Among the most popular genres within this "internet of animals" are animal attack videos and animal rescue videos. Since animals are not known to act in the way that professional actors do, the "reality effect" of these videos tends to precede the suspicion that they have been faked or altered. As with cinematic animals, the truth claims of digital video evoke a viewerly faith in the "co-presence," the "existential bond" believed to exist between the image and the object it depicts.[45] A GoPro camera–equipped swimmer encountering a shark is perceived to be encountering a real shark, not an actor in shark's clothing. It is understood that any editing took place later, but when swimmer faces shark in the same shot, the credibility of what is seen gives it its evident power over the viewer.

Yet the ease by which digital video can be altered, reedited, remixed, and otherwise manipulated, and then sent reeling along channels of multiplication, complication, deformation, and modulation, means that these videos' indexical status—the "reality effect" of the sense of presence they provide from the captured and recorded "real event"—will always be in tension with their malleability. The *truth* of the recorded moment and the *constructedness*, if not outright fakeness, of the uploaded product will typically be found in ambiguous mixtures that open up a wide berth for interpreting their meanings. Viewers of wildlife documentaries will by now be familiar with the "Making of . . ." genre of video add-ons, which have heightened awareness of how the filmmakers do not merely "capture" the worlds of wild animals, but may in various ways elicit, provoke, incite, or craft these worlds through sometimes painstaking and costly engagement with the animal "actors."[46] I have previously written of the making of big-budget documentaries like the *Planet Earth* series, which featured short "making of" vignettes at the end of its episodes, and of *Winged Migration*. The latter film provided a kind of artfully rendered, cinematic global tour showcasing the migrations of dozens of bird species, from bald eagles and Canada geese to Asian great cranes, Arctic gulls, and Antarctic penguins. To film these, the crew did not merely fly alongside and follow these birds with cameras. As revealed in *The Making of Winged Migration*, a companion video that accompanied the film on its DVD release, the filmmakers in some cases raised birds, from birth, to be part of a kind of human-avian-machine collective: they were "imprinted" on human "mothers"—crew members and graduate students hired to raise them—and trained to run and fly in interactive proximity with people and vehicles including remote-controlled aircraft, paragliders, hot air balloons, two-seater ultra-light aircraft, as well as trucks, motorcycles, remote-controlled all-terrain robots, and a French Navy warship.[47]

To some extent, this kind of sustained interplay is required for any cinematic or mediatic animal productions. In her analysis of National Geographic's *Crittercam* series, Donna Haraway outlines the many ways in which "each *Crittercam* project requires fast boats; expert pilots; and agile, jocular, well-muscled scientist-divers ready to jump off a moving boat and embrace a large swimming critter who is presumably not especially longing to embrace a human."[48] But this is never all it takes: on the other side of the ledger is always the coadaptive agency of the animals, to which humans with cameras must conform in some kind of "fugal accompaniment" if any insight into "critterworlds" is to be established.[49]

Of course, not all YouTube viewers will be familiar with the constructedness of "online nature." In any case, what we are concerned with here is not that nature is no longer "pure" and "undisturbed" (by humans)—that nature has "ended," as Bill McKibben provocatively, if misleadingly, put it in his 1989 book *The End of Nature*.[50] What's interesting, rather, is that wild animal lives continue in the nooks and crannies, margins, and presumptive "outsides" of the human worlds that have come to dominate our world, and that those lives intersect with ours at places that are increasingly sensible through the aid of technological apparatuses like cameras.

Among the more viral animal rescue videos, "Kayakers Help Save Seal Pups Entangled in Netting" (2019) is noteworthy.[51] In its first year, the 6-minute video received nearly 60 million views. The video compiles scenes of sea kayakers on and off the coast of Namibia rescuing sea lions from netting in which they have become entangled. Many of the comments (of which there are over 26,000) laud the rescuers for their efforts. Among the most popular (4,700 likes) is trevorphillips3293's comment, "Very good job. Well done. We need more people like you guys." When a snide commenter retorts, "Who are you to say 'we need . . .'. president of the world?" another responds, "Dude, calm down. He was congratulating his good deed." The snide commenter obtained 10 likes, their respondent 128 (the most of any reply to trevorphillips3293's comment). Some commenters shared their surprise that the rescuers carried scissors with them until one explained that this was their task. Fellow kayakers indicated that they will now bring scissors with them on their kayaking expeditions in case a similar situation might arise with an animal.

Other animal rescue videos have shown similar popularity. A Great Whale Conservancy video about a humpback whale being rescued from fishing nets has been viewed 38 million times. The 8-minute film's narrator, GWC cofounder Michael Fishbach, describes the whale's joyful and apparently grateful, hour-long "full-surface display" of "at least forty breaches as well as tail bobs, tail slaps, and pectoral fin slaps" after it was successfully released from the grip of the nets. The commentary largely shares in the joy of the whale and the rescuers, much of it noting the animal's intelligence, the emotional connections between the whale and the humans, and the rescuers' heroism.[52] A self-produced 2015 video documenting a fisherman's rescue of a screech owl, tangled in a fishing line and hanging from a tree, has attained 17 million views,[53] and a 3-minute video of an otter jumping repeatedly onto the safety of a small fishing boat, to escape a predatory orca, has gotten 21 million views in two years since being uploaded.[54] Another very short video (1 minute, 24 seconds) shared on the *Guardian News* web site, documents a Wisconsin family rescuing a bear with a plastic tub stuck on its head. While the YouTube video has garnered "only" three million views over a three-year period, the video has been shared in other social media, including the Facebook page where it was originally uploaded, and has triggered interesting discussions about the relationships between humans and bears in the Upper Midwest of the United States, where it was filmed.

Other human-animal encounters reveal a more mixed set of responses. One of the most viral of such videos, with over 90 million views to date (and almost a million likes), is the two-minute long video "Man Punches a Kangaroo in the Face to Rescue His Dog" (2016). The video shows an Australian boar-hunting crew come upon a kangaroo clutching one of their hunting dogs in an arm hold. A hunter, Greig Tonkins, runs up to confront the kangaroo, which lets the dog go but turns toward the hunter as if prepared to fight. The hunter then punches the kangaroo in the head, and the latter, stopping to apparently take in the situation, turns and hops away. Popular comments to the video divide along several lines. Some laud the film for its narrative qualities: "Everyone played a great role. The Roo (villain), the dog (victim in distress), the other dog (the coward friend) and the hero. The kangaroo's reaction is priceless" (6,300 likes); "The shock, the disbelieve [*sic*] in his eyes, the pain. It's art" (8,200 likes); and "I like how the kangaroo was acting like he couldn't believe the human hit him with a right hook" (36,000 likes). Others take the opportunity for ironic commentary on Australia and Aussies: "The most Australian thing I have ever seen" (87,000 likes); "Never underestimate a rouge [*sic*] Australian" (22,000 likes); "I like how the one guy's friend is like 'Let it go Tom' as if he's always squaring up to kangaroos" (5,100 likes); and "A wise man once said, 'Some things from Australia don't need an explanation because being from Australia is the explanation'" (4,500 likes). Some play with the irony of the human-kangaroo encounter: "Not many survived an encounter with a wild Australian like that. They are very dangerous. That kangaroo will be telling this story to his grandchildren" (2,600 likes); "Kangaroo wife: 'How was your day?' Kangaroo: 'I don't wanna talk about it.'" (24,000 likes).[55] The video has been replayed, reuploaded, and remixed in multiple venues, several of them reaching millions of further views. Australian animal activist organizations, including People for the Ethical Treatment of Animals (PETA), criticized Tonkins for punching the kangaroo, arguing that wild animals should never be attacked and that it could have led to greater violence. Dog lovers, meanwhile, tended to identify with Tonkins's defensive act, some noting that they would have done the same, or that they wished they would have had the "guts" to do what Tonkins did. As Australia's national animal, kangaroos have a symbolic function that catalyzed further debate, some of it ironic, about Australian wildlife, Australian masculinity, and national identity.

Human encounters with potentially dangerous predators tread into still more challenging terrain. Sharks and bears exemplify the kinds of creatures we are both supposed to fear and (unless one lives within a conservative media cocoon) to want to protect. As they did with the debates surrounding Werner Herzog's 2005 documentary *Grizzly Man* (which I examined in depth in *Ecologies of the Moving Image*)—debates that still continue online—it is these conflicting emotions that drive many of the conversations around YouTube encounters with such creatures. The 2016 video "Why I Don't Deep Sea Fish from a Kayak Anymore" (with 22 million views), itself a 2-minute excerpt from a 16-minute video with another four million views, seems to have gone through multiple waves of virality since its original upload, with viewership more than doubling in three years on YouTube and plentiful coverage in Facebook and elsewhere.[56] The video documents a kayaker's encounter with a hammerhead shark that appears to be following and harassing him over the course of at least a quarter of an hour. The video has elicited debate about whether or not the kayaker was in danger, or if it was his own fear that led him to provoke the shark and increase the risk. By contrast, the 2015 video "GREAT WHITE SHARKS SURFING" shows a group of paddleboarders exuding a calm excitement to see several great white sharks swimming beneath them.[57] Fear of sharks is a prominent theme in the comments, often coupled with irony: "I love how these dudes are smiling and laughing like the water can turn red in seconds everything's funny till it knocks you off your board" (234 likes); "90% of me wanted to see that shark go beast mode" (635 likes); and "How do you keep your balance on a paddle board with such big balls?" (2,100 likes). But these are somewhat balanced out by comments showing a clear appreciation for the surfers' calmness and curiosity: "Finally a shark encounter video that pays proper respect to these awesome predators!"; "As surfers, sharks go by us all the time. If you don't flail and panic they just kinda check you out, bump you maybe, and just kinda hang around sometimes because they're curious"; "Love how happy he is to see the shark. It's nice to see people happy and respectful when it comes to sharks for a change." (The latter have far fewer likes than the galeophobic, or shark-fearing, comments, yet they rise to the top in my own view of the commentary, which suggests something puzzling about YouTube's comment sorting algorithm even when my selection is to "Sort by Top comments.") Another video of an encounter with a great white shark, "Ocean Ramsey Encounters GIANT 20ft Great White Shark" (2019, with four million views), presents a more aestheticized rendition of a huge shark being circled and touched on its fin by free divers.[58] Since they are part of a diving team that monitors and works to conserve shark habitat and educate about them, the video raises questions about whether it goes too far in seeking contact with the species, questions we will turn to momentarily.

Bear encounters are not uncommon on YouTube, but for close encounters with polar bears we generally have to count on professional crews taking us to Arctic latitudes, such as the crew responsible for the documentary segment that has circulated virally under the title "Wild Polar Bear Tries to Break In" (2019). The 4-minute video clip attained at least 35 million views before being removed, but can still be found on other YouTube channels with millions of views.[59] The clip features a filmmaker, Gordon Buchanan, encased in a plexiglass cage within polar bear territory. A large, eight-foot-tall polar bear approaches the cage and attempts, over a reported 45-minute period, to get at the man inside. The bear sniffs at a crack in the cage, scratches the glass with its claws and breathes onto it as if it were ice that could melt, climbs up the side of the cage, and attempts to push it over. The video is informative and captivating, with Buchanan providing analysis of the bear's calculations even as he appears at risk of attack. The clip has inspired plentiful commentary on the danger of the situation, the bravery of the cameraman, the presence of an external camera (presumably on a tripod, though some commenters surmise a second cameraperson), and counterfactual scenarios in which the bear succeeds in claiming his victim. Interestingly, while the plight of polar bears is well known to be related to climate-related changes in their habitats, so the unmentioned context of diminishing polar bear food sources could be assumed from the short clip (something the longer documentary goes into greater detail on), none of the popular comments mention the impact of climate change on polar bear habitat.

## STAGING COMPANIONSHIP

If polar bears, sharks, and kangaroos find themselves in uneasy boundary zones between their wild habitats, which are diminishing, and cultural narratives about their fearfulness (in the case of sharks and bears) or their relationship to national identity (in the case of kangaroos), other animals are more vulnerable to the human longing for kinship. The exotic pet trade can be taken as a running index of social media's capacity to elicit a desire for interspecies companionship, with unfortunate results.

Among the animals who suffer as a consequence of those traits that make them appealing to us are slow lorises. These are small nocturnal primates, whose eight known species are all threatened either by habitat loss, a growing illegal trade, or both. Nekaris et al. conducted a comprehensive study of online commentary about a video, "Tickling Slow Loris," first uploaded to Vimeo.com in 2009, that shows a captive slow loris seemingly enjoying being tickled by its owner.[60] The video went viral, with celebrity endorsements coming from Ariana Grande, Ricky Gervais, Diedre Funk, and others. Eventually a copy of it uploaded by wired.com had generated over nine million views and over 12,000 comments by the time the web site took it down in early 2012, following a media backlash by conservationists and ecologists. The authors showed that far more commenters found the video to be "cute, adorable, or funny" (22.7%) or wanted to get a loris after seeing the video (11.2%) than cared or knew anything about its welfare. About 20% in total showed concern for the lorises' welfare, commented about their status as threatened and/or trade in lorises being illegal, or shared ecologically or biologically factual comments.

The study, like others, showed that the effects of animal videos are neither singular nor unidimensional—the actual effects of videos vary with the nature of the video (e.g., whether informative or entertaining), the comments accompanying it, the venue (e.g., YouTube, Vimeo, or other sites), and whether it results in celebrity endorsements and goes viral or not. The same authors later carried out a much broader investigation of one hundred videos featuring slow lorises across three video-sharing platforms (YouTube, Tudou, and Youku) and found that every single one of them showed evidence of at least one of five criteria indicating compromised welfare (human contact, daylight, signs of stress or ill health, an unnatural environment, and social isolation), with nearly a third of the videos showing all five criteria. The authors concluded that "the public were more likely to like videos where a slow loris was kept in the light [despite their nocturnal preference] or displayed signs of stress."[61]

As with slow lorises, so with kinkajous (a tropical mammal popularized by Paris Hilton), sea otters, lemurs, capuchin monkeys, galagos (bush babies), and other "cute" and, in social media terms, desirable wild animal species. Within a few years of the slow loris phenomenon, which died down following a "Tickling as Torture" campaign by animal welfare groups, researchers noted a marked increase in pet otter videos, coming especially from Southeast Asia and Japan. Over the period of 2009 to 2018, Harrington, Macdonald, and D'Cruze found an increase in viral content, often shared by a small number of influencers and increasingly aimed at English-language audiences, accompanied by frequent commentary about the "cute" and "adorable" creatures and often using phrases like "I want one." Almost all the videos studied "portrayed a picture of an affectionate 'easy to handle' animal in the house," thereby creating the misleading perception that otters are "suitable animals to be kept as pets." In fact, their territorial and dietary requirements—otters have extensive home ranges in the wild, and when held captive tend to develop abnormal repetitive behaviors—and serious conservation concerns in their Southeast Asian home environments make them highly inappropriate for this purpose.[62]

A 2020 study found an even more extreme upward curve in social media videos of galagos, nocturnal primates known as "bush babies," with a six-month period showing a nearly fivefold increase of posts, mostly from Japan, Thailand, and Russia. Ninety-five per cent of comments to the studied posts were deemed "positive," including the frequent "cute" and "I want one." The trend coincided with an increase in Google searches for the term "galago pet" and with the export of actual galagos.[63] A 2023 study found a similar trend with capuchin monkeys, with 1,138 capuchin-related videos on YouTube, of which 71% of the more popular ones (over 1 million views) portrayed them as pets. This coincided with an exponential growth since 2017 of news related to the trade, both legal and illegal, of capuchins for use as pets. Meanwhile, 18 of 22 capuchin species are listed by the International Union for the Conservation of Nature as vulnerable or at high risk of extinction due to habitat loss and fragmentation, risks to which commercial trade contributes.[64] Similar findings have been shown for social media videos of ring-tailed lemurs, macaques, vervet monkeys, squirrel monkeys, as well as tigers, lions, cheetahs, and other wild cats. Hundreds of YouTube videos depicting human interaction with (or "free handling" of) these creatures receive predominantly positive response. As Georgia Maloney and her coauthors note, such videos have the effect of supporting the "normalization, desirability and acceptability of exotic species as pets" even as the internet has "revolutionized" the exotic animal trade, making it much easier for consumers to purchase these animals legally or illegally.[65] Wildlife trafficking is considered the fourth largest illicit economy in the world, with trade routes for the import and export of live animals including Asia, Africa, South America, North America, and Europe.[66]

All of this suggests that viewing wild animals online can have negative consequences if it presents animals in an idealized manner—as "cute," "lovable," "adorable," and so on—but not as autonomous beings with their own needs and interests. Understanding the lives and needs of animals is typically not a priority for those who share or watch videos of animals. A 2018 study by Fidino, Herr, and Magle analyzed comments on the ten most viewed videos (respectively) of coyotes, Virginia opossums, and raccoons, three species that are more likely to be encountered in urban North Americans' lives than the exotic species we have been discussing thus far. The authors classified the comments into seven categories, following the social-ecological categories of ecophilosopher Stephen Kellert:

> naturalistic (concern for "wildlife and the outdoors"), ecologistic (concern for "environment as a system"), scientific (concern for "biological functioning of animals"), humanistic (concern for "individual animals, principally pets"), moralistic (concern for "right and wrong treatment of animals"), dominionistic (concern for "mastery and control of animals"), and negativistic ("indifference, dislike, or fear" of animals).[67]

They found that naturalistic, ecologistic, and scientific perspectives were the least commonly expressed, while humanistic, dominionistic, and negativistic opinions were the most common across all videos and species. Interestingly, YouTube users "held more dominionistic opinions toward coyotes, but more humanistic opinions toward opossum and raccoons."[68]

This relative lack of naturalistic, ecological, and scientific commentary is not surprising. It corroborates what studies of exotic pets have shown: namely, that viewers typically cannot easily tell whether or not an animal, like a lemur or slow loris, is actually enjoying its treatment by a human, such as being tickled or scratched. A 2022 report by the Social Media Animal Cruelty Coalition (SMACC) found 840 videos in social media, about half of them on Facebook and another quarter on YouTube, depicting endangered wild animals including macaques, tigers, and lions, being physically and psychologically tormented, and receiving a total of 11.8 billion views. Many show these wild animals being kept as pets.[69] While the volunteers who collected the videos reported them to the platforms, few were taken down.

The problem becomes more acute in the case of videos with staged interactions between wild animals and humans. Known to cause distress and injury to the animals, and to spread misconceptions to viewers, "fake animal rescue videos" have in recent years attained a certain notoriety thanks to the attention paid to them by animal welfare groups, media outlets including *National Geographic*, *Vice*, and *The Guardian*, and celebrities like Ricky Gervais.[70] Numerous animal welfare web sites now offer lists of signs that a rescue video has been staged, including the formulaic nature of its narrative; repeated locations, people, and rescue scenarios; clear presence of a camera crew (with multiple angles, editing, etc.); lack of narrative context and follow-up; and inconsistencies and inappropriate or unusual behaviors in the animals or people involved.[71] More recent studies of video viewership and commentary still show that exposure to staged animal rescue videos remains high and that many viewers "cannot identify (or are not concerned by) animal welfare or conservation issues."[72] That said, it is likely that public knowledge about the stagedness and scriptedness of some animal rescue videos is growing, as is the awareness of cruelty and suffering in these situations. Social media companies have also begun responding to calls to take down videos that display evident animal cruelty: as the authors of a 2023 study note, "all but two of the 241 videos included in the study were removed by YouTube" during the course of the study after National Geographic and members of the Social Media Animal Cruelty Coalition requested investigations. Moreover, 44 of 160 channels posting the staged rescue videos were terminated altogether. This response to the requests of the larger organizations contrasted with a frequent lack of response to individual complaints about web sites, and the review process for responding to complaints about animal cruelty for the most part remains opaque and inconsistent.[73] While YouTube's Community Guidelines prohibit "content where humans coerce animals to fight" and "content that shows animal rescue that is staged and puts the animal in harmful scenarios,"[74] these prohibitions are only as good as the detection, reporting, and enforcement of these rules, and the latter has not been particularly stringent.

The tension between the "real" and the "staged" is likely more palpable in instances where the familiarity of one or both of the creatures presents either a sense of shock or one of simple delight. "Golden Eagle Snatches Kid" is a classic of this genre.[75] The minute-long film (with 47 million views to date) shows what appears to be exactly that: a golden eagle circling around, swooping down and lifting a toddler, then dropping it on the ground several feet away as the camera-holding adult says "Oh, shit!" and runs, camera lens bobbing as it points to the ground, to pick up the frightened child. As James Leo Cahill describes it, the film "cannily cast[s] two of the most unruly subjects to film—babies and wild animals—in order to depict an encounter with the *real* in the form of the deadly and unpredictable business of the food chain."[76] Initial reactions to the video are often surprised and disbelieving—as in "what, really?" even if the video appears quite believable, as if this were a crazy act of God or of nature. Historically, it did not take long for the filmmakers to reveal that it was in fact a computer-assisted hoax. The video remains entertaining in part because of the way it raises the possibility of things like this happening. Cahill continues, "Videos of encounters with wild animals on YouTube act as the frontier between a well-stocked preserve for the cinema of the real in the digital era and the site where its boundaries are being re-negotiated. Real, fake, real, fake!"[77] Something similar could be said for "Pig Rescues Baby Goat," a 30-second video that seems to show a pig swimming to rescue a goat whose foot was stuck underwater at a petting zoo, but that was in time revealed to be carefully staged with about 20 crew members and an underwater track guiding the pig to the (never at risk) goat.[78]

What is not clear is to what extent this question of reality versus fakeness actually matters to viewers, who may have other motivations for watching these videos. Among the two more prevalent ones, I will suggest, are entertainment, naturally, but also the sheer speculative sense that all kinds of relationships and interactions remain possible in a world that is not entirely subsumed by humans.

## INTERSPECIES FRIENDSHIPS

Here is where the popularity of interspecies "animal friendship" videos comes into play. YouTube compilations featuring "animal odd couples," "unlikely animal friendships," the "best" or the "funniest animal friendships," and the like, are wildly popular. Some, like RealWild's "The World's Most Unlikely Animal Relationships" (with some 34 million views), include wildlife biologists explaining, or at least speculating about, what the videos show. Other animal "friends" become known characters in their own right. BLT, short for Baloo the black bear, Leo the African lion, and Shere Khan the Bengal tiger, were a bonded trio that "lived like brothers" for 15 years at Noah's Ark Animal Sanctuary after they were rescued and confiscated from a convicted drug dealer in Atlanta.[79] Other known "friends" include Bullet the Jack Russell terrier and Jag the jaguar, Hugo the bulldog and Igor the lion cub, Pippin the black-tailed deer and Kate the great dane, Pepper the cat and her suckling ducklings, Cheesecake the "foster super-mom" capybara and the litters of orphaned puppies she has adopted, and Hanuman the orangutan and her pet-like dog friend Roscoe. Videos document a variety of relationships—between polar bears and huskies, rhinos and sheep, a lioness and her adopted oryx calves, a troop of capuchin monkeys and their "pet" marmoset, and a male kudu antelope and the female giraffe he has repeatedly attempted to mate with—all of which show not only interspecies friendships but interspecies foster mothering, breastfeeding, game playing, sexual attraction, and lifetime bonding.[80]

What is especially interesting here is the role of digital media in triggering scientific interest in this phenomenon. As biologist Liz Bonnin explains in "The World's Most Unlikely Animal Relationships," it is videos on the internet that have alerted scientists to the commonality of interspecies relationships like these: "Videos getting hits in their millions are showing species interacting in ways that scientists didn't think were possible."[81] This is perhaps an overstatement: interspecies friendships are scientifically underresearched, but not unknown. More commonly referred to as interspecific "associations," "social bonds," or "social play," such relationships are thought to have multiple benefits related to cooperation over competition, stress reduction, hormonal regulation, substitute filiation (as when a parent is absent and another animal comes to perform some of the role of the missing parent), and play.[82] That aside, seeing such friendships remains surprising because we are accustomed to thinking of species as bounded categories, and cross-species friendships scramble those boundaries. Scientists themselves have not been immune to assuming those boundaries, since the models they operate with tend to focus either on individual species populations or on ecosystemic interactions.

Interspecies friendships may hardly be unnatural, then, but their prevalence is dependent on circumstances, and certain places—including captive animal sites such as zoos, safari parks, and animal rehabilitation centers—can present favorable conditions for such friendships to emerge. A study of one hundred YouTube videos showing "interspecies friendships" found that the vast majority occurred in captive rather than natural/wild environments, involved young animals (less than a year old), and appeared connected to a prior stress event such as being orphaned (80% of examples) or becoming separated from one's mother (13%).[83] To put this into a broader context: as human incursions on wildlife habitat deepen, these kinds of situations are arising more often, for individuals of many species. Three other trends arguably intersect with this one: first, human entanglements with individual animals are growing, both via the exotic pet trade and through animal rescue centers and other sites of interaction; second, cameras and other devices for visually capturing animal activities continue to spread and share images via social media; and third, at least hypothetically, a growing desire for interspecies friendship is encouraged and fed by the viral nature of online animal videos. As religion scholar Beatrice Marovich posits in her study of animal friendship videos, there is a kind of utopian undercurrent in the popular fascination with these "visions of interspecies kinship," which represent "the non-predational, creaturely, potentialities that might still emerge from these digital peaceable kingdoms."[84]

As a result of the feedback loops between such trends, both the digital visibility of interspecies friendships and the phenomenon itself is growing. This marks the sort of interaction Vinciane Despret had suggested might occur as "new forms of knowledge" and of subjectivity co-emerge with "new relational modalities" to alter the sense of what is possible between beings and across species. If digital media have brought wild animals closer to people, both as objects to be viewed and become curious about and as subjects to be interacted with, the question remains: what do we do with that closeness? What forms of interaction may or may not be appropriate in relation to wild animals?

## WILDLIFE SELFIES, VISUAL TROPHIES, AND CECIL THE LION

Videos of wild animals being shared online raise the question of what it takes for them to be encountered by camera-wielding humans. Lenzi, Speiran, and Grasso argue that "in order for a wild animal to" become "encounterable," there must first be " 'a series of severings' between the individual and their wild nature—including habituation and a loss of fear of humans."[85] In Anthropocenic times, of course, it is more and more difficult for wild animals to *avoid* encountering humans. It is perhaps for that reason that the human-animal boundary has become emotionally charged: it represents something that is increasingly being lost, and at the same time it evokes a past that can be glorified and idealized, ironically, both as a time of greater "harmony" between people and nature and as a time when nature remained "wild" and autonomous from human activities.

If the relationship between wild animals and humans was already a contentious one, the smartphone's entry into this dynamic, and especially the dawn of the selfie, has placed significantly greater pressure on that relationship. Photographic self-portraits arguably date back to a daguerreotype taken of himself by Robert Cornelius in 1839; painted self-portraits of course go back much further. The term "selfie" first seems to have been used in 2002, a year before the appearance of the first front-facing phone camera, a Sony Ericsson Z1010 that was intended not to enable quick self-portraits, but to enhance business meetings. In 2011, the first #selfie hashtag appeared on Instagram, and within three years Google was estimating that over 93 million selfies were taken every day on Google's own Android devices.[86] While selfies ostensibly are about the human subject—the self-portrait as an ideal-image, captured in an especially "live" moment—that image always comes flavored by the connotations of whatever it is shown to be encountering. Instagram has become a kind of central repository for selfies, and the platform has been described as "a vast gallery of animal exploitation," with many of its users, in Deborah Lupton's words, "seemingly unconcerned by—or, at the very least, unaware of—the suffering they are inflicting on animals by forcing them to be close to them, touching them, or even baiting them for the sake of a selfie."[87] Lupton details a history of celebrities with animal selfies: Rihanna cuddling a slow loris, Justin Bieber cradling a lion cub, and Kim Kardashian draped by a koala.[88]

As the desire to capture selfie moments increases, so do the risks associated with their pursuit. Epidemiological studies have documented close to four hundred accidental deaths caused by the effort to pose for a selfie between the years 2008 and 2021.[89] With wildlife selfies, the "temporary distraction" and "commensurate lack of situational awareness" that selfies encourage are exacerbated by a "desire for close and dramatic image capture," which can place both the selfie-taker and animals at greater risk.[90] In wildlife tourism contexts, such as the various "swim with" programs featuring marine megafauna (whales, dolphins, seals, and sharks), this can exacerbate harassment of animals. All of this puts into question the common assumption that wildlife photography is "nonconsumptive." Calculating the impacts of outdoor recreation and wildlife tourism on animals and ecosystems is not a simple matter, but it would at least have to include disruption of animals' living patterns alongside the broader ecological footprint of the transportation, accommodation, and consumption involved in tourist activities.

The pursuit of visual trophies is better known and more notorious in the case of game hunting, with its historical connotations of colonialism and masculinity. One of the most explosive image-events in recent animal rights history arose from an infamous photo of Minnesota dentist and game hunter Walter Palmer, who shot a lion named Cecil in July of 2015 in Zimbabwe's Hwange National Park. The term "image-event" has been used within literature on media activism to refer to processes "set in motion when a specific image or set of images erupts onto and intervenes in a social field, becoming a focal point of affective and discursive engagement across diverse publics."[91] In this case, it was not a single image but a constellation of them that set off this media event. The lion, it turned out, was a local celebrity, a photogenic animal unafraid of humans and a popular attraction and money-maker for the park. Palmer had reportedly paid $55,000 for the privilege of luring him with poisoned meat, shooting him with a crossbow, and then tracking the still-surviving animal for hours through the bush until he was shot dead, beheaded, and skinned, with the body left to rot.[92] Despite the Zimbabwean government's initial expressions of anger at the lion's death, this had all been done legally, with the hunting outfit (local hunting guide Theo Bronkhurst and landowner Honest Ndlovu) simply underestimating the public reaction that would ensue in the wake of the kill. Unbeknownst to them, Cecil was already part of the "internet of animals," outfitted with a GPS tracking device as part of an Oxford University conservation study. Palmer himself claimed he did not know that Cecil was a local favorite.

Picking up on the news of the lion's death, media organizations had plenty of images of Cecil to choose from: looking majestic on the Af-

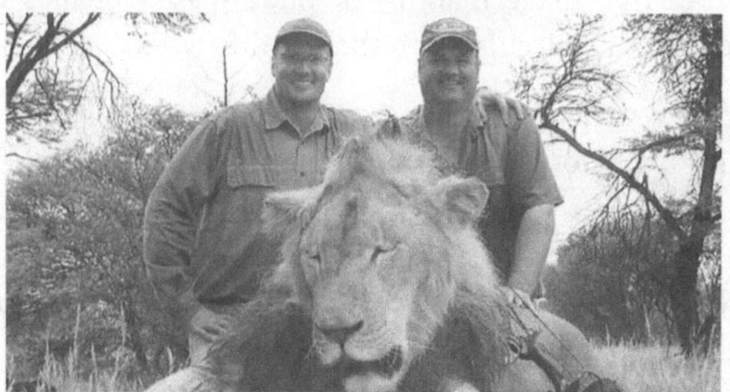


**FIGURE 6.4.** **Ricky Gervais/Facebook status, "It's not for food," featuring article on Dr. Walter Palmer, *The Telegraph*, 2015.**

rican plain, drinking by a watering hole, or "posing" with a female, a cub, or one of the lion coalition's other males. Palmer, meanwhile, was not shown with Cecil, but enraged animal rights activists quickly found images of the dentist posing with another lion he had killed. Moreover, Palmer, being "a man of his technological time," as Karla McManus puts it, had previously uploaded numerous images of himself posing with his hunting "trophies"—a rhino, a jaguar, a ram, and others—to Flickr and other web sites, and these quickly became fodder for social media memes and interventions. Photos of the kill are, after all, visual evidence of one's accomplishment.

In the viral photo of Palmer and another white hunter smiling behind the majestically large head and body of the dead lion, one can see the hunters' exhibitionary pride in the successful conquest of this "king of the beasts." Cajetan Iheka refers to the staged "frontality" of the image and its theatrical "to-be-seenness," which in the contest over meanings became "unbound" from the original intent behind the photograph. Instead of being a "self-performative" display of Palmer's hunting prowess, it became a pedagogical instrument in the hands of activists.[93] Others posted photos of Palmer from his practice's dental web site, so that his smiling face circulated regularly alongside Cecil's image, becoming, as McManus puts it, "a sinister reminder of Hannah Arendt's provocative description of the banality of evil," made famous in the wake of the trial of Nazi executioner Adolf Eichmann.[94] McManus describes the image macros, or photo-based memes combining image and text, that circulated in the ensuing weeks:

> Taking a pre-existing photograph from the web, often an image of Cecil from before his death, the maker would then add textual commentary and voila! Deeply hypersignified, these images are locked into a coded meaning informed by: majestic beauty, or carnivorous behaviour, or the tragedy of his fate at the hands of a small-town, small-minded schmuck. At times a twist is added, as in an image which shows a lion (not Cecil) licking his balls humorously paired with the phrase "moments before he was shot." Look, the image seems to say, Cecil is just like your own cat or dog. Other image macros mocked the viewer's sympathy for the dead lion, suggesting that only naive and sentimental bleeding-

> hearts think lions are not dangerous predators. But soon, the hypersignification shifted towards, as Shifman puts it, "highlighting the constructed, or even staged, nature of mediated realities" [. . .]. Images began to appear that reflected other sociopolitical concerns of the day: in the U.S. the Black Lives Matter movement became embroiled with Cecil's image, as did a scandal involving Planned Parenthood and the disposal of aborted foetuses by the organization. In reaction to the first wave of Cecil memes, from two different positions on the political spectrum, critical image macros appeared asking the same question: why do so many people get upset when one lion is killed?[95]

The entire episode encapsulated several lines of cultural tension at large both in the United States and in the world. It juxtaposed concerns over environmental disruption and the fate of endangered species with perceptions of racial privilege (it was hardly lost on audiences that Palmer was a wealthy, white American male) at a time when the politics of race were at a tipping point in the United States. The environmental concern led to an outpouring of support for conservation initiatives, raising over a million dollars for Oxford University's conservation research program in Hwange park.[96] As well, a petition calling for "Justice for Cecil" in Zimbabwe gained over a million signatories, and several major airlines agreed to stop transporting the pelts of the so-called Big Five of African megafauna: lions, leopards, rhinos, elephants, and buffalo.[97] Meanwhile, as Iheka describes, while Cecil's killing "generated outrage in the United States and across the West," little attention was paid to the incident in Zimbabwe or Africa more generally.[98] Left out of the picture, in more ways than one, were the Black laborers who assisted in the hunt, those serving the national park's conservation functions, the "Zimbabweans, and Africans more broadly, who feel that lions have more value than Black people in the Western imagination," and the "conservation refugees" across southern Africa, who "have been displaced to make room for animals and/or prohibited from cultivating land that their ancestors farmed for centuries."[99] The global politics of wildlife, environmental conservation, and human and animal welfare remain contested between more than just two sides.

## IN PURSUIT OF THE WILD SUBLIME

It is in this context that it is worth examining the work of Canadian photographer and filmmaker Gregory Colbert, even though its presence in social media has been somewhat muted. The only official YouTube site that carries his work, called AshesndSnowNY, was launched in 2006, when YouTube was young and Colbert's New York City exhibition of the *Ashes and Snow* project was still fresh. The three videos that were uploaded at the time are still on the site, having accrued 3.8 million views, but his videos can be found on other sites; and aside from books, the internet is the only place where his work can be readily found. My discussion of it in this context can thus serve both as a certain counterexample—the work of an artist who largely shies away from the digital world—and as the epitome of something that can be felt in so many videos that take place at the proverbial human-animal boundary. Its evident popularity—in spite of Colbert's notable avoidance of both the trappings of the art world and those of popular culture—speaks for itself. While the statistics cannot be verified, Colbert's claims that more than ten million people visited the *Ashes and Snow* exhibition on its global journeys, which make it the "most popular" and "most attended exhibition by any artist in history," underline the work's broad resonance with diverse publics.[100] I wish to argue that it epitomizes, and to some extent informs, a powerful tendency in the popular response to wildlife videos at a time when "nature" is presumed to be losing its battle against Anthropocenic humanity.

*Ashes and Snow* is a "nomadic museum," in Colbert's words, exhibited in purpose-built temporary structures consisting of recycled shipping containers, thick paper and bamboo tubes, and other reused materials, and shown for months at a time in Venice, New York City, Los Angeles, Tokyo, and Mexico City between 2002 and 2008. It consists of large-scale photographs, films, and a year-long novel-in-letters addressed by a traveling artist to his (presumably sedentary) wife. The more-than-50 photographs themselves are striking: sepia- and umber-toned black-and-whites, they are huge, measuring two-and-a-half by three-and-a-half meters in size, and hang suspended, unframed, by invisible cables from tubes and 34-foot high container ceilings. All feature seemingly wild animals: elephants, cheetahs, leopards, whales, falcons, zebras, caracals (African lynx), meerkats, manatees, and others, with no informational captions about location or subject. Together, the images make up Colbert's effort at creating what he calls a modern "bestiary," wherein animals are shown in their essential nature, as Colbert sees it, in stately grandeur, without fear, concern, or apparent hunger. Colbert sees his work as a form of "collaboration" with the animals: "I let the animals lead and invite them to express their own sensibilities in their own voices. A conversation with an animal begins by watching gestures and reading facial cues. It is a nonverbal conversation. You do not think an elephant. You try to feel it." He continues, "I try to create a climate of trust that opens the way for spontaneous interactions with animals."[101]

Far from leaving people out, however, Colbert incorporates humans in almost all of the images. Most are shown in poses that clearly depict a kind of submission to or entanglement with the animals: with eyes closed or in reverent or prayerful poses, cradled by animals (three monks reposing beneath a gently placed elephant's trunk), holding them in their arms, kneeling next to them, or swimming, dance-like, alongside and in contact with them (in the case of the whales). In the films, two monks drift in slow motion on a boat between two elephants, a child stands outside a temple as a hawk lands upon his back, African tribespeople sit and lie amongst leopards on a desert sand dune, a boy sleeps curled up next to a leopard, children swim alongside elephants. Like the animals, the humans are not identified; they are an ideal type, about which there is more to be said. (The exception is that in the film credits the animals are identified by species, while the "cast" members are identified by first names, with the exception of "23 Burmese monks.")

The show, in this sense, clearly depicts an idealized relationship—an ideal-image, to use this book's term, of a relationship of harmony between humans and the wild, natural world of animals. Sympathetic reviewers refer to the "timelessness" and "sense of wonder" evoked by Colbert's images, their "luminous, essential wisdom," "serenity" and "dreamlike calm," as the exhibition "operates in a parallel universe to ours, an earnest, refreshing, post-ironic world where pure wonder and awe still reside."[102] The exhibition, like the slow motion and ambient music of the films, aims to create a kind of ecstatic space for contemplation. As the *Smithsonian Magazine*'s Cathleen McGuigan wrote of the Pier 52 exhibition overlooking New York City's Hudson River,

> Entering it is a little like going to church: it is darkly dramatic, with the photographs lit and suspended on wires, so they seem to float in the nave-like space. They are stunning as objects, both in their scale—about 6 by 9 feet—and in their soft patina. Printing on handmade Japanese paper, Colbert uses beeswax or pigment to create a sense of age—or perhaps agelessness. The artist, who doesn't wear a watch (not even a Rolex), says, "I work outside of time."[103]

(Ironically, one of Colbert's leading patrons and underwriters has been Patrick Heiniger, the CEO of Rolex.)

As critics have pointed out, however, all of the people depicted with the exception of Colbert himself, shown free-diving in the underwater shots, are dark-skinned. Colbert claims that he is "working towards rediscovering the common ground that once existed when people saw themselves as part of nature and not outside of it," which suggests that those who are "part of nature" ought to look a certain way.[104] To critics, this is a simple regurgitation of colonialist tropes. As Nicole Shukin notes, apart from Colbert's occasional presence,

> only women and children appear, seminude or sumptuously draped in sartorial signifiers of a colonial era, such as white cottons and linens (no T-shirts and jeans here, no signs of corrupt coevalness with modernity and the West). They are shown either erotically or prayerfully entwined with animal bodies, as in the photo of a young South Asian boy reading to an elephant or that of an Asian child sitting in a meditative pose beside a leopard. Another photo of a young South Asian woman waist-deep in water, rapt in the phallic embrace of two elephant trunks, is an unabashed rendering of imperialist desire. Reiterating well-worn orientalist tropes, the East is both feminized and infantilized, semiographed as a terrain awaiting sexual discovery by the white male explorer. In virtually every photo, the eyes of the languid other are closed, enabling viewers of Colbert's exhibit to reproject imperialism's primal scene of intercourse with a passive virgin territory.[105]

By implication, the show also positions Colbert as the intrepid explorer and mediator of the relationships depicted, the one who has ventured out to the boundary of the human world and returned with these mythic images. There is a resonance here with the popularity of extreme sports and its cinematic relatives, mountaineering and adventure films like *Free Solo* (2018) and *Touching the Void* (2003), or viral YouTube shorts like Guillaume Néry's "One Breath Around the World" (2019, 27 million views), in which a free-diver appears to swim, unaided by breath breaks, across a multitude of underwater environments over a ten-minute period. Cultivating the persona of an elusive explorer and mystic, Gregory Colbert has studiously avoided the art circuit (and has largely been offline since about 2015). Prior to its 2002 installation at Venice's massive Arsenale shipyard, Colbert claims to have lived "off the grid" for over a decade as he traveled around the world "filming and photographing elephants, whales, birds, and other animals in India, Burma, Ethiopia, Sri Lanka, Kenya, Namibia, Egypt, the island of Dominica, Tonga, and Antarctica." The web site tells us that he in fact traveled to 34 countries over a period of 14 years. In the process, Colbert writes, "I have been tusked by an elephant, almost eaten by a sperm whale, knocked off my feet by a rhinoceros, embraced by a jaguar, given a haircut by a tiger shark, chased by a hippo and a black mamba, brought to my knees by malaria and dengue. But I was able to avoid the greatest danger of all. Never stop exploring the things that open you, or that you love."[106]

*Ashes and Snow* is in this sense a boundary object that is about the blurring of boundaries, even as it manifests its own boundedness. It attempts to blur the boundaries between people and nature, yet reasserts colonial conceptions (and perceptions) of who is "natural" and who is not. It blurs the boundary between the art object and the world, and between art and spirituality, even as it participates in global circulations—of itself between the artistic capitals of the world, of Colbert's photographs through sales to patrons (his supporters include Rolex's Heiniger and eco-entrepreneur Paul Hawken, and his photographs have been bought for substantial sums by actors including Brad Pitt and Laurence Fishburne), and of its own indebtedness to the celebrity-building capacity of traditional media and the word-of-mouth of social media.[107] As Karla McManus writes, "The internet, as a sight [*sic*] of uncurated mediation, offers the most complete fulfillment of Colbert's vision: the total work of art as exotic spectacle, rendered virtual into the hands of the admiring public."[108] It effaces Colbert himself through its cultivation of an "off the grid" persona, one who is dedicated to direct perception—no "digital collaging," retouching, or altering has taken place, he says; "The images record what [Colbert] saw through the lens of the camera"—even as it sets him up as a shamanic "obligatory passage-point" for its mystical vision of reunification with nature.[109]

This desire to touch nature and the animals that represent it, a desire to at least come close to them and bring something back—if not the animal itself (as a pet), then the wildlife selfie, the visual trophy of one's journey—haunts so much of the response to the wild animals of social media. At the same time, the proliferating conversations visible in so much YouTube commentary make it clear that questions around these desires cannot be avoided. It is, after all, in the comments beneath an online video that questions are most commonly raised: about the reality or fakeness of images; about whether animals, or in Colbert's case people, were treated respectfully and appropriately; about whether or not an artist's intent has been successfully captured in the multitude of audience responses; and about the many previous images—known from movies or, for that matter, from colonialist histories—that resonate with a given depiction. It is there where jokes, ironies, and sarcastic jibes are effectively negotiated by commenters. Colbert's personal choice to steer away from the interactivity of YouTube can be read as a desire to establish an ideal-image regime that can remain undefiled by the questions and messy debates that entanglement in social media generates. It is a choice that is indicative of the digital image-world's inhospitability to ideal-images except perhaps at the level of individualized tokens—selfies proclaiming one's own right to personally shape one's idealized public image. Social media provide a kind of unmanageable public sphere within which competing image-regimes, from the animate-image to the world moving-image, are contested by being subjected to each other. The ideal-image regime, which is the one in which Colbert attempts to operate, does not thrive in that environment. But I will try to argue, in this chapter's concluding section, that a certain, more animate kind of ideality *could* thrive.

## *PHOTOGÉNIE* OF THE EXTENDED ZOO-CINE-SENSORIUM

Film theorist Anat Pick, in an article called "Animal Life in the Cinematic *Umwelt*," has suggested that cinema has a particular "aptitude for showing the creaturely universes, or 'life-worlds' of human and nonhuman beings." She refers to this as cinema's "zoomorphic realism."[110] The "contours of an *Umwelt*," or life-world, Pick writes, "its coming into being as a subjective engagement between the living being and the objects around it, challenge anthropocentric conceits."[111] To the extent that online videos depicting animals show us glimpses of these animals' life-worlds, they contribute to the challenging of anthropocentric conceits, a process that may or may not continue as viewers respond to and reflect on their thoughts and feelings alongside those of other viewers and commenters.

If videos of animals always imply a relationship with the humans that film them or that, in the case of zoo-cams and critter-cams, set up the cameras that capture their images, there is always also a third player involved: the camera technology itself. Cameras, as I have been describing them, are part of networks that produce and reproduce images, collect and analyze them, and disseminate and interpret them. But they also take very material forms. In a twist on the animal video genre where the materiality of the camera comes to play an unusually prominent role, there are the videos in which cameras are attached to animals or, more interestingly, are taken by animals who then become unwitting filmmakers.

The "seagull stole my camera" genre has been especially popular, with herring gulls becoming its "pioneers," as Concepción Cortés Zulueta calls them, though a wide range of other camera-stealers have emerged, including sea turtles, octopuses, eagles, monkeys, squirrels, lions, belugas, elephants, otters, sea lions, foxes, and domestic dogs. Cameras, in turn, have been opened, dismantled, and even "devoured alive," resulting in jarringly non-anthropocentric perspectives whose "unconventions" can include feats of bizarre physicality that are impossible with humans or machines, as well as "extreme close-ups of isolated non-human eyes, hairy limbs, sharp claws, slippery tentacles, and suckers, or [. . .] the oozy inside of an oral cavity, fangs and fleshy tongue included," that "recall the conventions exploited by monster movies."[112]

There is a spectrum here between the (humanly) intentional and unintentional uses of cameras, and within the first category, between those oriented for scientific purposes and those intended for art or entertainment. Attaching cameras to the backs or bodies of animals for scientific purposes builds on the use of other electronic tracking equipment to give us a view of what an animal sees, or at least what it would see if it saw like a camera and not with its own eyes. The ideal is that the camera becomes an invisible eye, like Emerson's "transparent eye-ball" that *is* "nothing" but "see[s] all," or at least allows its human makers to see through the eyes of other animals in addition to our own.[113] But that ideal is disrupted when the camera's materiality is noticed: as in Sam Easterson's *A Sheep in Wolf's Clothing* (1998), when a sheep with a camera-equipped helmet on its head is treated as an outcast by the other sheep, who reject its entreaties to join their herd.[114] There is also a long tradition of art films that have sought animal, "nonhuman," or "machinic" perspectives on the world. Of many documentaries, Lucien Castaing-Taylor and Véréna Paravel's *Leviathan* (2012) is perhaps the most extreme in its use of dangling, swaying, and otherwise mobilized GoPro cameras, oblique and unusual angles, and other anthropodecentered audiovisual techniques employed toward creating an immersively visceral experience of an industrial fishing boat and its in- or extra-human impacts.

Videos that become popular on YouTube tend to have at least the bare elements of character, and even of narrative. "Dramatic Tarsier Stares at You for 10 Hours" pushes the limits of spectatorial endurance—it is in fact a loop, though not obviously so, of a close-up of a primate known for its enormous "staring" eyes (see image at the beginning of this chapter). Viewers note the humor as well as the "creepiness" in the sustained image, though some seem to have made it a point of competition to see how long they can "stare back" at the tarsier.[115] If the tarsier is the character in this film, one that begs the question "what is he or she thinking?", it is worth remembering that for the tarsier, it is the camera—"this strange thing I am looking at"—that is the character. This becomes much more obvious in compilation videos like "Animals Inspect Cameras" and "Animals Find the Live Cam," web sites like "9 Awesome Videos of Animals Discovering Cameras," and news stories like "This Black Bear Took Hundreds of 'Selfies' on a Wildlife

Camera."[116] Here it is animals' curiosity that becomes visible, a curiosity that—mediated by the camera and screen—mirrors our own curiosity as we watch. "Curious Chimp Checks Out Camera" is one of the more interesting, as a chimpanzee methodically probes at a wildlife camera first with a stick, then with a finger that leaves behind smudges, and then with an open hand, the chimp's intent gaze following its actions all along.[117] In "Prairie Dog Up Close!," it is the olfactory curiosity of two prairie dogs, visible in the sniffing action of their camera-facing noses, that meets the human-extending visual curiosity represented by the GoPro camera that has been placed just outside their mound.[118]

Other videos of animals actively discovering and then manipulating cameras display a photogenic beauty in their scenes of spontaneous camerawork, with its pure motion and novel perspectives. This happens in the seagull-carried camera in "Seagull Stole GoPro," a classic of the genre.[119] In the 1-minute-and-40-second nighttime video, a seagull picks up a camera and flies off with it, providing wobbly drone-like footage of the street-lit cityscape before it lands and, with a victorious yelp, drops the camera onto a roof. It then plays with it a bit more, providing an abstract series of floating-eyeball perspectives on itself (from below), the black sky behind it, and the roofscape, before wandering away. The soundtrack consists almost entirely of seagull squawks, loudly insistent

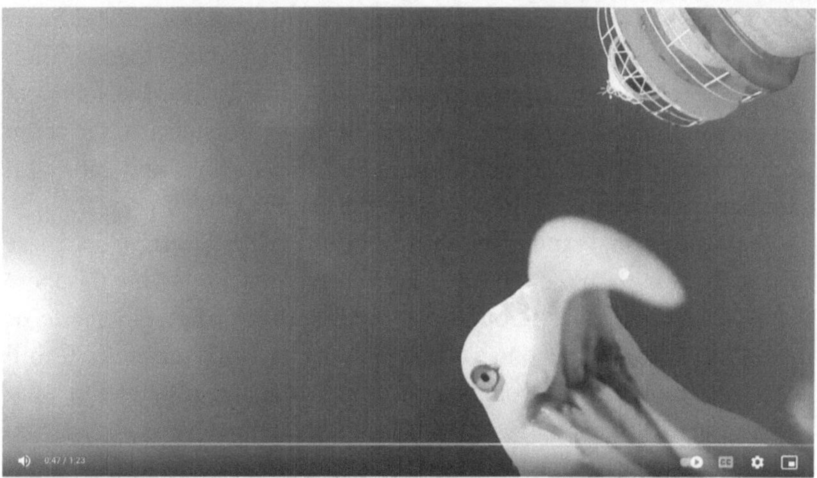

**FIGURE 6.5.** Screenshot from "GoPro: Seagull Stole My GoPro," by GoPro, YouTube, 2015.

in their alienness, except for an initial yell "Hey!" from the camera's human owner when the seagull lifted it. Videos like these excite in part because of the randomness that go into their making: there is no contract signed with the seagull that it will return the camera after the shoot, and it is only thanks to the persistence of its human owner that the video is ever retrieved and made shareable.

"Crab Makes a Movie" (aka "Oops! Dropped my Camera in the River!") (megyerdon/Ryan Strout, USA, 2011) begins when a dropped GoPro camera "films its own descent to the depths of the water." Later, as a crab hovers over it, its lens catches blurred images of the crab's carapace as, in James Leo Cahill's words, "fish dart past in the middle distance, and the murky shadows of humans appear as a recessed presence near the distant surface."[120] "Crab Steals a GoPro and Makes a Movie in His Lair" and the earlier "Crab Steals GoPro and You Won't Believe the Footage He Creates" are in a similar vein—all close-ups, chomping, and rich color. One could imagine a full-length, unedited version of these films passing for an experimental masterwork by a crustacean James Benning, a structural minimalist filmmaker intent on rendering a camera gaze on a nonhuman world. Other underwater videos are equally stunning in their otherworldly color: these include "Sea Turtle Finds Lost Camera" and the high-speed adventure tale "Octopus Steals My Video Camera and Swims Off with It (While It's Recording)." The land-based variation of the genre includes "Squirrel Steals GoPro and Carries It Up a Tree," "Eagle Steals Camera," "Haida Gwaii Bald Eagle Steals GoPro," and "Elephants Steal Go-Pro—Take Selfie Videos." "Crab Steals GoPro" begins with the slow and silent, horror film-like ascent of a crab from its underground hole, continues with its decision to wrap itself around the camera and bring it down into its hole, and ends with a human quickly emerging to retrieve the camera.[121]

The impersonal and non-anthropocentric perspectives in these scenes, along with the contextual layeredness of the human mediasphere that is always in the background, suggest that this is a new cinematic, or mediatic, genre. On the one hand, it harkens back, as James Leo Cahill argues, to the Vertovian goal of a pure cinematicism, a "Kino-Eye" that reveals the world through a novel, technological gaze. Multiplied across the camera-surveillance landscape, this gaze adds a new layer of technological visuality to the world, one largely unmediated by human control (except in the set-up) but mediated, rather, by the camera lens and the apparatus by which the gaze is shared and multiplied. It is part of the indexical world-picturescape that has grown alongside the development of digital technologies. On the other hand, it engages the agential and polymorphous multiplicity of a living, more-than-human world which has its own desires, goals, curiosities, and habits. Cahill argues that videos like the ones I have been describing are reviving a tradition of early French film theory focused on a *photogénie des bêtes*, or "animal *photogénie*," where silent animal and plant documentaries were celebrated as "marvelous witnesses to the enigmas of life."[122] While the term "photogenic" literally means "produced or precipitated by light" (or, in biology, producing or emitting light), and is commonly used to refer to things that are taken to be highly photographable, capturable in light, Cahill explains that the French theorists used the notion to assess cinema ontologically, phenomenologically, and technically so as to articulate a "critically re-evaluative vision of the world." *Photogénie* not only referred to "qualities of the profilmic world revealed by film," but also to "the spectator's cinematic experience" and "the effects of the cinematic apparatus in animating relays between world, spectacle and spectator."[123] For Jean Epstein, *photogénie* "reveals the non-identical nature of things, their perpetual becoming rather than their identity as fixed entities." For both Epstein and Louis Delluc it marked an autonomy of the technical apparatus, which could expand the limits of human perception even as it opened cinematic art to the contingency and indeterminacy of reality itself.[124] And with the proliferation of amateur as well as professionally produced videos on YouTube and other video aggregators, we see a dramatic increase in animal and wildlife videography that, in Cahill's words, "concentrates on the fleeting, contingent, non-narrative, untamed, wild and savage aspects of moving image media, but also presents examples of a literal photogénie des bêtes: an animal-generated photogénie."[125]

Some of this productivity has given rise to communities of followers who not only track newly uploaded videos, but seek out the creatures that star in those videos. As we have seen, the effects of this are not always laudatory. But when they are associated with local animal populations that are both pleasurable to observe and autonomous in their actions (and not particularly impacted by the observers), these efforts can contribute to learning about ecological environments. The massed flight of birds has long captivated its viewers, and among the more photogenic of species are starlings, whose murmurations (as they are called), when they are captured on video, have accrued tens of millions of views on YouTube and elsewhere.[126] The classic among these may still be Sophie Windsor Clive and Liberty Smith's "Murmuration" with 11.1 million views, which, from a wobbly camera in a moving canoe, captures masses of starlings forming and reforming in dynamic configurations in the sky above and around the two canoeists.[127] Videos like these are shared in social media groups such as the "Starling Murmuration Information (British Isles)" Facebook group, which had 28,000 members in early 2025, having nearly quadrupled in the four years preceding. The group, formed to share "locations, photos and videos of this wonderful natural occurrence," restricts itself to members in the United Kingdom and Ireland, but other geographically based groups do similar work elsewhere. It is this kind of geolocatedness of camera-equipped viewers of the natural world that may be contributing to Vinciane Despret's new interspecies "relational modalities."

In Sean Cubitt's *Ecomedia*, a book that laid the groundwork for so much scholarship in ecocinema and ecomedia studies, Cubitt argued on behalf of "a mode of looking that encourages the world's unmotivated upsurge to well up into us, clasp itself to us, merge with the salt water in our veins," a mode in which the earth, or in the case he was examining, "the ocean as a whole looks back, feels us as surely as we feel it." Echoing some of the arguments of Mark Hansen, Benjamin Bratton, and others referred to in chapter 3 of this book, Cubitt proposed that "techne" has become "the only route through which we now can sense the world, most especially that part of the world's conversations which are not conducted in wavelengths we can hear, see or otherwise apprehend." "If the core of such ethics" as are required today "is wonder," which arguably undergirds both the best science and the best art, "its corollaries are connectivity on the one hand—the imbrication of the human in the stories of the sea [and, we should add, the earth]—and on the other the sheer autonomy of this complex environment."[128] Cubitt saw such an expanded and reflexively more-than-human mode of looking prefigured in elements of BBC's *Blue Planet* series, and I have since written about how the later David Attenborough series *Planet Earth*, for all its limitations, continued with some of this sensibility. The previous chapter's examination of John Akomfrah's use of BBC's Natural History Unit videos shows us that that potential can be mobilized productively and somewhat disjunctively, even if it doesn't encapsulate an ideal of its own.

In this chapter I have tried to show that YouTube's sprawling world of animal-related videos presents a second dimension of this "mode of looking" premised, at once, on the connectivity of digital media and on an autonomy that opens itself to others-of-a-nonhuman-kind. There are within it many modes of looking, some quite contrary to others, and many modes of approaching the presumed boundary between humans and other animals. As Cubitt suggests, however, the technological infrastructure of the digital image-world has become an important part of the way in which relations between the human and the more-than-human are mediated. James Leo Cahill ends his essay on animal *photogénie* with the claim that cinema, and by extension the digital world of YouTube, does not generalize so much as it particularizes. Quoting Jean Epstein, he writes, "'An eye in close-up is no longer the eye, it is AN eye.' Animal photogénie theorises on the side of radical singularity," which means that for digital cinema there is no longer "the animal" but "*animals*, in all their diversity, singularity, and fleeting and unpredictable beauty."[129] If Gregory Colbert's *Ashes and Snow* displayed an attempt to create a singular bestiary, one that, I argued, must keep itself away from the unruly clamor of social media if it is to become the ideal-image Colbert desires, Cahill's thinking suggests that there is no singular logic to be found in the "post-cinema of animal attractions." It is all far less constrained than that.

Yet there are openings to the animacy of the world in its multiple singularities: this crab, that shark, this rash of starling murmurations, that strange friendship, this runaway horse (to cite one of Cahill's bestiary examples, a 27-second video in a which a horse appears running down a busy city sidewalk followed by a dog). Each video, as Cahill writes, "indexes the integration of the profilmic world," the world or event that was captured in the video, with the "mobile filming device, and larger communication networks and infrastructures."[130] Together, they make up a fluid and open-ended series of entanglements, one that is never fully graspable and always on the verge of disappearance (depending on the fate of the particular YouTube channel, video source, etc.). Some of the videos strike us with their animacy, they *move* us, as audiences were moved by the first moving images over a century ago. Others leave us wondering: what is this tarsier thinking, what would I do if I encountered that harassing shark, what will the chimpanzee do if he succeeds in extracting the camera from its mount? Some impress us with their expressiveness, but not always as products of their human creator; sometimes it is the animal that we are more impressed by. Some are sublime, in their own limited and eminently questionable ways. Many raise questions about how they were made and what they might tell us about the creatures they portray. They can in this sense be thought of as slivers of a fragmentary world-picture, each indexically connectible to the location it was spotted and the science that might shed light on its appearance, but incapable of being corralled into the kind of overarching synthesis feared by Heidegger and other critics of the modern world-picture regime.

For all its animate singularities and contingencies, and for all their unruly connectedness, there are wave-like patterns shaping what happens in data-worlds, whose algorithmic contours remain unexamined and unaccountable. They are by-products of economies premised on giving us more of what we like, so that our data can be sold to others who would give us even more of it. Before coming back to those algorithmic waveforms, let us first visit a third set of boundary relations, this one yet more elusive than the others.

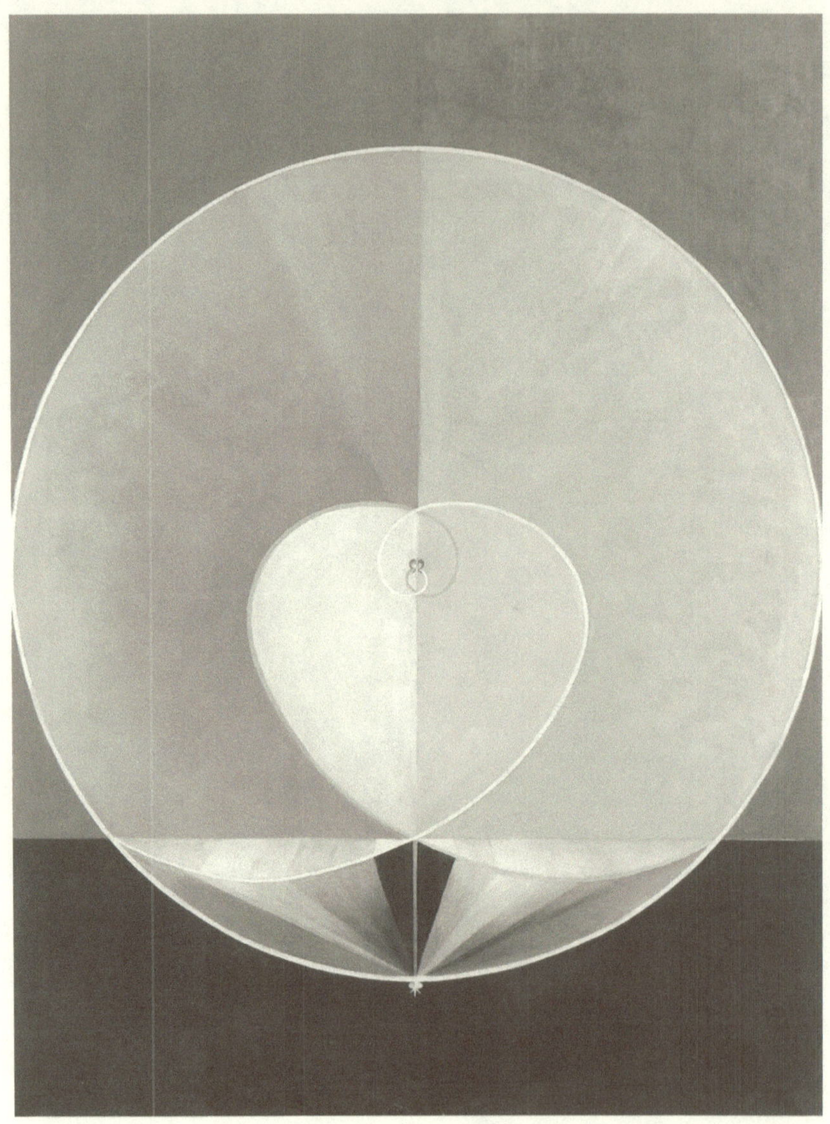

**FIGURE 7.1.** Hilma af Klint, Group IX/UW, *The Dove,* no. 2, 1915. Public domain image.

## Seven

# THEOSCENE

*At this moment I have knowledge of, in the living reality, that I am an atom in the universe that has access to infinite possibilities of development. These possibilities of development I want, gradually, to reveal.*

—*HILMA AF KLINT*[1]

*[M]an everywhere is still living in prehistory, indeed all and everything still stands before the creation of the world, of a right world.* True genesis is not at the beginning but at the end, *and it starts to begin only when society and existence become radical, i.e. grasp their roots. But the root of history is the working, creating human being who reshapes and overhauls the given facts. Once he has grasped himself and established what is his, without expropriation and alienation, in real democracy, there arises in the world something which shines into the childhood of all and in which no one has yet been: homeland.*

—*ERNST BLOCH*, The Principle of Hope[2]

• • • If the Therioscene stages surprising and sometimes transgressive interactions with wild animals, beings we know are out there but whose lives are best lived away from ours, there is another, less identifiable wilderness to be found in popular and subcultural media. For starters, this includes the wilderness of the religious, spiritual, and paranormal. Each of these terms fails to encompass the full array of the phenomena I intend to address. "Religion" itself has never been clearly and conclusively defined; "spirituality" fares even worse.[3] The paranormal, along with the occult and esoteric, directly suggests a less normative and more free-ranging spectrum of phenomena.[4] All of these are somehow opposed to the conception of a world that is "secular" and scientifically knowable, yet it is not clear to what extent that world has been secularized, as secularization theorists promised it would be, or has in fact become "post-secular."[5] It is arguably marked, rather, by multiple and incomplete transitions between one or both of these shifts: from the "religious" or "traditional" to the "modern" and "secular," and from the latter to the "post-secular," with all the ambiguities these categories allow for.

I have argued elsewhere for a conception of religion and of spirituality that sees the world as varying on a scale between the "polytropic" and the "monotropic," where "tropism" refers to the turning toward sources of "sustenance, hope, relief, or defence."[6] Polytropy, in Michael Carrithers's definition, refers to "the sense in which people turn toward many sources" for this.[7] My definition is broader than Carrithers's in that it takes this "sustenance, hope, relief, or defence"—one could add authority, deference, guidance, motivation, identity, and more—as not restricted to forms or practices conventionally termed religious. One could turn to science, to social recognition, to human history, to family or ancestry, to national or tribal identity, or to "the land" or "nature" for sustenance and guidance. Many people do, and most turn to multiple such sources, if not all at once, at least in different proportions and on varying occasions.

The present chapter concentrates its attention on those sources of sustenance that are not easily identifiable within a secular, modern, scientific worldview, one defined in part by the regime of the world-picture—the regime according to which only that which is visible or scientifically measurable is real. Rather, these sources appear at the peripheries of that world-picture, in marginal spaces and alternative or "occult geographies" where the modern world's official economies of knowledge (as adjudicated by scientific authorities), of trust (by political authorities), and of sanctity (by religious authorities) meet their respective "others" in the shadowy borderlands—those places where one finds "anomalous phenomena," suspicion and conspiracy theory, and various redistributions of the sacred and the profane.[8] Here one may find deities, especially those less well known and recognized than the tamed gods of public monotheism. Here also are spirits, specters, angels, aliens, ancestors, and other entities whom we might encounter by chance or by effort, or even be invaded and possessed by in acts of channeling or mediumship that may be sought for or may come unbidden. The key is that they are conceived as not lesser than but in key respects *greater* than humans, and so "turning" and "opening" toward them makes one a potential recipient or medium for information, knowledge, wisdom, or other qualities from such sources.

This section may therefore be better described as a Mediumoscene, a Spectroscene, an Etheroscene, or a Parascene; even naming it puts us on uncertain terrain. I am calling it a Theoscene in part to indicate that there are deities here, at least in the work of the artist on whom I will focus most directly (Hilma af Klint), but also to refer to the work of theosophy, both in its institutional forms (as Theosophy) and its noninstitutional practices. With respect to the latter, *theosophia* is commonly taken as a more intuitive and free-flowing partner to *theologia*: the knowledge (*logos*) of God is to be rationally sought and debated, while the wisdom (*sophia*) of God, or the gods, can only be inferred, intuited, or found through the gnosis of contemplation and direct experience. In its best known institutional form, however, the influence of the Theosophical Society is writ large on the modernist arts of the late nineteenth and early twentieth centuries. Two of its key ideas, thought-forms and spiritual evolution, will be important for us to consider here, as they continue to influence cultural and spiritual movements long after Theosophy had itself declined in its institutional form.

Since the subject matter of this chapter is more challenging to identify and circumscribe than that of the previous two (respectively, the Anthropocene and animals), it will take more theoretical untangling at the outset. Its case studies will also range across a broader field of media and artistic formats, so that we can better grasp the implications of the questions raised here. I will begin with an exploration of the generic question "Are we alone?" so as to identify what it means if we answer "no." Then I turn to the concept of thought-forms, contextualizing it within understandings of the imaginal and the imagination as these have arisen within religious studies and contemporary philosophy. I will examine in depth the tremendous surge in popularity of the work of Hilma af Klint (1862–1944) following her 2018–19 exhibition at the Guggenheim Museum; and will compare this to the work of later occult artists including painter and spiritual teacher Oberto Airaudi, founder of the Damanhur eco-community of northern Italy, and African-American pianist and composer Herman Blount, better known as Sun Ra. The latter's "Astro-black" mythology profoundly influenced the emergence of the Afrofuturist arts movement. Delving into Afrofuturism will allow me to consider the utopian potentials of music, and especially of improvisation, which I will relate to traditions of divination, or the interpretive opening towards more-than-human forms of otherness. The chapter will end with a return to the "oceanic" imagination, explored previously in reference to the video work of John Akomfrah, in the ecologically informed work of another Afrodiasporic artist, poet Alexis Pauline Gumbs.

## ARE WE ALONE YET?

Insofar as the very notion of an Anthropocene represents the culmination of an onto-epistemological humanism, a centering of collective humanity as the leading actor on the world stage, this question "Are we alone?" haunts the Anthropocenic imagination. Logically speaking, the question invites a series of answers, each of which has emerged in different guises.

Blaise Pascal's famous line "The eternal silence of these infinite spaces," that is, of the heavens, "frightens" or "terrifies me" exemplifies an affirmative response to the question: yes, we humans are alone in this universe.[9] For whatever reason, there is no other species that is our kin. We stand alone, and this marks our significance, our greatness, or perhaps our tragedy. We have no one to turn to except the figments of our own imagination and the results of our own creativity. (Presumably, AI would lie within that span.) Pascal went on to reason that the benefits of believing in a God, one whose inhabitation of those spaces would temper that fear, outweigh the benefits of disbelieving in such a God. But the very fact that he was able to raise the question tells us how far down the road of a species solipsism elite European thinking had reached by the seventeenth century.

Indigenous cultures around the world would likely recoil at the very question. Who is "we," they might ask? Do we not already inhabit a world rich with kin of many kinds? Setting these two in dialogue with each other suggests a range of other potential responses. At one end, then, we could simply answer yes and accept our human aloneness with solemnity, grace, befuddlement, or arrogant pretense; let's call this the ultra-humanist option. Secondly, we could answer no, that there are others out there and that we might one day, or have already, been in contact with them; the only thing preventing us from knowing this is the distance of Pascal's heavens. Let's call this the extraterrestrial, or "distant more-than-human," option. The very fact that there are hundreds of billions of Earth-like planets in our own galaxy, not to mention the hundreds of billions of other galaxies in the observable universe, suggests that the chances of us being alone in the universe are astronomical (no pun intended). Thirdly, we can answer no, that we aren't even alone *here*, as we have so many companions with such rich ways of making sense of their own worlds, neurocognitively similar or different from us and with sensory systems comparable in varying degrees; let's call this the "near more-than-human" option. (Where chatbots and other forms of technical persons might figure into this will be an open question.) Finally, we can push the latter approach further to simply ask, *Who do you mean by "we"?* and *What do you mean by "alone"?* Not only are there furry, finned, winged, webbed, vascular, rooted, and mycelial others; there are the many others of our dreams, our visions, and our mythological narratives. The question barely computes. Let's call this the "always much-more-than-human" option.

If these options were marginal, we could confidently pursue the ultra-humanist position, but they have never been marginal, and they are not that in the broader world today. The question then becomes what to do with the other-than-humans in our midst already. What is their ontological status relative to ours? If some of them are, like us, the kinds of evolved biophysical life forms studied and confirmed by evolutionary science over the last several decades, then what status do we assign those which are not—the spirits, deities, or whatever else, by all the names they have come and gone with—and how do we draw whatever boundaries may separate these categories? Are there empirically verifiable, scientifically researchable entities—particles, molecules, genes, organisms, and other measurable or theoretically positable forces—and then, in contrast, other kinds of things that humans posit, but that elude empirical verification through science? There is a long and distinguished tradition of bifurcating the world this way (to use Whitehead's term), distinguishing the empirically real from the imagined or merely experienced, and I have already made the case for rejecting this tradition. At any rate, some scholars today argue that this way of thinking overly privileges science as a way of knowing, at the expense of Indigenous and non-western ways of knowing. Yet the belief in multiple ways of knowing hardly makes things easier for us, for as long as we lack an agreeable means to bring those alternative ways into commensurability, that is, into a common framework of understanding whereby their differences can be navigated. If non-western ways of knowing (and many western ones, too) posit gods, spirits, or other forces as real entities with which we humans maintain relations, is there a common language for speaking about those relationships?

The ontological turn in anthropology has returned these questions to the forefront of that field. It is in the study of religion that these questions of ontology become particularly acute, even if they are conventionally left aside so that the study of religion can continue without too much discomfort. At the broadest, however, we can distinguish "essentialist" presumptions from "constructivist" challenges. Where some presume that the gods, spirits, angels, or other divinities—*some* if not *all* of them—are what believers say they are, or at least are something apart from human constructions, with some sort of agency of their own, others have long argued that they are nothing but social productions fabricated, imagined, and enacted into presence through individual and collective human activities. This opposition may be deeply ingrained, but it is not irreconcilable. Human activities clearly produce religion, but that does not necessitate that there aren't other things at play—agencies or "actants," to use Bruno Latour's agnostic formulation, with some of these being "natural" or accountable through current science and others not. If we are to follow our Whiteheadian premise, introduced at the outset of this volume, that the greenness of the trees is no less ontologically significant than the molecules, electromagnetic waves, and neuro-sensory processes that deliver that greenness to us, then we have to admit that the religious experiences of billions is *real experience* even if the theories that account for it are contestable (was it God who spoke to me, or my wish-fulfilling unconscious mind?). In this sense, the fact that millions of people around the world swear they have seen and even interacted with ghosts, spirits, or deities is an empirical fact of the same ontological status as the fact that scientists have failed to capture those ghosts in an empirically replicable way. And the reality that unidentified aerial phenomena continue to be witnessed, by reliable witnesses like military pilots no less, and that some of these appearances seem to deny what we know about current human technological capacities, is an empirical fact about which theories still elude any consensus.

Among the recent volumes that tackle this question of the ontology of gods, spirits, and other religious entities, religion scholar Tanya Luhrmann's 2020 book *How God Becomes Real: Kindling the Presence of Invisible Others* can be taken as a credible summary of a widespread scholarly position.[10] Luhrmann is a leading light in the anthropology of religion; she is widely interviewed and cited, pens *New York Times* op-eds, and her books win awards and lengthy *New Yorker* profiles. Her research has focused on so many different religious communities—American Evangelicals, Black and Latino Catholics, Orthodox Jews, Anglo-Cuban Santeria initiates, Indian Parsi Zoroastrians, Pentecostalists in India and Africa, and British neo-Pagan ritual magicians—that by now its insights can be considered well-honed and thoroughly road-tested. The book is in fact an excellent case study of how *practice* has become central in the scholarly interpretation of religion, so I will take it as a stand-in for a range of research in the practice of religion, and also for how difficult it is for even the best such research to shed the legacy of a kind of ultra-humanism.

As suggested by her title, *How God Becomes Real* presents an ontological constructivist perspective on religious beings, which are not real ipso facto (or ex nihilo; choose your metaphor), but must be *made* real. The reality of gods, spirits, and religious or invisible beings is something that is *accomplished* through the work and effort of their devotees, and this puts such entities on a different ontological plane than "ordinary," "factual" "things of the everyday world."[11] "Spirits," Luhrmann writes, "are different in kind from ordinary objects."[12] "Mundane beliefs adjust to the empirical details,"[13] whereas "supernatural beliefs" do not, because they are held much more tightly *due* to the cognitive and affective labor it has taken to produce them. Luhrmann has made this case in previous work, as with her 1989 account of contemporary ceremonial magicians, *Persuasions of the Witch's Craft*.[14] A key concept in that work was "interpretive drift," the activity by which one set of assumptions gets replaced by another through the repeated and communally supported effort at learning to see, hear, and perceive the world differently. One might, following Jacques Rancière (2004), call this a "redistribution of the sensible," and it is in its focus on sensibility, sensitivity, and their cultivation that Luhrmann's work continues to compel, even as she has applied it to such a disparate array of case studies.[15] At times this argument brings her into close contact with other forms of ontological constructivism, such as those of Bruno Latour, Philippe Descola, Eduardo Viveiros de Castro, and others she cites mostly in passing (and mostly approvingly).

The argument she weaves is expertly presented, with a tremendous array of empirical material to support it. There is a pitfall, however, that sneaks into her writing at key moments, where she appears to smuggle in unacknowledged and unquestioned assumptions about what religion is and is not. Recall that the key distinction in her argument is between things that are self-evidently real—things that are "natural," empirically perceived, and known to be part of the everyday furniture of the world—and others that manifestly are not, and that therefore have to be *made* real. Luhrmann's emphasis is always on the various activities that make them real: the building up of rich and detailed "paracosms" (via stories that can be serialized and reiterated in multiple forms), the "talent and training" it takes to learn to pay attention to how gods and spirits respond to one's prayers, to become absorbed in those responses such that they change one's life, and to otherwise make the "faith frame" (a key term in this book) as seemingly real as is ordinary reality. (A second volume could equally describe the same number of ways in which gods and spirits come to *lose* their reality—which would of course be a volume on secularization at the societal level, or "deconversion" at the individual level, and which would call for a third, on post-secularism. But that is asking too much of a single researcher.)

In a key passage, Luhrmann writes, "What rituals do is to remind people that gods and spirits matter":

> People need rituals because people do not in fact treat their religious beliefs [. . .] that a helpful god is real the same way they

> treat their beliefs that trees grow upward and coconuts fall down. [. . .] The idea that there is an invisible other who takes an active, loving interest in your life is in many ways preposterous and takes effort to maintain, even in a community that has never been secular. It takes intention and attention.[16]

In other words, there is "a mode of thinking in which gods and spirits really matter, and a mode of thinking about the *ordinary world of rocks and dogs and what to buy at the store*."[17] Luhrmann is drawing a line here between what is empirically self-evident, "ordinary," and "really out there," and what is not. "The deep anthropological puzzle," she writes in the book's closing sentence, "is how people come to feel intensely that invisible beings matter to their lives—how the invisible world comes close to humans and looks back, alive."[18]

But is it the *invisibility* of gods that makes us have to work harder with them, or is it what they *do* for us? The subatomic world that is "seen" by physicists through sophisticated machines in laboratory settings is no more visible to most people than the spirit world, yet the former doesn't amount to much (again, for most people), while the latter may if it brings results that count. The trees growing up and coconuts falling down do not matter much, unless of course they are essential to survival (or fatal, both of which they could be under the right conditions). There is, I would suggest, an important difference between the empirical visibility of "matters of fact," in Bruno Latour's parlance, and the existential presence of "matters of concern," but the two of them do not necessarily line up against the dichotomy of the visible and the invisible, or the obviously and not-so-obviously real.

What this dichotomy misses, then, is that the rituals are not just reminding people that their gods and spirits matter. It's the work those entities are believed to perform that matters, and that matters much more than those rocks and "what to buy at the store." For any deities worth their salt, this is the work of healing from illness, comforting in the depths of despair, and otherwise transforming their subjects in the midst of the most concerning crises and challenges of life. Whether it's done by gods and spirits (and their shamanic facilitators), or by hospitals, therapists, and modern medicine, those kinds of things—healing, repairing a community after a social rift or the sudden loss of an important leader's life—take time and effort. And just because that effort has been offloaded to medical laboratories, universities, and decades of research does not mean that the effort has not been made. There is no free lunch, one might say, when it comes to illness, death, grief, hunger, warfare, disaster, and life's other exigencies—which is where those gods and spirits (or medical and therapeutic powers) are needed most.

How they do that is not just by the tricks of the fiction writer's trade. (Luhrmann often compares religious beliefs to *Harry Potter* books or the "parasocial" reality taken on by television characters for their fans.) Luhrmann reassures us that "the evidence still suggests that invisible beings are understood as *differently real* from everyday objects everywhere";[19] they are of a different ontological order than "everyday objects." She acknowledges that "a god is not of course thought to be a fictional character by persons of faith," but then immediately slips up: "Nonetheless, the experience is parasocial because its content occurs largely inside the person's head, using his or her imagination"[20]—as if the lessons of the embodied, extended, embedded, enactive, affective, and imaginal turns in the cognitive study of religion were rendered irrelevant to where the experience of gods or spirits (or healing or transformation) was occurring.[21] The greater trajectory of Luhrmann's argument works its way out of this problem by clarifying that what matters is how the "inner" and "outer," or what we might call subjectivity and objectivity, get blurred—in an area she comes to call the "in-between." But she pays inadequate attention, in my reading, to the way in which the world itself is always already "in between."[22]

Matters of concern, then, may come couched in the symbolic language and efficacy of gods, or of science, or of energies, mana, spirit, orgone, or any other construct which is made real not because of its empirical elusiveness, but because it is central to how things that matter are made operant within a culture. How those things are made operant is what is important. For religious realities—or any realities—to "work" for people, they need to be lodged within a coherent network of activities, commitments, and "enchantments," as David Morgan describes them in *Images at Work* (which I discussed in chapter 4). And the efficacy of that network is real because it is coordinated, maintained, and kept in place by the world around us, a world of buildings and structural arrangements, relevant images and designs, and other material presences—a world that is not at all invisible, and that in fact mediates what will be visible and what will be rendered invisible for us. The world has its "distributions of the sensible," and the idea that religion is entirely different in its distributions than, say, a scientific, secular world is presupposed by Luhrmann, without being actually defended.[23] Her focus on what believers do to make their "faith frames" real is a welcome antidote to all the efforts asking why believers believe things that are evidently false, but it misses the ways in which faith frames are not just *religious* frames, but are all of the manifold ways in which worlds are shaped, enacted, and mediated by human and nonhuman objects and forces of all kinds, some of which are visible, or audible, and others of which are removed from sensory expression but built on relations of trust, persuasion, and delegation. One might say that to the extent that we live in a common world, whether religious or not, we live in a faith frame: we live committed to that world.

And that world has always included a range of negotiations around who or what is an agent within the world, and who or what can be appealed to for authority, insight, guidance, sustenance, and so on. The global world we share today is, by its nature, polytropic: it includes many significant agents or actants acknowledged by some and not by others, and the role of these actants—these sources of authority, guidance, and so on—is undeniable in people's navigation of the challenges posed by present circumstances. To get a sense of how this process works, the next section will focus on an important current of cultural creativity in renegotiating agency at an earlier time in the development of late modernity.

## THEOSOPHIC THOUGHT-FORMS AT THE TURN OF THE TWENTIETH CENTURY

In addition to being a time of technological innovation—we have already discussed the photographic and cinematographic revolutions that, respectively, marked the middle and end of the century—the late nineteenth century was a time of scientific and intellectual ferment. Broadly recognized scientific advances included the 1859 publication of Charles Darwin's work on evolution, Mendeleev's periodic table of chemical elements (1871), and the discoveries of electromagnetic waves (1886), X-rays (1895), radioactivity (1896), the electron (1897), and other subatomic particles (1899 and on). Technologies including the photograph, the telegraph, and the telephone all contributed to popular interest in the newly discovered invisible world of electromagnetic energies and radio waves, an interest that converged with rising interest in scientifically accounting for phenomena assumed to take place in the unseen worlds of religion and spirituality. If communication is possible across distance via telegraphic and telephonic media, the thinking went, why should it not be possible between the visible and invisible worlds?

Into this ferment stepped the Theosophical Society, which strove to articulate and embody an emerging science of the spiritual, a science that was not yet in place, but which could complement the emerging physical and biological sciences whilst addressing the question of their meaning for humans and for the future. Formed by Helena Petrovna Blavatsky and Henry Steel Olcott in 1875, the Theosophical Society aimed to synthesize eastern and western spiritual traditions into a unity appropriate for a scientific era. Inspired by the idea of evolution as not only a biological process but a spiritual process encompassing millennia-old efforts to advance human knowledge and wisdom, Theosophists preached the possibility of accessing higher knowledge from "ascended masters" whose aim is to guide the future evolution of humanity.[24] According to Blavatsky's *Cosmic Doctrine*, everything in the universe is alive and is part of a spiraling, cyclical evolutionary process, in which tensions between matter and spirit (and figuratively between masculine and feminine) provide the impetus that drives evolution forward. Theosophical ideas of spiritual evolution and of the unseen worlds of the "astral" and "etheric" "planes," whose more "subtle" dimensions encompassed what proceeded in thought, in feeling, and in imagination both prior to and apart from its manifestation in the physical plane, found broad resonance. At the same time as the late Victorian industry of spirit photography was believed by its practitioners to bring the living into contact with the dead, the idea of a fourth dimension offered a sense of proximity between living humans and those in a certain "beyond" that could be reached through séances and other forms of ritualized contact.

The list of artists, musicians, writers, and other cultural and intellectual leaders influenced by Theosophy and its immediate spinoffs (such as Rudolf Steiner's Anthroposophy) includes many of the leading figures of artistic modernism: Paul Gauguin, Vasily Kandinsky, Kasimir Malevich, Piet Mondrian, František Kupka, Marcel Duchamp, Franz Marc, Hans Arp, Paul Klee, Walter Gropius, Constantin Brancusi, Jackson Pollock, Joseph Beuys, and Harry Smith in the visual arts; Jean Sibelius, Aleksandr Scriabin, Cyril Scott, Gustav Holst, and Arnold Schoenberg in music; Rainer Maria Rilke, Leo Tolstoy, August Strindberg, William Butler Yeats, and T. S. Eliot in literature.[25] If one includes adjacent occult and esotericist movements of the time like Rosicrucianism, Spiritualism, Freemasonry, Christian Science, New Thought, Swedenborgianism, and the Gurdjieff "Work," the influence of some form of spiritual or religious thought on modern art becomes more of a rule than an exception. Artistic movements like Symbolism, Futurism, Suprematism, Constructivism, Dada, and Surrealism could hardly be imagined without them. (The fact that they *were* imagined that way is explainable by the decades-long hegemony of a certain notion of modern art as formalistic experimentation, a notion promulgated by critics and curators including New York's influential Museum of Modern Art, led by Alfred H. Barr Jr., and art historian Clement Greenberg. Historians of art have only recently begun to discard that hegemony.)[26] A list of the musical composers affected by these spiritual movements ranges from Wagner, Debussy, Stravinsky, Alan Hovhaness, and Dane Rudhyar to Olivier Messiaen and Karlheinz Stockhausen at mid-century; including Asian religions as well as Christianity and Judaism would cover many more including key minimalists (La Monte Young, Terry Riley, Steve Reich, Philip Glass) and "holy minimalists" (Arvo Pärt, Sir John Tavener, Henryk Górecki). In the performative and design arts we would find Frank Lloyd Wright, Jerzy Grotowski, and Peter Brook (all three closely connected to the Gurdjieff "Work") alongside Antonin Artaud, Tadeusz Kantor, and others. Historians of occultism such as Jeffrey Kripal and Christopher Partridge note the persistence of esoteric spirituality or "occulture" in the rock, jazz, and pop music of the 1960s through to today: for instance, in the music and thinking of John Coltrane, David Bowie, Van Morrison, Led Zeppelin, Leonard Cohen, Keith Jarrett, Bob Marley, Madonna, and so many others.[27]

Two related features of this spiritually influenced art, brought together particularly clearly in Theosophy, interest me here. The first is the idea that an artist can communicate directly, or "mediumistically," with spiritual, nonphysical, or discarnate sources of knowledge. (As a medium, the artist is the one who mediates between these sources and the human world at large.) The second is the idea that this communication can bring into physical form concepts, ideas, values, or principles that are intended to aid in the progress or evolution of humanity. The belief is that there are forms "needing to be" crystallized and embodied in visual or sensory form, and there are forces that aid in that effort. Among the methods for communicating with those forces were those designated as automatism, which ceded conscious control to nonhuman or discarnate entities. The notion of automatic writing and automatic drawing, as Tessel Bauduin writes, "sidesteps the rather thorny issue of *who* or *what* is actually doing the drawing—a spirit, a person's subconscious, the unconscious, or some alternate part of their personality." At the same time, it allows for an "opening" of a personal self that had become all too "bounded" within Victorian era metaphysics.[28]

One of the touchstones for both of these ideas, especially among visual artists in the early twentieth century, was the 1905 publication of Annie Besant's and Charles Leadbeater's work on "thought-forms." While today considered scientifically implausible, their idea that, as they put it, "thoughts are things," holds an unexplored resonance with the contemporary philosophical interest in objects, things, and matter, including Jane Bennett's notion of "vibrant matter," as well as an intriguing parallel with certain conceptualizations of images and the imagination.[29] The historical influence of their work on twentieth-century art is, moreover, undeniable.

By the time Besant and Leadbeater wrote their work on thought-forms, they were well known both within and outside Theosophical circles. Besant had been a socialist, union activist, and suffragist; living in India when the Theosophical Society was headquartered there, she became president of the Indian National Congress, campaigning for democracy and independence until her death in 1933. Leadbeater had been an Anglican priest, but left the priesthood to devote himself to Spiritualism and practices of clairvoyance. Both joined the Theosophical Society in part due to its (at the time) progressive and universalist ideals, which they saw as consistent with physical as well as spiritual evolutionary forces. Besant and Leadbeater developed the idea of thought-forms from H. P. Blavatsky's original theorization, drawn from the Platonic conception that geometrical Ideals precede and give rise to forms. As Blavatsky put it, "'Dots, Lines, Triangles, Cubes, Circles and finally 'Spheres'—why or how?" and continued, "Because, says the Commentary, such is the first law of Nature, and because Nature geometrizes universally in all her manifestations." Theosophy was the search for universals that lie behind and above the world of material forms and substances. For Theosophists, telepathy, clairvoyance, and telekinesis were all of a piece with the rapidly evolving sciences of magnetism, spectroscopy, sound waves, X-rays, photography, crystallography, subatomic physics, and electrochemistry. The visible world was considered the visible end of a much larger world of energies that could be perceived with the proper training and instrumentation. For those who believed in it, it could also be accessed and worked for the good of humanity by spiritually perceptive artists.

Besant's and Leadbeater's *Thought-Forms: A Record of Clairvoyant Investigation* proposes that thoughts and emotions can be seen as patterns of color, form, line, and density by those with clairvoyant perception, and that such perception could be developed and systematically investigated.[30] "Each definite thought," they wrote, "produces a double effect—a radiating vibration and a floating form."[31] The book lays out a set of illustrated descriptions of specific thought-forms including "affection," "devotion," "intellect," "ambition," "anger," "sympathy," "fear," and "greed," alongside "forms seen in those meditating" (which include "sympathy and love for all" and "an intellectual conception of cosmic order," among others), and "forms built by music" (with reference to Mendelssohn, Gounod, and Wagner). The book includes 57 color drawings that ostensibly represent the actual appearance (to clairvoyant vision) of thoughts, or as close as is possible to such appearance in two dimensions. In the terms we have used in this study, these reflect a combination of ideal-image, in their being representations of "higher realities," and world-picture, in their being equated with actuality.[32]

As a typology of the color and shape of specific thought-forms, the book could only ever be a beginning; since its value relied on the authority of the authors themselves, it would be subject to speculation, debate, and refinement. And while the correspondences Besant and Leadbeater proposed do not hold up to cross-cultural scrutiny, many carried a certain intuitive resonance, at least within the late Victorian

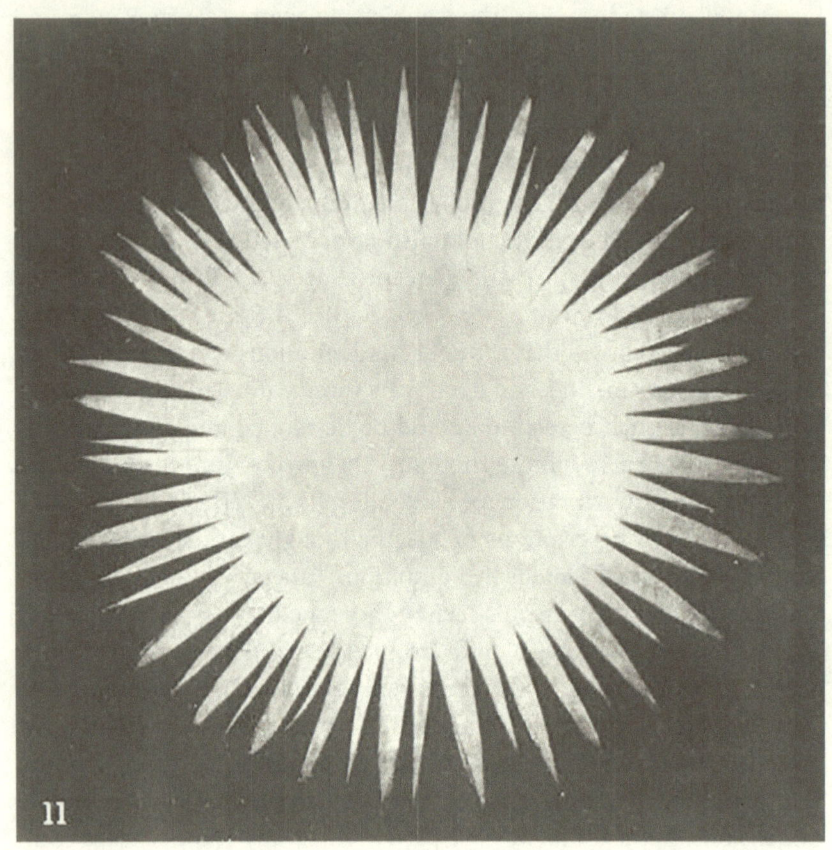


**FIGURE 7.2.** "Radiating Affection," from *Thought-Forms* by Annie Besant and C. W. Leadbeater.

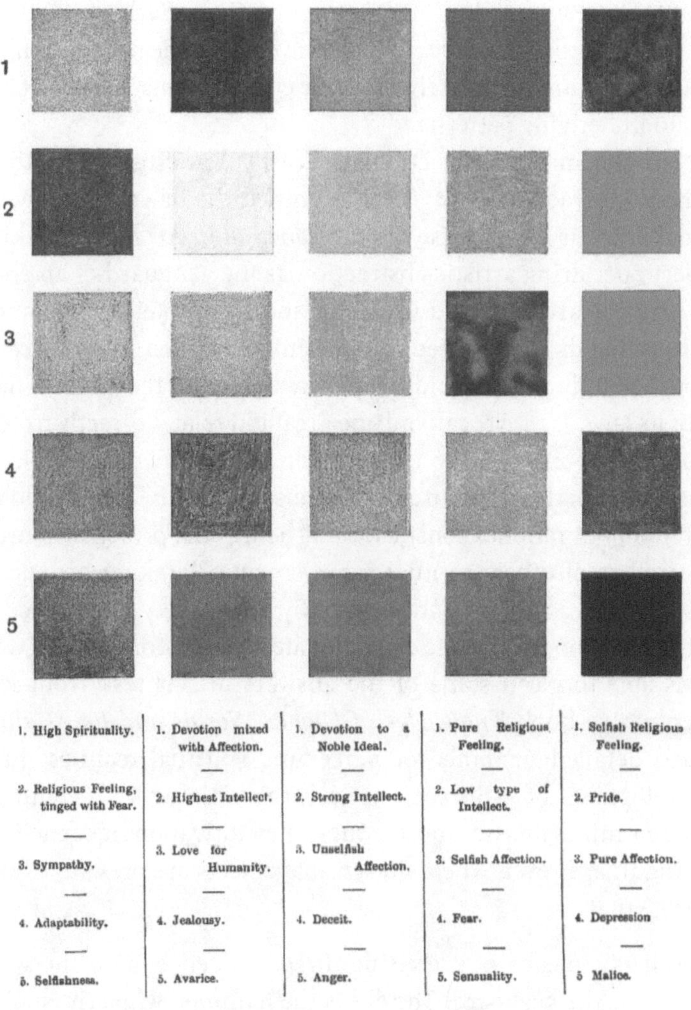


KEY TO THE MEANINGS OF COLOURS.

**FIGURE 7.3.** "Key to the Meanings of Colours," from *Thought-Forms* by Annie Besant and C. W. Leadbeater. Public domain image.

context: for instance, seeing affection as pink, anger as red, intellect as yellow, blue as the color of spiritual thoughts, and so on, and with vagueness in thinking resulting in a cloudiness of the image, while clarity and focus result in clear and distinct outlines. Early abstract painters took this theosophical search for universals to heart, assuming that abstract forms are not merely random cultural constructs, but correspond to underlying patterns.

Of all the major abstractionists, Vasily Kandinsky was the one for whom abstraction most clearly signified the dawn of a new, more spiritual era. His 1911 treatise *On the Spiritual in Art* became a kind of manifesto declaring artistic abstraction as the vanguard of an epochal shift, whereby artists would use color and form to elicit "vibrational" responses that directly related to something he called "inner necessity." "Abstract painting," for Kandinsky, "leaves behind the 'skin' of nature, but not its laws. [. . .] Art can only be great if it relates directly to cosmic laws and is subordinated to them."[33] For Kandinsky, "The work of art emanates 'out of the artist' in a mysterious way," with "feeling and inner orientation, not rational consideration" being "the principal sources of art as well as of other spiritual achievements."[34] Taking his cue from Theosophy and Steiner's Anthroposophy, Kandinsky was preoccupied with the question of how one can cultivate a perception of inner worlds. He was able to glean some of the answers to this task from Rudolf Steiner, whose book *Knowledge of Higher Worlds and Its Attainment* outlined detailed methods for perceiving spiritual realities through the development of skills such as "control of thoughts," "endurance," and "open-mindedness," and through the cultivation of capacities for "forming images even where no sensible objects are present." Kandinsky wrote that

> colour is a means of exercising direct influence upon the soul. Colour is the keyboard. The eye is the hammer, while the soul is a piano of many strings. The artist is the hand through which the medium of different keys causes the human soul to vibrate. It is, thus, evident that colour harmony can rest only on the principle of the corresponding vibration of the human soul. This basis can be considered as the principle of innermost necessity.[35]

As detailed by art historian Sixten Ringbom,

> The occult influences received during the first decade of the century affected [Kandinsky's] *basic outlook* more profoundly than any [. . .] other sources. The place of art in the spiritual development and the contribution of art to the future synthesis; the vibration theory; the correspondences between art, feeling and the cosmic laws; the notion of emancipated colours and forms as specific for the spiritual reality behind matter; and even some elements of Kandinsky's pictorial idiom; all these basic features are derived from theosophy or its confrontation with Goethean speculation in Steiner's teaching."[36]

Steiner's influence spread across a wide range of artistic circles and was a key influence on the art of Hilma af Klint, to which I will turn shortly. His own writing and teaching grew out of his studies of German idealist philosophy, inherited from Hegel, Schelling, Goethe, and others, but synthesized this base with theosophical and other esoteric ideas that were popular at the time. A central concept for Kandinsky was that of "inner necessity," which was driven by "laws common to nature and art" and in harmony with divinity: "the effect of the inner necessity," Kandinsky wrote, "is a continuous manifestation of the Eternally Objective in the Temporally Subjective."[37] Kandinsky followed Steiner's "Goethean aesthetics," for which "the real" would be grasped as it is and not "sink down to a means of expression."[38]

If all of this talk about spiritual realms, "cosmic laws," and transcendent, "eternal," or "objective" reality was but an episodic detour in western thought, one that has since been overcome and left behind, then we need not give it much attention today. That it remains with us, in various forms, is something I will pursue in the remainder of this chapter. The more important point is that it is neither exclusively western nor exclusively subcultural. It is a form of idealism related to what I have called the ideal-image regime, that is, an understanding of images as revealing or approximating real truths that exist on a prior or superior "plane" to that of mundane, everyday human perception.

These ideas have sometimes paralleled and, at other times, mixed with analogous ideas from non-western contexts. A prominent example of a thinker whose historiographic and interpretive work in the study of Islamic religion has helped shape an influential strand of contemporary religio-philosophical thought is French Iranologist Henry Corbin. Corbin's writings on the "imaginal" have significantly influenced popular depth psychology (as found, for instance, in the popular writings of Joseph Campbell, Thomas Moore, and others) and in the study of religion, in part through his collaborators and coparticipants at the Eranos conferences in Ascona, Switzerland, which have met annually since 1933. The list of high-profile Eranos figures from the middle decades of the last century reads like a "who's who" of contemporary religious studies: Carl Jung, Mircea Eliade, Gershom Scholem, Karl Kerényi, Heinrich Zimmer, Seyyed Hossein Nasr, Herbert Read, Joseph Campbell, and others.[39] Specializing in Iranian religious history, Corbin drew upon historical figures including Suhrawardi (1154–1191), Ibn Arabi (1165–1240), and Mulla Sadra Shirazi (1571–1635) to articulate the idea of the *mundus imaginalis*, the imaginal realm, which mediates between the "intellectual" and the "sensible" worlds. Where the sensible is perceived through the senses, the intellectual is defined theologically, usually according to Islamic tenets though Corbin's references range widely across religious and mystical traditions. He writes, for instance, that

> the *mundus imaginalis* is the place, and consequently the world, where not only the visions of the prophets, the visions of the mystics, the visionary events which each human soul traverses at the time of his exitus from this world, the events of the lesser Resurrection and of the Greater Resurrection "take place" and have their "place," but also the *gestes* of the mystical epics, the symbolic acts of all the rituals of initiation, liturgies in general with all their symbols, the "composition of the ground" in various methods of prayer (*oraison*), the spiritual filiations whose authenticity is not within the competence of documents and archives, and equally the esoteric *processus* of the Alchemical Work, in connection with which the First Imam of the Shi'ites was able to say "Alchemy is the sister of Prophecy."[40]

The imaginal, as mediating realm, provides entry for the senses to these intellectual or divine realms, whilst enabling the latter to interface through it with the world of the senses.

In our typology of images, Corbin's conception clearly falls into the ideal-image regime, with the *mundus imaginalis* mediating between human perception and an ideal or transcendent realm. His Islamic sources are more or less consistent with a longer lineage of thinkers going back to the emanationist Neoplatonism of third-century Hellenistic philosopher Plotinus. The latter's influence is in turn traceable to Europeans like Marsilio Ficino (1433–1499), Jakob Böhme (1575–1624), and Friedrich Schiller (1759–1805), and parallels the thinking of a long line of Indian philosophers, stretching from the writers of the early *Upanishads* to the subcontinent's arguably most significant medieval philosopher, Adi Shankara (Śaṅkara, c. 700–750 CE).[41] Sixten Ringbom, for instance, details connections such as Friedrich Schiller's taking up the Neoplatonic idea of "the Universe as a thought of God and the laws of nature as the symbolic language by which the Thinking Being becomes intellegible [*sic*]" to the writings of Blavatsky and Steiner, which in turn influenced Kandinsky and other early twentieth-century artists.[42] If the laws of nature are taken to be an intelligible language, then the ideal-image (of religion) becomes capable of reconciliation with the world-picture (of science), such that the indexicality of the latter comes to be readable through means that include aesthetic perception and artistic creation. To the extent that Romantic philosophers, Theosophists, and modernist artists could all have been seeking this kind of reconcordance of science and religion, they are arguably also seeking to overcome the "bifurcation of reality" that Alfred North Whitehead wrote about.

If Corbin's own writing on the imaginal appears overly theological, some recent interpreters have taken it into more speculative directions. In contemporary visual theory, film scholar Laura Marks has drawn directly on Mulla Sadra's philosophy of the imagination to articulate the "imaginal realm" as "collective, infinite, changing, expanding, and more real than matter."[43] She traces this "radically pro-image" conception to the Neoplatonic heritage that distinguishes a "lower, sensory imagination" from a "higher, intellective imagination that receives inspiration from above, as in divination and prophecy."[44] In contrast to the more substantialist philosophies of Islamic thinkers like Avicenna, Marks presents Sadra as a "process philosopher" for whom the imaginal is "ever changing, infinite, and populated by singularities." It is accessible to us through the psyche or soul, which is a "faculty of extreme presence, of intensification," the "active, vigorous, desirous soul constantly at work seeking the flow of Being."[45] If this represents an ideal-image regime, the ideal itself is changeable and dynamic, and the process of seeking it and opening to it becomes a crucial space for agency, and specifically for the discipline of cultivating attention to what is being presented by the "flow of Being." This is not inherently different from Corbin's conception of the imaginal, which can, in his view, "degrade" into "fantasy," and which requires the "discipline" of "active Imagination," a hermeneutic that is capable of "reconducting" the image to its "source," its "archetype" and "true reality," so as not to do that.[46] This discipline is something that is central to the work of Hilma af Klint, which I will examine next.

## ARTIST AS TIME CAPSULE: THE DISCOVERY OF HILMA AF KLINT

If the influence of Theosophy on Kandinsky, Kupka, Mondrian, and other leaders of artistic abstraction is now widely recognized, it is only in the last few decades that Hilma af Klint's work has come to be known at all, and only very recently recognized as similarly significant. This is largely because her abstract paintings failed to gain much publicity during her life, and in her will she specified that these works be kept secret for at least 20 years after her death. Yet she produced voluminously, leaving behind over 1,300 paintings and some 26,000 pages of text. The public emergence of her paintings in the late 1980s did not create the stir that it did once her work was given a major retrospective by the Moderna Museet in Stockholm in 2013. Five years later, New York's Guggenheim Museum organized a major exhibition that attracted some 600,000 museum-goers, breaking every record in that museum's history. The impact of the exhibition on the art world was dramatic. But we are getting ahead of ourselves.

On the surface, af Klint's artistic career was not too unusual for an artist whose upper-class upbringing enabled her to pursue a career that only provided modest and irregular support. Born near Stockholm in 1862, af Klint received an education that was unusual for women at the time, and became a classically trained artist, earning her living for the most part through her art. Like many attracted to spiritualist and

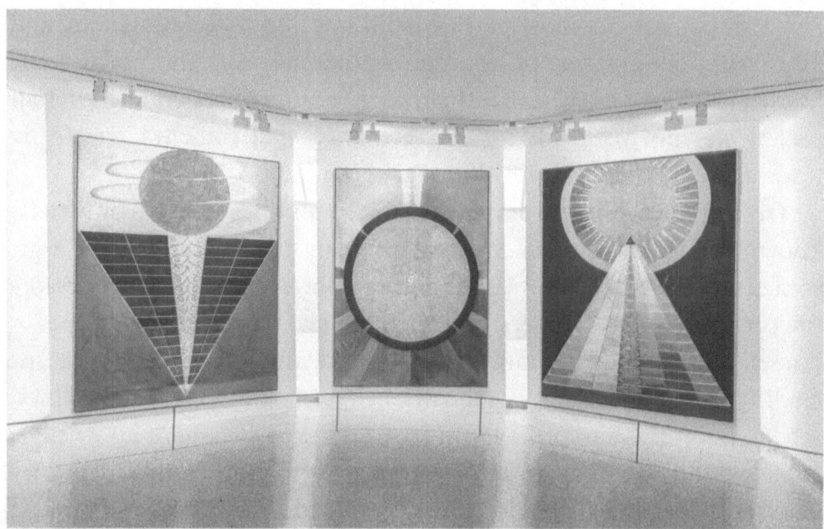

**FIGURE 7.4. Installation view: *Hilma af Klint: Paintings for the Future*, October 12, 2018–April 23, 2019, Solomon R. Guggenheim Museum, New York. Photograph by David Heald © Solomon R. Guggenheim Foundation, New York.**

theosophical movements, she was scientifically as well as religiously literate, and sought not only harmony between science and religion, but social progress, which she saw represented in the ferment of the time—workers' and women's suffrage movements, as well as the more specific revolutions arising in Russia and elsewhere. While she and her close friend and coworker Anna Cassel sometimes phrased their own work as bearing revolutionary aims, representing a "turning point in history" and including "liberation from the oppression of the higher classes,"[47] for her the revolution was always not merely material or political, but also spiritual.

Her singular devotion to producing an art that would revolutionize society, however, failed to achieve its goal in her lifetime. The reasons for that failure have been dissected by other commentators, and with the publication of Julia Voss's recent biography of af Klint, it can be clearly stated that she did not "hide" her work, as some have suggested.[48] Rather, she sought appropriate audiences who were prepared to understand the work, exhibiting it in Stockholm (in 1913) and London (in 1928), and sharing it with Rudolf Steiner and his associates in Dornach,

Switzerland. For the most part, she did not find those audiences, and as a result, her abstract or nonrepresentational work did not become known until long after her death, in part because of her conviction that society was not yet ready for the revolution that work was gesturing toward. What, then, was revolutionary about it?

On the surface, the work she produced and has now become most known for is marked by a consistency of scale (especially with the large, sometimes wall-sized paintings) and of effort, featuring strong colors (incorporating egg tempera and metallic leaf), geometrical shapes—circles, triangles, squares, and so on—and organic and related forms, including spirals, coils, waves, tendrils, helixes, snail forms, petals, vines, seedpods, lotuses and other floral forms, trees of life and of knowledge, chalices, and the like. An attention to polarity and complementarity between colors and shapes is legible, thanks to her symbols and profuse notes, as complementarity between male and female, spirit and matter, darkness and light, evolution upward and "involution" downward. Spirals appear to symbolize growth, change, development, and evolutionary progress. Her abstraction, in all of this, could be taken as not naturalistic but "ideal"—representational not of the material world but of ideals, principles, forces, and processes, with diagrammatic forms (such as trees, spirals, and androgynous figures) serving as midway points between realism and abstraction, as Jadranka Ryle argues.[49] Af Klint notably developed a language of colors, symbols, and letters that was peculiar yet somewhat consistent over time: blue indicating female and yellow male, the letters *u* for spirit and *w* for matter, and so on.

Among her best-known works today are *The Ten Largest*, a group of ten paintings created over 67 days in late 1907, whose total area spans 80 square meters. The paintings are titled after stages of life: two devoted to childhood, two to youth, four to adulthood, and two to old age, with background colors indicating the difference between them. Standing in the midst of them (as I did in the Tate Modern Museum in London), one experiences the paintings as large fountains of vibrant color, somewhat akin to Mark Rothko's color field paintings, but with the addition of shapes and forms in a kind of circulation of vibrating, sometimes spinning, energy. In these works, as Voss remarks, af Klint "succeeded" in giving "visual character to spirit and found enduring forms to show how everything changes, moves, and flows—buzzing, floating, fertilizing, mating, oscillating, flipping, gliding, growing. Everything happening at the same time, to the great and to the small; something is in motion in every corner, spinning. 'The form is the waves,' Hilma af Klint wrote later, 'behind the form is life itself.' "[50]

The predominant themes in her abstractions, then, appear to be principles of polarity and development, or evolution, underlying the living world as well as the social and spiritual world, and serving as a kind of unitary formulation of the movement of life and spirit. Voss describes the underlying concept as the "alchemical idea of a reunion of opposites," a reunion which is foreseen at multiple scales: between male and female, East and West, science and spirit, and so on.[51] The interest in the partnership of science and spirit is one af Klint shared with many artists and intellectuals of the time, which is part of what attracted her to the Theosophical Society and later the Anthroposophical Society, to both of which she was connected at various points. As noted earlier, the idea that geometrical figures could be a kind of language emerged in theosophical circles in the 1890s,[52] and by the early years of the twentieth century had become familiar through Leadbeater and Besant's writing on thought-forms.

Af Klint's interest in the natural world was evident from her early painting, and received greater impetus through her later readings of evolutionary biologist Ernst Haeckel, whose theory of embryonic recapitulation notably influenced her evolution paintings and much of her 1919 notebook "Flowers, Mosses, and Lichens." In that work, as Voss puts it, af Klint wrote that "by studying nature," one could "rise to the heights of thought without fear of former fallacies," "to turn inward and sense 'the force within oneself.' Microcosm and macrocosm were connected, and in constant interaction." In af Klint's words, "Behind the effervescent force of the plant is concealed the warmth of feeling, behind the mobility of the animal lies the force of thought. Thought and feeling are united in the gravity of the stone."[53] Daniel Birnbaum refers to af Klint's "vibrant geometries" as presenting "a kind of biological synesthesia (blue ether, moist moss, cool trees)," and Briony Fer refers to her work as a "spiritual herbarium" embodying a "vegetal poetics."[54]

If this were all there was to af Klint's art, the Guggenheim show might not have been nearly as dramatically received as it was, so we must ask: what about her makes her such a resonant figure for today, that is different from a century ago? The superficial answer is that she was a woman artist, whose work was overlooked while men—Kandinsky, Mondrian, Kupka, and others—came to be known as the "founding fathers" of high-modernist abstraction. But there are two other features of her life and work that make her more interesting for our purposes: the first is the way in which her positioning as a woman played itself out through her work; the second is her level of interaction with the forces that peopled her spiritual cosmos, a cosmos others may have pointed toward, but did not pursue as deeply or consistently as she did.

So much of the impetus for af Klint's creativity emerged in the context of group work among women, with a collective investment and exploration into "higher" goals playing a central role in this. She is best known for her work with De Fem, or The Five, a group of women who began meeting regularly for spiritualist séances on Easter Sunday in 1896, and who worked together in this way until 1907. The group emerged from earlier meetings among theosophists and spiritualists, whose participants trained themselves in methods of clairvoyance and mediumship that were popular at the time. Meetings of De Fem involved prayers, rituals, and extensive documentation of purported communication with "discarnate beings," with the different members playing different and sometimes changing roles: one serving as medium or "drawing instrument," another operating a tool they called a *psykograf* (akin to a Ouija board and planchette), a third taking notes, and so on. The drawings emerging from the group have been described as a "codified visual language" featuring "floral forms, spirals, tendrils, intersecting diagonal lines, delicate meandering S-shaped lines and repeated slender leaf-like shapes."[55] It was in this context that, on January 1, 1906, af Klint "received" the "commission" from one of the spirit beings, named Amaliel, to "transmit to humanity the images of the life that exists beyond everything."[56] Af Klint took this commission quite seriously, and the project would ultimately result in the 193 works known as *Paintings for the Temple,* painted by her between 1906 and 1915. In its own period of group work, De Fem produced a total of 1,789 pages of notes in seven volumes including transcribed spiritual communications and detailed descriptions of mediumistic methods. Af Klint was to produce a few thousand pages more on her own.

Af Klint continued to work, for many years, with circles of mostly women (with one or two men involved in later years), whose group size ranged up to 13. It is notable that her associations with women almost completely avoided any need for male approval. She in fact saw herself as both male and female, and found deep partnerships with women, both spiritual and in some cases physical relationships (lesbian *avant la letter,* though her own word appeared to be "Spartan"), including relationships that lasted for significant periods with Anna Cassel, Gusten Andersson, Sigrid Lancén, and Thomasine Anderson. The dynamics of the larger groups shifted over time, with interpersonal tensions sometimes accruing from individual relationships as well as divergent roles in relationship to the higher powers, rather as if a shifting constellation of relations was working itself out both microcosmically and macrocosmically, reflected in the communications "received" as well as the artwork produced.

A sociological explanation might account for the women's employment of "discarnate beings" as a compensation for their own lack of power in society—a presumed higher authority by which to promote the more gender-balanced society they were craving. Art, meanwhile, was one of the domains in which they could exercise some competency. This, however, does not diminish the radical nature of the goals they sought, the methods they employed, or the accomplishments of af Klint's artwork, which she pursued with single-minded devotion. Af Klint's methods in particular, which involved a kind of opening to influences outside of rational subjectivity, are what I would like to examine in greater depth.

## ARTIST AS MEDIUM: AF KLINT AND THE CREATIVE-IMAGE

Af Klint wrote about her *Paintings for the Temple*: "The pictures were painted directly through me, without any preliminary drawings and with great force. I had no idea what the paintings were supposed to depict; nevertheless, I worked swiftly and surely, without changing a single brushstroke."[57] The idea behind the "commission" from "Amaliel" was to "transmit to humanity the images of the life that exists beyond everything."[58] Working at a feverish pace, af Klint completed 111 paintings between November 1906 and April 1908, at which point she suspended them due, in part, to the need to take care of her mother but also, some have argued, to the response she obtained from Rudolf Steiner, who discouraged full mediumship in favor of an active and introspective relationship to spiritually perceived realities.[59] She completed much of the remainder of the *Paintings for the Temple* between 1912 and 1915.

This brings us to what we might call the ontological question surrounding af Klint, or any artist who works as a "medium": what is the status of the entities being "channeled" or communicated with? Put simply, who is doing the painting? And what does this imply for human agency? (This question bears on af Klint's relationship with Steiner, to which I will return.) It is perhaps a sign of the times that a University of Chicago book examining af Klint's artistic methods begins by informing readers that in 1906 "af Klint was *chosen by the higher powers* with whom The Five were in communication to create a series of largely abstract paintings known as *The Paintings for the Temple*."[60] There are no scare quotes, hesitations, or caveats here: the "higher powers" are simply described as agents actively intervening into the lives of af Klint and her four coworkers. But who are these higher powers?

Julia Voss describes af Klint's "spiritual cosmos" as "peopled with higher beings, vibrations, forces, waves, auras, chakras, elemental spirits, nature spirits, guardian spirits, angels and gnomes."[61] In spiritualist literature, discarnate entities were often the spirits or souls of those who had passed away, but in Theosophical and later variants, these become teachers, sages, saints, and something akin to angels and cosmic messengers. But none of this is helpful if we do not believe that it is possible to communicate with beings who are not physically present. Af Klint struggled with the question of who these beings were, yet she never relinquished the belief that they were real. It is notable that her *Paintings for the Temple*—which emerged from collective ritual and mediumship—were quite different from the paintings she made for public exhibition, which were naturalistic and easily appreciated at the time. If the genesis of these paintings is to be sought in artistic inspiration or "genius," the question still arises: where does this inspiration come from? If a secular modernist would insist the inspiration is psychological or social in nature, a postsecular perspective might argue it arrives across a somewhat "porous" boundary, to use Charles Taylor's term, between the self and a more-than-human world, or that it is co-constructed through a process that is both *social* among humans and potentially *relational beyond* the human. Af Klint's belief that the sources of her inspiration were not only real, but that they were on a "higher plane" and somehow *leading humanity forward*, makes her a practitioner of a particular version of the ideal-image. Let us consider this more closely.

Mediumship, or channeling, as it is popularly known today, is taken by its practitioners to be an opening to "higher sources"; it is a form of revelation. It typically includes the goal of overcoming one's own perceived limits—to step out of oneself and, in some sense, outside of one's cultural milieu—in order to access something that can provide insight, healing, solace, prophecy, or liberation of one kind or another, and thus to open oneself up to those incipient influences that are believed to exist in a realm that is otherwise inaccessible. If one "steps aside" and allows these influences to act through one's hands, words, or actions, as is done in the state of trance that accompanies most mediumship, then the question of *who* is acting becomes pertinent. As Tessel Bauduin recounts, when af Klint began working on the *Paintings for the Temple* in 1906, she painted "partly or fully entranced, and had known her paintings only in painting them. There was no (conscious) preconception and preparation; the Work was realized only and immediately in its creation."[62] Susan Tallman writes that "the crux of the Hilma af Klint dilemma" is the question, "To what degree does celebrating these things as works of art, and celebrating af Klint as their creator, invalidate everything she was hoping to achieve?"[63] In a review of the book and exhibition "World Receivers," which includes the mediumistic women artists Georgina Houghton and Emma Kunz, Tallman notes these artists' "deflection of authorship." Far from the art world's assumption that "the ultimate goal of pictures is to be hung in a museum," for these artists, Tallman writes, "these were not just images but *indexical evidence of another realm of existence*."[64] The paradox is that "*The Paintings for the Temple* may now be hailed as a work of genius, but where people were supposed to understand truth, most merely see beauty. Where they were supposed to understand 'spirit,' they recognize an artist." In other words, we are speaking here of the tension between artistry, or the expression-image, and the purest form of ideal-image these artists were aiming to embody in their work.

This tension was partly at work in af Klint's apparent disagreement with Rudolf Steiner. Of all the living people af Klint admired, Steiner was her most consistent authority on all things spiritual. She aspired to his approval, sending him letters seeking advice, and hoped to work alongside him as his equal. She continued looking up to him even after he showed minimal interest in her work, showing more interest in another (male) Swedish artist when he visited Sweden in 1908. According to Voss, Steiner's influence is evident in several paintings: for instance, af Klint noted that her *Tree of Knowledge* (1913) featured a "cosmic tree" that Steiner described as having "the roots go upwards, and the branches stretch down into all the members," and to which the brain is the "gateway."[65] Her interest in Steiner's teachings arguably grew stronger after his resignation from the Theosophical Society and his founding of Anthroposophy in 1913, and his community at Dornach, Switzerland, served as a kind of model for af Klint, her dream community. She was to visit it repeatedly, including after his death. That she received little attention in return should not be taken too harshly: Voss notes that Piet Mondrian had sent Steiner a manifesto and that Walter Gropius had sent him an invitation, with neither hearing back from the popular author and teacher. Voss writes that when Steiner died in 1925, "Nothing had been resolved: Steiner had offered vague encouragement but no real help."[66] Yet in the end, af Klint continued to compare herself to him, noting (in Voss's paraphrase) that while Steiner had "taught how to actively acquire knowledge 'above one's own earthly abilities,'" af Klint's life, in her own words, "comprises the understanding of how to receive help, and the struggle to make my own what I have already received."[67] Recall that Steiner had initially recommended against the pure receptivity of mediumship, and perhaps as a partial accommodation of his advice, af Klint continued to practice it, but actively engaged with it so as to make it "her own." There is clear evidence that she practiced some of the techniques Steiner taught in works like *Knowledge of the Higher Worlds and Its Attainment*, directed towards the development of clairvoyant vision.[68]

Af Klint's mediumship can be seen as both utterly non-modern, a seeming abdication of the rational, liberal, secular humanist self, and at the same time very modern in that the spiritual and religious movements that fed it could not have arisen without modernity; they accompanied it and paralleled it. In key respects these movements were fueled by modern developments and concerns—from the discovery of the invisible forces and powers of the atom, electromagnetism, the depths of geological and evolutionary time, and so on, to seemingly age-old questions of the relation between matter and spirit, animality and reason, warfare and the pursuit of progress. From religious fundamentalisms to the spiritualism, Theosophy, occultisms, and New Age spiritualities of the last 150 years, religious impulses have been a constant accompaniment of the modern era. Modernity has seeped out so many spiritualities even as its leading spokespersons have denied their value. (This might be an instance of Bruno Latour's "moderns" practicing something very different from what their theorists have preached.) At the same time, the capacity to appeal to "higher forces" could be seen as a kind of extension of one's agency, an act that allowed an artist to set aside the question of whether something was appropriate or not, and instead to pursue it beyond an otherwise socially acceptable limit. Tessel Bauduin suggests that "Maybe [we] should consider the spirit guides catalysts for the artist's self-actualisation, the mere *possibility* of their existence easing the way for af Klint to move beyond what she had been taught at the Academy." Mediumistic painting could, in this sense, be considered "a strategy towards dealing with the tension and demands of working in a style that was radically different and new," and to "go against gendered norms current in artistic circles and culture at large."[69]

As mentioned, then, af Klint's work can be seen as epitomizing the practice of artistic abstraction as an ideal-image. Sixten Ringbom, whose 1960s studies of Kandinsky proved paradigmatic in defining the theosophical impulse of the latter's work, proposes that af Klint's isolation makes her a kind of "one-person control group," whose output so clearly demonstrates the "visual potential of the theosophical teachings."[70] While many similarities can be found between af Klint and the others (Ringbom mentions the technique of "parallel representation"), it is the distinguishing features that may be of greater interest. In particular, there was a strong sense of utopian projection, or what Jadranka Ryle calls "visionary futurity," in af Klint's oeuvre. Unlike much mediumistic work, which reached back to deceased ancestors and other predecessors (past lives, with an interest in retrieving forms or wisdom from a past Golden Age, etc.), af Klint was oriented to the future, looking ahead to forms—thought-forms, image-forms, and ideals—that are at best only emergent, barely conceivable by humanity in her own time. Ryle and other sympathetic critics have interpreted af Klint's work as an employment of "diagrammatic abstraction" in service of a "utopian transformation of form" that both maps out a fusion of science and spirituality, and presciently prefigures an androgynously egalitarian gender politics.[71] Reviewing multiple sources on af Klint's oeuvre, Janice McNab notes that "nearly all of the post-1906 work has some iteration of this deconstruction of gendering through the creation of a new visual language for lived experience," and that it can be seen as "part of a revolutionary movement toward the visualization of a post-gender world that is also only now finding its audience."[72]

For this reason, I want to suggest a new kind of image to add to our taxonomy—that of the *creative-image*, which combines the expression-image and the ideal-image, with the ideal thereby becoming not something that is attainable or even singular, but something that is utopian, projective, and anticipatory, a creative and expressive stretching forward and outward to meet an Idea that may or may not be "accurate" (and therefore not a world-picture), but that is rooted in an "abduction," as Peirce would call it, of a desirable, "higher," or indeed *future*, reality.[73] Daniel Birnbaum writes that

> Rather than present a domain of static mathematical truths or Platonic forms, af Klint enacts a realm of vibrant life—of spiritual evolution and immanence alike. Her version of abstraction is compatible with the processes of teeming nature rather than the precision of heavenly geometries. Her visual cosmos can therefore sometimes appear to have more in common with the speculative biology of Ernst Haeckel or the process philosophy of Alfred North Whitehead than with the transcendental purity of Suprematism or the rigorous system of Neo-Plasticism. There are even moments when af Klint's biomorphic imagination seems remarkably in sync with today's experimental explorations of living form (think of the networks of artist Tomás Saraceno or architectural theorist Sanford Kwinter, among many other examples). In af Klint's trove, we find helical patterns in bright colors reminiscent of schematic seashells or microscopic genetic structures: the forms always evolving, growing, expanding outside her own

> obsession with traditional dualisms, to hint at a dimension of life emerging in matter as much as in the mind. [. . .] Form is never distinct from life in af Klint's art: The spiritual forces that sometimes emerge in purity in her paintings are, as her drawings and notes indicate, also present in everything that is alive.

Some of these judgments (such as the references to Saraceno and Kwinter) are only possible from the vantage point of the present, but even those referring to af Klint's own contemporaries (such as Haeckel and Whitehead) suggest a prescience in the ecological, even cybernetic, concerns that af Klint could be said to have anticipated. In this ability to prefigure and address a world that had not quite come to pass, Hilma af Klint gave expression to ideals that were chronologically ahead of her, that were still forming "in the ether," so to speak. This forward movement is something that all avant-garde art arguably aims to do. Af Klint, as several commentators have said, aimed to make the invisible visible, but in the end what she attained was a certain kind of reordering of the visible. Birnbaum writes, "Perhaps this is a new kind of mystical empiricism, one that has passed through the higher spheres only to return to the natural life surrounding an artist with a keen sense for form."[74]

## MEDIUMSHIP BETWEEN THE ANCESTRAL AND THE FUTURAL

Hilma af Klint's sudden ascent to art world stardom no doubt reflects on the gender implications of her until-recent invisibility in modern art history. In this it can be taken as emblematic of a certain #MeToo moment in western intellectual culture. That it resonates with a renewal of popular interest in spirituality—a more amorphous and individualized phenomenon than religion—has not hurt her popularity, but it threatens to obscure the fact that creativity and spirituality have gone hand-in-hand much more often than has been recognized.

Af Klint's work should be seen within a broader set of developments in modern religious and spiritual culture. I have referenced numerous high-profile twentieth-century artists whose religious or spiritual inclinations are undeniable (Kandinsky, Mondrian, Kupka, etc.). If these have not been traditionally seen as "mediumistic" in their practices, others, including surrealists like André Masson and Max Ernst and later artists like Joseph Beuys, at least flirted with automatism and other mediumistic or quasi-shamanistic practices. The art world's belated recognition for mediumistic art has found public outlet in recent exhibitions at the Venice Biennale, the Tate Modern, the Minneapolis Institute of Art, and other locations.[75] Individual artists like Tabita Rezaire, Zadie Xa, and Australian Aboriginal artist Hayley Millar Baker employ spiritual divination systems in association with digital technologies.

Beyond the professional art world, occult techniques are sometimes even more central to spiritually themed art.[76] Among the clearest examples of an artist whose work with occult techniques looks for inspiration both to the distant past and to the non-immediate future, and whose work has led to the growth of an actual new religious movement, is Oberto "Falco" Airaudi (1953–2013), founding leader of the Damanhur community in northwest Italy. Connected initially to the Movimento Arte Concreta in Turin, Airaudi founded the Horus Center for Parapsychological and Esoteric Research in 1975. By 1977, he and a dozen followers had begun to build the community they would name Damanhur, after an ancient Egyptian "City of the Sun," in the Chiusella Valley in the Piedmont foothills of the Italian Alps. By the 2000s, Damanhur had grown to include several villages of some six hundred residents, with its own constitution, government, schools, local currency, various businesses and creative ventures, and another four hundred or so affiliates living in nearby communities; all of this made it the "largest New Age communal group in the world," according to sociologist Pier-Luigi Zoccatelli.[77] To date, even after Airaudi's death in 2013, a tourist economy brings in tens of thousands of annual visitors, and satellite communities exist throughout Europe, the United States, Japan, and Australia. The community calls itself "a living laboratory for the Future, a Federation of spiritual communities, and a worldwide movement."[78]

There is much that could be said about Damanhur: for instance, about its idiosyncratic form of occult-magical spirituality, its utopian-millenarian vision of the future of humanity, its complicated internal authority structures, the secrecy that surrounds its doctrines and ritual-initiatic practices, the role of small businesses and eco-sustainable practices in its partially self-sufficient economy, and the significance the community places on experimentation and "continuous inner transformation" in personal as well as social-familial affairs. The latter is epitomized by its controversial "Game of Life," a kind of hybrid of field trip, magical battle, cathartic bonding ritual, and psychodrama-style group intensive.[79] Like many totalistic (or "cult-like") intentional communities, Damanhur has its share of detractors and "deconverts."[80] What I am interested in, however, is the role of art in the community and its vision. As an artist, Oberto Airaudi produced several thousand paintings over the course of his life. He came to call these "Selfica," which is the name given to the field of "spiritual science" by which Damanhurians "contact energies and intelligent beings from other dimensions and planets by using rituals and Selfic machines to mobilize the special energy associated with the spiral form."[81] Airaudi seemingly believed that he was in touch with higher powers from the future, and that his art could attract extraterrestrially sourced intelligent energies to its observers. He taught that spirals, among other signs, are a magical form, and that certain metals (including gold, silver, copper, and brass), colors, inks, and mineral crystals can be used to attract beings from other levels of reality. His paintings reflected this interest in organic forms, intense colors, and the use of substances that displayed differently under changing lighting conditions (provided by the community's exhibition space), all of which gave the paintings a sense of liveliness, animacy, and interactivity. As Damanhur's official "Ambassador," Esperide Ananas Ametista, writes in an introduction to a book of Airaudi's reproductions, each of Airaudi's paintings "is a door and the path that it opens, is different for every viewer. It is a dream dimension with new laws, an Alice's world, where everything is possible. Logic is turned upside down, multiple, non-linear and surprising." Each painting "is a mirror," its signs and lines altering under changing lighting conditions to create "spiritual Rorschach blots, in which everybody can grasp the reflections of themselves and their inner world."[82] This reference to Rorschach blots is one I will come back to, as it can represent a kind of transmission point from which a "network of enchantment" can be built. In this sense, Airaudi is working from the Rorschach of his own spiritual sources to create something that, in turn, becomes a Rorschach for others to make their own meanings from. It suggests an open-endedness of interpretation that, arguably, is belied by the intentionality of the art the community is best known for.

That art consists of Damanhur's temples and ceremonial structures, some of which are open-air, but the most famous of which are the Temples of Humankind. These make up a massive subterranean complex, encompassing 8,500 cubic meters on five underground levels, of thoroughly painted caverns and corridors, constructed in secrecy over a period of 13 years until a disgruntled former community member reported their existence to Italian authorities in 1991. Their "outing" led to court cases (their construction was in breach of zoning regulations), notoriety (with vehement attacks from some local Catholic clergy, who saw the group as a dangerous pagan cult), and ultimately acceptance, especially for their potential contribution to the local tourist economy. The Temples of Humankind are a remarkable structure. Author, anthropologist, and North Atlantic Books founder Richard Grossinger has described them as "like a transcultural time capsule, a glyphic and geometric compilation of the cumulative wisdom and memory of humanity."[83] The art on their walls, as he describes it (and having seen it myself, I would agree), is "as epic and detailed as in great Medieval and Renaissance cathedrals and mosques. It is painted on all the walls of immense rooms and includes sculptures, pottery, mosaic work, inlaid marble, terra-cotta," as well as stained glass, ornately carved pillars, marble columns, and three-dimensional walled inlays.[84] Its Hall of Mirrors includes a cathedral-like cupola that is "the world's largest Tiffany dome," and its Hall of Earth includes realistic portrayals of hundreds of creatures, with a particular emphasis on endangered species. There are Halls of Water, of Metals, of Spheres, a Blue Temple, and a Labyrinth Hall.

More than merely colorful, the entire temple complex, Grossinger writes, "is linked by nine hundred tons of intricately and carefully laid copper wiring plus large amounts of gold and silver, a mostly camouflaged circuitry that can be viewed in some of the chambers as golden metal filaments and knotty assemblages." These are connected with "radionic rooms" and "networked" by "globes of alchemical salts in fluids set into nodes cut in walls" to make up "a vast sending and receiving device, like a radio telescope or activated crop circle."[85] If this sounds like a Wakandan visionary fantasy from a *Black Panther* comic, Damanhurians take it quite seriously. This "cosmic machine," Grossinger writes, was "built comprehensively, piece by complicated piece, and tattooed meticulously and confidently *as if it absolutely works*."[86] He continues: "An unbelievable amount of work went into building a replica of a time machine, an imago of a cosmic transmission device, and making it look and track like exactly that rather than just the most ambitious and heroically illustrated New Age temple on Earth." He describes the impact of walking through the temples as the sense that " 'This machine is somehow alive and operating,' but more than that: 'We are men and women willing to place our lives and our deaths at its service and conveyance.' [. . .] Each Damanhurian has a clay statue of him- or herself and a handprint somewhere in the temples, and these are used in death ceremonies to guide passed ones through zones of the afterlife."[87]

Damanhur's art (if that's what we should call it) is certainly visionary, and clearly represents a cosmographic form of the ideal-image. It looks for its bearings to the deep past—especially that of Egypt, or what historian of occultism Christopher Lehrich calls "*Ægypt*," the Egypt of the nineteenth-century Romantic imagination, and even deeper to the mythical continent of Atlantis—and to the just-as-deep future, from which extraterrestrials are said to be communicating with the community. That both of these, perhaps more than af Klint's, are "imagined" temporalities, not those given to us by science or academic history, make it a kind of speculative fiction, one that takes itself extremely seriously even as it challenges its own seriousness through experimentation, ritualized role-playing, and a winking sense of irony and humor. As I have already argued, this imagining is done through networks of enchantment that are very material in their basis; they are similar in this to the networks of circulatory reference that science is based on (see chapter 5), with the difference that it makes some speculative leaps of interpretation that lack justification through indexical measures. There is, in any case, an element of play in the community's activities that makes their work *art* rather than *science*, despite what community members may call it (the term "spiritual science" being common).[88]

Taking the example of Damanhur as an outlier, however, it is still possible to argue that it is not someone like Airaudi or Hilma af Klint, the exemplary artist-as-medium, who has been anomalous. Rather, viewed on a world scale, it may be the modern western concept of art that is the anomaly. If we were to remove the boundaries that have framed modern conceptions of art—as creative products crafted by trained individuals who self-identify as artists, whose expressions originate from "within" themselves, and whose goals are restricted to aesthetic appreciation—and instead consider art to be a creative, imagistic practice performed by individuals or groups in the process of living, then we would find that individual artistry, and individualism per se, is hardly always at its core. Creative, image-based expression arises in groups and communities, ranging from traditional societies to groups like af Klint's De Fem and Airaudi's Damanhur (indeed, would Airaudi have continued with his artistic work without the community that made use of it?). And they take place within situations thoroughly embedded in relations involving more-than-human environments and other-than-human entities. Art can in this sense always be *mediumistic*. That is, in effect, the definition of the image that the first half of this book proposed. An image is a relation connecting three things: the "image itself," which becomes the medium for a relational action; the referent that it refers to; and the effect that is created in an observer or interpreter. An image is therefore an act that connects and relates, with resemblance being a key element in the way it does that. An animate-image, which is the most basic kind of image, carries agency: it shapes and modifies what it affects. A creative-image, being a combination of expression-image and ideal-image, expresses something of its shaper, its maker, or its mak*ing*, and at the same time points itself toward an ideal. That ideal need not be predetermined; the pointing may, in fact, be more akin to an antenna or satellite dish pointing itself in a certain direction skyward. In the meeting between the intention being extended outward, and whatever it is that may be "received," arises the creative-image.

If this were to be our model of artistic creativity, then many of the most celebrated artists would qualify as mediums. The difference is in what they point themselves toward. It can be something found within the human world alone, and, all too often, mainly within the artist's personal or immediately interpersonal world. Or it can be in the more-than-human, the other-than-human, the beyond-human. It is not necessary to go to the cosmic end of the scale, as Damanhur attempts to do, to find examples of contemporary artists engaging with the more-than-human. The emergence of the genre of art loosely known as "environmental art" or "eco-art," which in most accounts began with the Land Art of the late 1960s, testifies to the existence of art that aims to do this sort of thing by design.[89] But the "environmentalization" of art is better thought of as a historically specific effort to break down (or out of) the gallery space so as to allow the outside world, with its more-than-human expansiveness, into the art, and the art out into the world. Once that has happened it should become evident that art, however it be defined, has always existed "out in the world": in nature, in the land, in the country (as Aboriginal Australians would call it), in the community, in the world of kin-relations, other-relations, and layered spaces between the heavens above and the earth below. Art responds to the world and shapes it in turn. And the world that it responds to is always more-than-merely-human.

If European colonization was accompanied (in time) by a notion of art as individual creativity, worthy of celebrating for its genius or its mastery of technique, and of obtaining and trading for its commodity value, then it is to colonized peoples that we can look for the clearest indicator that art can evade these boundaries altogether. The work of Indigenous artists and artists of color today contains a great deal of evidence of the importance of ancestral connections to land—to specific territories, to the African continent, and so on.[90] It is when the *ancestral* comes to be linked to the *futural* (or futurist) that we get a sense of the centrality of the creative-image, that is, of the combination of expression-image and ideal-image. The Afrofuturist arts movement shows this combination, and it has become a model for other recent "futurisms" including Indigenous futurism(s), Chicana futurism, Latinx futurism, Xenofuturism, Indofuturism, Arabfuturism, ethno-futurism (of various kinds), queerfuturism, "Black Quantum Futurism," "Queer Muslim futurism," disabled or "crip" futurism, alongside other future-oriented genres such as ecotopianism, cyberpunk, solarpunk, and Qilombismo.[91]

In this context, I will next examine one of the acknowledged progenitors of what is now called Afrofuturism: the musician born as Herman Poole Blount, better known by his chosen name, Sun Ra. Over the course of a few decades, Ra developed a style of music and performance and an accompanying "Astro Black mythology" that came to influence later generations of African-American artists, from George Clinton and his Parliament/Funkadelic urban funk band to many in the Detroit techno scene (especially Drexciya); jazz musicians like Kamasi

Washington, Nicole Mitchell, and the Heliocentrics; rappers and hip-hop artists like Afrika Bambaataa, Digable Planets, Erykah Badu, Saul Williams, Ras G, Janelle Monáe, DJ Muggs, and Flying Lotus; and the *Black Panther* series of graphic novels and films. The connecting threads between Hilma af Klint, Oberto Airaudi, and Sun Ra, however distant they may seem otherwise, is the notion that an artist can act like a medium—all three touted their experience of "spirit worlds" or "higher worlds"—in order to simultaneously access the vision of a different future and to reconstruct a different past. Af Klint, in this sense, was not only a medium in her time: her images have come to the world now, in *her* future. At the same time they have enabled a reconstruction of the past, including the narrative of artistic modernism, which has been revised to include her work and that of similarly occult-inspired women artists such as Georgina Houghton (1814–1884), Anna Marie Howitt (1824–1884), Emma Kunz (1892–1963), Ithell Colquhoun (1906–1988), and Leonora Carrington (1917–2011). This ability to have an effect in the future that rearranges the past—and therefore to scramble temporal coordinates, bringing past, present, and future into heretofore unknown combinations—is something that is intentionally aimed for among Afrofuturists, as it is among those inspired to shape their own novel futurisms. It is something art critic T. J. Demos has called "chronopolitics," and it will be a central theme for the remainder of this chapter.[92]

## SUN RA, FREE JAZZ, AND THE AFROFUTURIST IMAGINARY

Afrofuturism is commonly understood as a creative reworking of pasts, presents, and futures in order to enable the emergence of alternatives to current trajectories of the present. As Ytasha Womack puts it, "Afrofuturism is where the past and future meet."[93] Reynaldo Anderson defines Afrofuturism as "a critical project with the mission of laying the groundwork for a humanity that is not bound up with the ideals of white Enlightenment universalism," a "Black speculative movement" of "creative intellectuals, mystics and artists" "challenging white racist normativity and Black parochialism" who are "in creative dialogue with the boundary of space-time."[94] Chip Linscott's account of John Akomfrah's *The Last Angel of History* (1996), a film that documents

Afrofuturism at a fairly early moment of its conception, captures this melding of future and past well. "In *The Last Angel*," Linscott writes, the film's fictional Data Thief "receives clues about the past: the 'black secret technology' of the blues, the 'Mothership Connection' of George Clinton and Parliament-Funkadelic," and others such as Sun Ra and Lee "Scratch" Perry. "Only in the past, it seems, can our future-hero find the answers he seeks, and the past he is revisiting was in fact already living in the future when he arrived back in time." The film and its musical subjects, Linscott continues, are "foundationally archaeological; they are attempts to uncover and reconstruct a history that has either been written out or was never written originally. The quest is met by remixing, by time travelling, by rewriting and reactivating history through experimentation, through sonic, musical, and audiovisual theory and praxis. It's a future-past, with seeds in the present."[95] These themes of past and future time travel, bricolage and "remixology," data hacking, and alienness are fixtures within the growing international movement of Afrofuturist arts.[96]

To understand Afrofuturism's relation to the past requires understanding a much longer tradition of Afro-diasporic culture. On the one hand, Afrofuturism continues in the line of intellectual activity marked by Black nationalism, the Harlem Renaissance, the Négritude movement, and the theorists of the Black Atlantic, with their efforts to unify the Afro-diasporic experience around cultural transformation (including musical expression) and emancipatory political activism.[97] On the other hand, it is related to spiritual cultures with deep roots in the African continent. Art and cultural historians including Robert Farris Thompson, Melville Herskovits, Alfred Metraux, Roland Abiodun, Roger Bastide, and others have documented a long-standing preoccupation within African diaspora communities surrounding a shared sense of creativity rooted in the recognition of a pervasive, spiritually enlivening vital force, sometimes referred to as *àse* (Yoruban), *ache* (Cuban), *axé* (Brazilian), or *ashé* (U.S.). This shared creative and spiritual impulse is found in more deliberate forms in African-derived religions like Santería, Espiritismo, Vodou, Candomblé, Palo Monte, and Shangó, but finds expression across African diasporic cultural traditions, from church-based religiosity, with its references to the "power of the spirit," to popular expression in music, dance, and the visual and plastic arts.[98] (I'll have more to say on this "channeling" of "spirit" momentarily.) Among others, New York City's Black Arts Movement (BAM) and Chicago's Association for the Advancement of Creative Musicians (AACM) precipitated African-American cultural creativity in the 1960s and 1970s, whilst Miles Davis, John Coltrane, Archie Shepp, Cassius Clay/Muhammad Ali, and civil rights leaders like Martin Luther King Jr. and Malcolm X brought African-American cultural concerns to the forefront of American society.

Sun Ra's (1914–1993) position in this cultural pantheon might have been marginal if it were not for the emergence of Afrofuturism as a movement, which took his legacy to be central. Born and raised in Alabama, Herman Blount moved to Chicago where he became a key figure as a composer and bandleader in the jazz scene in the late 1940s. Pursuing his own heterodox spiritual education, Blount, who formally changed his name to Le Sony'r Ra in 1952, became interested in various mystical and occult writings, from ancient Gnosticism and Kabbalah to the Theosophy of Helena Blavatsky and the writings of P. D. Ouspensky and G. I. Gurdjieff, to a line of African-American mystics including Theodore P. Ford, George Wells Parker, and George James, who looked back to Egypt as a source of Black spirituality. He disseminated many of these interests among his growing cadré of band members, and came to articulate a mythology centered around his alleged contact with "space men" who, in a visionary experience, took him to a planet he identified as Saturn.[99] As his "Arkestra" began to wear spacesuits and Egyptian robes for performances, Ra claimed an extraterrestrial origin for himself and his experimental music, which he described in interviews, during performances, in the 1973 film *Space Is the Place*, and in liner notes for albums bearing titles like *The Heliocentric Worlds of Sun Ra* (1965), *Other Planes of There* (1966), and *Cosmic Tones for Mental Therapy* (1967).[100] An eccentric crank to some, Ra became a spiritual initiate to others. "To his devotees," Darius James writes, Ra "was a respected visionary of multi-planed and inter-dimensional Afro-futures, who was an amalgam of mathematician, composer, mystic, poet, ritualist, and world teacher."[101] As Jason Bivins writes in *Spirits Rejoice! Jazz and American Religion*, Ra

> spent his life on Earth preparing ears to receive "these sound waves" that would scramble brains, doing so by locating ordering

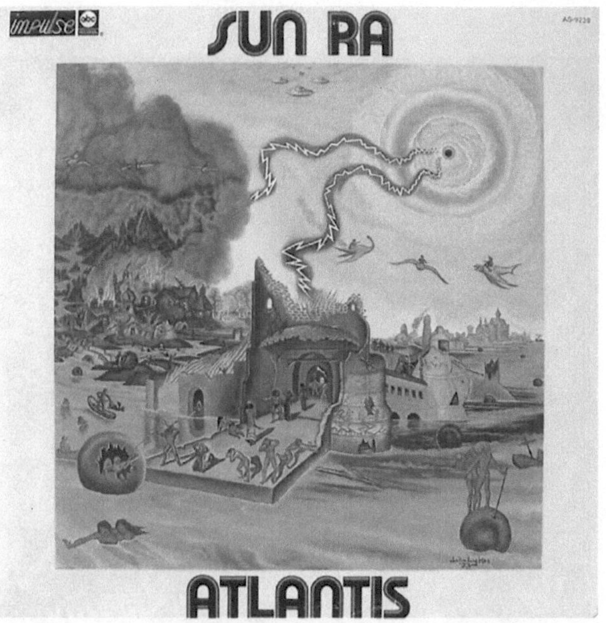


**FIGURE 7.5.** *Atlantis* cover art, Sun Ra, Impulse! 1973 reissue.

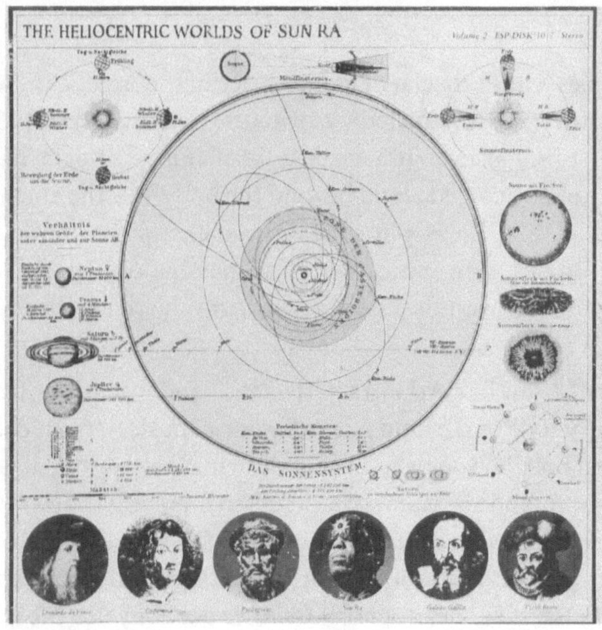


**FIGURE 7.6.** *Heliocentric Worlds of Sun Ra*, volume 2, cover art, ESP-Disk, 1965.

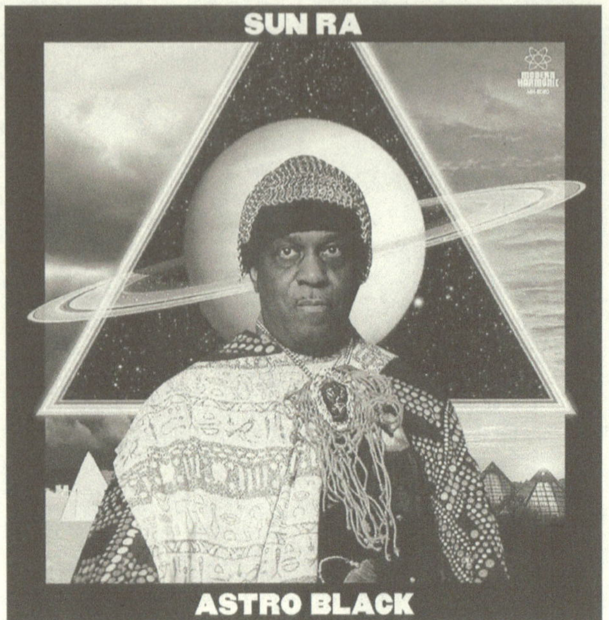


**FIGURE 7.7.** *Astro Black* cover art, Sun Ra, Impulse! 1973.

> principles within the flat or atonal space of the American twentieth century: a tone, a melody, a structure to things even if it is not audible to some, even if it made a lie of culture's bogus harmonies. Humans could ascend beyond the body, like the aliens who visited Ra, like Theosophy's mahatmas, like spirits on the astral plane. Bodies were sonic, too, combinations of vibrations that could resonate with the essence of things underlying the forms.[102]

Musically, Sun Ra's Arkestra of the 1960s and 1970s drew from practically every style of jazz and Afro-diasporic musics—from deep blues, gospel, and boogie-woogie to big band, swing, bebop, modal jazz, funk (on occasion), and African-style percussive polyrhythms—even as it melded them into a spacious and unpredictable weave of improvisation, tightly scripted orchestration, electronic as well as atonal experimentation, and the sheer heterophony (neither euphony nor cacophony) of pure sound. Sometime between their years in Chicago in the late 1950s and their relocation to the East Village of New York City in the early

1960s, the Arkestra came to crystallize the "space music" style, which cultural historian Paul Youngquist distills into three main qualities: "openness," especially "as a suspension of traditional conventions, in particular those regarding time"; "multiplicity," especially "of musical possibilities that occur without reference to a single regulative order"; and improvisation. "Improvisation," he writes, "extends what openness and multiplicity invoke: space as the medium of collective aspiration for better worlds."[103] As William Sites puts it, outer space becomes for Ra a metaphor for "an exploratory process, a set of pathways that are routinely traveled—in a strange yet everyday mode of utopian exploration—by the musician-workers," or "tone-scientists" as Ra referred to them, "who have created them." Ra embraced "de-familiarization" as a "strategy for challenging an oppressive reality with utopian assertion," and he did this both through the music and through performative theatrics.[104] In his colorful attire amalgamating African and Egyptian regalia with space suits and a kind of psychedelic, folk-cultural bricolage (metallic smocks, skull caps, and all manner of accoutrements), Ra came to embody the concept of "Astro-blackness," the mythology that Graham Lock describes as combining "the Astro of the outer space future" and "the Black of the ancient Egyptian past."[105] Lock's book *Blutopia* is aptly subtitled *Visions of the Future and Revisions of the Past in the Work of Sun Ra, Duke Ellington, and Anthony Braxton.* Ra, Ellington, and Braxton were in fact merely three points on a spectrum of Black artists and musicians who looked to reconstruct the past in reference to an open future.[106] Emerging within a racist mainstream culture, jazz, in Black musicians' hands, has commonly come to inhabit a space that is countercultural and critical of the mainstream, with sources seen to be beyond the present, located both in an ancestral African past and in a future unencompassed by North American modernity. The motto of the American Association for the Advancement of Creative Musicians (AACM) and its later torch-bearers, the Art Ensemble of Chicago, reflects this sensibility: "Great Black Music—Ancient to the Future." While the motto points back to the ancient roots of "Great Black Music," in its practice the AACM reflected a pursuit of what Fischlin, Heble, and Lipschutz call "life as possibility: the creation of new opportunities, the nurturing of new sources of hope for disadvantaged peoples," and "a utopia in sound."[107]

Perhaps most emblematic of this desire to weave past and future into a new and liberating synthesis, the prolific composer, music theorist, multi-instrumentalist, and AACM alumnus Anthony Braxton has drawn from Egyptology, astrology, numerology, pan-Africanism, ancient Gnostic and hermetic teachings, and white European philosophers and composers to develop a vision of the universe as a "vibrational" whole imbued with utopian and democratic potentials. In a three-volume work called *Tri-Axium Writings*, Braxton defined his key term "tri-axium" as an "attempt to gather axium tenets from the past and present—to get to the future."[108] Creativity is central for Braxton, as it is a "'doing' as a means to celebrate and 'affirm' the vibrational forms"—the "cosmic correspondences" and "higher forces"—that "dictate living."[109] In the words of musicologist Chadwick Jenkins, Braxton "proposes a mode of being (improvisation and creativity as a way to 'approach living') that allows for openness to change and an acknowledgment of the need for conflict even as one works to move beyond that conflict. Improvisation," for Braxton, "means being alive to the possibilities of the moment, recognizing the vestiges of the past as well as the trajectory of social change, and preparing the way for a future not *determined* by our collective decisions but in which those decisions will serve as the conditions of possibility for continual development and cultural renewal."[110]

Musicologists have long considered improvisation to be a fundamental feature of African diasporic musical cultures.[111] An improvising musician opens him or herself to what emerges spontaneously, impulsively, and unpredictably, and yet this opening is always made in reference to something that is already ongoing amidst the musicians one is playing with. At its core, this ongoingness has variously been characterized as "groove," "swing," "funk," a polyrhythmic "beat" or "breakbeat," or some other sense of motion or flow that one enters into relationship with.[112] Viewed more philosophically, this ongoingness can be taken to reflect the movement of collective history, which moves, as in the AACM's motto, from the "ancient" and ancestral African past "to the future" represented by collective freedom, creativity, and racial equality (if not superiority). In their ambitious attempt to theorize the free jazz movement that emerged among (mostly) African-American musicians in the early 1960s, Guerino Mazzola, Paul Cherlin, and their collaborators posit that this movement was rooted in the "romantic yearning for infinity" and "the human energy to ultimately transcend all finite barriers," which "at the same time is the desire to go home." For African-American musicians, "home" is of course represented by Africa and the lineage that connects them in multifarious ways to that continent; for others, it may be something different. Infinity, on the other hand, represents the freedom of creative expression and the multiplicity it opens up. "This romantic topos of infinity and intimacy," Mazzola et al. continue, "*creates a homeland* where political struggles and money do not threaten your life any more, and where the musical substance unfolds untouched and can flourish without being questioned by business and the contingencies of social life."[113] To these ends, the artists banded together in such collaborative organizations as the Black Arts Movement (BAM) and the Jazz Composers Guild in New York City, the AACM in Chicago, the Black Artists Group (BAG) in St. Louis, and Strata in Detroit.

I would like to take this "topos of infinity and intimacy" as a key to thinking about the significance of the creative-image in "freedom-seeking traditions" of cultural and artistic creativity. Insofar as the notion of tradition is backward-looking while freedom is forward-looking, this "topos of infinity and intimacy" represents a dialectic between a sense of rootedness within streams of ancestrality and, on the other hand, a sense of generative forward motion that enables expression toward the utopian potentials of an open universe. The noun I have emphasized in the previous paragraph—homeland—resonates with the work of utopian Marxist philosopher Ernst Bloch, whose mammoth multivolume work *The Principle of Hope* (*Das Prinzip Hoffnung*) ends with that very word. Bloch's concluding sentence in his nearly 1,400-page tome reads: "Once he has grasped himself and established what is his, without expropriation and alienation, in real democracy, there arises in the world something which shines into the childhood of all and in which no one has yet been: homeland (*Heimat*)."[114]

It is this intimation of a once-and-future homecoming, into a world that can hardly be anticipated let alone designed or projected, that nevertheless guides creative effort among the futurisms that arise in the face of present catastrophe. In this lie the chronopolitics of the creative-image.

## MUSIC AND IMMANENT UTOPIA

For all their critique of the present, neo-Marxist critical theorists like Bloch, Walter Benjamin, and Fredric Jameson have sought and found hope in utopian impulses uncovered both within long-standing cultural archives and in quotidian moments of everyday life. Bloch's *Principle of Hope* remains the encyclopedic distillation of this line of thinking. His hermeneutic grounds itself within Marxist class analysis, but it ranges widely across the entirety of western cultural history, and so it finds the felt anticipation of a brighter future—as he calls it, utopian aspirations of the "not-yet-conscious"—within the visual arts, music, architecture, religion, fairy tales, fashion, travel, and much else.

Bloch's writings on music capture the dialectic by which music both reflects social order and articulates that which would free itself from that order. "No art," Bloch writes, "is as socially conditioned as the supposedly spontaneous, indeed mechanically self-righteous art of music; it teems with historical materialism." His readings of western classical music generalize insightfully about the ways that "the very means and techniques" of music "are determined by the respective social conditions" and, at the same time, delineate what is uplifting and elusive about so many composers and forms. "To incipient free enterprise," he writes,

> corresponds the dominance of the melody-leading treble and the mobility of the other voices, just as cantus firmus in the middle and graded polyphony corresponded to society divided into estates. No Haydn and Mozart, no Handel and Bach, no Beethoven and Brahms, without their respective precisely varied social mandate; it extends from the form of the performance right to the characteristic style of the tonal material and its composition, to the expression, the meaning of the content. Handel's oratorios in their festive pride reflect rising imperialist England, its aptness to be the chosen people. No Brahms without the bourgeois concert society and even no music of "new objectivity," of supposed expressionlessness, without the gigantic rise of alienation, objectification and reification in late capitalism.[115]

Bloch's list here suggests iconic, indexical, as well as symbolic connections between social forces and the music they give rise to. Several pages later he is still elucidating the conditions from which emerged the innovations of equal temperament and symphonic and sonata form:

> The sonata form, with the conflict of two subjects, with keynote, development, recapitulation, presupposes capitalist dynamics; the stratified, completely undramatic fugue presupposes class, static society. So-called atonal music would not be possible in any other periods than those of late-bourgeois decline, it responded to this as bold helplessness. The twelve-tone technique, which leaves the dynamic relation between dissonance and consonance, modulation and cadence behind it to form still, severe sequences, would have been unthinkable in the age of free competition. Indeed it was only from 1600 onwards, in fact only from 1750 to 1900, that the history of music was a history of dissonance and cadence.[116]

But this dependence on history is continually punctured, for Bloch, by music's capacity to elude those same constraints. "At the same time music," he writes, "by virtue of its so immediately human capacity of expression, has more than other arts the quality of incorporating the numerous sufferings, the wishes and the spots of light of the oppressed class. And again no art has so much surplus over the respective time and ideology in which it exists, a surplus which of course certainly does not abandon the human layer. It is the surplus of hope-material."[117] About "*music itself as expression*" (all emphases here are his), which for Bloch "means the *entirety of its intending, signifying, depicting and of that which it depicts in such a clouded but, in both senses of the word, moving way,*" Bloch argues that music "ultimately" becomes "a *vice-regent for an articulation which goes much further than anything so far known.*" No one, he continues, "*has yet heard Mozart, Beethoven, Bach as they truly call, name, teach;* this will happen only much later, in the fullest after-ripening of these and of all great works. [. . .] The utopian art of music, in its polyphonic form still so young, is thus itself moving towards its own utopian career." Music, he writes, "is that art of pre-appearance which relates most intensively to the welling core of existence (moment) of That-Which-Is and relates most expansively to its horizon."[118]

In Bloch's immanent utopianism, human history is driven by a profound desire for that which it lacks, which could be characterized as a sense of egalitarian plenitude, an "anticipation of unalienated being-together," the "utopian excess" of "an open, processual world."[119] Music, being the most protean of the arts, is for Bloch also the most utopian. In music historian Beth Snyder's words, "Music is experienced as urgently present yet indeterminate, and as, in some sense, both material and immaterial." It "can better convey the emotive dimension of human existence because it shares the inceptive, surging quality of those emotional states that, in Bloch's words, '[press] for a solution.' Music is thus uniquely suited to the expression of desire more generally and to the feeling of hope in particular. And it enables us to experience a knowledge that is as inchoate as it is transformative."[120] Bloch's and Snyder's approach to music finds a strong parallel here to musicological writing inspired by Whiteheadian process philosophy, which I will take a moment to detail here.

Whitehead presented his most extended account of perception in the 1927 book *Symbolism, Its Meaning and Effect.*[121] There he distinguishes between three kinds of perception. One of these, "perception in the mode of presentational immediacy," refers to sensory perception in the clarity of its details; it is the "familiar immediate presentation of the contemporary world, by means of our projection of our immediate sensations, determining for us characteristics of contemporary physical entities."[122] It is what we generally consider to be sense-perception, consisting of colors, sounds, tastes, and the like. It is vivid and precise, and at the same time is "barren" of qualitative criteria, such as any understanding of the intrinsic nature of its sources. It is "that peculiar way in which contemporary things are 'objectively' in our experience."[123] The second, "perception in the mode of causal efficacy," is a kind of "general sense of things," a vague perception of the forward momentum of the world in which we find ourselves. It is "the conformation of the present to the immediate past," the sense in which "what is already made becomes a determinant of what is in the making."[124] It is more "primitive" or "primordial" than presentational immediacy, and is shared among all entities: "A flower turns to the light with much greater certainty than does a human being, and a stone conforms to the conditions set by its external environment with much greater certainty than does a flower."[125] Causal efficacy is at the root of our feelings and the significance they lend to our experience: "Anger, hatred, fear, terror, attraction, love, hunger, eagerness, massive enjoyment, are feelings and emotions closely entwined with the primitive functioning of 'retreat from' and of 'expansion towards.'"[126] The difference between these two modes of perception is significant: Whitehead claims that it is the "contrast between the comparative emptiness of Presentational Immediacy and the deep significance disclosed by Causal Efficacy" that "is at the root of the pathos which haunts the world."[127] The third form of perception, "symbolic reference," is that which synthesizes the first two, and which in combining the two also gives rise to the possibility of mistaken perception, and to the conflict and anxiety of situations where one's "feelings" appear contradicted by one's "senses."

This triad of Causal Efficacy, Presentational Immediacy, and Symbolic Reference corresponds in a general way to Peirce's categorical triad of firstness, secondness, and thirdness. Musical experience, like all experience, comes to us in all three registers: there is the sense of the forward momentum of what is felt (firstness, Causal Efficacy), the specific and determining perceived details of experience (secondness, Presentational Immediacy), and the synthesis that is made of the two (thirdness, Symbolic Reference). Music's specificity, however, is articulated well by Whiteheadian musicologist F. David Martin, who notes that "music more than any other art is perceived mainly in the mode of causal efficacy." By contrast, abstract painting, with its presentation of direct lines and colors, "more than any other art is perceived mainly in the mode of presentational immediacy." Martin continues, "In listening to music, we experience presentational immediacy because we hear the presently sounding tones. But there can be no 'holding' and we are swept up in the flow of process."[128] Music "forces us to *feel causal efficacy*, the *compulsion of process*."[129] Composer and musicologist Richard Elfin Jones explains that "music can make us feel process directly, since musical notes are presented successively," and that music's abstract nature means that its meanings are "embodied" rather than "designative" or "representational."[130]

It is this quality of embodied compulsion, which can sweep us up in its flow, that enables music to become a carrier for hopes as well as utopian aspirations. All of this is evident in the music of social movements, as with the civil rights movement and its anthems of justice-to-come (such as "We Shall Overcome"), the folk revival, anti-war movement, rock counterculture of the 1960s, the reggae of Bob Marley, and many others. It also animates the more abstract hopes infusing free jazz and collectively improvised music. Like Whitehead's process-relational philosophy, improvised music is about actively and creatively responding to the continual flow of sonic, rhythmic, melodic, and performative processes unfolding around and through oneself and one's collaborators in the collective creative act. Neither Bloch nor Whitehead wrote about jazz, predating the free jazz and Great Black Music movements by a few decades, but others have enthusiastically taken up that task.[131] For those who have written on the AACM, the Art Ensemble of Chicago, the Black Artists Group, Sun Ra, and the other musicians associated with these aesthetico-political movements—theorists as well as artists including George Lewis, Kodwo Eshun, Ytasha Womack, Reynaldo Anderson, Paul Youngquist, John Szwed, Alex Zamalin, and William Sites—the utopian dimension in their music has been central to their appeal.[132]

Making sense of this utopianism requires understanding the openness that is at the heart of the improvisational act. Even as improvisation involves self-expression, and is therefore a kind of expression-image unfolding in time, musicians associated with the free jazz movement—including John Coltrane, Ornette Coleman, Cecil Taylor, Archie Shepp, Albert Ayler, and various members of the AACM, the Black Artists Group, and the Art Ensemble of Chicago—have all referenced a broader collective context for their self-expression, a context that involved drawing from the past and moving toward a more open, freely shaped future. Most have, at one point or another, referenced spiritual sources of inspiration for their music. In chapter 1, I had discussed the ways in which music and sound scramble the Peircian categories of icon, index, and symbol by virtue of the fact that they are felt bodily in ways that seem to negate the separation of subject from object, and this blurring of the two is relevant here. Musicians have long characterized their own performance as a form of opening or submission to an external force, a force often characterized in religious or spiritual terms. In *Spirits Rejoice! Jazz and American Religion,* scholar of religion Jason Bivins documents a broad array of jazz musicians using the language of "surrendering," "channeling psychic energy," or becoming a "vessel," "terminal," "vehicle," "conduit," "instrument," or "receptacle" for a divine, universal, spiritual, or cosmic energy, power, or flow.

"These storms of energy and inspiration," Bivins writes, "the awareness of sound-spirit moving through the atmosphere into and out of you, are linked with processes like automatic writing, spirit mediumship, and consorting with angels."[133] Making music, he continues, is about "submission to those powers that bestow the gifts of sound and those patterns of tonal relation inherent in the religious fabric of things."[134]

"Submission to powers" raises questions about ontology and epistemology: which powers are being submitted to, what exactly are they, and how can one recognize them and approach them appropriately? So far I have referred to "ancestral" powers, those embodying the spirit of Africa and its rhythms and histories, but these should be considered as not only representing a past, but a forward movement oriented toward a desirable future. (Hilma af Klint's work is similarly guided by spirits who both embody a deep past and presage a possible future.) To broaden this discussion, it is necessary to speculate a bit further into how one might "open" to such powers. While some of the language referred to above may suggest that musicians are merely passive vehicles for a higher power (or perhaps a lower, more bodily one), few would deny that *activity,* and in fact *agency,* is required on their part. Collective improvisation demands active listening and creative participation; in the terms proposed by perceptual psychologist James J. Gibson, musicians selectively take up the "affordances" of their collectively produced and dynamically unfolding sonic milieu.[135] To play with others is always to read the signals coming from them, whether through the "groove," the melodies being traded and exchanged, or other articulations by which each of their contributions is being expressed, and to choose which of them to respond to and how to do that.

Collective musical improvisation is in this sense an interpretive, hermeneutic activity, but it differs semiotically from more linguistic forms of interpretation. Insofar as it involves the interpretation of sounds within systems of literary or cultural meanings—and playing "jazz" or "Great Black Music" always involves reference to such historically evolved systems—it is a form of *symbolic* interpretation and production. But being music, it also actively listens for icons and indexes—that is, for sounds that signify iconically, in and through their resemblance to other things, and indexically, in and through the ways they are directly produced. What sounds *sound like*, what rhythms *feel like*, what their *production* looks, sounds, and feels like (the visible and tangible nature of the instrumental acts of performance), and what the entire process of collective sound-making and "grooving" feels like to witness and participate within—these are all part of what gives free jazz and other forms of collectively improvised music its sense and meaning.

In all these things, the practice of collectively improvised music parallels the practice of what in other contexts is known as divination, augury, or prophecy—the reading of signs so as to intuit and recognize the ways they reveal hidden knowledge and point toward the future—and, in actively responding to these signs, the practice of magic. Let us explore these connections more directly.

## THE SEMIOTICS OF DIVINATION AND MAGIC

In his book *Divination and Human Nature,* classicist Peter Struck makes the case that divination, for many centuries, was not considered to be particularly unusual. It was a way of reading the signs of the world by those who were especially skilled at it, whose intuitive abilities made them better at accessing the "surplus knowledge" to be found through a nonrational scanning of given bits of informative materiality—the sensorially perceived materiality of dreams, stars, found objects, or living bodies. Struck writes,

> For many millennia and across the whole Old World, from Eastern to Western Eurasia, and from the tip of southern Africa to the highlands of Britannia, people were in the habit of practicing divination, or the art of translating information from their gods into the realm of the human. On a scale whose breadth we have yet to fully appreciate, they assumed that clandestine signs were buried in the world around them. Consultants perceived messages from temple-based oracles, like the one at Delphi, as well as in their dreams, the entrails of the animals they killed, lightning, fire, lots, pebbles, livers, fired tortoise shells, the stars, birds, the wind, and nearly anything else that moved.[136]

These practices, he continues, "were not, for the most part, considered esoteric or marginal. The inclinations of the divine, like the weather, were simply a part of the ancient atmosphere, and just about wherever we look in the sources, we find people trying to gauge the prevailing winds."[137] Consulting a diviner was something akin to how one may hire a consultant today, even if consulting the *best* diviners—say, the Oracle at Delphi—was rather more serious, requiring preparation of the sort that might have been intended in the two-word slogan that met them at the temple wall in Delphi: "Know yourself." While the divination itself referred to divinities believed to exist then and there, if not here and now, it was really a "reading" of the world, or a reading through and beyond the visible to the world's underlying patterns. If the diviner worked as a *medium* and not just an observer, it is because he or she knew themselves to be part of the world they were divining, a world made up of dreams, stars, found objects, living bodies, and indeed divinities.

There is a relationship here to the indexicality of the world-picture regime, described in part 1 of this book as a way of imaging the world through its directly traceable indices, captured in photographs and sensors of various kinds and recreated as images. The difference with divination is that it works not only with material that can be *pictured* (in sufficient clarity of detail such that it can be isolated, measured, tested, and circulated within methodologically consistent frameworks); it also works with relationships that can be sensed, felt, navigated, and negotiated with. If scientific methodology relies on clearly differentiating between causes and correlations, the better to manipulate its lines of causation, divinatory thinking revels in correlations—the more of them, the better. The world of the ancient diviner, the Siberian shaman, the Chinese geomancer, the Renaissance mage, or the Kabbalistic esotericist is a world of myriad patterns and correspondences within which one recognizes dynamically unfolding patterns so as to be able to incline oneself in their direction rather than against them, to "groove" with them (to use jazz terminology) and "tap" them to one's needs and concerns.[138] This is less a science than an art. It calls upon perceptual abilities, and thus the mode of perception Whitehead called Presentational Immediacy, but also upon intuitive perception and a kind of "submission" to the perception of Causal Efficacy—to interoceptive impulses, felt senses, hunches, affective currents, and so on. This is why shamanic or traditional healing techniques rely on a promiscuous array of sensory parameters: physical symptomatology, diet or fasting, ingestion of herbs, physical movement (dance, rhythmic swaying, and the like), sonic and olfactory stimulation, chanting or recitation, verbal locutions, visualizable narratives, exertion, duration, and so on. It is not any single one of them that leads to the eradication of an illness. It is the entirety of a performance, enlisted and endured over time, sometimes repeatedly, that refashions a situation in order to facilitate an appropriate outcome. A diviner is skilled in reading a multiplicity of signs—where almost anything could qualify, from marks on the skin, the flight paths of birds, the shapes of sticks and stones, and patterns of lines on a tree to the sounds of wind, letters in a random line of text, and dream images—in situations where what qualifies as a sign may not be knowable in advance, and when its signification may not be explainable or repeatable. It is an artful working within networks of relational ambiguity, dynamic Rorschach blots, we might say, or "unstructured fields of existing probabilities," as Diana Espirito Santo refers to them in her examination of Afro-Cuban spiritist oracles.[139]

From astrological horoscopes, Tarot cards, and Ouija boards to tea-leaf reading and bibliomancy, systems of divination remain immensely popular today. These practices commonly fall into the category loosely labeled "magic," though distinctions between magic and religion, on one hand, and between magic and science, on another, have historically been notoriously slippery and elusive.[140] Defining divinatory and magical practice as I am doing here, in any case, is bound to raise questions from those versed in the scientific values of empirical accuracy, theoretical precision, and experimental replicability. After all, the early modern development of science in sixteenth- and seventeenth-century Europe had already "tried" magic—many practicing scientists, from Paracelsus and Bruno to Galileo, Bacon, and Newton, were believing or skilled magicians of one kind or another (if magic is defined broadly enough to include alchemy, astrology, and similar now rejected fields)—and, according to the common story, had rejected it as untrue. If magic is something like the art of seeking correlational patterns within the "matters of concern" that face us, and learning to work with and through these to address our needs, the patterns may or may not reflect causal relationships that undergird the world, and extracting any perceived efficacy—which may be selective interpretation (wishful thinking), confirmation bias, placebo effect, and so on—from real causal forces is hardly possible without the methodological rigor of the sciences. As historian of science Brian Vickers puts it, the occult or magical system of correspondences "is based on resemblances, similarities, often heterogeneous and superficial," and while these may work within poetry or the arts, "the items in the correspondence grid are not metaphors at all" but "things, which, it is claimed, represent patterns of connection within reality."[141] Science, on the other hand, may start with a similar pattern-seeking impulse, but then works to identify specific causal relationships, so that these can be isolated from local circumstances and generalized into reliable "laws" explaining "matters of fact" and not mere "matters of concern." In the process, science comes to reject earlier beliefs and produce its own, with powerful empirical results to support them.

A process-semiotic perspective can shed helpful light on the similarities and differences between magic and science. In examining the regime of the world-picture, with its historical connection to the rise of modern science, I suggested, in chapter 2, that science is rooted in indexicality, the reading of signs in terms of the direct, causal relationships that they indicate. On its own, any single index will remain specific and limited. A weathervane—the classic example of an indexical sign—points in the direction that the wind is blowing, but it only does this if there *is* a wind, if no other factors impede it (if it isn't stuck, for instance), and if it is in fact a weathervane and not a fixed decoration that only *looks* like a weathervane. Grasping that the wind is coming from the West, and even that it often does that in a given location, tells us nothing about why westerlies are so common or what they depend on. Determining these broader patterns requires planting weathervanes—along with thermometers, barometers, hydrometers, and other measurement devices—at multiple locations, recording measurements over time, mapping the landscape with aerial technologies and satellites, analyzing streams of data, and doing this repeatedly over multiple and variable iterations. All of this builds upon the principle of indexicality—that something can be taken as a sign of something else—but comes to rely also on icons (such as maps, diagrams, graphs, and so on) and on symbols (words, arguments, theories), without which it cannot function. When it "works," it is because the networks of circulatory reference maintain their reversible indexicality: each node in the chain of transmissions is connected through a traceable transformation to the previous. Each is documented precisely enough that its work can be replicated and weaknesses in the chain strengthened over further iterations. In its aggregate, as with the science of meteorology, science produces results that no weather magic is able to match.

Magic, then, is not so different from science in principle—both manipulate the world based on observations of previous interactions—but its goals tend to be more pragmatic than systematic, depending as they do on the "matters of concern" of the practitioner or client. I've suggested that magic's reliance on signs is more promiscuous, in that anything can be taken as an indicator, and in this it favors those things that are most evident to our senses. This means it favors likenesses, resemblances, parallels, and analogues—things that look like, sound like, smell like, and taste like what we've experienced before; in other words, icons (in the Peircian sense), and therefore images. The commonplace that magic favors "invisible" or "supernatural" things is not quite correct: feelings, hunches, visions, voices, and all the other manifestations of the supernatural are *events of experience*, which are only *super*natural if "nature" is defined categorically as what is known to science. And in practice, magical divination doesn't always take just anything as an indicator; it looks for specific kinds of things that are prescribed by the traditions of thought it inherits from the past. (Magic and religion can be taken as overlapping categories here.) It is, in this sense, closer to human thought in its "natural" state, at least if we take contemporary neurophysiology seriously. As I recounted in chapter 1, humans, like other social mammals, have evolved to read signs quickly: to note resemblances and act on expectations derived from prior experience. This is how cognition works, according to neuroscientists for whom experience is a construction derived from the interaction of sensory input with a complex architecture of responses and expectations built from previous experience. As van Elk and Aleman summarize this perspective, "humans use prior cognitive models to predict and perceive the world, and these models are updated in case of conflicting predictions or sensory information." This implies that "the way in which we perceive the world is strongly determined by our prior expectations and beliefs," and that, therefore, in cultural contexts in which religious or "magical" ideas are powerful, these will in fact shape experience.[142]

All of this suggests that something like divination—the gleaning of meanings from ambiguous signs according to patterns of resemblance—comes naturally to humans, and that understanding these processes is important. Science may have tried to expunge certain habits of thought it considers magical or pseudoscientific, but its relatively short and, to many, checkered history has meant that its success has only been partial. (That checkered history includes such episodes as the Tuskegee experiment which, over a period of decades, observed hundreds of African-American men suffering from syphilis without informing them of their treatment options; or, of course, the atomic bombs and other technological "achievements" that have destroyed ecosystems and population centers.) Magic, as mentioned, may be nearly impossible to define, but popular accounts of it still rely on the categories proposed by turn-of-the-century armchair anthropologist Sir James G. Frazer, who distinguished what he called "sympathetic magic" into two forms. Frazer described them as following the two contrasting principles of "similarity" and "contagion": "First, that like produces like, or that an effect resembles its cause; and second, that things which have once been in contact with each other continue to act on each other at a distance after the physical contact has been severed."[143] The first describes a "homeopathic" magic reflecting an analogical, comparative logic that seeks parallelisms and patterns; the second, a logic of contiguity and connectedness. Perceptive readers may note that these two Frazerian principles of similarity and contagion parallel the iconic and indexical modes of signification: the first finds meaning in resemblance, the second in direct contact. Insofar as they involve generalization from similarity or contact, they also involve thirdness, or the formation of habits based on perceptual regularities. Social psychologists Paul Rozin and Carol Nemeroff, among others, have studied the persistence of these beliefs in contemporary society and hypothesized that they are rooted in adaptive natural tendencies: to generalize from experience ("this looks like that"), and to avoid microbial contagion ("this has touched that").[144] Experimental participants, for instance, tend to show disgust when exposed to replicas of disgusting objects, such as chocolate fudge in the shape of dog feces, and are negatively psychologically aroused when a photograph of someone or something they love is destroyed (both are iconic signs).[145] Analogously, an object given to them by a deceased loved one will be valued sentimentally (as an index of their relationship) even if its value in itself is nonexistent.

Where these may seem like sentimental attachments or even knee-jerk reactions, divinatory practices in traditional contexts tend to have more ontological bearing on their participants. Describing Ifá divination among Afro-Cuban diviners in Havana, anthropologist Martin Holbraad writes, "Rather than producing representations, diviners' truth-claims induce something resembling a eureka moment, by bringing the rich mythical narratives on which Ifá divination is based to bear on the personal circumstances of the client."[146] Instead of representing the world, then, "the oracle transforms it by interfering with its very meaning," which Holbraad calls "an ontological rather than an epistemic operation."[147] Divination thus consists of acts of "redefinition" that "effectively transform the world upon which they purport to comment."[148] To bring this back to the creation of music and art: just as the Tarot card reader and the Ifá diviner both work with images provided to create insightful and meaning-laden connections with the situation brought to them by a client, so an improvising musician works with available affordances to create artful and meaningful patterns in sound.[149] The musician's goal may include an effect on her listener, but it is also likely to include a hoped-for result on the musician herself, an effect that is affective and aesthetic in its nature. And inasmuch as certain musical forms, such as free jazz or certain forms of Hip Hop, have proposed radical goals, their hoped-for effect could be described as ontological.[150]

None of this is meant to suggest that divination or other forms of intuitive perception are in any way better than the measurable, repeatable results of scientific practice, or that any form of divination is as good as any other.[151] What it does suggest is that these forms of perception come naturally to us, and that communication, especially communication through images, is likely to be deeply reliant on them. I would like to propose that the divinatory arts, the arts of "opening to the spirits," can in fact facilitate a "channeling" of utopian aspirations *when aligned with* appropriate social and creative movements. They can, to be sure, be aligned with radically different societal trends. Examples of magic applied to racist or exclusionary ends are not hard to find: Nazi Germany was rife with them, as are many of today's far right political movements. Interpreting the rather different context of the capitalist marketplace, Joshua Ramey writes of a form of divination that, in his analysis, has usurped the traditional forms that have been practiced "from time immemorial." Where the latter consist of "procedures" of "conjecture and systematic inquiry" "by which human beings attempt to access knowledge of the unknown" through the "systematic solicitation" of chance, the new form of popular divination he describes is the neoliberal market form of "disingenuous" divination, by which entrepreneurs and traders systematically exploit risk and "weaponize" randomness "through the strategic production of uncertainty and instability."[152] "At the heart of neoliberalism," Ramey writes, "is a divinatory practice, a political theology that identifies arbitrary, unforeseeable changes in market conditions with divinely ordained order," and which in turn "justifies austerity, the maintenance of debts, and even ecological devastation, reading them as cosmic inevitabilities it is irrational to question."[153] Critical of such practice, Ramey advocates in its place a "decolonized" and "*expansive* politics of divination" that is "marked by curiosity, presumptive generosity, and genuine openness to transformation of present investments and attachments."[154]

In the spirit of such a decolonized divination, I would like to propose that we turn to certain of the "rich mythical narratives" that could be brought to bear onto the "circumstances of the client," with the client here being a collective one—humanity, of the Anthropocenic sort. More specifically, I mean a humanity that is prepared to learn from narratives cultivated by those who have already lived through the "end of the world," if not through multiple such "ends." As T. J. Demos puts it, "Current fears of the world's end" should be "contextualized by Indigenous voices that view them as a mode of settler anxiety, haunted by those centuries-old histories of colonial violence, climate-changing brutality, and genocide-directed militarism—forces that have long disrupted fragile ecologies integral to native lifeworlds and continue to do so in the present. Indeed, Indigenous peoples have already lived through many such apocalypses."[155] If anything, Indigenous, colonized, and formerly enslaved people suffer a "postapocalypse stress syndrome," as they live today in what Potawatomi scholar Kyle Whyte has called his "ancestors' dystopia now."[156] Their narratives are in this sense survivor narratives drawn from different temporalities than those guiding western modernity.

## EXPANDED KINSHIP, FROM LAND TO THE OCEANIC

As with my analysis of John Akomfrah's multichannel installations in chapter 5, I am emphasizing in this chapter the relevance of Afro-diasporic and other BIPOC perspectives in articulating a more complete analysis of the Anthropocene condition, with its historical relations to European colonialism and extractive capitalism. To capture the multiscalar complexities of this condition requires a chronopolitics that engages with time's nonlinear flows: with the ancestralities of humanity's multiple imagined communities; with futurities embodying not only modernity's hegemonically imagined progressive trajectory, but alternatives of varying hues; and with perceptions of ecological loss, trauma, and apocalypse *already lived through* and experienced, as well as those only foreseen in dystopian fiction. Afrofuturism, Indigenous futurism, and related artistic movements have aimed to work this spatial and temporal multiplicity into a more open-ended, cognitive and affective representation of possibilities. In their appeals to an expansive humanism—one that would explode the category of the human, or "Man," as it did in Afro-Caribbean philosopher Sylvia Wynter's writings—they naturally encompass ancestral as well as future humans who were typically left out of the picture of normative western humanism.[157] In some variants, these futurisms also include divinities as well as other kin relations that have never been included within modern notions of the human. In all of this, they reflect the "counter-hegemonic Anthropocene" described in chapter 5, as articulated by Stefania Barca and other left-decolonial theorists, with its centering of "other-than-master subjects" and "forces of reproduction."

Indigenous writings on land, sovereignty, and kinship have been especially forceful in making the case for expanding our understanding of the human.[158] To take just one example, Nishnaabeg artist and educator Leanne Betasamosake Simpson, in a much cited article entitled "Land as Pedagogy," writes that Nishnaabeg knowledge "originates in the spiritual realm, coming to individuals through dreams, visions, ceremony and through the process of gaaizhi-zhaawendaagoziyaang—that which is given lovingly to us by the spirits." Knowledge "comes *through* the land," which "is the place where our ancestors reside, where spiritual beings exist, and where the spirits of living plants, animals and humans interact. In order to gain access to this knowledge, one has to align themselves within and with the forces of the implicate order through ceremony, ritual and the embodiment of the teachings one already carries."[159] The broader context is the intimate one of an extended kinship network, which "requires long-term, stable, balanced warm relationship within the family, extended family, the community and all living aspects of creation. Intelligence," she continues, "flows through relationships between living entities," and meaning "is derived not through content or data" but "through a compassionate web of interdependent relationships."[160]

All of this is broadly congruent with the kinds of understandings long recognized by anthropologists, and more recently presented by Indigenous scholars, as central to Indigenous lifeways.[161] The slogan "We are the land, and the land is us" has been used repeatedly by Indigenous activists both to contrast with the settler view that the land can belong to a property owner, and be bought and sold by that person, and to make the case for a land-based Indigenous identity and political sovereignty.[162] Generalizing from the many hundreds of Indigenous cultures, and even generalizing about what it means to be Indigenous, is notoriously risky.[163] But there are sufficient commonalities to support the kind of argument made by Indigenous scholars Dei, Karanja, and Erger, who write that "in Indigenous philosophies and worldview, Land is a living entity and the source of Indigenous knowledges, pedagogies, cultures, languages and identities and includes the universe, all living and non-living entities and the spirit world."[164] Potawatomi scholar Robin Wall Kimmerer echoes this when she writes that Indigenous worldviews understand "the land as a web of relationships which are simultaneously spiritual and material," and according to which land is seen "as sustainer, as the dwelling place of non-human relatives, as a source of knowledge, as a pharmacy, as the intergenerational home of both ancestors and descendants," and as "the place where our moral responsibility to life is enacted."[165] Celidwen and Keltner describe an Indigenous "ethics of belonging" as consisting of the core elements of "kin relationality" and "ecological belonging." The first refers to an ontological sense of relatedness, with "living beings and phenomena" all "recognized as part of a family lineage" encompassing "larger collectives or systems, such as Lands, local ecosystems, and cosmic systems of meaning"; the second "conceptualizes the self as belonging to a kin relational, collective Earth system network—its ecosystems and life cycles." Both are grounded in what the authors call "self-transcendent emotions" including compassion, gratitude, and awe.[166]

Kinship and homeland are powerful concepts whose application is not unproblematic. They have been used by colonized and Indigenous peoples to articulate their claims to land taken away from them, and by ethnic communities claiming superiority over rivals in shared nation-states. They are hardly foreign to the blood-and-soil fascisms of the twentieth century or to the neoliberal ethnic nationalisms of the twenty-first. The "metaphysics of 'home'" is played by those seeking self-determination from colonial forces just as it is played by those seeking to prevent the entry of "foreigners" into the security of their own imagined national "homelands." It is therefore important to distinguish their uses in ways that can build viable communities rather than retreat to the closure of imagined pasts.[167] As explained by Cameroonian philosopher Achille Mbembe, neither the "community" nor "the republic nor democracy exist a priori"; all must be built within discourses of the past and the future:

> Even when [the community] referred to shared beliefs, such as the belief in myths of origin, it was nothing more than the name of a reciprocal responsibility between generations. At the two poles of the generational arc were the ancestors on one side and the generations to come on the other. Community-making consisted in mastering the art of making the link between the two. Weaving or composing the link was a processual affair. The communities were not rigid and closed collectives in themselves but processual assemblies in permanent recomposition, capable of digesting differences by means of permanent aggregations.[168]

If the metaphysics of "home" are to serve the building of viable communities today, this can only be done through a deep acknowledgment of the cultural disruptions and transformations of the past five centuries. "Home" is no longer simply home, if it ever was.

Here is where I would like to bring together strands from each of the last three chapters, with their respective examination of the interfaces between humanity and the Earth, humans and other creatures, and *present* humans and their *past and future more*-than-humans. (I use the term "more-than-human" to refer to divinities, since whatever else we may say about them, they are usually taken to be *more* of something or other: more powerful, more aware, "higher," "transcendent," and so on. But ancestors and descendants, being *differently* human from us, can qualify as well.[169]) In the context of a global world that has irredeemably transformed people's relationships to place and land, the nature of *land* can only be thought in relation to the nature of its constituting *other.* In elemental terms, this constituting other is most simply characterized as the *oceanic*: that is, as the planetary, encompassing water that shapes the land by bounding and enfolding it, by bringing otherness to it whether in the arrival of maritime colonizers and slaving ships or the promise of connections and potential routes outward, and by providing a stable point of reference only in its interminable *in*stability. While a terrestrial imagination keeps the ocean on the margins of our thought, a maritime vision, as Dilip Menon puts it, calls upon us "to engage with the persistent movement of people, goods, and ideas across the ocean which has always exceeded the remit of states and empires."[170] At a time when humanity and its land-based cohabitants are threatened by rising seas, the ocean in fact poses a threat to *any* fixed notion of land. When human relations with land are destabilized, movements of people increase, with some arriving along oceanic routes, crossing the Mediterranean and other seas. At the same time, human industrial activities threaten life *in* the oceans with toxification and rapid warming, with their resultant effects of coral bleaching, species decline, and ecological unraveling. As Elizabeth Deloughrey observes, the Anthropocene has made the ocean "a new space of empire" and "new 'El Dorado,'" with "territorial claims emerging with the melting of the Arctic ice, the planting of the Russian flag in the North Pole seabed, and the global expansion of submarine extractivism," as up to half of the world's oil and natural gas mining comes to be from undersea resources.[171]

Historically, understanding the emergence of Anthropocene conditions—the colonization of the Americas, the spread of the plantation system to grow cotton, sugar, and other products for expanding markets, inter-imperial competition, rapid industrialization, the global trade in fossil fuels and other products, carbon emissions and resultant climate change—requires understanding the maritime transportation that enabled all of these. In this respect, the out-of-Africa movement that paleo-anthropologists tell us shaped the evolutionary history of *Homo sapiens sapiens* finds a more recent analogue in the movement of millions of enslaved humans to serve the plantations that built the western world. As Tiffany Lethabo King points out, oceanic relations have been the constant undercurrent for all projects toward freedom and liberation of African-descendent peoples around the world: "evoking a space of connection, transit, passage, and flow, the ocean has also functioned as a complex seascape and ecology within Black diaspora studies that ruptures normative thought and European discourse." This can be seen in a series of critical-theoretical discourses which King enumerates as including "Hortense Spillers's notion of the 'oceanic,' Édouard Glissant's 'archipelagic thought,' Paul Gilroy's 'Black Atlantic,' Kamau Brathwaite's 'tidalectics,' Antonio Benítez-Rojo's 'rhythm,' and Omise'eke Natasha Tinsley's 'Black Atlantic, queer Atlantic.'" To these we can add Christina Sharpe's "wake work," King's own "black shoals," the vertiginous oceanic montage-thought of John Akomfrah (examined in chapter 5), and the "dub poetics" of Alexis Pauline Gumbs, to which we will turn next.[172]

In King's words, Brathwaite's "tidalectics" (along with the others) "confound the binary and dialectical thinking that would separate ocean from land and render Black people and Indigenous people as an antagonism."[173] King's concept of "the black shoals" is intended to serve as this kind of binary-confounding concept. As reefs, sandbars, and other sedimentations that, invisible from above, can slow the movement of vessels and present problems for maritime navigation, shoals are "spaces of contact, friction, and interaction among land and water," "in-between, ecotonal, unexpected, and shifting" spaces "of liminality, indeterminacy," and "suture" between divergent frames of reference.[174] Such spaces of contact and friction at which land and water meet, but whose meeting today is fraught with uncertainty, can serve as a kind of master metaphor for the Anthropocene condition. Land and water, solid and fluid, known and unknown, human and more-than-human: these are the confounding dualities that call today for new and different ways of navigating, divining, boundary-crossing, and communicating.

## DUB POETICS: GUMBS'S CREATIVE DIVINATION OF RELATIONS

One of the contemporary writers whose work most evocatively engages both with the oceanic imaginary of the Black Atlantic, and with the notion of a more-than-human ancestrality and futurity, is African-American poet Alexis Pauline Gumbs. In a trilogy of book-length poetic works, *Spill: Scenes of Black Feminist Fugitivity*, *M Archive: After the End of the World*, and *Dub: Finding Ceremony*, Gumbs employs what she describes as a "dub poetics," a music-modeled form of expressive writing that deploys "repetition with difference" as a citational and referential practice, a way of acknowledging a broad multiplicity of ancestors, from the Africans who made the transatlantic Middle Passage to more direct intellectual precursors. The trilogy focuses on three specific Black feminist interlocutors, treated both as intellectual forebears and as textual resources: literary critic Hortense Spillers in the case of *Spill*, writer and educator M. Jacqui Alexander in *M Archive*, and philosopher Sylvia Wynter in *Dub*. But it draws upon an expansive web of kinship relations in its simultaneously creative and divinatory methods.

*Dub: Finding Ceremony* takes its subtitle from Caribbean philosopher Sylvia Wynter's call, in the 1984 text "A Ceremony to be Found" and its 2015 follow-up "A Ceremony Found," for a new "cosmogony" that would suit the situation in which "for the first time in the history of humankinds we are now confronted with a common environment," a "post-atomic one" that "challenges us with the demand that we reinvent our present conflictive modes of group integration."[175] Gumbs's 252-page poem speaks in many voices, in lines freely playing off each other like bebop or free jazz: "we would like it if you wrote us poems," it begins, "we would like it if you wrote us long life sentences. We would like it if you broke sentences and gave us more life than you or we were told could be contained." And soon enough: "we promise to wake you up if we think you won't get the point of the dream." Then they, the voices, give instructions about what to "tell them" about, what to "gather," "what the coral said," "what the salt said," "what the seaweed kept," and about whale choruses, remembrances, arrivals, the smells upon arrival, and memories of Africa, of slavery, of violence, of longing, of love. The writing is musical and imagistic, its images flowing between what they invoke, as icons of what readers remember, and the rhythm of their flow, a rhythm that is continuous, sinuous, yet organized; the indexicality of their writing, its process revealed in lines reflecting the discipline of daily listening, noting, dreaming, and crafting; and the symbolic richness the words resonate with in their many connotations. It is music written in words, rhythmic and layered like a jazz musician soloing melismatically against the tonal drone of a history shot through with hopes, sacrifices, and possibilities remaining to be explored.

Gumbs's "dub poetics," as Isis Semaj-Hall describes them, provide a structure that "echoes the past, reflects the present, and anticipates the future in its very production." Through production techniques including "reverberation, mixing, talk-over, and muting," Jamaican-originated dub music enables an "unfamiliar encounter with the familiar."[176] Dub is a form of rhythmic citationality, a repetition with difference whereby repeated rhythms allow for the emergence of new figurations, morphings, and resonances. Gumbs's writing follows a dub stylistics when it thinks *with* its interlocutors rather than merely *about* them. In the introduction to *Spill*, Gumbs writes that she had intended to take phrases from Spillers's text *Black, White, and in Color* and to recontextualize them, but that when she "turned these phrases, doors opened and everyone came through. All the Black women writers Spillers wrote about and didn't write about. All the characters those Black women writers acknowledged and ignored. All the people living novelistic lives without arcs or arks to save them. As usual, the project took over and offered scene after scene out of time and invited voices and settings that I can't claim to have invented."[177] In line with the suggestive philosophies of Sylvia Wynter and others, Gumbs expresses, in the introduction to *M Archive*, the goal of "call[ing] pre-existing definitions of the human into question" and presenting "a possibility of being beyond the human."[178] In an outtake from *Dub* entitled "Being Ocean as Praxis" (the title is a reply to Wynter's much cited essay "Human Being as Praxis"), Gumbs describes "a species-unraveling encounter with the bottom of the ocean I experienced when I tried to listen to my ancestors."[179] Gumbs writes in the introduction to *Dub*:

> As I started doing the daily writing that would become this book, I started to hear from the perspective of my ancestors from the

> Caribbean region. And then my Irish ancestors who shipwrecked into the Caribbean and stayed. [. . .] My coastal whale-listening Shinnecock ancestors. My untraceable Arawak ancestors. My Ashanti ancestors who survived the Middle Passage. And then the ocean itself. In each case, I found myself confronting stories that I had been told, or that had been told around me, or that had been silently providing the context for my racial, national, and cultural existence. But these stories emerged in different voices, from submerged perspectives. And as I opened to a new and threatening listening (that often left me sitting at my computer in shock), my sense of who were and were not my ancestors shifted.
>
> [. . .] My listening began to include speakers who have never been considered human [. . .] my enslaved ancestors, my disabled ancestors, my queer and indigenous ancestors [. . .] it also generatively includes whales, corals, barnacles, bacteria, and more. Kindred beyond taxonomy.[180]

As Gumbs's pantheon of ancestors and relations becomes more expansive, her writing evolves to fit the calling. Describing some of her literary methods, she notes that the writing

> required me to let go of my voice and to surrender to language practices outside my memory and education. It required study into the political content and context of places I have never lived and during times that I have not been alive. It required repetition and giving over to the timing and rhythm of prayer, it has required me to read each page aloud at least a dozen times and to know that I am not the same person and the room is not the same place when these words have been spoken. It has required me to trust and know myself intimately and in the same moment to stop knowing who I am.[181]

The project, she writes,

> is an artifact and tool for breath retraining and interspecies ancestral listening. It is structured to ask, what if you could breathe like whales who sing underwater and recycle air to sing again before coming up for air? What if you could breathe like coral from a multitude of simultaneous openings connected to one source built upon the bones of all your dead? What if you could

> breathe like cyanobacteria who made the sky into oxygen millions of years ago and sent their contemporaries to a world of sulfur deep under ocean and ground?[182]

Ecocritics Henry Ivry and Max Karpinsky describe the "prophetic" register of Gumbs's writing as she invokes and engages a "distributed web of kinship ties" whilst perpetually "cut[ting], shift[ing], and modulat[ing] between scales."[183] Dub, they write,

> is a commitment to an understanding of the subject as constantly unsettled and recomposed, drawing and building on the labor of a capaciously imagined ancestry. The dub poetics that Gumbs develops through *Spill*, *M Archive*, and *Dub* simultaneously narrates and formalizes molecular transformation, calling into presence a mode of being that scales across the twinned crises of race and the environment that define the contemporary moment. Crucially, this is a mode of being that takes seriously the racial violence that has underwritten the emergence of this geological epoch, and the uneven distribution of violence, along racial lines, that continues to be subsumed in many discussions of global crisis. Gumbs's work, that is, offers a transformative vision of the Anthropocenic emphasis on relationality and non-human entanglements through the cultivation of a Black ontology for the contemporary moment.[184]

Toward the end of *Dub*, in the section called "blood chorus," Gumbs, they write, becomes "explicit" in her "unseating of human exceptionalism via an ever-expanding vision and mesh of kinship":[185] "who? us?" she writes, "we lost our names in fires and when the boat crashed and the crop broke . . . / me? i let them call me what they wanted to call me . . . / you? we made your name from fragments. from memories and accidents."[186] And then:

> at some point we all had to learn how to see the invisible. the unborn, the unremembered, the discounted, ourselves. we would have had to add the spirit to the air if it wasn't already thick with it. for us it was a matter of what you call love. thick relation. what you call ritual. repetitive action. . . . we made meaning out of the mess by what we did. and what we continued to do. once is

a moment. twice is time travel. there are very few things you are doing for the first time.[187]

Gumbs's writing could be considered a form of poetic musicality, a writing with words of musical thoughts, melodies, and refrains, drawn from a broad reading of history with its multiple forms of cultural and ecological connectedness. It is not unlike a verbal analogue to John Akomfrah's work with images: creative and expressive, not merely self-expressive but collectively expressive, with a recognition of the complex causalities behind the present, Anthropocenic predicament with its multiple ecological precarities. The legacies of colonialism, enslavement, and displacement that forcibly separated people from their homelands (in Africa, in the Americas, and elsewhere around the world) and drove them into a diasporic longing for the past, is connected here with memories of lost kinships and relationalities, but also with ideals rooted in the past yet oriented toward a different and more habitable future.

In her creative-divinatory strategy, Gumbs, like Hilma af Klint, Sun Ra, and others examined in this chapter, follows a kind of three-step method by which creative expression (the expression-image) encounters ideality (the ideal-image) to create animate-images that resonate on multiple levels with the current Anthropocene condition. The first step in the strategy is an opening to the multiple layers of causal and emotional preconditions and ancestral relationalities underlying the present, a "submission to the powers" in a process that unfolds over time. This may include the "repetition and giving over to the timing and rhythm of prayer" that Gumbs describes, which results in the "doors open[ing] and everyone [coming] through." (The "Acknowledgments" with which she ends the book *Dub* amount to a full seven pages of names and relations.) The second step is an extended engagement in the activities of listening, of receiving and divining, of reading and interpreting various kinds of signs: the voices of ancestors, of "whales, corals, barnacles, bacteria," and the "invisible," "unborn," and "unremembered," and in this sense also of descendants, the future attractors that shape our activities in the present by proffering a hope for a better world, the Blochian "not-yet-conscious" and "yet-to-come." Thirdly and finally, there is the art of participatorily navigating, an improvisatory "playing along," with the voices thus heard, images glimpsed, movements and perceptions felt, and so on. This is the creative act that follows the divinatory reading of what has been offered. If, as suggested in Laura Marks's processualist interpretation of Henry Corbin's and Mulla Sadra's imaginal realm, one can, through discipline, come to perceive and respond to the "flow of Being," this flow in its richness will be something akin to what these artists are approaching.

In *M Archive*, Gumbs writes that "we never put ourselves back together in the same way again. [I]t was a daily practice, slowly changing our sound from the inside, chanting and singing and listening deeper, moving in response to older harmonies than the reactive ones around."[188] In this search for "older harmonies," she is also searching for a reconcordance toward future harmonies. The work she does with verbal and poetic images is analogous to af Klint's work in visual forms and Akomfrah's in audiovisual moving images. This relatedness is found also in the efforts of other theosophically inspired early twentieth-century modernists, and then again in the mid-century Afrofuturists and avant-jazz explorers. Each pursued a kind of creatively divinatory method, where "divination" was a process of methodical opening to the obligations woven into relationships with ancestors and with descendants. For af Klint, Gumbs, and Akomfrah, these have also become relations with more-than-human kin and with the bio- and geological contexts that shape them. This is a relational opening to future worlds that may or may not come to pass, but within which we are poised to serve an ancestral function.

## HOMECOMINGS AND GOINGS-AWAY

None of this creative figuration of the ancestral and the futural is straightforward, and it is all too easy to lose a sense of specificity the deeper one goes into the (always imagined) past or future. Hilma af Klint's or Oberto Airaudi's futures are not the same as the futures envisioned by Afrofuturists and Indigenous writers and artists, and any articulation of desirable futures is likely to face contention over who they are desirable for, and at whose expense. The past is like that, too: even among those who look, for instance, to the African past for hints of its (or the world's) future, there is no consensus on which elements of that past to revive or draw from and which to leave behind. In *Lose*

*Your Mother*, her travelogue-cum-analytical-memoir tracing the routes of the Atlantic slave trade, Saidiya Hartman writes, "Unlike *we come together* or *we who fled* or *we who were liberated, African people* crossed the lines of raider and captive, broker and commodity, master and slave, kin and stranger. The capaciousness of these words—African people—was as dangerous as it was promising. [. . .] Africa was never one identity, but plural and contested ones."[189] The same is true of any imagined pasts and ancestralities, as it is for the futures we may build with them. It is the effort in opening to them, listening to them, and determining how to respond to them, ethically and creatively, that is important.

Hartman's cautionary note about her effort to find "home" is an important reminder for our thinking about chronopolitics and the Blochian search for a future "homeland" that could rearrange our sense of the past. If there is another key theorist of cultural homecoming that we have not yet heard from in these pages, it is Russian literary critic Mikhail Bakhtin, the philosopher par excellence of the dialogical and many-voiced nature of cultural production. Bakhtin's writing about speech genres is equally true about images, and his assertion that language is "essentially chronotopic as a treasure-house of images" perhaps suggests as much.[190] In an often cited passage Bakhtin wrote, "There is neither a first nor a last word"—and here we could add "nor image,"

> and there are no limits to the dialogic context (it extends into the boundless past and boundless future). Even *past* meanings, that is those born in the dialogue of past centuries, can never be stable (finalized, ended once and for all)—they will always change (be renewed) in the process of subsequent, future development of the dialogue. At any moment in the development of the dialogue there are immense, boundless masses of forgotten contextual meanings, but at certain moments of the dialogue's subsequent development along the way they are recalled and invigorated in renewed form (in a new context). Nothing is absolutely dead: every meaning will have its homecoming festival. The problem of *great time*.[191]

The final, grammatically incomplete sentence is not as frequently quoted as the one that precedes it, yet it is the last line of the final piece of writing Bakhtin completed before his death in 1975. In a 1971 interview, he elaborated on this term "great time" (большое время, in Russian), noting that "in great time nothing ever loses its significance. Homer, and Aeschylus, and Sophocles, and Socrates, and all the ancient writers and thinkers remain, with equal entitlement, in great time. [. . .] And it is in this sense that I consider that nothing dies, but everything is renewed. With every new step forward our previous steps acquire a new, additional meaning."[192]

Bakhtin's point is often taken as a celebration of the tradition of great writing and thinking. At times he seems to employ this notion of "great time" interchangeably with "great experience" and "great memory," which he sees as always "open" and "unfinalized" (*nezavershennoye*), a "memory of that which does not coincide with itself."[193] Following Bakhtin's insistence on the many-voicedness of human expression, Barry Sandywell interprets his "great time" as "the temporal equivalent of 'polyglossia' at the level of cultural traditions, [. . .] the time of collective, national, and civilizational processes, the time of 'human emergence and development' [. . .] the historicity of culture itself."[194] Bakhtin, elsewhere, relates this idea to a kind of collective memory of humanity:

> The model of the ultimate whole, the model of the world, lying at the basis of every artistic image. This model of the world is reconstructed over the c[ou]rse of centuries (or radically, of millennia). [. . . It contains] the great experience of humanity. [. . .] In great experience the world does not coincide with itself (it is not what it is), it is not closed and not finalized. In it there is memory that does not have borders, memory that descends and disappears into the pre-human depths of matter and inorganic life, the experience of the life of worlds and atoms. And for this memory the history of the individual person begins long before the awakening of his consciousness (his conscious I). In what forms and spheres of culture is this great experience, this great memory unlimited by practice, disinterested memory, embodied. Tragedy, Shakespeare—on the level of official culture—have their roots in the extra-official symbols of great popular experience. Language, the unpublishable spheres of discursive life, the symbols of laughter culture. The basis of myth, not reworked or rationalized by official consciousness. One must know how to

> capture the authentic voice of being, the whole of being, being that is more than human, not of a particular part of it, the voice of the whole and not of one of the parties to it. The memory of the supra-individual body.[195]

Bakhtin's capacious and, in this case, more-than-human embrace is echoed and amplified in the work of Gumbs and others like her. With her genuflections to countless ancestors and multiple progenitors, Gumbs both diversifies the "great traditions" already celebrated by Bakhtin and other "great humanists," and multiplies what *counts* as tradition, or *whose* traditions will count. The broader point, however, is that forward movements always bring elements of the past with them, reinterpreting and reshaping them as they go, with the latter effectively feeding forward into the new. This is done in order to respond to present conditions, and today's conditions, perhaps unlike those recognized in previous, more humanistically inclined eras, are also deeply ecological—and in this sense deeply resonant with Indigenous traditions that have not been well recognized or even known in the Eurocentric (or even more broadly, Eurasianist) pan-humanist lineages.

The more lasting cultural innovations respond not only to present needs but to future needs. There was little means of predicting that the painterly oeuvre of Hilma af Klint would arrive at its own "homecoming festival" so many decades after the paintings themselves were set aside and effectively hidden, time-capsule-like, for rediscovery in an alien future. That her work of a century ago drew on the past is evident through a consideration of her sources—in the sciences and the regularly reinvented theosophical traditions, which themselves reinterpreted the past according to *their* conditions. That her work somehow responds to *today's* needs is also difficult to deny, given its wide resonance. Which of today's creative artists, poets, authors, musicians, and performers will find their homecomings in a different future tomorrow? Predicting this may be impossible, but anticipating that it will take us outside of the boundaries of the present conjuncture—the modern, western "distribution of the sensible," to use Jacques Rancière's apt term—is virtually guaranteed.

This chapter has pursued the hunch that today's dominant distribution of the sensible, one that sees spirituality, religiosity, and divinity as either *out* of bounds or as fully and completely *tradition*-bound, is incomplete and needs reconfiguration. Seeking imagery to support this contention, I have examined a few instances of artists and artistic movements that provide helpful indications of where to look for signs of future-making creativity. To the extent that imagery produced in any aesthetic form—literary-poetic, painterly, musical, performative, or audiovisual—will genuinely animate viewers' engagement with the conditions and possibilities of their world(s), today or tomorrow, such imagery partakes of the regime of the animate-image, in which images take viewers along on a journey to a place that is different, that is *elsewhere*, from where they began. For better *and* for worse, that regime is extended today through the capacities offered by the digital image-world. It is to that and the mediations that it facilitates that I will return in the concluding section of this book.

## Afterimage

# ANIMISMS IN THE MEDIOCENE

*The challenge facing us is to understand—and practice—"image" no longer in terms of vision but in terms of relation. Freed from representation and unilateral subject/object relations, the image opens up to an "eco-relation," an oikos composed of the mutual relations between humans and non-humans. Contrary to the humanist period, what we need to reinvent is not our vision of the world, but our dwelling in the world, our living together on and with the planet. In this process, the next step is to abandon the old (and desiccated) humanist image and with it, the pillars of our existing visual culture, such as projection, resemblance, or objectivity. Only then can we imagine our entanglement in a mesh of protean relations among all worldly co-dwellers—and understand these relations as image.*

—*INGRID HOELZL AND REMI MARIE*, "No Image No Cry: On the Past, Present and Possible Futures of the Image"[1]

*For this is the final choice. Either repair or funeral arrangements. There will be no flight to any exoplanet. The Earth will be the oasis from which the "whole of humanity" will undertake the gigantic work of regenerating the living. Or it will be the universal tomb, its mausoleum, in keeping with the geological period of the history of the universe.*

—*ACHILLE MBEMBE*, Brutalism[2]

*To speak of the end of the world is to speak of the need to imagine, rather than a new world to replace our present one, a new people,* the people that is missing. *A people who believes in the world that it will have to create with whatever world we will have left them.*

—*DÉBORAH DANOWSKI AND EDUARDO VIVEIROS DE CASTRO*, The Ends of the World[3]

• • • As each of these quotes suggests, imagination is not peripheral to the existential choice that faces us today—the choice between the "universal tomb," to which we would consign ourselves all too quickly if we continue to speed ourselves toward the ecologically destructive end of the Anthropocene event, and the "gigantic work of regenerating the living." It is central to it.

And imagination today is both constrained and enabled by the media in which so much of our imaging takes place. As Marshall McLuhan and other media theorists have long argued, media are not incidental; they are formative and productive, rearranging the relationships that make up human society in its connection to the broader world. To the extent that they have become central to people's lives today, it would be appropriate to consider the term *Mediocene* as a descriptor for today's digitally mediated world.

"The concept of the Mediocene," note the organizers of a 2017 conference on the topic, "sees media and medial processes as epoch-making."[4] Intended to "decenter[. . .] the anthropocentric implications of the Anthropocene" in favor of "a primordial agency of mediality," the concept's defenders note that the "evolution of technical beings" operating through an array of "signaling and data processing techniques such as copying, messaging, intercepting, cutting up, doubling, etc." has "deepened" the primordial hybridity of "being and technology." More recently, the "emergence of global media systems" has "induced a synchronization of almost all cultures and collectives on the planet, which, together with a worldwide collectivization and interdependence of cultural and natural processes, has been further extended by means of communication via radio waves, satellites and global positioning systems." Media, by this account, are core to the processes encompassed within the notion of the Anthropocene, but what is credited with agency is not the singular humanity of the latter construct but a more "primordial" force that is both natural and technical.[5]

The problem with this description, however, is that it is not any less "naturalizing" than the Anthropocene concept which it would replace. It offers no way to distinguish between what has happened and what might *not* have happened. Even if its suggestion of continuity between the current global predicament and the long history of mediation (involving humans and not) is accepted, it would need to be supplemented with some way of distinguishing between rival or alternative "mediocenes." If "Anthropocene" suggests that humanity is the primary cause of our current situation—when, as critics point out, there have been divergent "humanities" with divergent environmental impacts—and "mediocene" suggests that media have naturally evolved to the current state, Burtynsky, Baichwal, and de Pencier's *Anthropocene Project* highlights the centrality of techno-industrial activities within the Anthropocene. In this, their depictions come closer to describing an Industriocene, and by extension a Capitalocene, as political economists have dubbed it.

My use of the words "Anthroposcene," "Therioscene," and "Theoscene" has been intended to decenter any historical claims about any of these as constituting new eras or epochs (-cenes), and instead to highlight their ways of framing—their *scenography*—and of thereby mediating the world. Each such mediation takes place within the present image-world, which at least qualifies as its own medio*scene.* Each of them posits a (re)mediated relationship as central: between humans and the planet (Anthroposcene), between humans and wild animals (Therioscene), between humans and divinities (Theoscene), and between media, inclusive of human medial processes (Medioscene). The question is whether this image-world, within which contending anthroposcenes, therioscenes, theoscenes, ecoscenes, and others play themselves out within the mediated digitality of a continuously evolving image-world, constitutes a new world order, a world-ecology, a historical epoch deserving of its own name: a Medio*cene.* Or are there other causal factors at play that are elided in that representation, factors that include industrial humanity, a capitalist world economy, colonial preconditions, patriarchal and anthropocentric assumptions, or others?

The question of the Mediocene thus remains an open one, even as its foregrounding of mediation is an important one to make in our time, when humans have ourselves become media for the generation and contestation of image regimes that constitute the human, the animal, the divine, and the earthly. There is a sense, however, in which Mediocene can be taken to describe not just a world that is thoroughly rearranged by media, but also a world in which mediation and even mediumship have become central. The previous chapter nodded to a certain counterhistory of mediumship, which has evolved alongside the emergence of new communication technologies. Let us recap a few of these developments.

Photography emerged to capture images of the living world, but soon enough it came to be used for capturing fleeting glimpses of what were thought to be spirits, auras, and mysterious fluids and ethereal energies in the unseen world. The telegraph adding an interest in telepathy and the possibility of decoding the mysterious "rapping" of unseen communicators; the telephone, of speaking with the dead; and television, of "channeling," that is, of tuning into broadcasts found on very different wavelengths, including from other worlds or from the distant past or future. Where in this sequence does the internet fall, and what desires for contact is it unleashing?

Contact, and the mediation of relationships, are central to much of the art that is arguably most advanced in articulating the interfolded problematics of our present moment: climate change, the global refugee crisis, massive inequality, and the legacies of colonization, capitalization, and industrialization that led to the Anthropocene predicament. Mediation, as I have been describing it, is always active, and it is what makes a sign signify. Images are one way of mediating between things: they connect iconically even as they may also connect indexically and symbolically. The digital image-world enables a profusion of imagistic mediation, and it does this in the midst of pressures to animate images in multiple ways. In some respects, it enables the emergence of what Benjamin Bratton has called a "planetary sapience," a planet-scale computation that might come to constitute Earth's "smart exoskeleton, a distributed sensory organ and cognitive layer capable of calculating" things that render the Earth continually habitable for humans and those species we ally with.[6] In other respects, however, this emergent planetary sapience is riven with conflicting agendas, deeply fractured and "borderized" (to use Achille Mbembe's term), and highly uneven in its positive and negative impacts. The sapience it enables is easy to manipulate toward the ends of the powerful, and not of the entire collectivity of humans and the nonhumans we depend on. Examining the promise and perils in this "planetary sapience" is a key task for our time, as digital technologies continue to develop at breakneck speed. Let us return to some of the challenges these new digital ecosystems pose.

## THE PROMISE AND PERIL OF DIGITAL "INTELLIGENCE"

We saw in chapter 3 that the emergence and growth of digital media as a pervasive presence in the background as well as the foreground of people's lives, and in the management of human relations with each other and with the nonhuman world, raises questions that have not been adequately answered. Digital media alter the human experience of the world, and they reshape how we communicate with each other and how we make sense of our realities. As our everyday lives have become more saturated with datafied images, those images, and perhaps *all* images, have become less reliable indicators of whatever it is that they represent. "Truth" has become more elusive, as has social trust in the institutions that have governed human lives. We have come to rely on new mediators—data platforms owned by private corporations with profit-motivated interests, whose use of our data is rarely transparent—even as the institutions that might protect us from risks, whether governments or nongovernmental organizations and social networks, have themselves become increasingly reliant on those same media (and, more often than not, under threat from reactionary governments).

Like the development of so-called Web 2.0, with its profusion of social media apps and platforms, in the first decade of this century, the development of artificial intelligence has been rapid, largely uncontrolled, and almost completely lacking in oversight. This is especially the case with "generative AI," artificial intelligence aimed at creating new content through machine learning. The companies that have led in these developments—OpenAI, Google/Alphabet, and Meta among others—have proceeded on the assumption that these technologies are so powerful and promising that nothing should constrain their development. In their rush to develop products whose value is derived from the massiveness of the databases on which they are "trained," they have datafied as much of the data on the internet as possible, from publicly accessible texts, images, audio, and video to paywalled and copywritten materials, with little concern for intellectual property rights or corporate user agreements. Each company has aimed to outcompete the others, even as their use of each other's data—OpenAI's use of Google-owned YouTube users' data, Google's use of its own YouTube despite the protections it ostensibly promised its users, and so on—has encouraged them to disregard each other's legally questionable actions. Like an arms race between rivals in which the arms makers always win, this AI arms race shows clear elements of monopolistic collusion.[7] The parallel with social media is instructive and foreboding. As Andrew Chow and Billy Perriog have noted, social media

> was built on the promise that connecting people would make our societies healthier and individuals happier. More than a decade later, we can see that its failures came not from that welcome connectedness, but the way tech companies monetized it: by slowly warping our news feeds to optimize for engagement, keeping us scrolling through viral content interspersed with targeted online advertising. True social connection has become increasingly sparse on our feeds. At the same time, our societies have been left to deal with the second-order implications: a gutted news business, a rise in misinformation, and a skyrocketing teen mental-health crisis.[8]

A similar history is being repeated with generative AI, which requires us to ask, what is being offered and at what potential cost?

Chatbots like OpenAI's ChatGPT, Microsoft's Copilot, Google's Gemini, and Meta's Llama 3, image generators like Dall-E, Stable Diffusion, and Midjourney, and a growing number of related tools promise the ability to generate content for practically any application. The implications are enormous for industries that depend on information and creative content generation: news and journalism, communication, the arts, academe, public relations and marketing, law, the military, security, medicine, and others. The known risks of these technologies include the threat of lost jobs and of entire professions, expected to particularly affect white-collar workers of all kinds; the consolidation of racial and gender bias, hate speech, and disinformation (or flawed attempts at mitigating such things, as occurred with Google's notorious Bard); the blurring of lines between truth and deception; the multiplication of opportunities for cybercrime and intensification of cyberwarfare; and unintentional consequences spiraling out of control even to the point of, in OpenAI CEO Sam Altman's words, the "extinction" of humanity.[9] The unknown risks remain, of course, unknown.

As I write, efforts to regulate AI and lawsuits against their makers' use of public and private data pose potential obstacles to their unfettered development. Meanwhile, promoters of AI continue to tout them as savior technologies that will not only enhance humanity's ability to meet present and future challenges, but potentially result in a kind of god-technology, a "technological singularity" in which "artificial general intelligence" surpasses human intelligence and proceeds to recreate the world according to its greater wisdom.[10] Leaving aside the more extreme projections of utopians and dystopians alike, it is safe to say that the future is uncertain. The rapid development of new tools by media corporations, startups, and governments around the world makes writing books about the topic risky, since anything one says is bound to be outdated by the time of publication. Perhaps the only certain trajectory is that these neural networks, as they become better able to teach themselves to spot patterns in huge datasets, will require more data to generate better results, so the data arms race can be expected to continue if left unregulated.[11] "Better results" here means more *plausible* results, since these technologies are essentially massive prediction engines, rather like human cognitive processing (according to the predictive model of cognition). In this respect, AI does not generate meaning so much as it generates data—primarily in the form of images and texts—for human end users to make use of as they see fit; those uses will in turn provide the data for further cycles of content generation. As AIs consume more and more data, they will be expected to generate their own data, so-called synthetic data, to "feed themselves" for their own training. This has led some to foresee the inevitability of a "peak AI" beyond which artificial intelligence will no longer be able to grow,[12] but others, like Sam Altman, confidently predict that this "synthetic data event horizon" will be overcome.[13] In this sense, the digital ecologies enfolding us are likely to continue growing, even as they become integrated in manifold ways with the sense-making practices that already shape the unstable world of today and tomorrow.

Where to, then, in this world of data-driven images and imagination(s)? And is there a story we can tell ourselves about where we have been and where we are going? The previous chapter emphasized the usefulness of chronopolitical narratives that look to the past and the future in order to find a different accounting of the present. It is time to revisit our examination of image regimes to see if there is a chronopolitics in the story this book has told.

## REGIME CHANGE: A STORY

I have emphasized all along that image regimes are not monoliths. The term is intended to help us identify ways of relating to images that become more or less established in specific cultural contexts. Some, such as the animate-image regime, have been with us all along, even if they are unrecognized or even formally denied. Others, like the world-picture regime, make their appearance when circumstances enable them to emerge. As "regimes" they are something between habits—sedimented ways of relating to images—and ensembles of relations that develop around specific imaginaries (such as Christianity's ideal-image regime, with its focal story of the passion and resurrection of Jesus).

It is possible, nevertheless, to make some historical generalizations, as long as we understand that these are abstractions from processes that are much more complicated. For starters, we could say that before the emergence of states and empires, the animate-image regime was widespread. This does not mean that all images were treated as living, agential, and interactive, but the images that *mattered most* likely were. We can, of course, not go back 12,000 years to see if this was true; it remains a useful speculation at best. Yet this way of relating to images is found in small-scale and traditional societies today, has been found historically, and is echoed in contemporary uses of images.

The rise of states and empires, and of imperial religions—those that spread not only through conquest but also through the cultural-ideological work of proselytization, recruitment, conversion, and discursive innovation—was facilitated by ideal-images. Insofar as they established their authority over multiple and previously disparate social communities, they did this by spreading sets of ideals that were embodied within "imaginal regimes." In certain times and places these were counteracted, or at least displaced and diffractively resisted, by expression-image forms. But the widespread adoption of expression-image regimes only arose in places where artists and artisans came to form professional groups recognized for their artistry. (The European Renaissance was one such period, but hardly the only one; artisan guilds were found in ancient Mesopotamia, China, Rome, and elsewhere.) Though the relationship is complex and variable, it should not be surprising if historical study shows that political democratization has tended to be accompanied by the spread of expression-image regimes. This is their nature: to highlight the creative potential of individuals. If this creative individualism may have seemed to reach a certain peak in the consumer-capitalist culture critiqued by Susan Sontag, it came as part of a culture of conformism that carried its own ideals ("democracy," "freedom," productivity, and so on) even as it constrained or subverted those ideals with other motivations, such as wealth accumulation, control over resources, and inter-imperial rivalry.

The world-picture regime emerged at a point in history when scientific labor was becoming recognized as a powerful mode for establishing truth. That is itself an ideal, but its methodology was instrumental and indexical. While the ideal-image regimes of imperialisms, nationalisms, and religion have never quite gone away, it is fair to say that the scientific world-picture established itself within the loose hegemony of western modernity as an essential partner, respected by political authorities and backed by emergent middle classes. By comparison, the expression-image regime has at best only supplemented this hegemony by functioning in part as an ideal—embodying individual rights, free expression, artistic creativity, and so on—though in the realm of ideology it was always contested by religious, nationalist, and other imaginaries. It may be more accurate to say that the expression-image regime has served more as a kind of "cultural filler," appealing in its various forms to elite as well as mass-cultural publics, but never seriously threatening the hegemonies of science or the Euro-colonial nation-state order. The moving-image regime, led by Hollywood, arose to supplement each of these functions whilst facilitating further buy-in around the world; in this sense it amplified this role of images as cultural filler (which served a purpose for the powers that be).

Where does the emergence of the digital image-world regime bring us? As I hope the previous chapters show, this new regime is not a mere supplement to what came before it. It builds upon the world-picture regime, but it also threatens to replace it by eliminating the "truth-bearing" basis of that regime. It is not that science is under serious threat; its achievements and productivity remain robust. But science's status as unassailable arbiter of reality—evident in the very picture of the world it brings us, from the astronomical to the microscopic levels—is challenged by the fact that the reliability of its images is no longer readily knowable. The reversible indexicalities that bring us the scientific world-picture can no longer be securely traced to their sources. The status of scientific claims—whether they be over climate change, viral contagion and its containment, or anything else—will have to be fought over by different means than in the past, as the picture-book version of science has lost its credibility.

Philosophers of science like Bruno Latour have argued for some time that the traditional image of science as the discovery of facts was never accurate. "Facts," as Latour put it, "remain robust only when they are supported by a common culture, by institutions that can be trusted, by a more or less decent public life, by more or less reliable media," and by an openness about the details of their construction through the "circulation of reference" between devices, inscriptions, translations, and confrontations that make up the scientific process.[14] What is yet to be widely recognized is that computation, artificial intelligence, and digital media in their very nature render the connections between the beginning and end of any particular operation practically untraceable. They do this even as they expand and multiply the possibilities for operationalizing data of all kinds. There may be skilled coders, hackers, and data analysts who can do their best to assess the veracity of any particular data point, criminal allegation, war image or video, political meme, or other contested fact. But in a world of high-stakes computational innovation, opaque algorithms, unstable political alliances, and multiplying vectors for obfuscation, encryption, and manipulation, it is practically impossible to create an infrastructure that would render the kind of transparency to content production that has, at least in principle, defined the scientific method. The general trend, then, points in the direction of a washing out of indexical truth. Truth can still be cobbled together, but it will take more diverse materials to do that successfully. It will take alliances built not only by scientists, but by politicians, journalists, citizens, activists, health workers, and others circulating images lodged within symbolic narratives that resonate with people's everyday experience.

Concluding this extended meditation will bring us back to the animate nature of the images that surround and shape us, even as the technological means by which they are animated makes them all the more elusive to our comprehension.

## IMAGINATION, BETWEEN ANIMISMS

This book has attempted to think through the nature of images and of imagination. To restate the book's central premise, the world today calls for reimagination. Understanding what this entails requires understanding what imagination is and what it consists of.

I have argued that imagination consists of images, which are one, and in many ways the predominant, type of sign. Signs, for their part, are what worlds are made of. It is only possible to inhabit a world if it is possible to generate the meanings that hold that world together. Worlds are dynamic, semiotic constructs, and they are lived by world-bearing beings. Images are a prime constituent of the world, *any* world, *all* worlds. We humans live images, breathe them, shape them, and are shaped by them. We do it in many ways: through thinking and talking, through bodily and aural communication, through social media, and so on. If images are how we make and communicate meaning, then we may as well get better at doing this: more creative, more articulate, and more responsible with regard to their uses and impacts.

Ultimately, "image" and "imagination" are words—which means that they are concepts: connective threads that make meaning possible through distinguishing differences and similarities across the spectrum of what it is possible for humans to experience. If these two words are to do the work I would like them to do, this is not because they are inherently better than other words that could be set to similar ends: creativity, say, or beauty, or truth, or love. Images connect through resemblance; they enable an echoing with variations, a repetition with differences. Their nature is dual: as Francesca Gosetti-Ferencei insists, they present the world to us, and by them the world is transformed.[15] At the interface of the perception and the creation is where we find ourselves, acting in and through our images *upon* the world we imagine into being. We shape them into image arrays, image formations, image regimes, each of which is intermeshed with other kinds of things: with words and concepts, with affects and habits, with collective movements and long-term trajectories.

We humans—we who address ourselves as "we" and who respond to that address, even as we negotiate the boundaries of who is being addressed and how—are already launched on myriad trajectories. One of these, or several, is that which is encompassed rather inadequately in what I have been calling the Anthropocene condition. That condition needs to be better understood today, and because it is a condition that is not sustainable for long—because the relations between human activities and the more-than-human world are threatening the support structures for their own continuation—it is a condition that also calls for being *unraveled*, and then *reraveled* into a more hospitable form. To do that requires an unfolding of some of its already thickly encrusted folds, a refolding into the critical assessment of coloniality, of instrumentality, of historical relations between imperial projects and creative forms of resistance, resilience, and adaptation.

If my claim is correct that images are in their nature animate—that the animate-image is a kind of original or foundational form taken by images—and that the digital image-world enables an increasingly complex animation of images, then we must return to the animate potential of images in order to reimagine our world. Describing the animist agency of objects in traditional African contexts, objects extracted from those contexts and now found in museums and collections around the world, Achille Mbembe writes that these objects "were vehicles of energy and movement. Living matter, they cooperated with life. Even when in themselves they were only utensils and devices, they had a part in life, physical life, psychic life, energetic life, the kind of life whose primary quality was circulation." "In certain circumstances," Mbembe continues,

> some of these objects played a properly philosophical role within the culture. They also served as mediators between humans and the vital powers. They were used by humans as a means to think their existence in common. Behind the technical gesture of making them, a particular horizon was hidden—the mutualization of generative resources in a way that did not endanger the whole ecosystem; the unconditional refusal to turn everything into commodities; the duty to open the door and give the floor to the dynamics of partner relationships, and to the uninterrupted creation of the commons. [. . .]
>
> Behind each of them were also crafts, and behind each craft a fund of knowledge and skills ceaselessly learned and transmit-

> ted, a technical and aesthetic thought, figurative information, a certain charge of magic, in short, the human effort to tame the very matter of life, its assortment of substances. One of their functions was to put in relation forms and forces while symbolizing them; to activate the powers which make it possible to move the world.[16]

The question we face as an emergent human collective in a more-than-human world—"a new people," in the words of Déborah Danowski and Eduardo Viveiros de Castro, "the people that is missing"—is how to enable the emergence of appropriate images, objects, and powers that would allow us to together reshape the world into one that is ecologically sustainable, socially just, psychologically nourishing, and politically feasible.[17] What objects are to play the role of mediators between us and "the vital powers," which would "activate the powers" that make it possible for us "to move the world" in the direction of greater conviviality? What role should our ever-more-mediating objects—computers, smartphones, and the rest—play in this, and how can they be crafted and managed in order to do that better? Could they be set in motion in ways that allow us to "feel" the "flow of the world" at a time of increasing uncertainty and precarity?

For all the questions his own filmmaking has raised and not quite answered, Werner Herzog phrased this problem as well as anyone. "Our civilization," he said in a 1979 interview, "doesn't have adequate images, and I think a civilization is doomed or is going to die out like dinosaurs if it does not develop an adequate language or adequate images." This is a "problem of the same magnitude" as the other "serious problems facing our civilization, like energy problems, or environmental problems, or nuclear power and all this, or over-population of the world."[18] The situation has barely improved in the nearly half-century since Herzog articulated this. The task of developing adequate images is an enormous one, but taking it on requires reckoning with the centrality of the imagination, the human capacity to shape images and meanings by which we recraft the world we are to share. The present time is reconfiguring the capacities of that imagination, and it is up to collective humanity to ensure that that is done with the rigor and sensitivity it requires.

Animate-images, as I have described them, have populated the world alongside and in the midst of the relations we humans have co-created with other, more-than-human agencies. They have served to connect humans and the more-than-human worlds into relational networks through materialities and practices that sustained communities over time. In the clashes between empires, societies, social classes, and cultural communities, animate-images have suffered from conquest, extraction, and demotion such that they have, in effect, become dead where once they were alive. This is what happens in a pluralistic world: images live and die just as do the relations and connections they make possible. The question before us is which images we should enable to live and to die today, to give birth to, to leave on the compost heap, or to redeem and bring home.

As Ernst Bloch suggested in *The Principle of Hope*, "The final will is that to be truly present. So that the lived moment belongs to us and we to it and 'Stay awhile' could be said to it."[19] Which of our images will be worthy of our saying "Stay awhile" to them, were we to find ourselves in the full, collective human presence that we have never, or not-yet ever, attained?

# NOTES

## Preface

1. Quoted in *Werner Herzog Eats His Shoe*, dir. Les Blank, 1980, https://www.imdb.com/title/tt0081746/.

2. Samuel R. Delany, *Starboard Wine: More Notes on the Language of Science Fiction*, rev. ed. (Wesleyan University Press, 2012), 14.

3. Chiara Bottici, *Imaginal Politics: Images Beyond Imagination and the Imaginary* (Columbia University Press, 2014), 61.

4. Alfred North Whitehead, *The Concept of Nature: The Tarner Lectures Delivered in Trinity College November 1919* (Cambridge University Press, 1920/1964), 21, emphasis added.

5. Quoted by Jean-Yves Chateau, "Preface: A Theory of the Image in Light of the Notion of Invention, a Theory of Invention in Light of the Notion of the Image," in Gilbert Simondon, *Imagination and Invention,* trans. J. Hughes and C. Wall-Romana (University of Minnesota Press, 2022), xxiv.

6. Jennifer Anna Gosetti-Ferencei's *The Life of Imagination: Revealing and Making the World* (Columbia University Press, 2018), 26, 28. This book is an ambitious, yet concise, recent overview of scholarship on imagination. Aside from its apparent restriction to *human* consciousness, Gosetti-Ferencei's definition of imagination coheres entirely with my own use of the word, and the "object or expression" with my own use of the word "image" (though I will suggest it is more like an event than an object). For somewhat overlapping arguments, see Kathleen Lennon, *Imagination and the Imaginary* (Routledge, 2015); and Chiara Bottici, *Imaginal Politics: Images Beyond Imagination and the Imaginary* (Columbia University Press, 2014). For a broad survey of philosophical approaches to imagina-

tion, see Amy Kind, ed., *The Routledge Handbook of Philosophy of Imagination* (Routledge, 2016).

Many others have probed the long history of concepts of the imagination. Richard Kearney's *The Wake of Imagination* (University of Minnesota Press, 1988), J. M. Cocking's *Imagination; A Study in the History of Ideas* (Routledge, 1991), and Eva Brann's *The World of the Imagination: Sum and Substance* (Rowman & Littlefield, 1991) all arguably err on the side of an all-too-Western history, rooted in ancient Greece and culminating in European Romanticism (or the French Renaissance, in Cocking's case), with a late modern or postmodern dénouement. Kearney's version of this is an incisive tale of a long rise, a sharp fall (via existentialism and postmodernism), and, as dénouement, the promise of an errant ethico-poetical wandering. In its 800 pages, Brann's volume is dauntingly comprehensive, and its definition of imagination, as an internal power or faculty that represents absent things as present by way of resemblance, deeply informs my own. To bring such a story up-to-date and place it within a more global, cross-cultural frame remains an open project. My work in this volume presumes that the result would be not only polymorphous and multilinear, but that the difficulty of defining its object (or subject, rather), "the imagination," would make it virtually untellable. The cognitive study of imagination is a case in point, with numerous competing approaches and little obvious consensus about what imagination is, let alone where it is neurologically located. I therefore begin from a fairly specific definition, with ontological presuppositions, and follow it where it leads me.

7. In my book *Shadowing the Anthropocene* (Punctum, 2018), and especially in that book's appendix on "Contemporary Process-Relational Thought: A Primer" (231–40), I outline a long genealogy of thinking along these lines, a genealogy that is as much "Eastern"—encompassing Buddhist, Daoist, and Hindu philosophers among others—as it is "western." That "the image" and "imagination" have tended to be topics of concern among professional philosophers, who have tended to be male, means that I will refer more to these philosophers than to Indigenous thinkers or to women (whose thought is in any case historically much less represented in literary form). But it should not imply that the concerns of the book are elitist; we all live in a world dense with images.

8. To mention just one strand of significant theory here, the feminist, would be to delve into the writings of a large number of important authors including Evelyn Fox Keller, Sandra Harding, Donna Haraway, Silvia Federici, and Val Plumwood. The same could be done for Marxist and socialist theorists, postcolonial and decolonial thinkers, and environmental philosophers, many of whose names will come up here and there throughout the book. My previous writings have delved more deeply into some of these sources of critical theory. Among the twentieth-century critical theorists who have emphasized the centrality of imagination in human experience, whose influence is felt here but not explicitly referred to much, are Cornelius Castoriadis, Gaston Bachelard, Gilbert Simondon, and Richard Kearney (see also note 6 above).

9. For a recent effort, see Adam Frank, Marcelo Gleiser, and Evan Thompson, *The Blind Spot: Why Science Cannot Ignore Human Experience* (MIT Press, 2024).

10. Mihnea Mircan and Jonas Staal, "Let's Take Back Control! Of Our Imagination," *Stedelijk Studies* 6 (2018), accessed June 12, 2023, https://stedelijkstudies.com/journal/lets-take-back-control-of-our-imagination/.

11. Readers of my book *Ecologies of the Moving Image: Cinema, Affect, Nature* (Wilfrid Laurier University Press, 2013) may wonder how this triad maps against the one that organized the previous book. While that one paid attention to the construction of and movement across boundaries, the division of its three central chapters was premised on a differentiation of the "geomorphic" (geographic/geological), "biomorphic" (biological), and "anthropomorphic" (human) dimensions of the production of cinema worlds. In this book, I focus more directly on the boundaries between the human, on one side, and the geological/geographic (geomorphic), the animal (a subset of the biomorphic), and—what is novel here—the "theomorphic." In this, I hope the book is resonant with work in decolonial theory and the "pluriversal politics," as Arturo Escobar calls it, of a less Eurocentric future. See Escobar, *Pluriversal Politics: The Real and the Possible* (Duke University Press, 2020).

**Chapter 1**

1. Hans Belting, *An Anthropology of Images: Picture, Medium, Body,* trans. Thomas Dunlap (Princeton University Press, 2011), 6.

2. Gilbert Simondon, *Imagination and Invention,* trans. Joe Hughes and Christophe Wall-Romana (University of Minnesota Press, 2022), 9.

3. Jean-Luc Nancy, *The Ground of the Image,* trans. Jeff Fort (Fordham University Press, 2005), 4, emphasis in original.

4. Hans Belting, *Likeness and Presence: A History of the Image Before the Era of Art* (University of Chicago Press, 1994); Peter Burke, *Eyewitnessing: The Uses of Images as Historical Evidence* (Cornell University Press, 2001); James Elkins, *On Pictures and the Words That Fail Them* (Cambridge University Press, 1998); James Elkins, *The Domain of Images* (Cornell University Press, 1999); Roy F. Fox, *Images in Language, Media, and Mind* (National Council of Teachers of English, 1994); James J. Gibson, "The Ecological Approach to the Visual Perception of Pictures," *Leonardo* 11 (1978): 227–35; Carolyn Bailey Gill, ed., *Time and the Image* (Manchester University Press, 2000); Ernst Hans Gombrich, *Art and Illusion: A Study in the Psychology of Pictorial Representation*, 2nd ed. (Princeton University Press, 1960); E. H. Gombrich, *The Image and the Eye: Further Studies in the Psychology of Pictorial Representation* (Phaidon Press, 1982); Robert Hopkins, *Picture, Image, and Experience: A Philosophical Inquiry* (Cambridge University Press, 1998); Stephen Kosslyn, *Image and Brain: The Resolution of the Imagery Debate* (MIT Press, 1996); John V. Kulvicki, *Images* (Routledge, 2014); Erwin Panofsky, *Studies in Iconology: Humanistic Themes in the Art of the Renaissance* (Harper & Row, 1939/1972); Sunil Manghani, *Image Studies: Theory and Practice* (Routledge, 2013); Sunil Manghani,

ed., *Images: Critical and Primary Sources,* 4 vols. (Bloomsbury, 2013); Sunil Manghani, Arthur Piper, and Jon Simons, eds., *Images: A Reader* (Sage, 2006); Colin McGinn, *Mindsight: Image, Dream, Meaning* (Harvard University Press, 2006); Colin Renfrew and Iain Morley, *Image and Imagination: A Global Prehistory of Figurative Representation* (McDonald Institute for Archaeological Research, 2007); Patricia Spyer and Mary Margaret Steedly, eds., *Images That Move* (School for Advanced Research Press, 2013); Barbara Maria Stafford, *Echo Objects: The Cognitive Work of Images* (University of Chicago Press, 2007).

5. Jonathan Crary, *On Vision and Modernity: Techniques of the Observer in the Nineteenth Century* (MIT Press, 1990); Elkins, *The Domain of Images*; James Elkins, *Visual Studies: A Sceptical Introduction* (Routledge, 2003); James Elkins and Maja Naef, eds., *What Is an Image?* (Pennsylvania State University Press, 2011); Hal Foster, ed., *Vision and Visuality* (Dia Art Foundation, 1988); Martin Jay, *Downcast Eyes: The Denigration of Vision in Twentieth-Century French Thought* (University of California Press, 1993); Jacques Rancière, "Do Pictures Really Want to Live," *Culture, Theory, and Critique* 50.2 (2009): 123–32.

6. Richard M. Rorty, *The Linguistic Turn: Essays in Philosophical Method* (University of Chicago Press, 1967); Richard M. Rorty, *Philosophy and the Mirror of Nature* (Princeton University Press, 1981).

7. Gottfried Boehm, *Was its ein Bild?* (Brill, 1994); Gottfried Boehm and W.J.T. Mitchell, "Pictorial Versus Iconic Turn," *Culture, Theory and Critique* 50 (2009): 103–21; Neal Curtis, ed. *The Pictorial Turn* (Routledge, 2010); W.J.T. Mitchell, *Iconology: Image, Text, Ideology* (University of Chicago Press, 1987); W. J. T. Mitchell, *Picture Theory: Essays on Verbal and Visual Representation* (University of Chicago Press, 1994); W. J. T. Mitchell, *What Do Pictures Want? The Lives and Loves of Images* (University of Chicago Press, 2005).

8. Jessica Evans and Stuart Hall, eds., *Visual Culture: The Reader* (Sage, 1999); Nicholas Mirzoeff, *An Introduction to Visual Culture* (Routledge, 2009).

9. The idea of "iconoclashes" comes from a 2002 exhibition of that title, held at the Center for Art and Media Karlsruhe, Germany, and followed by the mammoth anthology *Iconoclash: Beyond the Image Wars in Science, Religion, and Art,* edited by Bruno Latour and Peter Weibel (MIT Press, 2002), which charts out so much of the current terrain of conflicts over images and their meanings. See also Liza Bakewell, "Image Acts," *American Anthropologist* 100.1 (1998): 22–32; James Elkins, *Pictures and Tears: A History of People Who Have Cried in Front of Paintings* (Routledge, 2001); David Freedberg, *The Power of Images: Studies in the History and Theory of Response* (University of Chicago Press, 1989); Serge Gruzinski, *Images at War: Mexico from Columbus to* Blade Runner *(1492–2019)* (Duke University Press, 2001); Sunil Manghani, *Image Studies: Theory and Practice* (Routledge, 2013); David Morgan, *Visual Piety: A History and Theory of Popular Religious Images* (University of California Press, 1998); David Morgan, *Images at Work: The Material Culture of Enchantment* (Oxford University Press, 2018); Sthaneshwar Timalsina, *Tantric Visual Culture: A Cognitive Approach* (Routledge, 2015).

10. James J. Gibson, "Foreword: A Prefatory Essay on the Perception of Surfaces Versus the Perception of Marking on a Surface," in Margaret A. Hagen, ed., *Varieties of Realism: Geometries of Representational Art*, xi–xviii;(Cambridge University Press, 1980), xv–xvii.

11. W.J.T. Mitchell, "What Is an Image?" *New Literary History* 15.3 (1984): 503–37; 504, 505.

12. Kulvicki, *Images*, 3.

13. Belting, *An Anthropology of Images*, 6.

14. E.g., C. S. Peirce, *The Essential Peirce, Selected Philosophical Writings, Volume 1 (1867–1893)*, ed. N. Houser and C. Kloesel (Indiana University Press, 1992); C. S. Peirce, *The Essential Peirce, Selected Philosophical Writings, Volume 2 (1893–1913)*, ed. Peirce Edition Project (Indiana University Press, 1998).

15. In his later writings, Peirce used the word "image" to describe one type of iconic sign, in contradistinction to two others, which he called "diagrams" and "metaphors." While other interpretations have been made, I find Farias and Queiroz's clarification of this terminology particularly useful. They define these three forms of "iconic signs," or "hypoicons," as "instantiated icons, participating in sign relations, due mainly to some kind of likeness they share with their existing objects." In this "instantiation" and "participation in sign relations," these "iconic signs" more or less fit my definition of the image. They argue that this makes them "iconic sinsigns," in Peircian parlance, which is one of three general types of icons (and a small subset of the 66 types of signs Peirce identified in his later writings). Farias and Queiroz clarify the difference between the three types by defining images as "instantiated icons of immediate, apparent, or superficial qualities," diagrams as "hypoicons whose similarity with their objects is mostly based on shared structural or relational qualities," and metaphors as "instantiated icons of habits, conventions, or laws." They note that the three constitute a hierarchy of firstness, secondness, and thirdness, which means that the latter two categories incorporate the first in one way or another. My use of the term "image" could be applied to all three, but is particularly aimed at the first. It is, in any case, roughly equivalent to the Peircian term "iconic sign." See Priscila Farias and João Queiroz, "Images, Diagrams, and Metaphors: Hypo-icons in the Context of Peirce's Sixty-Six Fold Classification of Signs," *Semiotica* 162 (2006), 287–307; 294.

16. Gilles Deleuze, *Difference and Repetition*, trans. P. Patton (Continuum International, 1968/1994). What Deleuze accomplishes ontologically Jacques Derrida accomplishes epistemologically: namely, that difference, or *différance* in Derrida's rendition—the slippage in meaning by which words and signs can never fully summon forth anything without appeal to additional words and signs, from which they differ and to which their meanings must be "deferred"—is part and parcel of the possibility of meaning. This is true for Peirce's semiotics as well. All are processual philosophies that attempt to account for the dynamism and active interdependence of the world of our experience, a dynamic interdependence

that Buddhists (as I argued in *Shadowing the Anthropocene*) named *Pratītya-samutpāda*, the conditioned arising of all things.

17. The argument has also been made that imaging begins with animal forms of camouflage, that is, with the creation and display of "forms that refer to something else." See Caroline van Eck, "Camouflage, Zoomorphism, and the Origins of Image-Making," in *Images, Thought, and the Making of Social Worlds*, ed. David Wengrow, 99–114 (Freiburger Studien zur Archäologie & Visuellen Kultur 3, Propylaeum, 2022), 93. As this form of image-making arguably involves an intention to deceive, I would call it more "advanced" than the echo.

18. Adrian Ivakhiv, *Ecologies of the Moving Image: Cinema, Affect, Nature* (Wilfrid Laurier University Press, 2013); Adrian Ivakhiv, *Shadowing the Anthropocene: Eco-Realism for Turbulent Times* (Punctum, 2018).

19. I define the "process-relational" tradition of thought in an appendix to *Shadowing the Anthropocene* (Punctum, 2018). Whitehead is often considered the quintessential process philosopher, with the term "process-relational" commonly used to describe his metaphysics; e.g., C. Robert Mesle, *Process-Relational Philosophy: An Introduction to Alfred North Whitehead* (Templeton Press, 2008). Peirce is generally recognized as a process philosopher by those who write about that tradition; see, e.g., Nicholas Rescher, *Process Metaphysics: An Introduction to Process Philosophy* (State University of New York Press, 1996); Carl Hausman, "Charles Peirce's Evolutionary Realism as a Process Philosophy," *Transactions of the Charles S. Peirce Society* 38.1/2 (2002): 13–27. Besides Peirce and Whitehead, representatives of this tradition who have most influenced my thinking include Henri Bergson, William James, Gilbert Simondon, Gilles Deleuze, William Connolly, Brian Massumi, Isabelle Stengers, and Michel Weber. I should note that an anonymous reviewer of this manuscript expressed skepticism that process philosophy could adequately "articulat[e] ontology with history." But if process philosophy is taken to include the work of such scholars as Deleuze and Guattari, Massumi, Connolly, Manuel De Landa, and John Protevi, then its ability to do justice to ontology, history, *and* politics is complex and insightful; see, e.g., Gilles Deleuze and Félix Guattari, *Capitalism and Schizophrenia: Anti-Oedipus*, trans. R. Hurley, M. Seem, and H. R. Lane (University of Minnesota Press, 1983); Gilles Deleuze and Félix Guattari, *Capitalism and Schizophrenia: A Thousand Plateaus*, trans. B. Massumi (University of Minnesota Press, 1987); Manuel De Landa, *A Thousand Years of Nonlinear History* (Zone Books, 1997); John Protevi, *Political Affect: Connecting the Social and the Somatic* (University of Minnesota Press, 2009).

20. Alf Hornborg, *The Power of the Machine: Global Inequalities of Economy, Technology, and Environment* (AltaMira/Rowman & Littlefield, 2001); Tim Ingold, "Culture and the Perception of the Environment," in E. Croll and D. Parkin, eds., *Bush Base: Forest Farm. Culture, Environment and Development* (Routledge, 1992).

21. Alfred North Whitehead, *Adventures of Ideas* (The Free Press, 1933/1967); Alfred North Whitehead, *Process and Reality: Corrected Edition*, ed. D. R. Griffin and D. W. Sherburne (The Free Press, 1933/1978). Whitehead termed the "end"

of the process of prehension "concrescence." For our purposes, the distinction between prehension and concrescence is not an important one to parse. I'll simply refer to "prehension" for the entire process.

22. See note 14 above; and C. S. Peirce, "The Principles of Phenomenology: The Categories in Detail," in *Collected Papers of Charles Sanders Peirce,* vol. 1, ed. by C. Hartshorne and P. Weiss, 148–80 (Harvard University Press, 1931–58).

23. Claus Emmeche and Kalevi Kull, eds., *Towards a Semiotic Biology: Life Is the Action of Signs* (Imperial College Press, 2011); Donald Favareau, ed., *Essential Readings in Biosemiotics: Anthology and Commentary* (Springer, 2010); Jesper Hoffmeyer, *Signs of Meaning in the Universe,* trans. B. Haveland (Indiana University Press, 1996); Thomas A. Sebeok, *Global Semiotics* (Indiana University Press, 2001).

24. Quoted by W. E. Hocking (from a recollected conversation) in "Whitehead on Mind and Nature," in P. A. Schilpp, ed., *The Philosophy of Alfred North Whitehead* (Tudor Publication, 1951), 385.

25. This idea of images as the access points between agents finds a rough parallel in object-oriented philosophy (see Graham Harman, *Object-Oriented Ontology: A New Theory of Everything* [Routledge, 2018]; Timothy Morton, *Realist Magic: Objects, Ontology, Causality* [Open Humanities Press, 2013]), which distinguishes between "real" objects (which are, effectively, agents) and "sensual" objects (which are what I call images). On the differences between object-oriented and process-relational ontologies, see Adrian Ivakhiv, "Beatnik Brothers? Between Graham Harman and the Deleuzo-Whiteheadian Axis," *Parrhesia* 19 (2014): 65–78; Adrian Ivakhiv, *Shadowing the Anthropocene: Eco-Realism for Turbulent Times* (Punctum, 2018), 151ff.

26. Wendy Wheeler, *The Whole Creature: Complexity, Biosemiotics, and the Evolution of Culture* (Laurence & Wishart, 2006).

27. Immanuel Kant, *Critique of Pure Reason,* trans. P. Guyer and A. Wood (Cambridge University Press, 1998). And see Rolf-Peter Horstmann, *Kant's Power of Imagination* (Cambridge University Press, 2018); Samantha Matherne, "Kant's Theory of the Imagination," in *The Routledge Handbook of Philosophy of Imagination,* ed. Amy Kind, 55–68 (Routledge, 2016).

28. The imagination has long been the subject of philosophy, and a different book—not this one with its focus on images and image regimes, but one specifically devoted to the philosophy of imagination—would dedicate whole chapters to Kant, Schelling, Husserl, Heidegger, Sartre, and more recent interpreters such as Castoriadis and Casey. In the preface (see note 6), I mentioned a few of the books that detail some of this history, by Eva Brann, J. M. Cocking, Richard Kearney, and others. For another overview, see Kind, *Routledge Handbook of Philosophy of Imagination.*

29. James Hillman, "Back to Beyond: On Cosmology," in *Archetypal Process: Self and Divine in Whitehead, Jung, and Hillman,* ed. D. R. Griffin, 213–32 (Northwestern University Press, 1989).

30. Rather late in the process of writing this book, I came across the work of Thomas Nail, which shares a strongly process-oriented sensibility with mine. Nail's *Theory of the Image* (Oxford University Press, 2019) approaches images, including the "history of images," in ways that run parallel to mine in this book. But the core of our respective ontologies is subtly yet significantly different. His foundational concept is motion, or kinesis, of which both matter and images are expressions; mine is becoming, which is the conjoined process of subjectivation and objectivation. I find motion at once too abstract (like force, energy, activity, etc.) and too insufficient a concept, as it begs the question "what is it that is in motion?" The more important question for me is "motion to what end?" Becoming is *motivated* motion, motion (or action) in response to relational prompts and in pursuit of satisfactions triggered by those prompts. As a result, subjects become, and objects are taken into the becoming of subjects. At the core of everything, for me, is not motion *in itself* but motion *in response*. This is more closely affiliated with the idea of "desiring-production" that underpins the historico-materialist analyses of Gilles Deleuze and Félix Guattari's collaborative volumes, which Nail and I share among our inspirational starting points. There is more to be said in comparing our projects, especially on the typology of images, but I leave that aside for a future effort.

31. See David Howes, *Sensorial Investigations: A History of the Senses in Anthropology, Psychology, and Law* (Pennsylvania State University Press, 2023); Fiona Macpherson, "Taxonomising the Senses," *Philosophical Studies* 153.1 (2011): 123–42; Fiona Macpherson, *The Senses: Classical and Contemporary Philosophical Perspectives* (Oxford University Press, 2011); Ed Yong, *An Immense World: How Animal Senses Reveal the Hidden Realms Around Us* (Random House, 2022).

32. Jack Goody, "The Anthropology of the Senses and Sensations," *La ricerca folklorica* 45 (2002): 17–28.

33. Francois Bonnet, *The Order of Sounds: A Sonorous Archipelago* (Urbanomic, 2016). On musical and auditory images, see also Robert J. Zatorre and Andrea R. Halpern, "Mental Concerts: Musical Imagery and Auditory Cortex," *Neuron* 47.1 (2005): 9–12.

34. Suzanne Langer, *Feeling and Form: A Theory of Art* (Charles Scribner's Sons, 1953), 121, 125.

35. One of the currently most influential neurological explanations of perception takes our moment-to-moment experience of the world to be constructed through a complex predictive process based on previous experience. See Lisa Feldman Barrett, *How Emotions Are Made: The Secret Life of the Brain* (Houghton Mifflin Harcourt, 2017).

36. See Barrett's *How Emotions Are Made,* mentioned above, which I reviewed in "Emotional Practices, Part 1: Affective Neuroscience" and "Emotional Practices, Part 2: Affective Construction, the Triune Self, and the Art of Joyful Deliberation," *Immanence*, August 16 and August 25, 2020, https://blog.uvm.edu/aivakhiv/2020/08/16/emotional-practices-part-1-affective-neuroscience/ and https:

//blog.uvm.edu/aivakhiv/2020/08/25/emotional-practices-part-2-affective-construction-the-triune-self-the-art-of-joyful-deliberation/.

37. Susan Sontag, "The Image-World," in *On Photography* (Penguin, 1978), 180.

38. E.g., Oliver Grau with Thomas Veigl, *Imagery in the 21st Century* (MIT Press, 2011); Manghani et al., *Images: A Reader*; Mitchell, *Iconology: Image, Text, Ideology*; Mitchell, *What Do Pictures Want?*; Latour and Weibel, *Iconoclash*.

39. Belting, *Likeness and Presence*; Richard H. Davis, *Lives of Indian Images* (Princeton University Press, 1997); Graham Howes, *The Art of the Sacred: An Introduction to the Aesthetics of Art and Belief* (I. B. Tauris, 2007); Albert C. Moore, *Iconography of Religions: An Introduction* (Fortress, 1977); Morgan, *Visual Piety*; David Morgan, *The Sacred Gaze: Religious Visual Culture in Theory and Practice* (University of California Press, 2005); Nico Tassi, " 'Dancing the Image': Materiality and Spirituality in Andean Religious Images," *Journal of the Royal Anthropological Institute* 18 (2012): 285–310.

40. Félix Guattari, *The Three Ecologies*, trans. I. Pindar and P. Sutton (Athlone, 2000); Stefan Helmreich, *Alien Ocean: Anthropological Voyages in Microbial Seas* (University of California Press, 2009); Adrian Ivakhiv, *Ecologies of the Moving Image* (Wilfrid Laurier University Press, 2013); Melody Jue, *Wild Blue Media: Thinking Through Seawater* (Duke University Press, 2020); Sarah Kember and Joanna Zylinska, *Life After New Media: Mediation as Vital Process* (MIT Press, 2014); Manghani, *Image Studies: Theory and Practice*; David Morgan, "The Ecology of Images: Seeing and the Study of Religion," *Religion and Society* 5 (2014): 83–105; John Durham Peters, *The Marvelous Clouds: Towards a Philosophy of Elemental Media* (University of Chicago Press, 2015); Andrew Ross, *The Chicago Gangster Theory of Life: Nature's Debt to Society* (Verso, 1994).

41. Jessica Smartt Gullion, *Diffractive Ethnography: Social Sciences and the Ontological Turn* (Routledge, 2018); Martin Holbraad and Morten Axel Pedersen, *The Ontological Turn: An Anthropological Exposition* (Cambridge University Press, 2017); Bruno Latour, *An Inquiry into Modes of Existence: An Anthropology of the Moderns*, trans. C. Porter (Harvard University Press, 2013).

42. On ecological metaphors see Ivakhiv, "Three Ecologies: Ecomediality as Ontology," in *The Routledge Handbook of Ecomedia Studies*, ed. A. Lopez et al. (Routledge, 2023); Erich Hörl, ed. *General Ecology: The New Ecological Paradigm* (Bloomsbury Academic, 2017); C. M. Raymond et al., "Ecosystem Services and Beyond: Using Multiple Metaphors to Understand Human-Environment Relations," *BioScience* 63.7 (2013): 536–46.

43. David Morgan, *Images at Work: The Material Culture of Enchantment* (Oxford University Press, 2018), 51.

44. Ivakhiv, *Ecologies of the Moving Image*, 33–42.

45. Maurice Merleau-Ponty, *The Visible and the Invisible*, trans. A. Lingis (Northwestern University Press, 1968).

46. I develop this tri-ecological view of media more fully in Ivakhiv, "Three Ecologies: Ecomediality as Ontology" (also see note 42).

47. For that, I would recommend starting with David Freedberg's *The Power of Images: Studies in the History and Theory of Response* (University of Chicago Press, 1989).

**Chapter 2**

1. Anselm Franke, "Much Trouble in the Transportation of Souls, or the Sudden Disorganization of Boundaries," in *Animism*, vol. 1 (Sternberg Press, 2010), 26.

2. Charles W. Hendel, "Introduction," in Ernest Cassirer, *The Philosophy of Symbolic Forms*, vol. 1, *Language*, 1–65 (Yale University Press, 1965), 62.

3. See Régis Debray, *Vie et mort de l'image: Une histories du regard en Occident* (Gallimard, 1992). The book's main theses are summarized in Régis Debray and Eric Rauth, "The Three Ages of Looking," *Critical Inquiry* 21.3 (1995): 529–55.

4. In the later stages of writing this book, I came across John Lechte's *Genealogy and Ontology of the Western Image and Its Digital Future* (Routledge, 2012), a book which comes closer to the genealogy of "image regimes" I am aiming for. Lechte's approach is more obviously historical and western in its focus, though its rich readings of a series of intellectual conceptualizations of the image—ancient Greek and Platonic, Byzantine, Renaissance, Enlightenment era, and "Industrial"—are fascinating and informative.

5. An anonymous reviewer of this manuscript compared my method to that of "an intellectual Buster Keaton, teaching the reader, by example, modesty in the face of conceptual complexity and the recalcitrance of the world it tries to nail down." He noted in particular the "almost slapstick relation between [my] urge to schematise [my] categories, in text and tables, and the way they keep breaking down and dissolving." Thankfully, the reviewer referred to this as "a strength."

6. Edward Tylor, *Primitive Culture* (G. P. Putnam's, 1920).

7. Kaj Århem and Guido Sprenger, *Animism in Southeast Asia* (Routledge, 2016); Miguel Astor-Aguilera and Graham Harvey, ed., *Rethinking Relations and Animism: Personhood and Materiality* (Routledge, 2020); Christopher Braddock, *Animism in Art and Performance* (Palgrave Macmillan, 2017); Anselm Franke, ed., *Animism*, vol. 1 (Sternberg Press/Extra City-Kunsthal Antwerp, 2010); Harry Garuba, "On Animism, Modernity/Colonialism and the African Order of Knowledge: Provisional Reflections," in *Contested Ecologies: Dialogues in the South on Nature and Knowledge*, ed. L. J. F. Green, 42–52 (HSRC Press, 2013); Jacob W. Glazier, *Arts of Subjectivity: A New Animism for the Post-Media Era* (Bloomsbury, 2020); Graham Harvey, *The Handbook of Contemporary Animism* (Routledge, 2014); Deborah Bird Rose, "Val Plumwood's Philosophical Animism: Attentive Interactions in the Sentient World," *Environmental Humanities* 3.1 (2013): 93–109; Isabelle Stengers, "Reclaiming Animism," *e-flux* 36 (2012), https://www.e-flux.com/journal/36/61245/reclaiming-animism; Arne Johan Vetlesen, *Cosmologies of the Anthropocene: Panpsychism, Animism, and the Limits of Posthumanism* (Routledge, 2019).

8. Bruno Latour, *Reassembling the Social: An Introduction to Actor-Network-Theory* (Oxford University Press, 2005), 37ff.

9. David Morgan, *Images at Work: The Material Culture of Enchantment* (Oxford University Press, 2018), 56.

10. Chinua Achebe, "The Igbo World and Its Art," in *African Philosophy: An Anthology*, ed. Emmanuel Chukwudi Eze, 435–37 (Blackwell, 1998), 436.

11. Diana Eck, *Darsan: Seeing the Divine Image in India*, 3rd ed. (Columbia University Press, 1998), 3.

12. Lauren Kendall, *Mediums and Magical Things: Statues, Paintings, and Masks in Asian Places* (University of California Press, 2021), 6.

13. Nico Tassi, "'Dancing the Image': Materiality and Spirituality in Andean Religious 'Images,'" *Journal of the Royal Anthropological Institute* 18 (2012): 285–310; 289.

14. Tassi, "Dancing," 290–91, emphasis mine.

15. Tassi, 292.

16. David Freedberg, *The Power of Images: Studies in the History and Theory of Response* (University of Chicago Press, 1991), 31.

17. Freedberg, *The Power of Images*, 42.

18. Something like this argument is made by Alfred Gell in *Art and Agency: An Anthropological Theory* (Clarendon Press, 1998) and Louis Marin, *Des pouvoirs de l'image: Gloses* (Seuil, 1993). I will come back to its primordiality in chapter 4.

19. David Morgan, *Images at Work: The Material Culture of Enchantment* (Oxford University Press, 2018), 67.

20. Morgan, *Images at Work*, 60.

21. Morgan, 75.

22. Max Weber, *The Vocation Lectures*, ed. D. S. Owen and T. B. Strong, trans. R. Livingstone (Hackett, 2004/1918); Max Horkheimer and Theodor Adorno, *The Dialectic of Enlightenment: Philosophical Fragments*, ed. G. S. Noerr, trans. E. Jephcott (Stanford University Press, 2002/1947). For a sampling of views leaning to the first position on enchantment, see Jane Bennett, *The Enchantment of Modern Life: Attachments, Crossings, and Ethics* (Princeton University Press, 2001); Lorraine Daston and Katharine Park, *Wonders and the Order of Nature* (New York, 1998); Saurabh Dube, ed., *Enduring Enchantments*, special issue of the *South Atlantic Quarterly* 101.4 (October 2002); Joshua Landy and Michael Saler, ed., *The Re-Enchantment of the World: Secular Magic in a Rational Age* (Stanford University Press, 2017); Alex Owen, *The Place of Enchantment: British Occultism and the Culture of the Modern* (Chicago, 2004); and to the second, see Morris Berman, *The Reenchantment of the World* (New York, 1988); Christopher H. Partridge, *The Re-enchantment of the West: Alternative Spiritualities, Sacralization, Popular Culture, and Occulture* (Edinburgh, 2005). For a useful overview, see Michael Saler, "Modernity and Enchantment: A Historiographic Review," *American Historical Review* 111.3 (2006): 692–716.

23. Morgan, *Images at Work*, 75.

24. Morgan, 92.

25. Morgan, 94.

26. Stephen T. Asma and Rami Gabriel, *The Emotional Mind: The Affective Roots of Culture and Cognition* (Harvard University Press, 2019), 293. Asma and Gabriel's definition is nearly identical to Graham Harvey's: that animists "recognize that the world is full of persons, only some of whom are human, and that life is always lived in relationship to others" (Harvey, *Animism: Respecting the Living World* [Hurst & Company, 2005], xi).

27. Asma and Gabriel, 294. For other examples of the "animist," or animated and enchanted, use of images around the world, see Kendall, *Mediums and Magical Things*; Franke, *Animism*.

28. Quoted in Freedberg, *The Power of Images*, 165.

29. Susanne Küchler, "Why Images Prevail," in *Images, Thought, and the Making of Social Worlds*, ed. by David Wengrow, 9–38 (Freiburger Studien zur Archäologie & Visuellen Kultur 3, Propylaeum, 2022), 30.

30. Küchler, "Why Images," 34.

31. Martin Jay, *Downcast Eyes: The Denigration of Vision in Twentieth-Century French Thought* (University of California Press, 1993).

32. Jacques Rancière, *The Politics of Aesthetics: The Distribution of the Sensible* (Continuum, 2004).

33. Certain religious images are sometimes called aniconic. For instance, in her analysis of Hindu divine images, Diana Eck refers to "aniconic images" as "those symbolic forms which, although they refer to a deity, do not attempt any anthropomorphic form or any representational likeness." Examples include the Christian cross or the *lingam* stone representing Shiva. By my definition, these are images; they are not anthropomorphic images of the deities they represent, but they are icons of something that has come to be a metonym or symbol of that deity (the cross on which Jesus was crucified; the cylindrical or phallic-shaped vertical object representing Shiva's generative power, frequently paired with the horizontal *yoni* of his consort, Shakti). See Diana Eck, *Darsan: Seeing the Divine Image in India*, 3rd ed. (Columbia University Press, 1996), 32.

34. John Tresch, "Technological World-Pictures: Cosmic Things and Cosmograms," *Isis* 98 (2007), 84–99, 92–93. See also Melik Ohanian and Jean-Christophe Royoux, eds., *Cosmograms* (Sternberg Press, 2005).

35. Tresch, "Technological World-Pictures," 93, emphasis added.

36. Robert Farris Thompson, *Flash of the Spirit: African and Afro-American Art and Philosophy* (Vintage/Random House, 1984), 108; MacGaffey is quoted there.

37. Thompson, *Flash of the Spirit*, 109ff.

38. See Alexander Studholme, *The Origins of Om Manipadme Hum: A Study of the Karandavyuha Sutra* (State University of New York Press, 2002); Lama Anagarika Govinda, *Foundations of Tibetan Mysticism According to the Esoteric Teachings of the Great Mantra* Om Mani Padme Hum (Weiser, 1969).

39. I adopt this way of speaking of "Durkheimian religion" from Charles Taylor, *A Secular Age* (Harvard University Press/Belknap, 2007), 442ff. For my detailed critique of Taylor, see Adrian Ivakhiv, *Shadowing the Anthropocene* (Punc-

tum, 2018), 159–78; and for a more global perspective on the issues he raises, see Miriam Künkler, John Madeley, and Shylashri Shankar, ed., *A Secular Age Beyond the West: Religion, Law and the State in Asia, the Middle East and North Africa* (Cambridge University Press, 2018).

40. Hans Belting, *Likeness and Presence*, trans. Edmund Jephcott (University of Chicago Press, 1994), 7.

41. W. J. T. Mitchell, *Image Science: Iconology, Visual Culture, and Media Aesthetics* (University of Chicago Press, 2015), 70.

42. Tresch, "Technological World-Pictures," 93–94.

43. Jonas Staal, *Propaganda Art in the 21st Century* (MIT Press, 2019).

44. W. J. T. Mitchell, "What Is an Image?" *New Literary History* 15.3 (1984): 503–37; 528–29.

45. On the sublime in contemporary visuality, see Temenuga Trifonova, ed., *Contemporary Visual Culture and the Sublime* (Routledge, 2018).

46. Hans Belting, *Likeness and Presence: A History of the Image Before the Era of Art*, trans. E. Jephcott (University of Chicago Press, 1994); Fredrika Jacobs, "Rethinking the Divide: Cult Images and the Cult of Images," *Renaissance Theory*, ed. James Elkins and Robert Williams (Routledge, 2008); Sylvia Perino Pagden, "From Cult Images to the Cult of Images: The Case of Raphael's Altarpieces," in *The Altarpiece in the Renaissance*, ed. Peter Humphrey and Martin Kemp, 165–89 (Cambridge University Press, 1990).

47. Belting, *Likeness and Presence*, xxi.

48. See, e.g., Charles Barber, "From Image into Art: Art After Byzantine Iconoclasm," in "The History of Medieval Art Without 'Art'?," ed. H. Maguire, special issue, *Gesta* 34.1 (1995): 5–10.

49. Henry Maguire, "Medieval Art Without 'Art': Introduction," *Gesta* 34.1 (1994): 3, cited in Roland Betancourt, "Medieval Art After Duchamp: Hans Belting's *Likeness and Presence* at 25," *Gesta* 55.1 (2016): 5.

50. Ellen Dissanayake, "Roots and Route of the Artification Hypothesis," *AVANT* 8.1 (2017): 15–32, 20; and Dissanayake, "Born to Artify: The Universal Origin of Picturing," in *Origins of Pictures: Anthropological Discourses in Image Science*, ed. Klaus Sachs-Hornbach and Jeorg R. J. Schirra, 230–49 (Halem, 2013), 232, 233.

51. Martin Heidegger, "The Age of the World Picture," in *The Question Concerning Technology and Other Essays*, trans. William Lovitt, 115–54 (Harper & Row, 1977), 134, emphasis added. I leave aside Heidegger's Nazism, which has been dealt with in detail excruciating enough (for Heidegger scholars) to discredit previous interpretation of his work by some of the prominent philosophers of the last century. See Richard Wolin's *Heidegger in Ruins: Between Philosophy and Ideology* (Yale University Press, 2023). Heidegger's influence on the resurgent political far right can also not be denied. None of that alters my point about the historical influence that Heidegger's critique of modernity has had.

52. Jennifer Anna Gosetti-Ferencei, *The Life of Imagination: Revealing and Making the World* (Columbia University Press, 2018), 128.

53. William Mills Ivins, *On the Rationalization of Sight, with an Examination of Three Renaissance Texts on Perspective* (Metropolitan Museum of Art, 1938).

54. But on the complexities in early modern visuality, see Martin Jay, "Scopic Regimes of Modernity," in *Vision and Visuality,* ed. Hal Foster (Bay Press, 1988); Stuart Clark, *Vanities of the Eye: Vision in Early Modern European Culture* (Oxford University Press, 2007).

55. Gosetti-Ferencei, *Life of Imagination,* 130.

56. E.g, Stan Brakhage, *Metaphors on Vision* (Anthology Film Archives, 1963/2017). Brakhage arguably combines the world-picture regime with the sublime variant of the ideal-image.

57. Michel Foucault, *Les mots et les choses* (Editions Gallimard, 1966); C. S. Lewis, *The Discarded Image: An Introduction to Medieval and Renaissance Literature* (Cambridge University Press, 1964); Eustace M. Tillyard, *The Elizabethan World Picture: A Study of the Idea of Order in Shakespeare, Donne, and Milton* (Vintage/Random House, 1959); Frances Yates, *The Occult Philosophy in the Elizabethan Age* (Routledge and Kegan Paul, 1979). A lucid discussion of the strengths and weaknesses of Foucault's work on the Renaissance *episteme* is found in chapter 3 of John Lechte's *Genealogy and Ontology of the Western Image and Its Digital Future* (Routledge, 2012).

58. I take the term "anthropocosmic" from studies of the traditional cosmology of China by Tu Weiming, John Grim, and others. See, e.g., Wei-ming Tu, *Confucian Thought: Selfhood as Creative Transformation* (State University of New York Press, 1985).

59. Bruno Latour, *We Have Never Been Modern,* trans. Catherine Porter (Harvard University Press, 1993), 106.

60. Bruno Latour, *Pandora's Hope: Essays on the Reality of Science Studies* (Harvard University Press, 1999), 195–96.

61. This is what Lechte, in his *Genealogy and Ontology of the Western Image and Its Digital Future*, describes as the "industrial image," or "an image having a transductive relation to a technical support," 84.

62. Susan Sontag, "The Image-World," in *On Photography* (Penguin, 1978), 153, 154.

63. Sontag, "The Image-World," 172.

64. Sontag, 170.

65. Sontag, 172.

66. Sontag, 173.

67. Sontag, 156.

68. Horkheimer and Adorno, cited/retranslated in Simon Ferdinand, Irene Villaescusa-Illán, and Esther Peeren, *Other Globes: Past and Peripheral Imaginations of Globalization* (Palgrave Macmillan/Springer, 2019), 2.

69. Michel Foucault, *Discipline and Punish: The Birth of the Prison,* trans. Alan Sheridan (Vintage/Random House, 1977); Gilles Deleuze, "Postscript on the Societies of Control," *October* 59 (1992): 3–7.

70. Sontag, "Image-World," 176.

71. Jussi Parikka, *Operational Images: From the Visual to the Invisual* (University of Minnesota Press, 2023), 12. The term "operational" or "operative image" was first used by filmmaker and artist-critic Harun Farocki in his 2000 exhibition *Eye/Machine*. See Aud Sissel Hoel, "Operative Images: Inroads to a New Paradigm of Media Theory," in *Image—Action—Space: Situating the Screen in Visual Practice*, ed. by Luisa Feiersinger, Kathrin Friedrich, and Moritz Queisner, 11–27 (De Gruyter, 2018).

72. Sontag, "Image-World," 176.

73. In *Picture Theory: Essays on Verbal and Visual Representation* (University of Chicago Press, 1994), W. J. T. Mitchell distinguishes between images and pictures, with the latter being *physical* images or "the concrete, representational objects in which images appear" (4). In this sense, the "world-picture" is the regime that equates the *image* with the *picture*, that is, the thing itself with its "picturable" appearance. Note that in translation to German, where both "image" and "picture" are translated as *Bild*, the distinction gets lost.

74. See Bart Testa, "Review-Essay: *The Cinema of Attractions Reloaded*," *Canadian Journal of Film Studies* 16.2 (2007): 119–26; Tom Gunning, "The Cinema of Attraction: Early Film, Its Spectator, and the Avant-Garde," in *Film and Theory: An Anthology*, ed. R. Stam and T. Miller, 229–35 (Blackwell, 2000).

75. Quoted in Teresa Castro, "An Animistic History of the Camera: Filmic Forms and Machinic Subjectivity," *A History of Cinema Without Names* (Film Forum, 2016), 247–55; 248.

76. On the spectrum of realist and anti-realist theories of film, see Martin Seel, "Realism and Anti-Realism in Film Theory," *Critical Horizons* 9.2 (2008): 157–75; and the "Film and Reality" section of Leo Braudy and Marshall Cohen, ed., *Film Theory and Criticism*, 6th ed. (Oxford University Press, 2004), 135–282.

77. Francesco Casetti, *Eye of the Century: Film, Experience, Modernity* (Columbia University Press, 2005), 2.

78. Adrian Ivakhiv, *Ecologies of the Moving Image: Cinema, Affect, Nature* (Wilfrid Laurier University Press, 2013). On the idea of the "world-motion-picture," see also Adrian Ivakhiv, "The Age of the World Motion Picture: Cosmic Visions in the Post-*Earthrise* Era," in *The Changing World Religion Map*, ed. S. D. Brunn, 129–44 (Springer, 2015); and on the "cognitive and affective journeys" of cinema, see Adrian Ivakhiv, "Cinema of the Not-Yet: The Utopian Promise of Film as Heterotopia," *Journal for the Study of Religion, Nature, and Culture* 5.2 (2011): 186–209.

79. See Erkki Huhtamo, "Natural Magic: A Short Cultural History of Moving Images," in *The Routledge Companion to Film History*, ed. William Guynn, 3–15 (Routledge, 2010).

80. Bill Gorman, "U.S. Television Households By Season," 2007, https://web.archive.org/web/20130613173153/http://tvbythenumbers.zap2it.com/2007/08/28/us-television-households-by-season/273/; Brian Stelter, "Ownership of TV Sets Falls in U.S.," *New York Times*, May 3, 2011, https://www.nytimes.com/2011/05/

03/business/media/03television.html; The Nielsen Company, "Nielsen Estimates 121 Million Homes in the U.S. for the 2020–2021 TV Season," https://www.nielsen.com/us/en/insights/article/2020/nielsen-estimates-121-million-tv-homes-in-the-u-s-for-the-2020-2021-tv-season/; NationMaster, "Households with Television: Countries Compared," https://www.nationmaster.com/country-info/stats/Media/Households-with-television.

81. See Cecelia Tichi, *Electronic Hearth: Creating an American Television Culture* (Oxford University Press, 1992). On cultures of television viewing, see Ron Lembo, *Thinking Through Television* (Cambridge University Press, 2000). On television ontology, see Lorenz Engell, *The Switch Image: Television Philosophy* (Bloomsbury Academic, 2021).

82. Stanley Cavell, "The Fact of Television," *Daedalus* 111.4 (1982): 75–96.

83. "Signals: How Video Transformed the World," an exhibition at the Museum of Modern Art, New York City, March 5–July 8, 2023, quoted in Jed Perl, "The Chilliest Mystique," *New York Review of Books,* May 11, 2022, 67–77; 70.

84. Gilles Deleuze, *Cinema 1: The Movement Image*, trans. Hugh Tomlinson and Barbara Habberjam (Athlone Press, 1989); Deleuze, *Cinema 2: The Time Image*, trans. Hugh Tomlinson and Robert Galeta (Athlone Press, 1989).

85. Lorenz Engell, *The Switch Image: Television Philosophy* (Bloomsbury Academic, 2021).

86. While her definition of montage (as ideologically prescriptive) is at times overly restrictive, I find Magda Dragu's differentiation between montage and collage to be informative; see her *Form and Meaning in Avant-Garde Collage and Montage* (Routledge, 2020).

87. Francesco Casetti, *Eye of the Century: Film, Experience, Modernity,* trans. Erin Larkin and Jennifer Pranolo (Columbia University Press, 2008), 107.

88. See Patricia Pisters, *The Neuro-Image: A Deleuzian Film-Philosophy of Digital Screen Culture* (Stanford University Press, 2012); Ingrid Hoelzl and Rémi Marie, *Softimage: Towards a New Theory of the Digital Image* (Intellect, 2015); Ingrid Hoelzl and Rémi Marie, "From Softimage to Postimage," *Leonardo* 50.1 (2017): 72–73; Steven Shaviro, *The Rhythm Image: Music Videos and New Audiovisual Forms* (Bloomsbury Academic, 2022); Steen Ledet Christiansen, "The Morph-Image: Four Forms of Post-Cinema," in *Philosophy and Film*, ed. Christina Rawls, Diana Neiva, and Steven S. Gouveia, 49–63 (Routledge, 2019); Daniel Rubinstein and Katrina Sluis, "A Life More Photographic: Mapping the Networked Image," *Photographies* 1.1 (2008): 9–28; Jacob T. Watson, "The Page in the Screen: Visualized Information and the Aesthetics of the Digital Image" (Ph.D. dissertation, University of North Caroline at Chapel Hill Graduate School, 2019); Shane Denson, *Discorrelated Images* (Duke University Press, 2020).

89. Motion Picture Association of America, *THEME Report 2017* (MPAA, 2018), 9.

90. Shane Denson and Julia Leyda, *Post-Cinema: Theorizing 21st-Century Film* (REFRAME, 2016).

91. Lev Manovich, *The Language of New Media* (MIT Press, 2001), 78–79.

92. Dana Rodowick, *The Virtual Life of Film* (Harvard University Press, 2007), 27.

93. Manovich, *The Language*, 86.

94. Manovich, *The Language*: "raw material for further compositing," 301; "an isolated accident," 308; "Born from animation," 302, italics his. Manovich repeats the same verdict about digital cinema and animation in "What Is Digital Cinema?" in *Post-Cinema*.

**Chapter 3**

1. Irmgard Emmelhainz, "Conditions of Visuality Under the Anthropocene and Images of the Anthropocene to Come," *e-flux Journal* 63 (2015), https://www.e-flux.com/journal/63/60882/conditions-of-visuality-under-the-anthropocene-and-images-of-the-anthropocene-to-come/.

2. Bruno Latour, *We Have Never Been Modern*, trans. C. Porter (Harvard University Press, 1993), 37.

3. Susan Sontag, "The Image-World," in *On Photography* (Penguin, 1978), 160.

4. Sontag, "Image-World," 156.

5. Sontag, 178–79.

6. Sontag, 179–80.

7. Martin Hand, *Ubiquitous Photography* (Malden, 2012), 1.

8. I take this list from Vincent Miller, *Understanding Digital Culture*, 2nd ed. (Sage, 2020), though its essence can be found in a range of texts on the topic.

9. On the physicality of digital media, see J. Allen-Robertson, "The Materiality of Digital Media: The Hard Disk Drive, Phonograph, Magnetic Tape and Optical Media in Technical Close-Up," *New Media & Society* 19.3 (2015): 455–470; Sean Cubitt, *Finite Media: Environmental Implications of Digital Technologies* (Duke University Press, 2016); Jennifer Gabrys, *Digital Rubbish: A Natural History of Electronics* (University of Michigan Press, 2011); Nicole Starosielski, *The Undersea Network* (Duke University Press, 2015).

10. Paula Albuquerque, *The Webcam as an Emerging Cinematic Medium* (Amsterdam University Press, 2018), 16.

11. Jonathan Beller, *The Cinematic Mode of Production: Attention Economy and the Society of the Spectacle* (University Press of New England, 2006); Francesco Casetti, *Eye of the Century: Film, Experience, Modernity*, trans. Erin Larkin and Jennifer Pranolo (Columbia University Press, 2008); Steen Ledet Christiansen, "The Morph-Image: Four Forms of Post-Cinema," in *Philosophy and Film*, ed. Christina Rawls, Diana Neiva, and Steven S. Gouveia, 49–63 (Routledge, 2019); Shane Denson and Julia Leyda, eds., *Post-Cinema: Theorizing 21st-Century Film* (REFRAME, 2016); Matthew Fuller, *Media Ecologies: Materialist Energies in Art and Technoculture* (MIT Press, 2005); Ingrid Hoelzl and Remi Marie, *Softimage: Towards a New Theory of the Digital Image* (Intellect, 2015); Luciana Parini and Tiziana Terranova, "A Matter of Affect: Digital Images and the Cybernetic Re-

Wiring of Vision," *Parallax* 7.4 (2001): 122–27; Steven Shaviro, *The Rhythm-Image*, unpublished paper presented at Society for Cinema and Media Studies 2015 annual meeting, accessed April 14, 2024, http://www.shaviro.com/Presentations/Third/#/; James W. Marcum, "Beyond Visual Culture: The Challenge of Visual Ecology," *Portal: Libraries and the Academy* 2.2 (2002): 189–206.

12. John Lechte, *Genealogy and Ontology of the Western Image and Its Digital Future* (Routledge, 2012), 54.

13. Jens Eder and Charlotte Klonk, ed., *Image Operations: Visual Media and Political Conflict* (Manchester University Press, 2017), 12.

14. Jussi Parikka, *Operational Images: From the Visual to the Invisual* (University of Minnesota Press, 2023), 96.

15. Harun Farocki, "Phantom Images," *Public* 29 (2004), 18.

16. Simon Rothöhler, "Calm Images: The Invisible Visual Culture of Digital Image Distribution," in *Images on the Move. Materiality—Networks—Formats*, ed. Olga Moskatova, 73–86 (Bielefeld, 2021), 74; John May, *Signal. Image. Architecture.* (Columbia University Press, 2019); Adrian Mackenzie and Anna Munster, "Platform Seeing: Image Ensembles and Their Invisualities," *Theory, Culture & Society* 36.5 (2019): 3–22.

17. Operationality and processability are Birgit Schneider's terms, cited in Rothöhler, "Calm Images," 76. Programmability and operability come from Hoelzl and Marie, *Softimage*.

18. On "image operations," see Eder and Klonk, *Image Operations*.

19. Parikka, *Operational Images*, 18, 20.

20. Rothöhler, "Calm Images," 76.

21. Paul Frosh, *The Poetics of Digital Media* (Polity, 2018), 167–68.

22. Frosh, *Poetics*, 164.

23. Timothy Erik Ström, "Capital and Cybernetics," *New Left Review* 135 (May-June, 2022): 23–41, quote on 23. Other adjectives used include computational, biopolitical, telematic, metabolic, emotional, and neuro-capitalism. See, e.g., Giorgio Griziotti, *Neurocapitalism: Technological Mediation and Vanishing Lines* (Minor Compositions, 2018); Eva Illouz, *Cold Intimacies: The Making of Emotional Capitalism* (Polity, 2007); Adrian Ivakhiv, "Weathering Global Futures: Ecology, Economy, and the Unruly Tropics of the 'Global,'" *Topia* 4 (2001): 5–26; and other books cited herein.

24. Jonathan Zittrain, *The Future of the Internet and How to Stop It* (Yale University Press, 2008), 12.

25. Thomas Poell, David Nieborg, and José van Dijck, "Platformisation," *Internet Policy Review* 8.4 (2019): 1–13. On platform capitalism, see Nick Srnicek, *Platform Capitalism* (Polity, 2016).

26. Steven Shaviro, *Post-Cinematic Affect* (Zero Books, 2010), 131–32, italics added.

27. See Ignas Kalpokas and Julija Kalpokiene, *Deepfakes: A Realistic Assessment of Potentials, Risks, and Policy Regulation* (Springer, 2022); Graham Meikle,

*Deepfakes* (Polity, 2022); Nina Schick, *Deepfakes and the Infocalypse: What You Urgently Need to Know* (Octopus, 2020).

28. Meikle, *Deepfakes*, 145–46.

29. Jennifer Gabrys, *Program Earth: Environmental Sensing and the Making of a Computational Planet* (University of Minnesota Press, 2016), 16. And see Gabrys, *How to Do Things with Sensors* (University of Minnesota Press, 2019). "Smartification" and "sensorization" are Gabrys's terms. For examples of urban sensorization, see the Senseable City Lab, https://senseable.mit.edu.

30. Mark Hansen, *Feed-Forward: On the Future of Twenty-First Century Media* (University of Chicago Press, 2015), 23, emphasis added.

31. Shane Denson, *Discorrelated Images* (Duke University Press, 2020), 41ff.

32. Andrea Pinotti, "Towards An-iconology: The Image as Environment," *Screen* 61.4 (2020): 594–603; 602. Pinotti's use of the hyphen in "an-iconic" is meant to indicate a tension between the ontological pictoriality of these images and their phenomenological status as real and non-pictorial.

33. Hansen, *Feed-Forward*, 26.

34. Hansen, 267, 269.

35. Hansen, 269.

36. Shoshana Zuboff, *The Age of Surveillance Capitalism: The Fight for a Human Future at the New Frontier of Power* (Public Affairs, 2019).

37. Adrian Ivakhiv, "The Art of Morphogenesis: Cinema In and Beyond the Capitalocene," in *Post-Cinema: Theorizing 21st Century Film*, ed. Shane Denson and Julia Leyda, 724–47 (REFRAME, 2016).

38. This point is well made by Tom Boellstorff in "For Whom the Ontology Turns: Theorizing the Digital Real," *Current Anthropology* 57.4 (2016): 387–407.

39. See, e.g., Wendy Chun, *Programmed Visions: Software and Memory* (MIT Press, 2011); James W. Potter, *Digital Media Effects* (Rowman & Littlefield, 2021); Andy Ruddock, *Digital Media Influence: A Cultivation Approach* (Sage, 2020).

40. See Sean Cubitt, *Finite Media: Environmental Implications of Digital Technologies* (Duke University Press, 2016).

41. Trevor Paglen, "Invisible Images (Your Pictures Are Looking at You)," *The New Inquiry*, December 8, 2016, https://thenewinquiry.com/invisible-images-your-pictures-are-looking-at-you; n.p., emphasis added.

42. Antonio Somaini, "On the Altered States of Machine Vision: Trevor Paglen, Hito Steyerl, Grégory Chatonsky," *AN-ICON: Studies in Environmental Images* 1 (2022), 91–110; 96–97.

43. Somaini, "On the Altered," 95; Romain Beaumont, "LAOIN-5B: A New Era of Open Large-Scale Multi-Modal Datasets," *LAION*, March 31, 2022, https://laion.ai/blog/laion-5b.

44. Paglen, "Invisible Images," n.p.

45. Denson, *Discorrelated Images*.

46. Karen Weise and Cade Metz, "When A.I. Chatbots Hallucinate," *New York Times*, May 1, 2023, https://www.nytimes.com/2023/05/01/business/ai-chatbots

-hallucination.html; Wikipedia, "Hallucination (Artificial Intelligence)," accessed May 9, 2023, https://en.wikipedia.org/wiki/Hallucination_(artificial_intel ligence). Artists like Refik Anadol play with this idea of machine-generated "hallucination"; see his series "Unsupervised: Machine Hallucination," Museum of Modern Art, https://refikanadol.com/works/unsupervised.

47. Matthew Fuller and Eyal Weizman, *Investigative Aesthetics: Conflicts and Commons in the Politics of Truth* (London: Verso, 2021).

48. Fuller and Weizman, *Investigative Aesthetics*, 25–26; 17.

49. See Fuller and Weizman, *Investigative Aesthetics*; Paolo Cirio, ed., *Evidentiary Realism: Investigative, Forensic, Documentary Art* (Lulu Press, 2019); Kate Crawford, *Atlas of AI: Power, Politics, and the Planetary Costs of Artificial Intelligence* (Yale University Press, 2021); T. J. Demos, *Beyond the World's End: Arts of Living at the Crossing* (Duke University Press, 2020); Miren Gutiérrez, *Data Activism and Social Change* (Palgrave Macmillan, 2018); David Houston Jones, *Visual Culture and the Forensic: Culture, Memory, Ethics* (Routledge, 2022); Susan Schuppli, *Material Witness: Media, Forensics, Evidence* (MIT Press, 2020); Antonio Somaini, "On the Altered States of Machine Vision"; Eyal Weizman, *Forensic Architecture: Violence at the Threshold of Detectability* (Zone Books, 2017).

50. Anna Weiner, "Infinite Art," *New Yorker*, November 20, 2023, 40–47; 42; Jerzy Lewandowski, "Exploring the Boundaries of Art with AI: Holly Herndon's Journey into Generative Media," *TS2*, November 13, 2023, https://ts2.space/en/exploring-the-boundaries-of-art-with-ai-holly-herndons-journey-into-genera tive-media.

51. Benjamin H. Bratton, *The Stack: On Software and Sovereignty* (MIT Press, 2015).

**Chapter 4**

1. Anselm Franke, "Much Trouble in the Transportation of Souls, or the Sudden Disorganization of Boundaries," in *Animism*, vol. 1 (Sternberg Press, 2010), 26.

2. Gilbert Simondon, *Imagination and Invention*, trans. J. Hughes and C. Wall-Romana (University of Minnesota Press, 2022), 18.

3. The notion of the "operating table" and the quote that follows are from Michel Foucault, *The Order of Things: An Archaeology of the Human Sciences* (Pantheon, 1970), xv–xvii; xv.

4. On the interplay of immanence and transcendence in South Indian uses of religious images, see Richard H. Davis, *Lives of Indian Images* (Princeton University Press, 1997), 27–29. Davis contrasts this with medieval Christian uses of images (pp. 32–33), which correlate more closely with what I am calling the ideal-image regime. On "immanent transcendence," see Patrice Haynes, *Immanent Transcendence: Reconfiguring Materialism in Continental Philosophy* (Bloomsbury, 2012); Kenneth Inada, "Immanent Transcendence: The Possibility of an East-West Philosophical Dialogue," *Journal of Chinese Philosophy* 35.3 (2008), 493–510; Jan Engberts, "Immanent Transcendence in Chinese and Western Process

Thinking," *Philosophy Study* 2.6 (2012), 377–83; and Adrian Ivakhiv, *Shadowing the Anthropocene* (Punctum, 2018), 89–92.

5. David Lewis-Williams, "Overview," in Daniel Lewis-Williams et al., "Review Feature: *The Mind in the Cave: Consciousness and the Origins of Art*," *Cambridge Archaeological Journal* 13.2 (2003): 263–79; 266.

6. Jacques Derrida, *Positions*, trans. A. Bass (University of Chicago Press, 1981); Jacques Derrida, *Limited, Inc.*, trans. J. Mehlmand and S. Webr, ed. J. Graff (Northwestern University Press, 1988).

7. Melissa K. Nelson, *Indigenous Science and Traditional Ecological Knowledge Persistence in Place* (Routledge, 2014); K. David Harrison, *When Languages Die: The Extinction of the World's Languages and the Erosion of Human Knowledge* (Oxford University Press, 2007).

8. On some of the richness of these forms of scriptural imaging, see David Wengrow, ed., *Images, Thought, and the Making of Social Worlds* (Freiburger Studien zur Archäologie & Visuellen Kultur 3, Propylaeum, 2022).

9. See Alfred Newen, Leon De Bruin, and Shaun Gallagher, eds., *The Oxford Handbook of 4E Cognition* (Oxford University Press, 2020); John Protevi, *Political Affect: Connecting the Social and the Somatic* (University of Minnesota Press, 2009).

10. See Lambros Malafouris, *How Things Shape the Mind: A Theory of Material Engagement* (MIT Press, 2013); Carl Knappett and Lambros Malafouris, ed., *Material Agency: Towards a Non-anthropocentric Perspective* (Springer, 2008); Lambros Malafouris and Colin Renfrew, eds., *The Cognitive Life of Things: Recasting the Boundaries of the Mind* (McDonald Institute Monographs, 2010). On material religion, see the work of Birgit Meyer, S. Brent Plate, David Morgan (cited in note 14), and others associated with the journal *Material Religion: The Journal of Objects, Art, and Belief.* On religion and "the new materialisms," see Catherine Keller and Mary-Jane Rubenstein, *Entangled Worlds: Religion, Science, and the New Materialisms* (Fordham University Press, 2017).

11. Malafouris, *How Things Shape the Mind*, 44.

12. Wouter J. Hanegraaff, "Imagining the Future Study of Religion and Spirituality," *Religion* 50.1 (2020): 72–82.

13. Ivakhiv, *Shadowing the Anthropocene*; and Adrian Ivakhiv, "Reimagining Religious Imagination, in Theory and in Practice," *Journal for the Study of Religion, Nature and Culture* 15.3 (2021): 390–408, from which some of this section is adapted.

14. David Morgan, *Visual Piety: A History and Theory of Popular Religious Images* (University of California Press, 1998); *The Sacred Gaze: Religious Visual Culture in Theory and Practice* (University of California Press, 2005); *The Lure of Images: A History of Religion and Visual Media in America* (Routledge, 2007); *The Embodied Eye: Religious Visual Culture and the Social Life of Feeling* (University of California Press, 2012); *Images at Work: The Material Culture of Enchantment* (Oxford University Press, 2018). See also his contributions to James Elkins and

David Morgan, eds., *Re-Enchantment* (Routledge, 2008) and his chapter "The Sensory Web of Vision: Enchantment and Agency in Religious Material Culture," in *The Oxford Handbook of History and Material Culture*, ed. Ivan Gaskell and Sarah Anne Carter, 254–74 (Oxford University Press, 2020).

15. Morgan, *Images at Work*, 60.

16. Morgan, 92.

17. Morgan, 11, 20.

18. Morgan, 68.

19. Morgan, 30.

20. Morgan, 169.

21. Morgan, 29, 173.

22. Morgan, 69.

23. This assumption is found not only in skeptical analyses of religion, but also very sympathetic ones. In chapter 7 I will critically analyze how T. M. Luhrmann's *How God Becomes Real: Kindling the Presence of Invisible Others* (Princeton University Press, 2020) is marred by such an assumption.

24. Morgan, *Images at Work*, 75.

25. Peter Berger, *The Sacred Canopy: Elements of a Sociological Theory of Religion* (Doubleday, 1967).

26. Morgan, *Images at Work*, 171, 172.

27. I examined the debate over the enchantment, disenchantment, and re-enchantment of modernity in Ivakhiv, *Shadowing the Anthropocene*, part 3, "Engaging Images: Building Common Worlds." See also Jane Bennett, *The Enchantment of Modern Life: Attachments, Crossings, Ethics* (Princeton University Press, 2001); Jason Josephson-Storm, *The Myth of Disenchantment: Magic, Modernity, and the Birth of the Human Sciences* (University of Chicago Press, 2017); Joshua Landy and Michael Saler, eds., *The Re-Enchantment of the World: Secular Magic in a Rational Age* (Stanford University Press, 2009); Birgit Meyer and Peter Pels, *Magic and Modernity: Interfaces of Revelation and Concealment* (Stanford University Press, 2003); Alex Owen, *The Place of Enchantment: British Occultism and the Culture of the Modern* (University of Chicago Press, 2004); Christopher Partridge, *The Re-Enchantment of the West*, vols. 1 and 2 (London: Continuum, 2005–2006); Steve Pile, *Real Cities: Modernity, Space, and the Phantasmagorias of City Life* (Sage, 2005); Randall Styers, *Making Magic: Religion, Magic, and Science in the Modern World* (Oxford University Press, 2004).

28. Charles Hartshorne, "Whitehead's Revolutionary Concept of Prehension," *International Philosophical Quarterly* 19.3 (1979): 253–63; 257, emphasis added.

29. Vincent Michael Colapietro, *Peirce's Approach to the Self: A Semiotic Perspective on Human Subjectivity* (State University of New York Press, 1988), 87.

30. Colapietro, *Peirce's Approach*, xx.

31. Colapietro, 77.

32. Colapietro, 79.

33. Quoted in Stango, "'I' Who? A New Look at Peirce's Theory of Indexical Self-Reference," *The Pluralist* 10.2 (2015): 220–46; 227.

34. This is explained in Stango, "'I' Who? A New Look," which also critically assesses the various perspectives on Peirce's account of subjectivity.

35. Charles Taylor, *A Secular Age* (Belknap Press of Harvard University Press, 2007), 33, 34. And see Taylor, *Sources of the Self: The Making of the Modern Identity* (Harvard University Press, 1989).

36. Taylor, *A Secular Age,* 135.

37. For my in-depth critique of Taylor, see Ivakhiv, *Shadowing the Anthropocene,* 164–80.

38. Judith Butler, *The Psychic Life of Power: Theories in Subjection* (Stanford University Press, 1997), 32, 2.

39. Kim Sang Ong-Van-Cung, "Critique and Subjectivation: Foucault and Butler on the Subject," *Actuel Marx* 49.1 (2011), par. 30, https://www.cairn-int.info/article-E_AMX_049_0148--critique-and-subjectivation.htm.

40. Mabel Berezin, *Making the Fascist Self: The Political Culture of Interwar Italy* (Cornell University Press, 1997).

41. On ancient Chinese cities as "cosmo-magical symbols," see Paul Wheatley, *The Pivot of the Four Quarters: A Preliminary Enquiry into the Origins and Character of the Ancient Chinese City* (Edinburgh University Press, 1971). On modern urban architecture seen in a similar light, see Michael Minkenburg, ed., *Power and Architecture: The Construction of Capitals and the Politics of Space* (Berghahn, 2014).

42. Olga Moskatova, "Introduction: Trajectories of Images," in *Images on the Move: Materiality—Networks—Formats,* ed. by O. Moskatova, 7–28 (Bielefeld: transcript, 2021), 13.

43. My Ph.D. dissertation focused on what I called "charismatic landscapes"; it was later published in modified form as Adrian Ivakhiv, *Claiming Sacred Ground: Pilgrims and Politics at Glastonbury and Sedona* (Indiana University Press, 2001). See also Elise Hunchuck, "Olafur Eliasson: Planetary Metabolism and the Charismatic Landscapes of the Cryosphere," *Flash Art* 331 (2020), https://flash---art.com/article/olafur-eliasson-planetary-metabolism-and-the-charismatic-landscapes-of-the-cryosphere/; Nigel Thrift, "The Material Practices of Glamour," *Journal of Cultural Economy* 1.1 (2008): 9–23.

44. Jan Assmann, "Monotheism and Polytheism," in *Ancient Religions,* ed. Sarah Iles Johnson, 17–31 (Harvard University Press, 2007), 24.

45. Jan Assmann, *The Price of Monotheism*, trans. Robert Savage (Stanford University Press, 2010), 24.

46. Assmann, "Monotheism and Polytheism," 27.

47. Assmann, "Monotheism and Polytheism," 28.

48. I'm indebted for this reading of the Templo da Humanidade to John Tresch's wonderful article, cited earlier, "Technological World-Pictures: Cosmic Things and Cosmograms," *Isis* 98 (2007): 84–99.

49. In addition to the five rules of thumb described here, we could speak also of a sixth: *the relationship between text and image evolves as image regimes evolve.* Images arguably preceded texts, even if textuality as a kind of system or network

of images and meanings emerged alongside the use of images. Images serve alongside texts, but in certain situations they can become opposed to text as well: for instance, with Religions of the Book, it is the words and not the images that are taken to be holy, to the point that for some images become the epitome of profanity, the very opposite of holiness. Images and texts work together, therefore, but also against each other in the same way that images themselves can conjoin into networks of enchantment, but these will always be opposed or counteracted by others. In the digital image-world, this takes on such a multitude of relations—between data and metadata, between data and algorithm, and so on—to the point of becoming opaque and unknowable.

50. Mark Hansen, *Feed-Forward: On the Future of Twenty-First Century Media* (University of Chicago Press, 2014), 2, 1 (the final quote cites Alex Galloway and Eugene Thacker).

51. This was later revised and appeared as a chapter in W. J. T. Mitchell, *What Do Pictures Want? The Lives and Loves of Images* (University of Chicago Press, 2005).

52. Mitchell, *What Do Pictures Want?*, 30.

53. Latour, *We Have Never Been Modern*, trans. Catherine Porter (Harvard University Press, 1993).

54. First quote cited in Jay Hetrick, "Video Assemblages: 'Machinic Animism' and 'Asignifying Semiotics' in the work of Melitopoulos and Lazzarato," *Footprint* 8 (2014): 53–68; 61; second quote from Stengers, "Reclaiming Animism," *e-flux* 36 (2012), https://www.e-flux.com/journal/36/61245/reclaiming-animism/. Stengers's "reclaimed animism" aligns well with others commonly considered among the "new animists," such as Eduardo Kohn, Tim Ingold, Philippe Descola, Eduardo Viveiros de Castro, and Graham Harvey. See Arianne Conty, "Animism in the Anthropocene," *Theory, Culture & Society* 39.5 (2022): 127–53; Philippe Descola, *Beyond Nature and Culture*, trans. J. Lloyd (University of Chicago Press, 2013); Graham Harvey, *Animism: Respecting the Living World* (Columbia University Press, 2005); Tim Ingold, "Rethinking the Animate, Re-animating Thought," *Ethnos: Journal of Anthropology* 71.1 (2006): 9–20; Eduardo Kohn, *How Forests Think: Toward an Anthropology Beyond the Human* (University of California Press, 2013); and the references to animism in chapter 2 in this book.

55. Déborah Danowski and Eduardo Viveiros de Castro, *The Ends of the World*, trans. Rodrigo Nunes (Polity, 2017), 71.

56. David R. Boyle, *The Rights of Nature: The Legal Revolution That Could Save the World* (ECW Press, 2017); Peter Burdon, ed., *Exploring Wild Law: The Philosophy of Earth Jurisprudence* (Wakefield, 2011); Timothy Cadman, Margot Hurlbert, and Andrea C. Simonelli, eds., *Earth System Law: Standing on the Precipice of the Anthropocene* (Routledge, 2021).

57. Achille Mbembe, *Brutalism*, trans. by Steven Corcoran (Duke University Press, 2024), 7.

**Part II**

1. Jedediah Purdy uses "condition"; see Purdy, *After Nature: A Politics for the Anthropocene* (Harvard University Press, 2015), 4. I favor "predicament" (Adrian Ivakhiv, *Shadowing the Anthropocene* [Punctum, 2018]).

2. See Adrian Ivakhiv, *Ecologies of the Moving Image: Cinema, Affect, Nature* (Wilfrid Laurier University Press, 2013), 37–42, 341–45.

3. Each of these questions can be further broken down into multiple registers. I detail the relationship between these three ecologies and the three "normative sciences" as Peirce called them—of aesthetics, ethics, and logic, or "ecologic"—in *Ecologies of the Moving Image*, in the second part of Adrian Ivakhiv, *Shadowing the Anthropocene*, and in the chapter "Three Ecologies: Toward Ecomediality" in *The Routledge Handbook of Ecomedia Studies*, ed. A. Lopez et al. (Routledge, 2023).

4. David Morgan, *Images at Work: The Material Culture of Enchantment* (Oxford University Press, 2018).

5. Morgan, *Images at Work*, 27–30.

6. See Steven E. Jones, *Against Technology: From the Luddites to Neo-Luddism* (Routledge, 2006); John Zerzan, *Twilight of the Machines* (Feral House, 2008).

7. Lewis Mumford, *The Myth of the Machine* (Harcourt, Brace and World, 1970).

8. Adrian Ivakhiv, "Is the Post- in Posthuman the Post- in Postmodern? Or, What Can the Human Be?" *Critical Theory* 4.2 (2020), 43–59.

**Chapter 5**

1. Christophe Bonneuil and Jean-Baptiste Fressoz, *The Shock of the Anthropocene: The Earth, History and Us,* trans. David Fernbach (Verso, 2016), 29.

2. Donna Haraway, *Staying with the Trouble: Making Kin in the Chthulucene* (Duke University Press, 2016), 100.

3. I first used the term "Anthropo-scene" in the context of a course and blog in 2014; see "Anthropo(s)cene and Beyond," *A(S)CENE: Eco-Arts, Media, and Culture for the Anthropo(s)cene,* January 21, 2014; https://blog.uvm.edu/aivakhiv-acene/2014/01/21/anthroposcene-beyond/. Unbeknownst to me at the time, Christian Schwägerl had used the term "Anthropo-scene" at Next Nature blog as early as April, 2013; see "Anthropo-scene #1: From Rocks to Thoughts," April 29, 2013; https://nextnature.net/story/2013/anthropo-scene-1-from-rocks-to-thoughts. Other uses of this compound term are examined in Jamie Lorimer, "The Anthropo-scene: A Guide for the Perplexed," *Social Studies of Science* 47.1 (2017): 117–42.

4. See Franciszek Chwalczyk, "Around the Anthropocene in Eighty Names—Considering the Urbanocene Proposition," *Sustainability* 12 (2020), 4458; Elizabeth M. DeLoughrey, *Allegories of the Anthropocene* (Duke University Press, 2019); Jan Jagodinski, *Interrogating the Anthropocene: Ecology, Aesthetics, Pedagogy, and the Future in Question* (Palgrave Macmillan, 2018); Kathryn Yusoff, *A Billion Black Anthropocenes or None* (University of Minnesota Press, 2019); Malcom Ferdinand, *Decolonial Ecology: Thinking from the Caribbean,* trans. A. P. Smith (Polity Press, 2022).

5. Déborah Danowski and Eduardo Viveiros de Castro, *The Ends of the World* (Polity, 2016), 107.

6. Achille Mbembe, "Futures of Life and Futures of Reason," *Public Culture* 33.1 (2021): 11–33; 11–12. And see Mbembe, *Brutalism*, trans. S. Corcoran (Duke University Press, 2024).

7. My classification of perspectives on the Anthropocene loosely follows Delf Rothe's distinction between "planetary realists," "eco-catastrophists," and "eco-modernists," except that critics of the Anthropocene (environmentalists and left-decolonialists) do not always fall into the "catastrophist" category, and scientists while in principle being "realists" sometimes do fall into that category. See Rothe, "Governing the End Times? Planet Politics and the Secular Eschatology of the Anthropocene," *Millennium* 48.2 (2020): 143–64. More moderate ecomodernists would include associates of the Breakthrough Institute (such as Ted Nordhaus and Michael Shellenberger) and the Long Now Foundation (such as Stewart Brand). On the more technophilic extreme we would find venture capitalists Elon Musk, Marc Andreessen, and, further still, "singularity" proponent Ray Kurzweil—though at that point the "eco" suffix is completely overshadowed by the "techno."

8. Angela Zottola and Claudio de Majo, "The Anthropocene: Genesis of a Term and Popularization in the Press," *Text & Talk* 42.4 (2022): 453–73.

9. Zottola and de Majo, 268, "The Anthropocene."

10. Libby Robin, Dag Avango, and Helmuth Trischler, "The Galleries of the Anthropocene," *The Anthropocene Review* 1.3 (2014): 207–24; Libby Robin and Cameron Muir, "Slamming the Anthropocene: Performing Climate Change in Museums," *reCollections: Journal of the National Museum of Australia* 10.1 (2015), https://recollections.nma.gov.au/issues/volume_10_number_1/papers/slamming_the_anthropocene; Leslie Sklair, ed., *Anthropocene in Global Media: Neutralizing the Risk* (Routledge, 2020).

11. Max Ritts and Karen Bakker, "New Forms: Anthropocene Festivals and Experimental Environmental Governance," *Environment & Planning E: Nature and Space* 5.1 (2022): 125–45; 131.

12. While based in Berlin, the *Anthropocene Curriculum* included events around the world, including in Montreal, Chicago, Melbourne, Lisbon, Venice, New Delhi, Cape Town, and at various places along the Mississippi River. The project wrapped up in late 2022 as I was working on this book in Berlin; I was able to attend a few of its culminating events. See Christoph Rosol, "Finding Common Ground: The Global *Anthropocene Curriculum* Experiment," *Anthropocene Review* 8.3 (2021): 221–29; Bernd Scherer, "Curating the Anthropocene at Berlin's Haus der Kulturen der Welt," in *Altered Earth: Getting the Anthropocene Right*, ed. Julia Adeney Thomas, 209–19 (Cambridge University Press, 2022).

13. Ritts and Bakker, "New Forms," 125, 138.

14. Stefania Barca, *Forces of Reproduction: Notes for a Counter-Hegemonic Anthropocene* (Cambridge University Press, 2020). For related critical and creative responses to the "master" Anthropocene narrative, see Hiuwai Chu, Meagan Dawn,

Nkule Mabaso, Pablo Martinez, and Corina Oprea, eds., *Climate: Our Right to Breathe* (L'Internationale and K. Verlag, 2022); Heather Davis and Zoe Todd, "On the Importance of a Date, or Decolonizing the Anthropocene," *ACME: An International E-Journal for Critical Geographies* 16.4 (2017): 761–80; Elizabeth Deloughrey, Jill Didur, and Anthony Carrigan, eds., *Global Ecologies and the Environmental Humanities: Postcolonial Approaches* (Routledge, 2015); Jennifer Mae Hamilton, Susan Reid, Pia van Gelder, and Astrida Neimanis, eds., *Feminist, Queer, Anticolonial Propositions for Hacking the Anthropocene* (Open Humanities Press, 2021); Axelle Karera, "Blackness and the Pitfalls of Anthropocene Ethics," *Critical Philosophy of Race* 7.1 (2019); Achille Mbembe, *Brutalism*, trans. Steven Corcoran (Duke University Press, 2024); Kathryn Yusoff, *A Billion Black Anthropocenes or None* (University of Minnesota Press, 2019). For a useful genealogy of discourses of globalism, alongside concepts of "earth," "world," and "planet," see Simon Ferdinand, Irene Villaescusa-Illán, and Esther Peeren, "Introduction," in *Other Globes: Past and Peripheral Imaginations of Globalization* (Palgrave Macmillan/Springer, 2019).

15. Barca, *Forces of Reproduction*, 5–6.

16. Barca, 14.

17. Elizabeth Kolbert tells the story well in "The 'Epic Row' over a New Epoch," *The New Yorker*, April 20, 2024, https://www.newyorker.com/news/the-weekend-essay/the-epic-row-over-a-new-epoch.

18. This account ignores the history of geological pursuits in their intimate connections to colonialism and capitalist extractivism. Kathryn Yusoff's already mentioned *A Billion Black Anthropocenes or None* (University of Minnesota Press, 2019) presents a helpful synthesis of this larger picture.

19. Bruno Latour, *Pandora's Hope: Essays on the Reality of Science Studies* (Harvard University Press, 1999), 71; and Joshua Malitsky, "Science and Documentary: Unity, Indexicality, Reality," *Journal of Visual Culture* 11.3 (2012): 244.

20. Katrin Klingan, ed., *Earth Indices—Processing the Anthropocene: Guilia Bruno and Armin Linke, May 19–Oct 17 2022* (Haus der Kulturen der Welt, 2022), 9.

21. Klingan, *Earth Indices*, 31.

22. Klingan, 8.

23. Anthropocene Curriculum, "Anthropocene Working Group," accessed March 21, 2024, https://www.anthropocene-curriculum.org/contributors/anthropocene-working-group.

24. Klingan, *Earth Indices*, 16.

25. Sigal Samuel, "Why Did Geologists Reject the 'Anthropocene' Epoch? It's Not Rock Science," *Vox*, March 20, 2024, https://www.vox.com/future-perfect/2024/3/7/24092675/anthropocene-climate-change-epoch-geology.

26. The notes refer several times to a "series of complex votes," "continued rounds of voting and data analysis," and the like.

27. Erle Ellis, Letter to Anthropocene Working Group (AWG), Subcommission on Quaternary Stratigraphy, ICS, IUGS, July 12, 2023, https://anthroecology.org/wp-content/uploads/2023/07/ellis_AWG_resignation_2023_07_12.pdf.

28. Colin Waters, "Chair's Column," *Newsletter of the Anthropocene Working Group* 13: Report of Activities 2023, March 16, 2024, 4. Waters later compared the process to "a palace coup"; see Kolbert, "The 'Epic Row' over a New Epoch."

29. See Damian Carrington, "Quest to Declare Anthropocene an Epoch Descends into Epic Row," *The Guardian,* March 7, 2024, https://www.theguardian.com/science/2024/mar/07/quest-to-declare-anthropocene-an-epoch-descends-into-epic-row; Alexandra Witze, "Geologists Reject the Anthropocene as Earth's New Epoch—After 15 Years of Debate," *Nature,* March 6, 2024, https://www.nature.com/articles/d41586-024-00675-8; Alexandra Witze, "It's Final: The Anthropocene Is Not an Epoch, Despite Protest After Vote," *Nature,* March 20, 2024, https://www.nature.com/articles/d41586-024-00868-1.

30. International Union of Geological Sciences, Facebook, March 21, 2024, https://www.facebook.com/iugspage.

31. Matthias Grotkopp, "Tipping the Scales: The Interfering Worlds of *Anthropocene: The Human Epoch,*" *Interfaces* 50 (2023): 19, https://journals.openedition.org/interfaces/8114.

32. Cited in Sophie Hackett, "Far and Near: New Views of the Anthropocene," in *Anthropocene,* ed. Edward Burtynsky with Jennifer Baichwal and Nicholas de Pencier, 13–33 (AGO/Goose Lane, 2018), 14.

33. Cited in Hackett, "Far and Near," 14.

34. Hackett, 14.

35. Edward Burtynsky, "Life in the Anthropocene," in Burtynsky et al., *Anthropocene,* 189–95; 191–92.

36. Karla McManus, "How Anthropo-scenic! Concerns and Debates About the Age of the Human," in Burtynsky et al., *Anthropocene,* 45–53; 52.

37. Gerda Cammaer, "Edward Burtynsky's *Manufactured Landscapes*: The Ethics and Aesthetics of Creating Moving Still Images and Stilling Moving Images of Ecological Disasters," *Environmental Communication* 3.1 (2009): 121–30; T. J. Demos, *Against the Anthropocene: Visual Culture and the Environment Today* (Sternberg, 2017); Jennifer Peeples, "Toxic Sublime: Imaging Contaminated Landscapes," *Environmental Communication* 5.4 (2011): 373–92; Robert Shore, "Toxicity's Sublime Seductions," *Elephant: The Art Culture Magazine* 28 (2016); Soenke Zehle, "Dispatches from the Depletion Zone: Edward Burtynsky and the Documentary Sublime," *Media International Australia* 127.1 (2008): 109–15.

38. Kelly Oliver, *Earth and World: Philosophy After the Apollo Missions* (Columbia University Press, 2015), 24.

39. Jennings Bryant and Mary Beth Oliver, *Media Effects: Advances in Theory and Research,* 3rd ed. (Routledge, 2009); Finis Dunaway, *Seeing Green: The Use and Abuse of Environmental Images* (University of Chicago Press, 2015); Lynda Walsh, "The Visual Rhetoric of Climate Change," *WIREs Climate Change* 6.4 (2015): 361–68.

40. Carol Diehl, "The Toxic Sublime," *Art in America* 94.2 (2006): 118–23; Jennifer Peeples, "Toxic Sublime" (see note 37).

41. On the "god trick," see Donna Haraway, "Situating Situated Knowledges: The Science Question in Feminism and the Privilege of Partial Perspective," *Feminist Studies* 14. 3 (1988): 575–99; 581. On "techno-imperialist logistics," see Zoë Druick, "'A Wide-Angle View of Fragile Earth': Capitalist Aesthetics in the Work of Yann Arthus-Bertrand," *Open Cultural Studies* 2 (2018): 396–405; 397. For an astute analysis that finds The Anthropocene Project failing to account for the "ideological baggage and omissions of the colonial histories" of such representation, see Selmin Kara, "The Anthropocene Project and the Archiviolithic Imaginary," *Screen* 61.2 (2020): 315–21; 320.

42. Jennifer Baichwal, "Our Embedded Signal," in Burtynsky et al., *Anthropocene*, 197–203; 197.

43. Baichwal, "Our Embedded Signal," 198.

44. Jennifer Baichwal interviewed by Alenda Chang, in "Anthropocene: The Human Epoch," YouTube (Carsey Wolf Center/University of California Television, March 31, 2020), c. 7'00"–8'00", https://www.youtube.com/watch?v=8kLkJVLRQoo.

45. November 20, 2018.

46. Baichwal, interviewed by Chang, c. 8'00"–8'30".

47. CBC Radio/The Current, "Anthropocene Project Highlights the Apocalyptic Beauty of Humans' Effect on the Planet," September 26, 2018, https://www.cbc.ca/radio/thecurrent/the-current-for-september-26-2018-1.4838781/anthropocene-project-highlights-the-apocalyptic-beauty-of-humans-effect-on-the-planet-1.4838811.

48. Robert Enright, "'What More Is There to Say?' Review of *Anthropocene: The Human Epoch*," *Border Crossings* 148, December 2018, https://bordercrossingsmag.com/article/what-more-is-there-to-say.

49. Enright, "What More."

50. Audre Lorde, *The Master's Tools Will Never Dismantle the Master's House* (New York: Penguin, 2018).

51. Grotkopp, "Tipping the Scales," 13 (see note 31).

52. Grotkopp, 14.

53. For an astute critique, see Sara B. Pritchard, "Dangerous Beauty: Aesthetics, Politics, and Power in *Anthropocene: The Human Epoch*," *Environmental History* 25.2 (2020): 377–82.

54. Shannon Stevens and Richard Wainwright, "A Review of 'The Anthropocene Project': Treachery in Images," *Art/Research International: A Transdisciplinary Journal* 5.1 (2020): 567–84; 574.

55. On the toxic sublime, see Peeples, "Toxic Sublime." On the variety of contemporary "sublimes," see Temenuga Trifanova, ed., *Contemporary Visual Culture and the Sublime* (Routledge, 2017).

56. Kino Lorber, "Anthropocene – Official U.S. Trailer," YouTube, accessed May 13, 2022, https://www.youtube.com/watch?v=ikMlCxzO-94.

57. See, e.g., Rayson K. Alex and S. Susan Deborah, eds., *Ecodocumentaries:*

*Critical Essays* (Palgrave Macmillan, 2016); John A. Duvall, *The Environmental Documentary: Cinema Activism in the 21st Century* (Bloomsbury, 2017); Helen Hughes, *Green Documentary: Environmental Documentary in the Twenty-First Century* (Intellect, 2014).

58. There's some debate over the attribution of the quip: even Jameson himself, in 2003, referred to "someone once" saying it, though in 1994, Slavoj Žižek attributed it to Jameson. See Slavoj Žižek, "Mapping Ideology," in *The Spectre of Ideology*, ed. Slavoj Žižek (Verso, 1994), 1; Fredric Jameson, *The Seeds of Time* (Columbia University Press, 1994), xii; Fredric Jameson, "Future City," in *The Ideologies of Theory* (Verso, 2008), 473.

59. Andrew Ross, "The Ecology of Images," *South Atlantic Quarterly* 91.1 (1992): 215–38; 220.

60. Birgit Schneider, "Burning Worlds of Cartography: A Critical Approach to Climate Cosmograms of the Anthropocene," *Geo: Geography and Environment* 3.2 (2016), e00027.

61. There are audiences that are already engaged with "ideals" of the sort found within traditions of the ideal-image: that is, with religious, cultural, or political narratives to which followers naturally turn in interpreting the unfamiliar. Cognizant of the importance of providing sources of sustenance and hope for change, some artists are working to forge *new* modes of image interpretation based on the cultivation of affective relations toward the Earth. Among these are the ones described by observers of "spiritual ecology," "dark green religion," and other forms of compelling and religion-resembling environmental and ecojustice work; see, e.g., Roger S. Gottlieb, *A Greener Faith: Religious Environmentalism and Our Planet's Future* (Oxford University Press, 2006); Leslie Sponsel, *Spiritual Ecology: A Quiet Revolution* (Bloomsbury, 2012); Bron R. Taylor, *Dark Green Religion: Nature Spirituality and the Planetary Future* (University of California Press, 2009). When Anthropocene images land on the screens of those who are already poised to act, because they already affiliate with the promise of a more viable human coexistence with the Earth, they may in fact have the effect of nourishing further desire for transformative action. The images alone, however, in separation from the broader social and perceptual ecology of social and ecological activism, may not have much more effect than to provoke the "worry," "sadness," and "anger" seen in respondents to the *Anthropocene* exhibition; even more likely, they will get lost in the din of an already oversaturated image-world.

62. See Jihoon Kim, *Documentary's Expanded Fields: New Media and the Twenty-First-Century Documentary* (Oxford University Press, 2022); and for some earlier examples, Catherine Russell, *Experimental Ethnography: The Work of Film in the Age of Video* (Duke University Press, 1999).

63. I discussed the essay film in chapter four of Adrian Ivakhiv, *Ecologies of the Moving Image* (Wilfrid Laurier University Press, 2013). See also Nora Alter, *The Essay Film After Fact and Fiction* (Columbia University Press, 2018); Brenda Hollweg and Igor Krstic, *World Cinema and the Essay Film: Transnational Perspectives*

*on a Global Practice* (Edinburgh University Press, 2020); Volker Pantenburg, *Farocki/Godard: Film as Theory* (Amsterdam University Press, 2015); Laura Rascaroli, *How the Essay Film Thinks* (Oxford University Press, 2017).

64. See Jihoon Kim, *Documentary's Expanded Fields: New Media and the Twenty-First Century Documentary* (Oxford University Press, 2022); Georgia Wallace-Crabbe, "The Earth and the Elements: Multi-Screen Documentary and How the Cinema Migrates" (doctorate of creative arts thesis, University of Wollongong, 2015); Erika Balsom and Hila Peleg, *Documentary Across Disciplines* (MIT Press, 2016).

65. Asbjørn S. Grønstad, *Rethinking Art and Visual Culture: The Poetics of Opacity* (Springer, 2020), 78.

66. John Akomfrah, "Memory and the Morphologies of Difference," in *Politics of Memory: Documentary and Archive*, ed. Marco Scotini and Elisabetta Galasso, 23–36 (Berlin: Archive Books, 2014), 29.

67. Haley Weiss, "John Akomfrah and the Image as Intervention," *Interview*, June 27, 2016, https://www.interviewmagazine.com/film/john-akomfrah.

68. Dan Barrow, "*Vertigo Sea* by John Akomfrah," *Dandelion* 8.1 (2017):1–4; 3.

69. See Akomfrah, "Memory and the Morphologies of Difference," 29.

70. Anthony Downey, "Vital Materialism: Filming the Anthropocene—John Akomfrah in Conversation with Anthony Downey," *Third Text*, accessed March 5, 2022, http://thirdtext.org/akomfrah-downey.

71. Ian Bourland, "John Akomfrah: Multichannel Prehensions," *Nka, Journal of Contemporary African Art* 45 (2019): 128–39; 132.

72. Jakob Nilsson, "Capitalocene, Clichés, and Critical Re-enchantment: What Akomfrah's *Vertigo Sea* Does Through BBC Nature," *Journal of Aesthetics and Culture* 10 (2018): 2.

73. Cited in Eleanor Byrne, "Migration, Disaster, and the Globalized Mediterranean: Between *Barca Nostra* and *Vertigo Sea*," *Parallax* 27.1 (2021): 46–62; 58.

74. Mother Tongue, "Spectres of the Deep," *MAP* 42 (January 2018), https://mapmagazine.co.uk/spectres-of-the-deep.

75. Nilsson, "Capitalocene, Clichés, and Critical Re-enchantment," 9.

76. Quoted in T. J. Demos, "Unspeakable Moments: An Interview with John Akomfrah," *Atlántica* 54 (2014), 59.

77. Alexander Kluge, "On Film and the Public Sphere," trans. Thomas Levin and Miriam Hansen, *New German Critique* 24/25 (1981–1983): 206–20; 206, 219.

78. James Harvey, *John Akomfrah* (British Film Institute, 2023), 164.

79. Harvey, *John Akomfrah*, 171.

80. Anuradha Vikram, "Underneath the Black Atlantic: Race and Capital in John Akomfrah's *Vertigo Sea*," *X-Tra* 21.3 (Spring 2019), accessed July 20, 2023, https://www.x-traonline.org/article/underneath-the-black-atlantic-race-and-capital-in-john-akomfrahs-vertigo-sea.

81. Christina Sharpe, *In the Wake: On Blackness and Being* (Duke University Press, 2016), 21.

82. T. J. Demos, "On Terror and Beauty: John Akomfrah's Vertigo Sea," *Atlántica,* accessed July 23, 2023, https://www.revistaatlantica.com/en/on-terror-and-beauty-john-akomfrahs-vertigo-sea/.

83. Downey, "Vital Materialism."

84. See Schneider, "Burning Worlds of Cartography," on global heat maps.

85. Akomfrah refers to *Purple* as a "fugue" and discusses his method as more "contrapuntal" in his interview with Anthony Downey; see Downey, "Vital Materialism."

86. Kass Banning and Ekow Eshun, eds., *John Akomfrah: Purple* (London: Barbican Center, 2017), 42–43.

87. T. S. Eliot, *Four Quartets* (Harcourt, 1943).

88. Nilsson, "Capitalocene, Clichés, and Critical Re-enchantment," 9.

89. Downey, "Vital Materialism," n.p.

90. On the ambiguous nature of Akomfrah's "figures of stillness," see also Alessandra Raengo's "Cosmopolitanism, Contemplation, and the Ontopolitics of Movement in John Akomfrah's Gallery Practice," in *Black Film British Cinema II,* ed. Clive Nwonka and Anamik Saha, 143–61 (London: Goldsmiths Press, 2021).

91. James Harvey, *John Akomfrah* (British Film Institute, 2023), 150.

**Chapter 6**

1. John Berger, "Why Look at Animals," in *About Looking*, 1–26 (Pantheon, 1980), 24.

2. Alexander Pschera, *Animal Internet: Nature and the Digital Revolution*, trans. Elisabeth Lauffer (New Vessel Press, 2016), EPUB, 15.

3. Important scholarly studies of YouTube include Jean Burgess and Joshua Green, *YouTube,* 2nd ed. (Polity, 2018); Anandam Kavoori, "Making Sense of YouTube," *Global Media Journal* 13.24 (2015); Paul A. Soukup, "Looking At, Through, and With YouTube," *Communication Research Trends* 33.3 (2014): 3–34; and Kevin Munger, *The YouTube Apparatus* (Cambridge University Press, 2024).

4. YouTube is the world's second most visited web site, second only to Google Search. Both are owned by Google/Alphabet. See Similarweb, "Top Websites Ranking," accessed July 12, 2023, https://www.similarweb.com/top-websites/; and Global Media Insight, "YouTube User Statistics 2023," May 26, 2023, https://www.globalmediainsight.com/blog/youtube-users-statistics/.

5. See Greg Garrard, *Ecocriticism*, 2nd ed. (Routledge, 2011), 154ff. For primers in critical animal studies in relation to media, see Núria Almiron, Matthew Cole, and Carrie P. Freeman, eds., *Critical Animal and Media Studies: Communication for Nonhuman Animal Advocacy* (Routledge, 2018); Amber E. George and J. L. Schatz, eds., *Screening the Nonhuman: Representations of Animal Others in the Media* (Lexington, 2016); and Claire Parkinson, *Animals, Anthropomorphism, and Mediated Encounters* (Routledge, 2020). For the framework I describe here, see the chapter "Anima Moralia" in Adrian Ivakhiv, *Ecologies of the Moving Image: Cinema, Affect, Nature* (Wilfrid Laurier University Press, 2013), especially

pages 244–52. And for issues surrounding human-nonhuman animal relations in the Anthropocene, see Bernice Bovenkirk and Jozef Keulartz, eds., *Animals in Our Midst: The Challenges of Co-existing with Animals in the Anthropocene* (Springer, 2021).

6. Shane Denson and Julia Leyda, *Post-Cinema: Theorizing 21st-Century Film* (REFRAME, 2016).

7. Lev Manovich, *The Language of New Media* (MIT Press, 2001), 302; in the original this line is emphasized using italics.

8. Henry Jenkins, "YouTube and the Vaudeville Aesthetic," Confessions of an Aca-Fan, November 19, 2006, http://henryjenkins.org/blog/2006/11/youtube_and_the_vaudeville_aes.html.

9. Paul Sheehan, "Against the Image: Herzog and the Troubling Politics of the Screen Animal," *SubStance* 37.3 (2008): 117–36; 119.

10. James Leo Cahill, "A YouTube Bestiary: 26 Theses on a Post-Cinema of Animal Attractions," *The New Silent Cinema*, ed. by Paul Flaig and Katherine Groos (AFI/Routledge, 2015), 263–93.

11. The term "ethnographic taxidermy" is Fatimah Tobing Rony's; see Rony, *The Third Eye: Race, Cinema, and Ethnographic Spectacle* (Duke University Press, 1996). I discuss this in reference to ethnographic film in chapter 4 of Ivakhiv, *Ecologies of the Moving Image*.

12. Vinciane Despret, *What Would Animals Say If We Asked the Right Questions?* (University of Minnesota Press, 2016), 195.

13. ICARUS, "Data from Space Unveils a Global View of Animals on the Move," *ICARUS: Global Monitoring with Animals*, March 20, 2022, https://www.icarus.mpg.de/115079/news_publication_18465516_transferred?c=63759.

14. See https://movebank.org/cms/movebank-main.

15. See http://animalinternet.earth, accessed June 18, 2023. See also Alexander Pschera, *Animal Internet: Nature and the Digital Revolution*, trans. Elisabeth Laufer (New Vessel Press, 2016).

16. Marek Jancovic, "Animal Technics: On Borders and the Labour of Knowing the World," SITUATIONS, Fotomuseum Winterthur, July 3, 2018. https://www.fotomuse-um.ch/en/explore/situations/154932.

17. Cahill, "A YouTube Bestiary," 269.

18. Parts of this chapter are based on a study of YouTube videos that I carried out, with the aid of research assistant Michael McGuire, in the summer of 2020, with follow-up study in the spring and summer of 2023. It involved analysis of popularity data (views, likes, comments) as well as key themes in the commentary, with an eye to teasing out the relative preponderance and popularity of "anthropocentric" versus "theriocentric" (animal-sympathetic), informed versus uninformed, sincere versus ironic (satirical, mocking, etc.), politically motivated, and other perspectives in the commentary.

19. Jessica Gall Myrick, "Emotion Regulation, Procrastination, and Watching Cat Videos Online: Who Watches Internet Cats, Why, and to What Effect?" *Com-*

*puters in Human Behavior* 52 (2015): 168–76; 168. Myrick's source documents that there were already more than two million cat videos posted on YouTube, with nearly 26 billion total views, making for an average of 12,000 views per video.

20. These statistics are from YouTube, July 4, 2023. See also vidIQ's statistics and rankings for the YouTube "Pets and Animals" category, http://vidiq.com/youtube-stats/top/category/pets.

21. Yuliya Kisora and Clemens Driessen, "Interpreting the YouTube Zoo: Ethical Potential of Captive Encounters," in *Animals in Our Midst: The Challenges of Co-existing with Animals in the Anthropocene.* ed. Bernice Bovenkerk and Jozef Keular, 323–40 (Springer, 2021).

22. For the negative, see Christian Lenzi, Siobhan Speiran, and Chiara Grasso, "'Let Me Take a Selfie': Implications of Social Media for Public Perceptions of Wild Animals," *Society & Animals* 31 (2023): 64–83; and G. K. Moloney, J. Tuke, E. Dal Grande, T. Nielsen, and A. Chaber, "Is YouTube Promoting the Exotic Pet Trade? Analysis of the Global Public Perception of Popular YouTube Videos Featuring Threatened Exotic Animals," *PLOS ONE,* April 13, 2021, https://doi.org/10.1371/journal.pone.0235451. For the potentially positive, see J. M. Beall et al., "The Influence of YouTube Videos on Human Tolerance of Sharks," *Animal Conservation* 26.2 (2023): 154–64; William R. Casola et al., "How Do YouTube Videos Impact Tolerance of Wolves?" *Human Dimensions of Wildlife* 25.6 (2020): 531–43.

23. Andrew Burke, "ZooTube: Streaming Animal Life," in *The Zoo and Screen Media: Images of Exhibition and Encounter,* ed. Michael Lawrence and Karen Lury, 65–83 (Palgrave Macmillan, 2016), 74.

24. Burke, "ZooTube," 68.

25. Burke, 78.

26. Kisora and Driessen, "Interpreting the YouTube Zoo," 337; Burke, "ZooTube," 337.

27. Kisora and Driessen, 334.

28. Crystal Pineda, "Beluga Mesmerized by Violin," YouTube, uploaded June 24, 2015, accessed April 13, 2023, https://www.youtube.com/watch?v=N3JRNvQi4Oc. A similar video is "Beluga Whale Mesmerized by the Violin," https://www.youtube.com/watch?v=MsfKifGisIg.

29. LADbible Extra, "Beluga Whale Retrieves Girl's Phone," YouTube, May 7, 2019, https://www.youtube.com/watch?v=qA3iainpIzs. The most popular comment to the video (with 90,000 likes) is "Get your trash out of my house," imagined to be the beluga's words to the girl.

30. See Shedd Aquarium, "Penguin Adventures" series of videos, YouTube, https://youtu.be/i8l4fShUmho.

31. Benjamin Schultz-Figueroa, "Abandoned Attractions: Online Animal Aquariums During Quarantine," *Journal of Environmental Media* 1 Supplement, 5.1–5.8; quotes on pp. 5.6, 5.7.

32. Bram Büscher, *The Truth About Nature: Environmentalism in the Era of Post-Truth Politics and Platform Capitalism* (University of California Press, 2021).

33. Büscher, *The Truth*, 126.

34. Bram Büscher, "Nature 2.0: Exploring and Theorizing the Links Between New Media and Nature Conservation," *New Media & Society* 18.5 (2016): 726–43; Büscher, *The Truth About Nature*, 128.

35. Büscher, *The Truth*, 138.

36. Jeffrey Kluger, "When Animals Attack—and Defend," *Time*, June 7, 2007, https://content.time.com/time/health/article/0,8599,1630667,00.html.

37. Kluger, "When Animals Attack"; Drew Millhon, "Video Captures Animal Battle for Survival," August 1, 2007, ABC News Video Ventures, http://web.archive.org/web/20160813005056/http://abcnews.go.com/icaught/story?id=3418552&page=1.

38. Brian Stelter, "You've Seen the YouTube Video; Now Try the Documentary," *New York Times*, May 10, 2008, https://www.nytimes.com/2008/05/10/arts/television/10kruger.html.

39. Stelter, "You've Seen the YouTube Video."

40. Ximena J. Nelson and Natasha Fijn, "The Use of Visual Media as a Tool for Investigating Animal Behaviour," *Animal Behaviour* 85 (2013): 525–36.

41. Despret, *What Would Animals Say*, 196 (see note 12).

42. Despret, 197–98.

43. Despret, 200.

44. Anne MacConnell, "A is for Anecdotes, Amateurs, and Anomalies: Vinciane Despret's Case for Exceptional Interspecies Relations," *Humanities* 11 (2022): 9, https://doi.org/ 10.3390/h11010020.

45. Cahill, "A YouTube Bestiary," 275.

46. Guy Hawkins and Ben Dibley, "Provoking Animal Realities on TV: Exploring the Affinities between STS and Screen Studies," *Science, Technology, and Human Values* 46.4 (2021): 695–718.

47. For my analysis of the film and others in the nature documentary genre, see chapter 5 of Ivakhiv, *Ecologies of the Moving Image*, especially pp. 212–14.

48. Donna Haraway, *When Species Meet* (University of Minnesota Press, 2008), 255.

49. "Fugal accompaniment": Haraway, *When Species Meet*, 261.

50. Bill McKibben, *The End of Nature* (Random House, 1989).

51. Newsflare, YouTube, September 16, 2019, https://www.youtube.com/watch?v=sKjBKMtuWE8.

52. Wake Up World, "Humpback Whale Shows AMAZING Appreciation After Being Freed from Nets," YouTube, July 17, 2011, accessed July 13, 2023, https://www.youtube.com/watch?v=tcXU7G6zhjU.

53. BankFishing, "Rescuing a Screech Owl Tangled in Fishing Line, New Jersey—09/06/2015," YouTube, accessed July 13, 2023, https://www.youtube.com/watch?v=CDpnyedAJvg.

54. T & T Creative Media, "Otter Jumps onto Boat Escaping Orca with Seconds to Spare," YouTube, accessed July 13, 2023, https://www.youtube.com/watch?v=jeyXRF_1FOE.

55. ViralHog, "Man Punches a Kangaroo in the Face to Rescue His Dog (Original HD)," YouTube, https://www.youtube.com/watch?v=FIRT7lf8byw.

56. Kayamping, "Why I Don't Deep Sea Fish from a Kayak Anymore," YouTube, uploaded Dec 10 2016, https://www.youtube.com/watch?v=UcLV2CWi8oI, 21 million views as of July 16, 2023; Mr. Markus, "Kayak Fisherman Fights Off Aggresive [*sic*] Hammerhead Shark!!! (full video), YouTube, uploaded September 23, 2015, https://www.youtube.com/watch?v=JUldotszSG8, 4 million views as of July 16, 2023.

57. Ruby the Nature Girl, "GREAT WHITE SHARKS SURFING," YouTube, uploaded June 27, 2015, https://youtu.be/VvvTs70h6Ow, 6 million views as of July 12, 2023.

58. Explore Live Nature Cams, "Ocean Ramsey Encounters GIANT 20ft Great White Shark," YouTube, uploaded January 20, 2019, accessed July 14, 2023, 4.2 million views, https://www.youtube.com/watch?v=BMsyssBXRsQ.

59. Animal Channel, "Wild Polar Bear Tries to Break In—BBC Earth," YouTube, uploaded August 4, 2019, 2.26 million views, https://www.youtube.com/watch?v=9G1aHkLHQ2I&t=2s. It had previously received at least 35 million views on a site that is no longer available: https://www.youtube.com/watch?v=RJraofcMsVU, accessed July 2020.

60. K. Anne-Isola Nekaris et al., "Tickled to Death: Analysing Public Perceptions of 'Cute' Videos of Threatened Species (Slow Lorises—*Nycticebus spp.*) on Web 2.0 Sites," *PLOS ONE* 8.7 (2013), e69215.

61. K. Anne I. Nekaris, Louisa Musing, Asier Gil Vasquez, and Giuseppe Donati, "Is Tickling Torture? Assessing Welfare Towards Slow Lorises (*Nycticebus spp.*) Within Web 2.0 Videos," *Folia Primatologica* 86.6 (2016): 534–51; 534.

62. Lauren A. Harrington, David W. Macdonald, and Neil D'Cruze, "Popularity of Pet Otters on YouTube: Evidence of an Emerging Trade Threat," *Nature Conservation* 36 (2019): 17–35; 31–32.

63. Magdalena Svenson, Thais Morcatty, Vincent Nijman, and Chris Shepherd, "The Next Exotic Pet to Go Viral: Is Social Media Causing an Increase in the Demand of Owning Bushbabies as Pets?" *Hystrix: Italian Journal of Mammalogy* 33.1 (2022): 51–57.

64. Vitória Fernandes Nunes, Priscila R. M. Lopes, and Renata Gonçalves Ferreira, "#capuchinmonkeys on Social Media: A Threat for Species Conservation," *Anthrozoös* 36.4 (2023): 665–83.

65. G. K. Moloney, J. Tuke, E. Dal Grande, T. Nielsen, and A. Chaber, "Is YouTube Promoting the Exotic Pet Trade? Analysis of the Global Public Perception of Popular YouTube Videos Featuring Threatened Exotic Animals," *PLOS ONE*, April 13, 2021, https://doi.org/10.1371/journal.pone.0235451. And see Tara A. Clarke, Kim E. Reuter, Marni LaFleur, and Melissa S. Schaefer, "A Viral Video and Pet Lemurs on Twitter," *PLOS ONE*, January 9, 2019, https://doi.org/10.1371/journal.pone.0208577.

66. Moloney et al., "Is YouTube Promoting," 12; Rashi Shrivastava, "Hundreds Of Social Media Videos with Billions of Views Show Wild Animals Being Tor-

tured, Report Finds," *Forbes,* November 22, 2022, https://www.forbes.com/sites/rashishrivastava/2022/11/22/hundreds-of-social-media-videos-with-billions-of-views-show-wild-animals-being-tortured-report-finds/.

67. Cited in Lenzi et al., "'Let Me Take a Selfie,'" 1–20; 6.

68. Mason Fidino, Seth W. Herr, and Seth B. Magle, "Assessing Online Opinions of Wildlife Through Social Media," *Human Dimensions of Wildlife* 23.5 (2018): 482–90; 488.

69. Social Media Animal Cruelty Coalition, *SMACC Spotlight Report. Wild Animal "Pets" on Social Media: A Vicious Cycle of Suffering* (SMACC/Asia for Animals Coalition, 2022).

70. Dina Fine Maron, "How Fake Animal Rescue Videos Have Become a New Frontier for Animal Abuse," *National Geographic,* June 30, 2021, https://www.nationalgeographic.com/animals/article/how-fake-animal-rescue-videos-have-become-a-new-frontier-for-animal-abuse; Koh Ewe, "Fake Rescues and Animal Torture Are Disturbingly Common on Social Media," *Vice,* September 1, 2021, https://www.vice.com/ en/article/akg9pz/fake-rescues-and-animal-torture-are-disturbingly-common-on-social-media; Jamie Doward, "YouTube Must Remove Videos of Animal Cruelty, Says Charity," *The Guardian,* December 19, 2020, https://www.theguardian.com/world/2020/dec/19/youtube-must-remove-videos-of-animal-cruelty-says-charity.

71. See, for instance, World Animal Protection, "How to Spot a Fake Animal Rescue Video," July 6, 2021, https://www.worldanimalprotection.org.au/news/how-spot-fake-animal-rescue-video; FOUR PAWS International, "Fake Animal Rescue Videos: How to Spot Orchestrated Animal Rescues," March 4, 2021, https://www.four-paws.org/our-stories/publications-guides/fake-animal-rescue-videos; Cat Protection Society of New South Wales, "Factsheet—Animals on the Internet," accessed July 13, 2023, https://catprotection.org.au/cat-care-factsheets/factsheet-animals-on-the-internet/.

72. Lauren A. Harrington, Angie Elwin, Suzi Paterson, and Neil D'Cruze, "The Viewer Doesn't Always Seem to Care—Response to Fake Animal Videos on YouTube and Implications for Social Media Self-Policing Policies," *People & Nature* 5 (2023): 103–18; 103.

73. Moloney et al., cited earlier ("Is YouTube Promoting the Exotic Pet Trade?," 13), offer some recommendations for combating these trends. These include the development of software and artificial intelligence systems for identifying the depiction of threatened exotic species in social media, as well as advertisement and information campaigns and the strengthening of social media guidelines. Of course, a large part of the problem is YouTube's economic model: to make money via ads, owners of YouTube channels need to have a minimum of a thousand subscribers and 4,000 hours of viewership during the preceding year. This puts the pressure on them to bring in more views and clicks and to care less for accuracy or obligation to the sources of the images shown.

74. Google, "YouTube Policies: Violent or Graphic Content Policies," accessed

March 26, 2022, https://support.google.com/youtube/answer/2802008?hl=en&ref_topic=9282436.

75. MrNuclearCat, "Golden Eagle Snatches Kid," YouTube, 2012, accessed July 14, 2023, https://www.youtube.com/watch?v=9feAQtgX1fw.

76. Cahill, "A YouTube Bestiary," 282.

77. Cahill, 282.

78. Jebdogrpm, "Pig Rescues Baby Goat," YouTube, September 19, 2012 (11 million views), accessed July 14, 2023, https://www.youtube.com/watch?v=g7WjrvG1GMk.

79. Amy Pilkington, "Lion, Tiger, and Bear Lives Like Brothers for Fifteen Years—Oh My," Diply, September 8, 2021, https://diply.com/106795/lion-tiger-and-bear-lived-like-brothers-for-15-years-oh-my.

80. And see Jennifer S. Holland, *Unlikely Friendships: 47 Remarkable Stories from the Animal Kingdom* (Workman Publishing, 2011).

81. Real Wild, "The World's Most Unlikely Animal Relationships: Animal Odd Couples," YouTube, December 16, 2016, https://www.youtube.com/watch?v=_BvB0182xag&t=109s, 2' 37" to 2' 50".

82. See Heather J. B. Brooks and Gordon M. Burghardt, "A Review of Interspecific Social Play among Nonhuman Animals," *Neuroscience & Biobehavioral Reviews* 151 (2023), https://doi.org/10.1016/j.neubiorev.2023.105232; Marc Bekoff, "Odd Couples: Compassion Doesn't Know Species Lines," *Psychology Today* (blog), October 28, 2012, https://www.psychologytoday.com/us/blog/animal-emotions/201210/odd-couples-compassion-doesnt-know-species-lines; Lauren J Brent, Steve W Chang, Jean-Francois Gariépy, and Michael Platt, "The Neuroethology of Friendship," *Annals of the New York Academy of Sciences* 1316.1 (2014): 1–17.

83. Nadil Silva, "Interspecies Animal 'Friendships' "( master's thesis, Swedish University of Agricultural Sciences Dept. of Animal Environment and Health, 2017).

84. Beatrice Marovich, "Peaceable Kingdoms in the Digital World," *Relegere: Studies in Religion and Reception* 7.102 (2018): 93–113; 93.

85. Lenzi et al., " 'Let Me Take a Selfie,' " 10.

86. Jonnathan Coleman, "10 Pivotal Moments in the History of the Selfie," *Medium,* April 10, 2018, https://jonnathancoleman.medium.com/10-momentous-moments-in-the-history-of-the-selfie-169d7183c21d; Anne Quito, "Front Facing Cameras Were Never Intended for Selfies," *Quartz,* October 26, 2017, https://qz.com/1104742/front-facing-cameras-were-never-intended-for-selfies.

87. Deborah Lupton, *The Internet of Animals: Human-Animal Relationships in the Digital Age* (Polity Press, 2023), 124.

88. Lupton, *Internet of Animals,* 125.

89. Manuel Linares et al., "Selfie-Related Deaths Using Web Epidemiological Intelligence Tool (2008–2021): A Cross-Sectional Study," *Journal of Travel Medicine* 29.5 (2022), https://doi.org/10.1093/jtm/taab170; Mohit J. Jain and Kinjal J. Mavani, "A Comprehensive Study of Worldwide Selfie-Related Accidental Mor-

tality," *International Journal of Injury Control and Safety Promotion*, 2017, DOI: 10.1080/17457300.2016.1278240.

90. Chantal Denise Pagel and Michael Lück, "#Wildlifeselfies: Insights into the Ocular Consumption of Marine Wildlife," *Tourism Recreation Research* (2022), published online January 28, 2022, https://doi.org/10.1080/02508281.2022.2026151.

91. Karen Strassler, *Demanding Images: Democracy, Mediation, and the Image-Event in Indonesia* (Duke University Press, 2020), 9–10. See also John W. Delicath and Kevin Michael deLuca, "Image Events, the Public Sphere, and Argumentative Practice: The Case of Radical Environmental Groups," *Argumentation* 17.3 (2003): 315–33; Kevin Michael DeLuca, "The Force of Images as Events," *JAC* 28.3/4 (2008): 663–73.

92. I'm especially indebted to Karla McManus's and Cajetan Iheka's treatments of the event and its media afterlife. See Karla McManus, "Cecil the Lion's Networked Image: The Post-Photographic Media Ecology of Environmental Concern," *Captures* 1.1 (2016), https://id.erudit.org/iderudit/1059821ar; Cajetan Iheka, *African Ecomedia: Network Forms, Planetary Politics* (Duke University Press, 2021), 156–72.

93. Iheka, *African Ecomedia*, 160–61.

94. McManus, "Cecil the Lion's Networked Image," 6, 5.

95. McManus, 9.

96. Iheka, *African Ecomedia*, 162.

97. McManus, "Cecil the Lion's Networked Image," 11.

98. Iheka, *African Ecomedia*, 169.

99. Iheka, 171, 176.

100. "Gregory Colbert's Ashes and Snow" press kit, accessed July 13, 2023, https://gregorycolbert.com/images/press/pdf/Full_press_kit.pdf, 1, 16.

101. Gregory Colbert, "In the Field," accessed July 17, 2023, https://gregorycolbert.com/in-the-field/.

102. Simon Houpt, "Canadian Artist Gregory Colbert's Photographs Are the Subject of a Giant Exhibit in Venice," *Globe & Mail*, Toronto, April 9, 2002, Arts section; other reviews cited in Wikipedia, "Ashes and Snow," accessed July, 2023, https://gregorycolbert.com/press-room/.

103. Cathleen McGuigan, "Animal Magnetism," *Smithsonian Magazine*, June, 2005, https://www.smithsonianmag.com/arts-culture/animal-magnetism-75357925/.

104. Gregory Colbert, "Ashes and Snow," accessed July 17, 2023, https://gregorycolbert.com/ashes-and-snow/.

105. Nicole Shukin, *Animal Capital: Rendering Life in Biopolitical Times* (University of Minnesota Press, 2009), 195.

106. Unless otherwise noted, all quotes are from his web site: https://gregorycolbert.com, accessed July 17, 2023.

107. McGuigan, "Animal Magnetism.".

108. Karla Kit McManus, "Questionable Moral Geographies: The Human-Animal Landscape of Gregory Colbert," *Psychogeographies*, 2011, 6.

109. Gregory Colbert, "Ashes and Snow," accessed July 17, 2023, https://gregorycolbert.com/ashes-and-snow/. The term "obligatory passage-point" is taken from actor-network theory. See Michel Callon, "Some Elements of a Sociology of Translation: Domestication of the Scallops and the Fishermen of St Brieuc Bay," *Sociological Review* 32.51 (1984): 6–233.

110. Anat Pick, "Animal Life in the Cinematic *Umwelt*," in *Animal Life and the Moving Image*, ed. Michael Lawrence and Laura McMahon, 221–37 (Palgrave/British Film Institute, 2015), 221.

111. Pick, "Animal Life," 233.

112. Concepción Cortés Zulueta, "That Seagull Stole My Camera (and My Shot)!: Overlapping Metaphorical and Physical Distances in the Human-Animal-Camera Triad," in *Critical Distance in Documentary Media*, ed. G. Cammaer, B. Fitzpatrick, and B. Lessard (Springer, 2018), 241.

113. Ralph Waldo Emerson, "Nature," in *Selected Writings of Ralph Waldo Emerson*, ed. Robert D. Habich (Broadview, 2017), 50.

114. Zulueta, "That Seagull Stole," 236.

115. e7magic, "Dramatic Tarsier Stares at You for 10 Hours," YouTube, uploaded September 21, 2012, accessed July 17, 2023, https://www.youtube.com/watch?v=xF1RhuoegMI.

116. Explore Live Nature Cams, "Animals Find the Live Cam: Memorable Moments," February 1, 2023, https://www.youtube.com/watch?v=1KBJskfAG-E; StoryTrender, "Animals Inspect Cameras," July 9, 2015, https://www.youtube.com/watch?v=BNy6CvyI3r4; Jacquelyne Germain, "This Black Bear Took Hundreds of 'Selfies' on a Wildlife Camera," *Smithsonian Magazine*, January 30, 2023, https://www.smithsonianmag.com/smart-news/this-black-bear-took-hundreds-of-selfies-on-a-wildlife-camera-180981534/; Erin McCarthy, "9 Awesome Videos of Animals Discovering Cameras," *Mental Floss*, October 1, 2014, https://www.mentalfloss.com/article/59230/9-awesome-videos-animals-discovering-cameras; all accessed July 17, 2023.

117. SuperSukutube, "Curious Chimp Checks Out Camera," uploaded February 5, 2010, https://www.youtube.com/watch?v=juWNZGSW-_M.

118. mrzhao5, "Prairie Dog Up Close!", uploaded March 13, 2013, https://www.youtube.com/watch?v=uQwE8p4Vb7A.

119. Lukas Karasek, "Seagull Stole GoPro," YouTube, uploaded June 23, 2011, https://www.youtube.com/watch?v=rIu5B3Fsstg&t=1s, 3.7 million views as of July 17, 2023.

120. Cahill, "A YouTube Bestiary," 272.

121. "Crab Makes a Movie" is no longer online. Rumble Viral, "Crab Steals a GoPro," 2020, https://www.youtube.com/watch?v=-iC2hWquUYE; Rumble Viral, "Crab Steals GoPro and You Won't Believe," 2018, https://www.youtube.com/watch?v=HNaA7Zlceos; Sea Turtle and Dick de Bruin and Paul Shultz, "Sea Turtle Finds," 2010, https://older.xray-mag.com/content/sea-turtle-finds-lost-camera; Victor Huang, "Octopus Steals My Video," 2010, with 7.5 million views, https:/

/www.youtube.com/watch?v=x5DyBkYKqnM; Newsflare, "Squirrel Steals," 2011, with 11 million views, https://www.youtube.com/watch?v=xIEWgxuaPyA; Mason Colby, "Eagle Steals Camera," 2014, https://www.youtube.com/watch?v=r5mo5o OyO1M; James Williams, "Haida Gwaii Bald Eagle," 2019, https://www.youtube .com/watch?v=EuNZjB6QGHA; Elephants Alive, "Elephants," 2020, https://www .youtube.com/watch?v=7jeSCvEyk2g; Diederick Ryan, "Crab Steals," 2013, https:// www.youtube.com/watch?v=YJLJxnDvq3M.

122. James Leo Cahill, "Animal Photogénie: The Wild Side of French Film Theory's First Wave," in *Animal Life and the Moving Image,* ed. Michael Lawrence and Laura McMahon, 23–41 (Palgrave/British Film Institute, 2015), 23.

123. Cahill, "Animal Photogénie," 26.

124. Cahill, 27.

125. Cahill, 36. Laura McMahon's *Animal Worlds: Film, Philosophy and Time* (Edinburgh University Press, 2019) makes a strong case for the possibilities of "slow," contemplative, and experimental film styles in revealing the perceptual worlds of animals.

126. On the aesthetics of flocking birds, see Susan McHugh, "Unknowing Animals: Wild Bird Films and the Limits of Knowledge," in *Animal Life and the Moving Image,* ed. Michael Lawrence and Laura McMahon, 271–87 (Palgrave, 2015).

127. Sophie Windsor Clive and Liberty Smith, "Murmuration (Official Video)," YouTube, uploaded December 2, 2011, https://www.youtube.com/watch?v=iRNqh i2ka9k.

128. Sean Cubitt, *Ecomedia* (Brill, 2005), 59–60.

129. Cahill, "Animal Photogénie," 36–37.

130. Cahill, "A YouTube Bestiary," 268.

**Chapter 7**

1. Hilma af Klint, cited in Catherine de Zegher and Hendel Teicher, ed., *3 x Abstraction: New Methods of Drawing by Hilma af Klint, Emma Kunz, Agnes Martin* (Yale University Press, 2005), 26.

2. Ernst Bloch, *The Principle of Hope,* trans. Neville Plaice, Stephen Plaice, and Paul Knight (MIT Press, 1995), 1375–76.

3. On religion, see Talal Asad, *Genealogies of Religion: Discipline and Reasons of Power in Christianity and Islam* (Johns Hopkins University Press, 1993); Carlin Barton and Daniel Boyarin, *Imagine No Religion: How Modern Abstractions Hide Ancient Realities* (Fordham University Press, 2016); Hent de Vries, ed., *Religion: Beyond a Concept* (Fordham University Press, 2009); Timothy Fitzgerald, ed., *Religion and the Secular: Historical and Colonial Formations* (Equinox, 2007); Adrian Ivakhiv, "Toward a Geography of 'Religion': On the Spatial Dimension of Significance," *Annals of the Association of American Geographers* 96.1 (2006): 169–75; Tomoko Masuzawa, *The Invention of World Religions, or, How European Universalism Was Preserved in the Language of Pluralism* (University of Chicago

Press, 2005); Brent Nongbri, *Before Religion: A History of a Modern Concept* (Yale University Press, 2013); Benson Saler, *Conceptualizing Religion: Immanent Anthropologists, Transcendent Natives, and Unbounded Categories* (Brill Academic, 1993); Francesca Schussler Fiorenza, "Religion: A Contested Site in Theology and the Study of Religion," *Harvard Theological Review* 93.1 (2000): 7–34. On spirituality, see Boaz Huss, "Spirituality: The Emergence of a New Cultural Category and Its Challenge to the Religious and the Secular," *Journal of Contemporary Religion* 29.1 (2012): 47–60; Lucy Bregman, *The Ecology of Spirituality: Meanings, Virtues, and Practices in a Post-Religious Age* (Baylor University Press, 2014).

4. One of the more compelling guides to the literature on the occult, esoteric, and paranormal is Rice University religion professor Jeffrey J. Kripal; see his *Authors of the Impossible: The Paranormal and the Sacred* (University of Chicago Press, 2011) and *Secret Body: Erotic and Esoteric Currents in the History of Religions* (University of Chicago Press, 2017). Kripal's book *How to Think Impossibly: About Souls, UFOs, Time, Belief, and Everything Else* (University of Chicago, 2024), in which he presents a full-fledged "theory of the imagination," came into my hands as this book was already undergoing its last touches. Fortunately, the book doesn't seem to deviate much from Kripal's earlier work, which I reviewed in Adrian Ivakhiv, "Reimagining Religious Imagination, in Theory and in Practice," *Journal for the Study of Religion, Nature and Culture* 15.3 (2021): 390–408. For an earlier but sociologically sophisticated examination of the paranormal, see David J. Hess, *Science in the New Age: The Paranormal, Its Defenders and Debunkers, and American Culture* (University of Wisconsin Press, 1993).

5. On secularization theory, see Steve Bruce, ed., *Religion and Modernization: Sociologists and Historians Debate the Secularization Thesis* (Oxford University Press, 2002). On the post-secular, see Hent de Vries and Lawrence E. Sullivan, eds., *Political Theologies: Public Religions in a Post-Secular World* (Fordham University Press, 2006); Philip Gorski, David Kyuman Kim, John Torpey, and Jonathan VanAntwerpen, eds., *The Post-Secular in Question: Religion in Contemporary Society* (New York University Press, 2012); Adrian Ivakhiv, "Religious (Re-)Turns in the Wake of Global Nature: Toward a Cosmopolitics," in *Nature, Science, and Religion: Intersections Shaping Society and the Environment,* ed. C. Tucker, 213–30 (SAR Press); Michael Rectenwald, Rochelle Almeida, and George Levine, eds., *Global Secularisms in a Post-Secular Age* (de Gruyter, 2015).

6. Michael Carrithers, "On Polytropy: Or the Natural Condition of Spiritual Cosmopolitanism in India: The Digambar Jain Case," *Modern Asian Studies* 34.4 (2000): 831–61; 834; and see Adrian Ivakhiv, "Image Ecologies, Spiritual Polytropy, and the Anthropocene," *The Journal for the Study of Religion, Nature and Culture* 13.4 (2019): 479–509.

7. Carrithers, "On Polytropy," 834.

8. Ivakhiv, "Image Ecologies."

9. In its original, Pascal wrote "Le silence éternel des ces espaces infinis m'effrai."

10. T. M. Luhrmann, *How God Becomes Real: Kindling the Presence of Invisible*

*Others* (Princeton University Press, 2020). I reviewed the book in Ivakhiv, "Reimagining Religious Imagination, in Theory and in Practice" (see note 4 above), and parts of the section that follows are taken from that article.

11. Luhrmann, *How God Becomes Real*, 19.

12. Luhrmann, 14.

13. Luhrmann, 10.

14. Luhrmann, *Persuasions of the Witch's Craft: Ritual Magic in Contemporary England* (Harvard University Press, 1991).

15. Jacques Rancière, *The Politics of Aesthetics: Distributions of the Sensible*, trans. Gabriel Rockhill (Continuum, 2004).

16. Luhrmann, *How God Becomes Real*, 17.

17. Luhrmann, 21.

18. Luhrmann, 184.

19. Luhrmann, 19, emphasis added.

20. Luhrmann, 20.

21. The 4E approach to cognition is well established; see Albert Newen, Leon de Bruin, and Shaun Gallagher, eds., *The Oxford Handbook of 4E Cognition* (Oxford University Press, 2018). The addition of the fifth A for "affective" has been used in reference to the work of cognitive scientists and philosophers including Andy Clark, Shaun Gallagher, Michael Wheeler, and John Protevi. The addition of "imaginal" is my own suggestion.

22. More nuanced understandings of the practical, aesthetic-sensorial, and affective work of reality-making can be found, for instance, in Giovanna Parmigiani, "Magic and Politics: Conspirituality and COVID-19," *Journal of the American Academy of Religion* 89.2 (2021): 506–29; and Sabina Magliocco, "Beyond Belief: Context, Rationality and Participatory Consciousness," *Western Folklore* 71.1 (2012): 5–24. Both see reality as a product of processes of cognitive, affective, and communal engagement aimed not so much at explanation (of what is real) but at participation. Science and ordinary common sense are ways of participating in a world; so are magic and religion. All carve up what needs to be treated as relationally real, significant, and personal (whether gods or just other humans) and what does not (and can therefore be treated as part of the "furniture" of the world). If climate, weather systems, and other earthly forces are taken to be part of the world's furniture, not something to be respectfully engaged with and obliged, then they themselves will push back. This materiality is also engaged in David Morgan's *Images at Work: The Material Culture of Enchantment* (Oxford University Press, 2018), discussed earlier in this book.

23. This of course ignores the many forms of naturalistic religiosity and modern enchantment that scholars like Bron Taylor, Michael Saler, Jane Bennett, and others have in various ways pointed to. See, e.g., Joshua Landy and Michael Saler, eds., *The Re-Enchantment of the World: Secular Magic in a Rational Age* (Stanford University Press, 2009); Bron R. Taylor, *Dark Green Religion: Nature Spirituality and the Planetary Future* (University of California Press, 2009).

24. There were certainly elements of Theosophical Society doctrine that are outdated and linked to colonial and even anti-Semitic sentiments. I have no interest in reviving Theosophy as a doctrine, so I leave these aside in my discussion.

25. On the influence of Theosophy on artistic modernism, see especially Sixten Ringbom, *The Sounding Cosmos: A Study in the Spiritualism of Kandinsky and the Genesis of Abstract Painting* (Bokförlaget Stolpe, 2022 [1970]); and Sixten Ringbom, "Art in the 'Epoch of the Great Spiritual': Occult Elements in the Early Theory of Abstract Painting," *Journal of the Warburg and Courtauld Institute* 29 (1966): 386–418. See also Zoe Alderton, "Colour, Shape, and Music: The Presence of *Thought Forms* in Abstract Art," *Literature and Aesthetics* 21.1 (2011): 236–58; Tessel M. Bauduin, "Abstract Art as 'By-Product of Astral Manifestation': The Influence of Theosophy on Modern Art in Europe," in *Handbook of the Theosophical Current,* ed. Olav Hammer and Mikael Rothstein, 429–51 (Brill, 2013); John Bramble, *Modernism and the Occult* (Palgrave Macmillan, 2015); Massimo Introvigne, "New Religious Movements and the Visual Arts," *Nova Religio* 19.4 (2016): 3–13; Jay Johnston, "Theosophical Bodies: Colour, Shape and Emotion from Modern Aesthetics to Healing Therapies," in *Handbook of New Religions and Cultural Production,* ed. C. M. Cusack and Alex Norman, 153–70 (Brill, 2012); Roger Lipsey, *An Art of Our Own: The Spiritual in Twentieth Century Art* (Shamballa, 1997); Mark C. Taylor, *Disfiguring: Art, Architecture, and Religion* (University of Chicago Press, 1992); Maurice Tuchman, "Hidden Meanings in Abstract Art," in *The Spiritual in Art: Abstract Painting 1890–1985,* ed. E. Weisberger, 17–61 (Abbeville Press, 1986). On the influence of Theosophy more generally, especially on the modern study of religion, see Jason Ananda Josephson Storm, "A Theosophical Discipline: Revisiting the History of Religious Studies," *Journal of the American Academy of Religion* 89.4 (2021): 1153–63; Olav Hammer and Mikael Rothstein, eds., *Handbook of the Theosophical Current* (Brill, 2013).

26. Artists weren't alone in their preoccupation with such heterodox pursuits. So were prominent scientists, such as astronomer Camille Flammarion, chemist William Crookes, and physicist Oliver Lodge, all of whom were interested in the occult and associated with the Society for Psychical Research. See Richard Noakes, *Physics and Psychics: The Occult and the Sciences in Modern Britain* (Cambridge University Press, 2019).

27. And working backwards, we could include William Blake, Victor Hugo, and many others. Among other sources, see Christopher H. Partridge, *The Lyre of Orpheus: Popular Music, the Sacred, and the Profane* (Oxford University Press, 2014).

28. Tessel M. Bauduin, "The Occult in the Visual Arts," in *The Occult World,* vol. 1, ed. Christopher Partridge (Routledge, 2015). I take the term "bounded self" from Charles Taylor, whose *Sources of the Self: The Making of the Modern Identity* (Harvard University Press, 1992) and his later *A Secular Age* (Harvard University Press, 2007) assess the development of modern selfhood as a restriction of the more open and "porous" sense of self that had historically preceded liberal,

secular modernity. This is critically analyzed in Adrian Ivakhiv, *Shadowing the Anthropocene* (Punctum, 2018), 164–80.

29. Annie Besant and C. W. Leadbeater, *Thought-Forms: A Record of Clairvoyant Investigation* (Theosophical Publishing House, 1905). On its publication date, sometimes incorrectly attributed to 1901, see John Crow, "Thought Forms: A Bibliographic Error," *Theosophical History* 16.3/4: 126–27. An especially satisfying edition was published in 2020 by Sacred Bones Records. Quote from 1905 edition, p. 73.

30. Besant and Leadbeater, *Thought-Forms*.

31. Besant and Leadbeater, *Thought-Forms* (Project Gutenberg edition, 2005), 9.

32. Photography was similarly used by Spiritualists to document physically present but invisible realities such as auras, ethereal energies, fluids, and other presences. Here the indexicality is taken to be more clear.

33. Vasily Kandinsky, "Interview with Karl Nierendorf" (1937), in *Kandinsky: Complete Writings on Art,* vol. 2, ed. Kenneth C. Lindsay and Peter Virgo (G. K. Hall, 1982), 807.

34. Sixten Ringbom, "Art in 'The Epoch of the Great Spiritual': Occult Elements in the Early Theory of Abstract Painting," *Journal of the Warburg and Courtauld Institutes* 29 (1966): 386–418; 407.

35. Vasily Kandinsky, *On the Spiritual in Art* (Solomon R. Guggenheim Foundation, 1946).

36. Ringbom, "Art in "The Epoch of the Great Spiritual," 408, italics in original.

37. Ringbom, "Occult Elements in Abstract Painting," 391–92.

38. Ringbom, 392.

39. On popular depth psychology, see, e.g., Joseph Campbell, *The Hero with a Thousand Faces,* 3rd ed. (New World Library, 2008); Clarissa Pinkola Estes, *Women Who Run with the Wolves* (Ballantine, 1992); Thomas Moore, *The Re-enchantment of Everyday Life* (Harper Perennial, 1997). On the Eranos conferences, see Steven M. Wasserstrom, *Religion After Religion: Gershom Scholem, Mircea Eliade, and Henry Corbin at Eranos* (Princeton University Press, 1999).

40. Henry Corbin, "Towards a Chart of the Imaginal," Prelude to the second edition of *Corps Spiritual et Terre Célest de l'Iran Mazdén à l'Iran Si'ite,* in *Spiritual Body and Celestial Earth: From Mazdean Iran to Shi'ite Iran,* 5th printing (Princeton University Press, 1989), xi.

41. See, e.g., Paulos Mar Gregorios, ed., *Neoplatonism and Indian Philosophy* (State University of New York Press, 2001).

42. Ringbom, *The Sounding Cosmos,* 59.

43. Laura Marks, "Real Images Flow: Mulla Sadra Meets Film-Philosophy," *Film-Philosophy* 20 (2016): 24–46; 25.

44. Marks, "Real Images," 25, 28.

45. Marks, 36. The last phrase is a quote from J. W. Morris, *The Wisdom of the Throne: An Introduction to the Philosophy of Mulla Sadra* (Princeton University Press, 1981), 138.

46. Corbin, "Towards a Chart of the Imaginal," ix–x.

47. Julia Voss, *Hilma af Klint: A Biography* (University of Chicago Press, 2022), 135; and see 233ff.

48. Voss, *Hilma af Klint.*

49. Jadranka Ryle, "Reinventing the Yggdrasil: Hilma af Klint and Political Aesthetics," *Nordic Journal of Art and Research* 7.1 (2018), http://dx.doi.org/10.7577/information.v7i1.2629.

50. Voss, *Hilma af Klint,* 143.

51. Voss, "Five Things to Know About Hilma af Klint," in *Hilma af Klint: Visionary,* ed. Kurt Almqvist and Louise Belfrage (Bökforlaget Stolpe, 2020), 36.

52. Voss, *Hilma af Klint,* 93.

53. Voss, 227.

54. Daniel Birnbaum, "Universal Pictures: The Art of Hilma af Klint," *Artforum* 51.5 (January, 2013), https://www.artforum.com/print/201301/universal-pictures-the-art-of-hilma-af-klint-38217; Briony Fer, "A Vegetal Universe," in *Hilma af Klint and Piet Mondrian: Forms of Life,* ed. Nabila Abdel Nabi, Briony Fer, and Laura Stamps (Tate, 2023), 11, 16.

55. Simon Grant, "Hilma af Klint and The Five," in Nabila et al. *Hilma af Klint and Piet Mondrian,* 104.

56. Hilma af Klint, notebook, HAK 555, 23, 7.5, 1906, cited in Iris Müller-Westermann, "Hilma af Klint—Artist, Researcher, Medium," in *Hilma af Klint: Artist, Researcher, Medium,* ed. Iris Müller-Westermann and Milena Høgsberg (Moderna Museet, 2020), 29.

57. Cited in Müller-Westermann and Høgsberg, *Hilma af Klint,* "Hilma," 26.

58. Cited in Müller-Westermann and Høgsberg 29.

59. Emily Virginia Leon, whose master's thesis provides a "big data" digital analysis of documents produced by and about af Klint, argues that Steiner's role in af Klint's art and thinking has been exaggerated, and that others (such as Goethe, Blavatsky, and Darwin) were more influential on her all along. See Emily Virginia Leon, "Analyzing the Crisis of Hilma af Klint: The Digital and Analog Analysis of Spirituality, Abstraction, and Art" (master's thesis, Department of Art, Art History, and Visual Studies, Duke University, 2018). Whether Steiner actually saw any of af Klint's art in 1908 or 1910, as has been widely surmised, has not been demonstrated; see Hedvig Martin, "Hilma af Klint and Rudolf Steiner: An Ambiguous Encounter," in Nabila et al., *Hilma af Klint and Piet Mondrian,* 100–103; and Voss, *Hilma af Klint.*

60. Iris Müller-Westermann, "Introduction," in *Notes and Methods,* ed. Christine Burgin (University of Chicago Press, 2018), 8, italics added.

61. Julia Voss, "Five Things to Know About Hilma af Klint," in *Hilma af Klint: Visionary,* ed. Kurt Almqvist and Louise Belfrage (Bökforlaget Stolpe, 2020), 36.

62. Tessel M. Bauduin, "Seeing and Depicting the Invisible: On Hilma af Klint's Modern Art and Spiritual Paintings" (original: "Að sjá og sýna hið ósýnilega. Um nútímalist og andleg verk Hilmu af Klint," *Ritið* (January 2017): 187–224, trans.

Eva Dagbjört Óladóttir, https://pure.uva.nl/ws/files/15573067/Tessel_M._Bauduin_Seeing_and_Depicting_the_Invisible_untranslated_original_draft_2017.pdf.

63. Susan Tallman, "Painting the Beyond," *New York Review of Books,* April 4, 2019.

64. Tallman, "Painting the Beyond," emphasis added.

65. Voss, *Hilma af Klint,* 188.

66. Voss, 240.

67. Voss, 284–85.

68. Rudolf Steiner, *Knowledge of the Higher Worlds and Its Attainment,* trans. George Metaxa (SteinerBooks, 1947/orig. 1904); David Adams, "The Esoteric Botany of Hilma af Klint," accessed March 8, 2024, https://static1.squarespace.com/static/5ced44211046fc000115a804/t/5e8cb3298e92871e73abf17f/1586279211614/EsotericBotany+of+HilmaafKlint-DavidAdams.pdf.

69. Bauduin, "Seeing and Depicting the Invisible," 18–19.

70. Sixten Ringbom, "Transcending the Visible: The Generation of the Abstract Pioneers," in *The Spiritual in Art: Abstract Painting 1890–1985,* ed. Maurice Tuchman et al., 131–53 (Abbeville Press/Los Angeles County Museum of Art, 1985), 143.

71. Jadranka Ryle, "Feminine Androgyny and Diagrammatic Abstraction: Science, Myth and Gender in Hilma af Klint's Paintings," in *The Idea of North: Myth-Making and Identities,* ed. Frances Fowle and Marja Lahelma, 70–87 (The Birch and the Star, 2019), 85.

72. Janice McNab, "Review Essay: Hilma af Klint and the Need for Historical Revision," *Religious Studies Review* 47.1 (2021): 35–40; 37–38.

73. In an M.A. thesis called "Of Light and Empty Space: Hilma af Klint's 'Flowers, Mosses, and Lichens'" (Rice University, 2022), Zachary Schwarze proposes the idea of an "inspired image," which he defines as "images created in the context of visionary aspiration or experience" (117), which are "both a representation of knowledge and mode of knowledge production" (127). Exemplars of this kind of imagery, in Schwarze's account, include medieval mystic-artists Hildegard of Bingen and John of Morigny alongside modern occult artists like af Klint, Georgiana Houghton, Lady Frieda Harris, and Austin Osman Spare.

74. Daniel Birnbaum, "Universal Pictures: The Art of Hilma af Klint," *Artforum* 51.5 (January 2013), https://www.artforum.com/print/201301/universal-pictures-the-art-of-hilma-af-klint-38217.

75. See, e.g., Lisa Slominski, "Spiritual Art Is Back, Again," *Hyperallergic,* February 26, 2023, https://hyperallergic.com/803561/spiritual-art-is-back-again/; J. J. Charlesworth, "The Return of Magic in Art," *ArtReview,* May 30, 2022, https://artreview.com/the-return-of-magic-in-art/; Museum of Contemporary Art Tucson, "Blessed Be: Mysticism, Spirituality, and the Occult in Contemporary Art," accessed April 23, 2024, https://moca-tucson.org/exhibition/blessed-be-mysticism-spirituality-and-the-occult-in-contemporary-art/.

76. See, e.g., Everton de Oliveira Maraldi, Wellington Zangari, Fatima Regina Machado, and Stanley Krippner, "Anomalous Mental and Physical Phenomena

of Brazilian Mediums: A Review of the Scientific Literature," in *Talking with the Spirits: Ethnographies from Between the Worlds*, ed. J. Hunter and D. Luke, 259–301 (Daily Grail, 2014).

77. PierLuigi Zoccatelli, "'All the Heavens in Your Hands': Oberto Airaudi and the Art of Damanhur," *Nova Religio* 19.4 (2016): 145–62; 147.

78. http://damanhur.org, accessed April 13, 2024.

79. For studies of these, see Francesca Fois, "Enacting Experimental Alternative Spaces," *Antipode* 51.1 (2019): 107–28; Georgia Gaia, "Damanhur: The Ecology of Spirit" (master's thesis in cultural and social anthropology, University of Amsterdam, 2014); Eva Meijerink, "The Game of Life: The Significance of Play in the Commune of Damanhur," *Journal of Contemporary Religion* 18.2 (2003): 155–68; Jeff Merrifield, *Damanhur: The Story of the Extraordinary Italian Artistic and Spiritual Community* (Hanford Mead, 2006); Stefania Palmisano and Nicola Pannofino, eds., *Damanhur: An Esoteric Community Open to the World* (Palgrave Macmillan, 2023); Kara M. Salter, "Structure and Anti-Structure: Communitas in Damanhur, Federation of Communities" (Ph.D. thesis in anthropology, University of Western Australia, 2015).

80. See Mario Cardano and Nicola Pannofino, "Taking Leave of Damanhur: Deconversion from a Magico-Esoteric Community," *Social Compass* 65.3 (2018): 433–50.

81. Zoccatelli, "'All the Heavens in Your Hands,'" 154.

82. Esperide Ananas, "A Sign in Time," *Quadri Selfici di Oberto Airaudi*, ed. Eraldo Tempia Valenta (Parsifal) (Il Mettifoglio Torino, 2004), v.

83. Richard Grossinger, "Visiting the Cosmic Machine on Earth: Pages from the Travel Journal of Richard Grossinger," in *The Traveler's Guide to Damanhur: The Amazing Norther Italian Eco-Society*, ed. Esperide Ananas and Stambcco Pesco (North Atlantic Books, 2009), 82.

84. Grossinger, "Visiting," 90.

85. Grossinger, 82–83.

86. Grossinger, 87.

87. Grossinger, 88.

88. See "A Fantastic Story and a Beautiful Comic: Q & Q with Massimo Introvigne on Sharing Damanhur's Spiritual Vision," in Ananas and Pesco, *The Traveler's Guide to Damanhur*, 187–93; and previously mentioned writing by Eva Meijerink, Kara Salter, and Francesca Fois.

89. The literature on land art, environmental art, and eco-art is voluminous. See, for instance, Amanda Boetzkes, *The Ethics of Earth Art* (University of Minnesota Press, 2010); Nicholas Bourriaud, *Planet B: Climate Change and the New Sublime* (Radicants, 2022); Heather Davis and Etienne Turpin, *Art in the Anthropocene: Encounters Among Aesthetics, Politics, Environments and Epistemologies* (Open Humanities Press, 2015); Jeffrey Kastner and Brian Wallis, *Land and Environmental Art* (Phaidon, 1998); Alan Sonfist, ed., *Art in the Land: A Critical Anthology of Environmental Art* (Plume, 1983); Nathaniel Stern, *Ecological Aesthetics: Artful Tactics for Humans, Nature, and Politics* (Dartmouth College Press, 2018);

Linda Weintraub, *To Life! Eco-Art in Pursuit of a Sustainable Planet* (University of California Press, 2013).

90. For instance, on Indigenous art, see Kate Morris, *Shifting Grounds: Landscape in Contemporary Native American Art* (University of Washington Press, 2019); Yale University Art Gallery, *Place, Nations, Generations, Beings: 200 Years of Indigenous North American Art* (Yale University Art Gallery, 2019); Jaune Quick-to-See Smith, ed., *The Land Carries Our Ancestors: Contemporary Art by Native Americans* (Yale University Press/National Gallery of Art, 2023). On African-American art, see Eddie Chambers, *World Is Africa: Writings on Diaspora Art* (Bloomsbury Visual Arts, 2021); H. Ike Okafor-Newsum, ed., *Soulstirrers: Black Art and the Neo-Ancestral Impulse* (University Press of Mississippi, 2016); Richard J. Powell, *Black Art: A Cultural History* (Thames & Hudson, 2021); Alvia J. Wardlaw, *Black Art, Ancestral Legacy: The African Impulse in African-American Art* (Dallas Museum of Art, 1990).

91. Priya Bandodkar, "Activating Indofuturism: Applying a Lens Adapted from Postcolonial Futurisms" (master's thesis in design in digital futures, OCAD University, 2021); Zulfikar Ali Bhutto, "Searching for the Next Intifada: Exercises in Queer Muslim Futurism," *Meridians* 20.2 (2021): 443–65; Bodhisattva Chattopadhyay, "Manifestos of Futurisms," CoFUTURES, July 2021, https://www.researchgate.net/publication/356192403_Manifestos_of_Futurisms; Grace L. Dillon, "Imagining Indigenous Futurisms," in *Walking the Clouds: An Anthology of Indigenous Science Fiction*, ed. G. Dillon (University of Arizona Press, 2012); Natasha A. Kelly, ed., *The Comet—Afrofuturism 2.0* (Orlanda Verlag, 2020); Anders Kreuger, "Ethno-Futurism: Leaning on the Past, Working for the Future," *Afterall* 43 (2017): 116–33; Henrietta Lidchi and Suzanne Newman Fricke, eds., "Future History: Indigenous Futurisms in North American Visual Arts," Special Issue of *World Art* 9.2 (2019); Audra Mitchell and Aadita Chaudhury, "Worlding Beyond 'the' 'End' of 'the World': White Apocalyptic Visions and BIPOC Futurisms," *International Relations* 34.3 (2020): 309–32; Alexandra Munoz, "Chicanafuturist Poetics and a Mestiza Future" (M.A. thesis, California State University San Marcos, Literature and Writing Studies, 2022); Lindsay Nixon, "Visual Cultures of Indigenous Futurism," in *Otherwise Worlds: Against Settler Colonialism and Anti-Blackness*, ed. Tiffany Lethabo King, Jenell Navarro, and Andrea Smith (Duke University Press, 2020); Rasheedah Phillips, ed., *Black Quantum Futurism: Theory & Practice* (AfroFuturist Affair, 2015); Bonaventure Soh Bejeng, Ndikung, Olga Schubert, and Eric Otieno Sumba, eds., *O Qilombismo Reader* (Haus der Kulturen der Welt, 2023); Claire Elise Thompson, "From Afrofuturism to Ecotopia: A Climate-Fiction Glossary," *Grist*, September 14, 2021, https://grist.org/fix/climate-fiction/afrofuturism-to-ecotopia-climate-fiction-glossary/.

92. T. J. Demos, *Radical Futurisms: Ecologies of Collapse, Chronopolitics, and Justice-to-Come* (Sternberg Press, 2023).

93. Cited in Frédéric Neyrat, "The Black Angel of History: Afrofuturism's Cosmic Techniques," trans. Daniel Ross, *Angelaki* 25.4 (2020): 120–134; 128.

94. Reynaldo Anderson, "Afrofuturism 2.0 and the Black Speculative Arts Movement: Notes on a Manifesto," *Obsidian* 42.1/2 (2016): 228–236; 230, 228–29.

95. Charles P. "Chip" Linscott, "The Ghosts of John Akomfrah," *Liquid Blackness* 1.4 (2015): 14–27; 24.

96. See Henriette Gunkel and kara lynch, *We Travel the Space Ways: Black Imaginations, Fragments, and Diffractions* (Transcript Verlag, 2019); Sofia Samatar, "Toward a Planetary History of Afrofuturism," *Research in African Literatures* 48.4 (2017): 175–91; and the other sources cited in the references for this section.

97. Paul Gilroy, *The Black Atlantic: Modernity and Double Consciousness* (Verso, 1993).

98. See Melville Herskovits, *The New World Negro: Selected Papers in AfroAmerican Studies* (Minerva Press, 1966); Addison Gayle Jr., ed., *The Black Aesthetic* (Doubleday, 1971); Zora Neale Hurston, *Tell My Horse: Voodoo and Life in Haiti and Jamaica* (Harper and Row, 1990/1966); Alfred Metraux, *Voodoo in Haiti* (Schocken, 1972); Rowland Abiodun, "Understanding Yoruba Art and Aesthetics: The Concept of Ase," *African Arts* 27.3 (1994): 68–102; Margarite Fernandez Olmos and Lizabeth Paravisini-Gebert, eds., *Sacred Possessions: Vodou, Santeria, Obeah, and the Caribbean* (Rutgers University Press, 1997); Robert Farris Thompson, *Flash of the Spirit* (Vintage Books, 1974); Marta Moreno Vega, "The Ancestral Sacred Creative Impulse of Africa and the African Diaspora: Ase, the Nexus of the Black Global Aesthetic," *Lenox Avenue: A Journal of Interarts Inquiry* 5 (1999): 45–57. On the Africanist aesthetics of Hip Hop culture, see Imani Kai Johnson, *Dark Matter in Breaking Cyphers: The Life of Africanist Aesthetics in Global Hip Hop* (Oxford University Press, 2023); in Black comics, see Paul Humphrey, "Myth, Afrodiasporic Spirituality, and the Oceanic Archive in Independent Comics," in *Myth and Environmentalism: Arts of Resilience for a Damaged Planet*, ed. Esther Sánchez-Pardo and María Porras Sánchez, 127–50 (Routledge, 2023).

99. The story is recounted in interviews documented in John F. Szwed's *Space Is the Place: The Lives and Times of Sun Ra* (Pantheon, 1997). See also Paul Youngquist, *A Pure Solar World: Sun Ra and the Birth of Afrofuturism* (University of Texas Press, 2016).

100. William Ramsey, *Let All the Children Boogie: Occult Presences Through the Musical Performances of Sun Ra, David Bowie, Magma, and Janelle Monáe* (master's thesis, Department of Religious Studies, University of Colorado, 2014).

101. Darius James, "'Uncle Snookum's Astral Odditorium & Psychic Haberdashery': Sun Ra & the Occult," in *Animism*, vol. 1, ed. Anselm Franke, 172–77 (Sternberg Press, 2010), 172.

102. Jason C. Bivins, *Spirits Rejoice! Jazz and American Religion* (Oxford University Press, 2013), 94.

103. Youngquist, *A Pure Solar World*, 182, 183, 186.

104. William Sites, "'We Travel the Spaceways': Urban Utopianism and the Imagined Spaces of Black Experimental Music," *Urban Geography* 33.4 (2012): 566–92; 584.

105. Graham Lock, *Blutopia: Visions of the Future and Revisions of the Past in the Work of Sun Ra, Duke Ellington, and Anthony Braxton* (Duke University Press, 1999), 14. And see John Corbett, Anthony Elms, and Terri Kapsalis, eds., *Pathways to Unknown Worlds: Sun Ra, El Saturn, and Chicago's Afro-Futurist Underground 1954–68* (Whitewalls, 2006); Daniel Kreiss, "Performing the Past to Claim the Future: Sun Ra and the Afro-Future Underground, 1954–1968," *African American Review* 45.1/2 (2012): 197–203; Erik Steinskog, *Afrofuturism and Black Sound Studies: Culture, Technology, and Things to Come* (Palgrave Macmillan, 2018).

106. Szwed, *Space Is the Place.*

107. Daniel Fischlin, Ajay Heble, and George Lipsitz, *The Fierce Urgency of Now: Improvisation, Rights, and the Ethics of Cocreation* (Duke University Press, 2013), 36–37.

108. Quoted in Lock, *Blutopia*, 173.

109. Quoted in Lock, 174. And see Gerald J. Frederic, "The African Aesthetic in World Creativity: Anthony Braxton's Philosophy of Vibrational Affinity Dynamics," *Journal of Black Studies* 38.2 (2007): 130–41.

110. Chadwick Jenkins, "The Sounds of Now, Part Three: Anthony Braxton and the Ethics of Improvisation," *Pop Matters*, January 22, 2007, https://www.popmatters.com/the-sounds-of-now-part-three-anthony-braxton-and-the-ethics-of-improvisatio-2495789808.html.

111. See Fischlin et al., *The Fierce Urgency of Now.* This is not to suggest that all theorists of jazz agree that improvisation is essential to it; for instance, André Hodeir, in *Jazz: Its Evolution and Essence,* trans. David Noakes (Grover Press, 1956), argues that since there is jazz that lacks improvisation, it is not essential to the musical form.

112. See Mark Abel, *Groove: An Aesthetic of Measured Time* (Brill, 2014); Tony Bolden, "Groove Theory: A Vamp on the Epistemology of Funk," *American Studies* 52.4 (2013): 9–34; Kodwo Eshun, *More Brilliant Than the Sun: Adventures in Sonic Fiction* (Quartet Books, 1998); Charles Keil and Steven Feld, *Music Grooves* (University of Chicago Press, 1994); Tiger C. Roholt, *Groove: A Phenomenology of Rhythmic Nuance* (Bloomsbury, 2014); Alexander G. Weheliye, *Phonographies: Grooves in Sonic Afro-Modernity* (Duke University Press, 2005).

113. Guerino B. Mazzola and Paul B. Cherlin (in collaboration with Mathias Rissi and Nathan Kennedy), *Flow, Gestures, and Spaces in Free Jazz: Towards a Theory of Collaboration* (Springer, 2009), 21–22, emphasis added.

114. Ernst Bloch, *The Principle of Hope,* trans. by Neville Plaice, Stephen Plaice, and Paul Knight (MIT Press, 1986, orig. 1954–1959), 1375–76.

115. Bloch, *The Principle of Hope,* vol. 3, 1063.

116. Bloch, 1071.

117. Bloch, 1063.

118. Bloch, 1070.

119. "Anticipation": Ivan Boldyrev, *Erns Bloch and His Contemporaries: Locating Utopian Messianism* (Bloomsbury Academic, 2014), 23. "Utopian excess": Ben

Anderson, "A Principle of Hope: Recorded Music, Listening Practices and the Immanence of Utopia," *Geografiska Annaler: Series B, Human Geography* 82.3/4 (2002): 211–27. I take the term "immanent utopianism" from Anderson.

120. Beth M. Snyder, "The Not-Yet-Conscious: Music as a Way of Knowing," *Journal of the American Musicological Society* 70.3 (2017): 825–29; 829.

121. Alfred North Whitehead, *Symbolism, Its Meaning and Effect* (Macmillan, 1927). On the continuing relevance of Whitehead's book, see Roland Faber, Jeffrey A. Bell, and Joseph Petek, eds., *Rethinking Whitehead's* Symbolism: Thought, Language, Culture (Edinburgh University Press, 2017).

122. Whitehead, *Symbolism*, 13–14.

123. Whitehead, 23, 25.

124. Whitehead, 46.

125. Whitehead, 42.

126. Whitehead, 45.

127. Whitehead, 47.

128. F. David Martin, *Art and the Religious Experience: The "Language" of the Sacred* (Bucknell University Press, 1972), 147.

129. Martin, *Art and the Religious*, 94, emphasis added.

130. Richard Elfyn Jones, "AN Whitehead and Music: Real Time," *The Musical Times* 141.1873 (2000): 47–52; 49.

131. That said, Whitehead's influence on improvisational forms of poetry and abstract painting are described in Daniel Belgrad's *The Culture of Spontaneity: Improvisation and the Arts in Postwar America* (University of Chicago Press, 1998). And for a Blochian approach to Sun Ra, see William Sites, "'We Travel the Spaceways': Urban Utopianism and the Imagined Spaces of Black Experimental Music," *Urban Geography* 33.4 (2012): 566–92.

132. Reynaldo Anderson and Charles E. Jones, *Afrofuturism 2.0: The Rise of Astro-Blackness* (Lexington, 2016); Reynaldo Anderson and Clinton R. Fluker, eds., *The Black Speculative Arts Movement: Black Futurity, Art+Design* (Lexington, 2019); George Lewis, *A Power Stronger Than Itself: The AACM and American Experimental Music* (University of Chicago Press, 2008); William Sites, *Sun Ra's Chicago: Afrofuturism and the City* (University of Chicago Press, 2020); Ytasha Womack, *Afrofuturism: The World of Black Sci-Fi and Fantasy Culture* (Chicago Review Press, 2013); Alex Zamalin, *Black Utopia: The History of an Idea from Black Nationalism to Afrofuturism* (Columbia University Press, 2019); and previously cited work by Corbett et al., *Pathways to Unknown Worlds*; Eshun, *More Brilliant Than the Sun*; Lock, *Blutopia*; Sites, "'We Travel the Spaceways'"; Szwed, *Space Is the Place*; Youngquist, *A Pure Solar World* (see notes 103–105, 112).

133. Jason Bivins, *Spirits Rejoice! Jazz and American Religion* (Oxford University Press, 2014), 207; these quotes are primarily found on pp. 206–10, but characterize much of the flavor of Bivins's book-length survey.

134. Bivins, *Spirits Rejoice!*, 218.

135. James J. Gibson, *The Ecological Approach to Visual Perception* (Houghton

Mifflin, 1979); Adrian Ivakhiv, "Toward a Multicultural Ecology," *Organization & Environment* 15.4 (2002): 389–409.

136. Peter T. Struck, *Divination and Human Nature: A Cognitive History of Intuition in Classical Antiquity* (Princeton University Press, 2016), 3–4. And see André Caquot and Marcel Leibovici, *La Divination*, 2 vols. (Paris Presses Universitaires de France, 1968); Philip M. Peek, ed., *African Divination Systems* (Indiana University Press, 1991).

137. Struck, *Divination and Human Nature*, 4.

138. Historians of esoteric spiritual traditions generally agree on this characterization of esotericism; see Antoine Faivre, *Access to Western Esotericism* (State University of New York Press, 1994); Nicholas Goodrick-Clarke, *The Western Esoteric Traditions: A Historical Introduction* (Oxford University Press, 2008); Wouter J. Hanegraaff, *Western Esotericism: A Guide for the Perplexed* (Bloomsbury, 2013). On the parallels as well as the global connections between western esotericism and related non-western systems of thought and practice, see Julian Strube, "Religious Comparativism, Esotericism, and the Global Occult: A Methodological Outline," the introduction to a special issue of the *Interdisciplinary Journal for Religion and Transformation in Contemporary Society*, advance article, published August 1, 2023, 1–24.

139. Diana Espirito Santo, "Fluid Divination: Movement, Chaos, and the Generation of 'Noise' in Afro-Cuban Spiritist Oracular Production," *Anthropology of Consciousness* 24.1 (2013): 32–56; 35.

140. On "magic" and its relationship to science, modernity, and religion, see Matteo Benussi, "Magic," *The Open Encyclopedia of Anthropology*, ed. Felix Stein, 2023 (2019), http://doi.org/10.29164/19magic; Edward Bever and Randall Styers, eds., *Magic in the Modern World: Strategies of Repression and Legitimization* (Pennsylvania State University Press, 2017); Brian P. Copenhaver, *Magic in Western Culture: From Antiquity to the Enlightenment* (Cambridge University Press, 2015); Christopher I. Lehrich, *The Occult Mind: Magic in Theory and Practice* (Cornell University Press, 2007); Randall Styers, *Making Magic: Religion, Magic, and Science in the Modern World* (Oxford University Press, 2004); Kocku von Stuckrad, "Magic," in *The Wiley Blackwell Companion to the Study of Religion*, 2nd ed., ed. Robert A. Segal and Nickolas P. Roubekas (Blackwell, 2021), https://doi.org/10.1002/9781119092797.ch21.

141. Brian Vickers, "On the Function of Analogy in the Occult," in *Hermeticism and the Renaissance*, ed. Ingrid Merkel and Allan G. Debus, 265–92 (London: Associated University Presses, 1982), 272, 276.

142. Michael van Elk and André Aleman, "Brain Mechanisms in Religion and Spirituality: An Integrative Predictive Processing Framework," *Neuroscience and Biobehavioral Reviews* 73 (2017): 359–78; 361. The predictive processing model of mind has its critics. For a review of its status, see Kevin S. Walsh, David P. McGovern, Andy Clark, and Redmond G. O'Connell, "Evaluating the Neurophysiological Evidence for Predictive Processing as a Model of Perception," *Annals of the New York Academy of Sciences* 1464.1 (2020): 242–68.

143. James G. Frazer, *The Golden Bough: A Study in Comparative Religion*, 2 vols. (Macmillan, 1890), 19b.

144. Carol Nemeroff and Paul Rozin, "The Makings of the Magical Mind: The Nature and Function of Sympathetic Magical Thinking," in *Imagining the Impossible*, ed. K. S. Rosengren, C. N. Johnson, P. L. Harris, C. N. Johnson, and P. L. Harris, 1–34 (Cambridge University Press, 2000).

145. Ze Hong, "A Cognitive Account of Manipulative Sympathetic Magic," *Religion, Brain and Behavior* (2022): 3, https://doi.org/10.1080/2153599X.2021.2006294.

146. Martin Holbraad, *Truth in Motion: The Recursive Anthropology of Cuban Divination* (University of Chicago Press, 2012), xxiii.

147. Holbraad, *Truth in Motion*, xviii.

148. Holbraad, xxiii.

149. On some uses of the Tarot and its history, see Ronald Decker and Michael Dummett, *A History of the Occult Tarot* (Gerald Duckworth & Co., 2013); Helen Farley, *A Cultural History of Tarot* (Bloomsbury Academic, 2019); Danny L. Jorgensen, *The Esoteric Scene, Cultic Milieu, and Occult Tarot* (Garland, 1992).

150. I capitalize "Hip Hop" here to indicate the more specific culture that has grown out of the musical genre of "hip-hop." See Danielle Hyams, "The Three Natures of Hip Hop," EpicenterNYC, June 6, 2023, https://epicenter-nyc.com/the-3-natures-of-hip-hop/.

151. There is a connection to be made as well to the arts of "not knowing," a notion some artists as well as scholars have found productive. See Elizabeth Fisher and Rebecca Fortnum, eds., *On Not Knowing: How Artists Think* (Black Dog, 2013); Maria Korolkova and Simon Bowes, "Mistake as Method: Towards an Epistemology of Errors in Creative Practice and Research," *NECSUS: European Journal of Media Studies* 9.2 (2010): 139–57.

152. Joshua Ramey, *Politics of Divination: Neoliberal Endgame and the Religion of Contingency* (Rowman & Littlefield, 2016), 5, 158.

153. Ramey, *Politics of Divination*, 6.

154. Ramey, 157.

155. T. J. Demos, *Beyond the World's End: Arts of Living at the Crossing* (Duke University Press, 2020), 9–10.

156. Kyle Powys Whyte, "Our Ancestors' Dystopia Now: Indigenous Conservation and the Anthropocene," in *Routledge Companion to the Environmental Humanities*, ed. Ursula Heise, Jon Christensen, and Michelle Niemann (Routledge, 2017). And see Deborah Danowski and Eduardo Viveiros de Castro, *The Ends of the World*, trans. Rodrigo Nunes (Polity, 2017); Heather Davis and Zoe Todd, "On the Importance of a Date, or Decolonizing the Anthropocene," *ACME: International E-Journal for Critical Geographies* 16.4 (2017): 761–80; Anselm Franke, Elisa Giuliano, Denise Ryner, Claire Tancons, and Zairong Xiang, eds., *Ceremony (Burial of an Undead World)* (Spector Books, 2022).

157. See Katherine McKittrick, ed., *Sylvia Wynter: On Being Human as Praxis* (Duke University Press, 2015).

158. See, for instance, Miguel Astor-Aguilera and Graham Harvey, eds., *Rethinking Relations and Animism: Personhood and Materiality* (Routledge, 2018); Yuria Celidwen and Dacher Keltner, "Kin Relationality and Ecological Belonging: A Cultural Psychology of Indigenous Transcendence," *Frontiers in Psychology*, October 20, 2023, https://doi.org/10.3389/fpsyg.2023.994508; Enrique Salmon, "Kincentric Ecology: Indigenous Perceptions of the Human-Nature Relationship," *Ecological Applications* 10.5 (2000): 1327–32; Lauren Tynan, "What Is Relationality? Indigenous Knowledges, Practices and Responsibilities with Kin," *Cultural Geographies* 28.4 (2021): 597–610; Matt Wildcat and Daniel Voth, "Indigenous Relationality: Definitions and Methods," *AlterNative* 19.2 (2023), https://doi.org/10.1177/11771801231168380.

159. Leanne Betasamosake Simpson, "Land as Pedagogy: Nishnaabeg Intelligence and Rebellious Transformation," *Decolonization: Indigeneity, Education & Society* 3.3 (2014): 1–25; 9–10.

160. Simpson, "Land as Pedagogy," 10, 11.

161. See Brian Burkhart, *Indigenous Philosophy Through the Land: A Trickster Methodology for Decolonizing Environmental Ethics and Indigenous Futures* (Michigan State University Press, 2019); George J. Sefa Dei, Wambui Karanja, and Grace Erger, "Land as Indigenous Epistemology," in *Elders' Cultural Knowledges and the Question of Black/ African Indigeneity in Education*, 113–26, Critical Studies of Education, vol 16. (Springer, 2022); Robin Wall Kimmerer, *Braiding Sweetgrass: Indigenous Wisdom, Scientific Knowledge, and the Teaching of Plants* (Milkweed, 2020).

162. See Damon B. Akins and William J. Bauer, Jr., *We Are the Land: A History of Native California* (University of California Press, 2022); Mandy Bayha, "We Are the Land and the Land Is Us: Indigenous Women Accompany NASA Campaign Studying Arctic Climate Change," *ASK NASA Climate*, November 6, 2018, https://climate.nasa.gov/explore/ask-nasa-climate/2824/we-are-the-land-and-the-land-is-us-indigenous-women-accompany-nasa-campaign-studying-arctic-climate-c/; Dian Million, "'We Are the Land, and the Land Is Us': Indigenous Land, Lives, and Embodied Ecologies in the Twenty-First Century," in *Racial Ecologies*, ed. Leilani Nishime and Kim D. Hester Williams, 19–33 (University of Washington Press, 2018).

163. See Manvir Singh, "It's Time to Rethink the Idea of the 'Indigenous,'" *The New Yorker*, February 20, 2023, https://www.newyorker.com/magazine/2023/02/27/its-time-to-rethink-the-idea-of-the-indigenous.

164. Sefa Dei et al., "Land as Indigenous Epistemology," in *Elders' Cultural Knowledges*, 113.

165. Robin Wall Kimmerer, "The Covenant of Reciprocity," in *The Wiley Blackwell Companion to Religion and Ecology*, ed. John Hart (John Wiley & Sons, 2017), 370.

166. Celidwen and Keltner, "Kin Relationality and Ecological Belonging, 2–3.

167. Donna Haraway's intervention into discussions of kinship and relational-

ity has been influential; see Donna J. Haraway, *Staying with the Trouble: Making Kin in the Chthulucene* (Duke University Press, 2016).

168. Achille Mbembe, *Brutalism,* trans. by Steven Corcoran (Duke University Press, 2024), 119–20.

169. The term "more-than-human" is used by some to refer to nonhumans of any kind, but this usage begs too many questions. Why is *more* assumed to be better than *less*? More of what: more confused, more determined, more voracious? On this, see my blog post "More-or-less-(than)-human," *Immanence,* October 19, 2022, https://blog.uvm.edu/aivakhiv/2022/10/19/more-or-less-than-human.

170. Dilip M. Menon, "Oceanic Histories: From the Terrestrial to the Maritime," in *Ocean as Method: Thinking with the Maritime,* ed. Dilip M. Menon, Nishat Zaidi, Simi Malhotra, and Saarah Jappie (Routledge, 2022), 2.

171. Elizabeth M. Deloughrey, *Allegories of the Anthropocene* (Duke University Press, 2019), 140. I am drawing in this section upon insights from recent writing in the "blue humanities," especially those with a decolonial emphasis. See Sidney I. Dobrin, *Blue Ecocriticism and the Oceanic Imperative* (Taylor & Francis, 2021); Stefanie Hessler, *Tidalectics: Imagining an Oceanic Worldview Through Art and Science* (MIT Press, 2018); Steve Mentz, *An Introduction to the Blue Humanities* (Routledge, 2024); Dilip Menon et al., *Ocean as Method*; Serpil Oppermann, *Blue Humanities* (Cambridge University Press, 2023).

172. Tiffany Lethabo King, *The Black Shoals: Offshore Formations of Black and Native Studies* (Duke University Press, 2019), 5.

173. King, *The Black Shoals,* 7.

174. King, 3–4.

175. Sylvia Wynter, "The Ceremony Must Be Found: After Humanism," *boundary 2* 12.3 (1984): 19–70; 51–52.

176. Isis Semaj-Hall, "Constructing a Dub Identity: What It Means to Be 'Back Home' in Jamaica." *Cultural Dynamics* 30.1/2 (2018): 96–108; 96–97.

177. Alexis Pauline Gumbs, *Spill: Scenes of Black Feminist Fugitivity* (Duke University Press, 2016), xii.

178. Alexis Pauline Gumbs, *M Archive: After the End of the World* (Duke University Press, 2018), xi.

179. Alexis Pauline Gumbs, "Being Ocean as Praxis: Depth Humanisms and Dark Sciences," *Qui Parle* 28.2 (2019): 335–52; 336.

180. Gumbs, *Dub,* xi–xii.

181. Gumbs, xii–xiii.

182. Gumbs, xiii.

183. Henry Ivry and Max Karpinsky, "Blackness After the End of the World: Alexis Pauline Gumbs's Dub Ecologies," *ISLE: Interdisciplinary Studies in Literature and Environment* 30.1 (2023): 77–101; 13, 18.

184. Ivry and Karpinsky, "Blackness," 19.

185. Ivry and Karpinsky, 12.

186. Gumbs, *Dub,* 205.

187. Gumbs, 212.

188. Gumbs, *M Archive*, 78.

189. Saidiya Hartman, *Lose Your Mother: A Journey Along the Atlantic Slave Route* (Farrar, Straus and Giroux, 2007), EPUB, 198.

190. Cited in David Shepherd, "A Feeling for History: Bakhtin and 'The Problem of Great Time,'" *SEER* 84.1 (2006): 32–51; 38.

191. M. M. Bakhtin, *Speech Genres and Other Late Essays*, trans. V. W. McGee, ed. C. Emerson and M. Holquist (University of Texas Press, 1986), 170.

192. Cited in Shepherd, "A Feeling for History," 33–34.

193. Cited in Shepherd, 43.

194. Barry Sandywell, "The Shock of the Old: Mikhail Bakhtin's Contributions to the Theory of Time and Alterity," in *Bakhtin and the Human Sciences*, ed. Michael Bell and Michael Gardiner, 196–213 (SAGE Publications, 1998), 208.

195. Cited in Shepherd, "A Feeling for History," 40–41.

**Afterimage**

1. Ingrid Hoelzl and Remi Marie, "No Image No Cry: On the Past, Present and Possible Futures of the Image," January 1, 2020, https://generalhumanity.org/2020/01/01/no-image-no-cry-by-ingrid-hoelzl.

2. Achille Mbembe, *Brutalism*, trans. S. Corcoran (Duke University Press, 2024), 149.

3. Déborah Danowski and Eduardo Viveiros de Castro, *The Ends of the World*, trans. Rodrigo Nunes (Polity, 2017), 123.

4. Internationales Kolleg für Kulturtechnikforschung und Medienphilosophie Weimar, "The Mediocene," Bauhaus-Universität Weimar, https://ikkm-weimar.de/en/events/the-mediocene/the-mediocene/.

5. Internationales Kolleg, "The Mediocene."

6. Benjamin Bratton, "Planetary Sapience," *Noema*, June 17, 2021.

7. *The New York Times* has reported on this repeatedly; see The Daily, "A.I.'s Original Sin," April 16, 2024, https://www.nytimes.com/2024/04/16/podcasts/the-daily/ai-data.html; Cade Metz, Cecilia Kang, Sheera Frenkel, Stuart A. Thompson, and Nico Grant, "How Tech Giants Cut Corners to Harvest Date for A.I.," *New York Times*, April 6, 2024, https://www.nytimes.com/2024/04/06/technology/tech-giants-harvest-data-artificial-intelligence.html.

8. Andrew R. Chow and Billy Perrigo, "The AI Arms Race Is Changing Everything," *Time*, February 16, 2023, https://time.com/6255952/ai-impact-chatgpt-microsoft-google.

9. Samantha Kelly, "Sam Altman Warns AI Could Kill Us All. But He Still Wants the World to Use It," *CNN Risk Takers*, October 31, 2023, https://www.cnn.com/2023/10/31/tech/sam-altman-ai-risk-taker/. For a sober academic appraisal of risks and potential benefits, see Avyay Casheekar et al., "A Contemporary Review on Chatbots, AI-powered Virtual Conversational Agents, ChatGPT: Applications, Open Challenges and Future Research Directions," *Computer Science Review* 52

(2024), https://www.sciencedirect.com/science/article/abs/pii/S1574013724000169.

10. Ray Kurzweil's *The Singularity Is Near: When Humans Transcend Biology* (Viking, 2005) is generally considered the public announcement of this vision of AI-led super-intelligence. For a recent critical consideration, see Matthew Hutson, "Can We Stop Runaway A.I.?" *The New Yorker,* May 16, 2023, https://www.newyorker.com/science/annals-of-artificial-intelligence/can-we-stop-the-singularity.

11. This was the argument made in the industry-influencing paper by OpenAI associates Jared Kaplan, Sam McCandlish, and coauthors, "Scaling Laws for Neural Language Models," January 2020, https://arxiv.org/pdf/2001.08361.pdf.

12. See The Daily, "A.I.'s Original Sin"; and Edward Zitron, "Have We Reached Peak AI?" Where's Your Ed At?, Substack, March 18, 2024, https://www.wheresyoured.at/peakai/.

13. See Metz et al., "How Tech Giants Cut Corners."

14. Quote from Ava Kofman, "Bruno Latour, the Post-Truth Philosopher, Mounts a Defense of Science," *New York Times,* October 28, 2018, https://www.nytimes.com/2018/10/25/magazine/bruno-latour-post-truth-philosopher-science.html. See Bruno Latour, *Pandora's Hope: Essays on the Reality of Science Studies,* trans. C. Porter (Harvard University Press, 1999), among other works of his.

15. Jennifer Anna Gosetti-Ferencei, *The Life of Imagination: Revealing and Making the World* (Columbia University Press, 2018).

16. Mbembe, *Brutalism,* 141.

17. Danowski and Viveiros de Castro, *The Ends of the World*, 123.

18. Herzog quoted in the film *Werner Herzog Eats His Shoe,* directed by Les Blank, 1979.

19. Ernst Bloch, *The Principle of Hope,* vol. 1, trans. Neville Plaice, Stephen Place, and Paul Knight (MIT Press, 1996), 16.

# INDEX

*f* marks a figure; *t* marks a table

... **Sensing Media**

**Aesthetics, Philosophy, and Cultures of Media**

EDITED BY WENDY HUI KYONG CHUN AND SHANE DENSON

What does it mean to think, feel, and sense with and through media? In this cross-disciplinary series we present books and authors exploring this and related questions: How do media technologies, broadly defined, transform artistic practices and aesthetic sensibilities? How are practices, encounters, and affects entangled with the deep infrastructures and visible surfaces of the media environment? How do we "make sense"—cognitively, perceptually, and culturally—of media?

We are especially interested in contributions that open our understanding of media aesthetics beyond the narrow confines of Western art and aesthetic values. We seek works that reestablish the environmental connections between art and technology as well as between the aesthetic, the sensible, and the philosophical. We invite alternative epistemologies and phenomenologies of media rooted in the practices and subjectivities of Black, Indigenous, queer, trans, and other communities that have been unjustly marginalized in these discussions. Ultimately, we aim to sense the many possible worlds that media disclose.

—

Maja Bak Herrie, *Thinking Through Data: How Outliers, Aggregates, and Patterns Shape Perception*

The DISCO Network, *Technoskepticism: Between Possibility and Refusal*

Timon Beyes, *Organizing Color: Toward a Chromatics of the Social*

Edmund Mendelssohn, *White Musical Mythologies: Sonic Presence in Modernism*

Ioana B. Jucan, *Malicious Deceivers: Thinking Machines and Performative Objects*

Vilém Flusser, *Communicology: Mutations in Human Relations?*, edited by Rodrigo Maltez Novaes, foreword by N. Katherine Hayles

Mark Amerika, *My Life as an Artificial Creative Intelligence*

The authorized representative in the EU for product safety and compliance is:
Mare Nostrum Group
B.V Doelen 72
4831 GR Breda
The Netherlands

www.ingramcontent.com/pod-product-compliance
Lightning Source LLC
LaVergne TN
LVHW041057080826
845145LV00007B/1604

* 9 7 8 1 5 0 3 6 4 3 9 8 7 *